Anthropology
and
Civilizational
Analysis

SUNY series

Pangaea II: Global/Local Studies

Saïd Amir Arjomand and Wolf Schäfer, editors

Anthropology and Civilizational Analysis

Eurasian Explorations

EDITED BY

JOHANN P. ARNASON AND CHRIS HANN

Published by State University of New York Press, Albany

For information, contact State University of New York Press, Albany, NY
www.sunypress.edu

Library of Congress Cataloging-in-Publication Data

Names: Árnason, Jóhann Páll, 1940- editor. | Hann, C. M., 1953- editor.
Title: Anthropology and civilizational analysis : Eurasian explorations / edited by Johann P. Arnason and Chris Hann.
Description: Albany : State University of New York, 2018. | Series: Suny series, Pangaea II. Global/local studies | Includes bibliographical references and index.
Identifiers: LCCN 2017024530 (print) | LCCN 2017051580 (ebook) | ISBN 9781438469416 (e-book) | ISBN 9781438469393 (hardcover : alk. paper)
Subjects: LCSH: Ethnohistory. | Historical sociology. | Comparative civilization. | Civilization—Philosophy.
Classification: LCC GN345.2 (ebook) | LCC GN345.2 .A58 2018 (print) | DDC 909/.04—dc23
LC record available at https://lccn.loc.gov/2017024530

10 9 8 7 6 5 4 3 2 1

The editors and contributors would
like to dedicate this book to the memory
of two distinguished anthropologists,

JACK GOODY AND JOEL S. KAHN,

who passed away during the interval
between the Halle conference and the
publication of its revised papers.

Contents

Acknowledgments | ix

INTRODUCTION | xiii
Making Contact and Mapping the Terrain
Johann P. Arnason

CHAPTER 1 | 1
Mauss Revisited: The Birth of Civilizational Analysis
from the Spirit of Anthropology
Johann P. Arnason

CHAPTER 2 | 35
Approaching Civilization from an Anthropological Perspective:
The Complexities of Norbert Elias
Hans Peter Hahn

CHAPTER 3 | 53
Civilizational Analysis and Archaeology:
Prospects for Collaboration
Yulia Prozorova

CHAPTER 4 | 75
The Use and Abuse of Civilization: An Assessment from
Historical Anthropology for South Arabia's History
Andre Gingrich

CHAPTER 5 | 99
Civilization as a Key Guiding Idea in South Asia
David N. Gellner

CHAPTER 6 | 121

Indian Imbroglios: *Bhakti* Neglected; Or, The Missed
Opportunities for a New Approach to a Comparative
Analysis of Civilizational Diversity
Martin Fuchs

CHAPTER 7 | 155

The Indianization and Localization of Textual Imaginaries:
Theravada Buddhist Statecraft in Mainland Southeast Asia and
Laos in the Context of Civilizational Analysis
Patrice Ladwig

CHAPTER 8 | 193

Frontier as Civilization?: Sociocultural Dynamics in
the Uplands of Southeast Asia
Oliver Tappe

CHAPTER 9 | 219

Anthropology, Civilizational Analysis, and the Malay World
Joel S. Kahn

CHAPTER 10 | 233

Chinese Civilization in Comparative Perspective:
Some Markers
Stephan Feuchtwang

CHAPTER 11 | 259

Technological Choices and Modern Material Civilization:
Reflections on Everyday Toilet Practices in Rural South China
Gonçalo Santos

CHAPTER 12 | 281

Theoretical Paradigm or Methodological Heuristic?:
Reflections on *Kulturkreislehre* with Reference to China
YANG Shengmin and WU Xiujie

CHAPTER 13 | 303
Nomads and the Theory of Civilizations
Nikolay N. Kradin

CHAPTER 14 | 323
The "Orthodox," "Eurasian," or "Russian Orthodox" Civilization?
Milena Benovska-Sabkova

AFTERWORD | 339
Anthropology, Eurasia, and Global History
Chris Hann

Contributors | 355

Index | 357

Acknowledgments

This volume arises out of a Workshop with the same title convened by the editors in late June 2012 at the Max Planck Institute for Social Anthropology (Halle/Saale). We thank all our contributors for their patience and willingness to revise their papers. We also thank Krishan Kumar (University of Virginia, Charlottesville) and Jean-Claude Galey (EHESS, Paris), who presented rich papers in the opening session of the Workshop and have continued to support the project ever since. Thanks are also due to Michael Rowlands and David Wengrow of the Centre for Research into the Dynamics of Civilisation (CREDOC) at University College, London; to Saïd Amir Arjomand, an editor of this series, for his interest and support; to the publisher and its anonymous reviewers; to Jennifer Cash for assistance with language editing; and, last but not least, to Anke Meyer at the MPI, without whose coordination this work would never have been completed.

Introduction

MAKING CONTACT AND MAPPING THE TERRAIN

Johann P. Arnason

The present work should be read as an attempt to establish connections between two apparently distant and unequally developed currents of scholarship. We refer to anthropology in a very broad sense, comprising not only social as well as cultural anthropology, but also the variously and often vaguely defined historical anthropology that has gone beyond the traditional focus on stateless, nonurban, and oral cultures. Mention will also be made of archaeology, sometimes (by Marcel Mauss, among others) seen as the discipline most capable of compensating for the lack of anthropological evidence on the past of human societies. There is no consensus on the unity or the ideals of inquiry on this side of the field. We have no fundamental objection to Clifford Geertz's description of anthropology as an estranged double of philosophy, "a combination of a diffuse and miscellaneous academic identity and an ambition to connect just about everything with everything else and get thereby to the bottom of things" (Geertz 2000, ix). But we can presuppose general acquaintance with certain well-known names (from Boas and Malinowski to Lévi-Strauss, Geertz, and beyond), a number of landmark works, and the broader cultural echoes that document some kind of disciplinary progress. It is different with the other side of the field. Civilizational analysis is anything but a household notion, and some clarification of its claims will be needed.

Civilizational Approaches

As defined by Shmuel Eisenstadt (2003, 23–56), the civilizational dimension of human societies involves the intertwining of cultural visions of the world with institutional frameworks of social life, and thus, more specifically, with forms of social power. Civilizational analysis is, first and foremost, the comparative study of such configurations. As it begins with the demarcation of an analytical level, it can allow for a variety of concrete formations within that frame of reference, and some of those may be seen as civilizations in a more emphatic sense than others. The ancient Greek world, imperial China, and medieval Western Christendom are cases in point. Their historical record also highlights another aspect of the civilizational dimension: the configurations in question, at least the major ones, are large-scale and long-term patterns of social-historical reality, encompassing a plurality of coexisting and successive social formations. That was precisely the perspective from which Durkheim and Mauss discovered civilizations as "families of societies" (see Schlanger 2006). As they also understood, the multisocietal groupings that they proposed to analyze as civilizations were spatiotemporal phenomena. Civilizations emerge and unfold in history, but they have their distinctive historical contours and rhythms, differing from case to case. Contrasts between ancient Egypt and ancient Greece, or Western and Byzantine Christendom, can serve to illustrate varying patterns of historical existence and historical consciousness. As for the spatial contours of civilizations, regional boundaries are often easy to identify, as in the case of the East Asian region centered on China, or the expanding European domain of medieval Western Christendom; but both these civilizational regions also exemplify the internal differentiation of smaller historical-geographical ones, such as Northern, Western, and Central Europe.

It may be objected that these spatial perspectives are not equally relevant to all civilizations. In particular, the markedly translocal and transregional dynamic of Islam seems to set it apart from more circumscribed formations. But on closer examination, two geographical aspects stand out as crucial features of Islamic history. On the one hand, Islam, as a civilization crystallized within a region with a long multicivilizational history (the Near East, or the "Nile-to-Oxus region," as Marshall Hodgson [1974] described it), achieved an unprecedented in-depth cultural unification of this area, and expanded from there. On the other hand, Islam was the only premodern civilization that expanded from the western to the eastern extremity of the Afro-Eurasian macroregion and continued to gain ground in its southern parts. This is the specific historical-geographical meaning of the global thrust often attributed to Islam, and it is a fact of major importance that sustained territorial growth was not, in the early modern era, followed by any overseas expansion.

Civilizational analysis is, at least for the most notable recent and contemporary scholars in the field, within the domain of historical sociology. The contributions of authors such as Benjamin Nelson (2011) and Shmuel Eisenstadt (2003), who have linked their research programs to insights and anticipations of the sociological classics, have done most to define the orientations of further work. The academic status and autonomy of historical sociology are still somewhat uncertain (historical anthropology has been more effectively recognized in some countries, including Germany, but here too the overall picture is unclear). This applies a fortiori to civilizational analysis. We are dealing with a project still in the process of defining its tasks and encountering some skepticism from more established disciplines. The problem is compounded by an ambivalent legacy. Alongside the historical-sociological pedigree, other ways of thinking about civilizational issues have left their mark on the context of discussion. It may be going too far to speak of a metahistorical tradition, but that term has—because of their speculative bent and a loose relationship to the empirical record—been used to describe the well-known works of both Oswald Spengler and Arnold Toynbee. Their names stand for very different approaches; although nobody advocates a return to their visions of history, their continued invocation suggests that some of their questions are still relevant to lasting concerns. We may therefore consider these alternative approaches as unexhausted sources of inputs to the civilizationist project.

Finally, the historical-sociological view of civilizations—our primary frame of reference—can draw on the work of historians who discuss civilizations without precise conceptual markers or clear demarcation from other formations. Fernand Braudel's writings are perhaps the most prominent example. His reputation rests most of all on two massive works, the first on the Mediterranean in the second half of the sixteenth century (but with copious references to a longer history) and the second on capitalism and material life in the early modern world (Braudel 1996; 1981–84). In the former case, varying accounts of civilizational divisions within the Mediterranean reflect unresolved questions about the very concept of civilization. In the latter, the French original uses the term *civilisation matérielle* to refer to what the English version calls material life, that is to say, the most basic networks of economic activity. But in the same volume, civilizations in the plural are invoked as large-scale formations that impose different patterns on societies and their economies, without any further clarification of the relationship between the two concepts. Braudel can, however, at least be credited with highlighting two aspects of civilizations in the plural: he stressed the centrality of religion as well as the importance of geo-economic and geopolitical infrastructures.

No representative author has ever suggested that civilizational analysis should develop a methodology of its own. There are no good grounds for attempting anything of the kind. Civilizational analysis is an interdisciplinary research program, with particularly strong links to historical sociology, and it draws on the whole spectrum of methods applied in the human sciences. Within that framework, it will require and develop its specific combinations of methods in response to particular issues. Given the state of the art, it would be premature to propose a systematic survey of these approaches (Max Weber's emphatic warnings against methodological constructions preceding substantive studies are still relevant), but a few basic orientations may be outlined. Because of the focus on cultural patterns and their interpretive as well as institutional implications, civilizational studies have inevitably tended to stress the significance of key traditional texts, and thus to rely extensively on a variety of hermeneutical approaches. This leaves us with a double legacy. On the one hand, a more balanced line of inquiry will strive to move beyond texts and situate them in the social and historical contexts that co-determine their effective interpretation. On the other hand, civilizational analysis can learn from the efforts of hermeneutical thinkers to show that the interpretation of texts provides guidance for hermeneutical work on other levels, from tacit cultural premises to the overt logic of action.

Another major task is the clarification and integration of processual analysis. This approach was developed in the sociological tradition, most seminally by Norbert Elias, in close connection with a critique of causal, functional, and structural explanations (Elias 2000; 2012). It can link up with philosophical reflections in the same vein, notably with the work of Alfred North Whitehead and his disciples. Processual dynamics were shown to have patterns of their own, irreducible to the more familiar models. The human sciences have yet to fully assimilate the insights of processual thought. In the particular case of civilizational analysis, this is one of the most urgent preconditions for further progress. Understanding civilizations as historical processes is a necessary complement to the emphasis on cultural patterns. This leads to a third methodological observation. Contingency is an integral aspect of processes. In the context of civilizations, it involves internal as well as external factors. Choices between possibilities open to civilizations may be decided by contingent events; interactions between different civilizations unfold in historical settings, where complex chains of events can result in epoch-making events. A historical sociology of civilizations that takes due notice of these dimensions will move toward narrativist modes (currently exemplified by the work of Michael Mann; see Mann 1986–2012). But the narratives will include the dynamics of cultural patterns and power formations; here again, Braudel should be acknowledged as a pioneer.

Anthropological Landmarks

If anthropology and civilizational studies are characterized in these very broad terms, a closer analysis of their interrelations would have to deal with wide-ranging questions. Mutual borrowings did occur, sometimes in surprising contexts. One of the most widely read anthropological texts, Ruth Benedict's *Patterns of Culture* (Benedict 1993), relies on a holistic concept of culture that is explicitly indebted to Spengler. A work written in the wake of the Boasian turn to ethnography thus aligns itself with a particularly speculative version of comparative civilizational analysis. Moreover, Benedict argued that Spengler's model, overly ambitious in his chosen field, could be put on a stronger footing within the anthropological universe of discourse. Spengler's conception of cultural integration through "destiny ideas," exemplified by his image of Faustian man in quest of infinity, was incompatible with the multiple strands and complex patterns of European history, but anthropologists were dealing with societies simple enough for this kind of unifying perspective to be applicable. On a more recent note, the most controversial offshoot of the civilizationist revival, Samuel Huntington's *Clash of Civilizations*, uses an anthropological metaphor to underline its main point: civilizations are the "ultimate tribes" (Huntington 1996). Once again, this deservedly contested view has unmistakable affinities with Spengler's notion of mutually incommensurable symbolic universes. It is unnecessary to search for further examples of this kind; what we want to highlight is an overall trend and an inconclusive result of changing relations between the two lines of inquiry.

The classical beginnings of civilizational analysis have a strong anthropological background. Although this ancestry was later forgotten, a reappraisal of the French sociological tradition has shown that Émile Durkheim and Marcel Mauss developed clearer conceptual guidelines for the study of civilizations than anybody else at the time, and that this step beyond their original image of society was closely linked to a growing interest in anthropological research (Schlanger 2006). Mauss continued to reflect on these issues after Durkheim's death, and their joint legacy influenced some later works in the French tradition.

The dominant aspect of twentieth-century developments in the field, however, was an increasing mutual estrangement of anthropology and civilizational studies. Those who adopted the civilizational approach and tried to put it to comparative use tended to accept—without further argument—a historical boundary of their domain: civilizations were distinguished from prehistorical, stateless, or primitive societies, and equated with the state- and city-centered formations that developed from the fourth millennium BCE onward, first in the Near East and subsequently in other regions. Particular emphasis was then placed on later civilizations with more complex cultural articulations. The Axial Age, commonly identified with a few centuries around the middle of the last millennium BCE, was proffered as a paradigm of civilizational efflorescence. This perspective (most significantly elaborated by S. N. Eisenstadt [1986], following Karl Jaspers) was, in spirit if not in specific terms, akin to the comparative studies of Max Weber, whose substantive contribution to civilizational analysis went far beyond the French classics, but who was less focused on basic concepts. Weber did not relate to anthropology in any significant way. His "cultural worlds" (*Weltkulturen*) were those of the major Eurasian civilizational complexes, especially the Occident (implicitly understood as extending from Greek and Jewish origins to the modern Euro-Atlantic zone), the Chinese, and the Indian traditions. Although Weber's main emphasis was on the contrasts and divergences that set the Occident apart from other geocultural units, the comparative perspective was also extended to affinities and differences between non-Western cases. Seen from a later vantage point, the framework leaves much to be desired; there is no doubt that Weber vastly oversimplified the interplay of sociocultural forces and underestimated the historical transformations of both Chinese and Indian civilizations. To note another shortcoming, the emergence of a larger Indian (or Indianized) world is analyzed only in relation to Buddhism, and there is no discussion of the regional configuration that developed around China. A planned work on

Islam was never completed, but would clearly have portrayed this neighbor of the West as a later and somewhat less than equal entrant to the Eurasian field. That said, the general line of argument, and more precisely the effort to link interpretations of and attitudes to the world with institutional and practical patterns, are clear enough to constitute an enduring example for contemporary civilizational studies.

As for the anthropologists, the self-definition of their discipline underwent major changes, but none of these led to a civilizational turn. E. B. Tylor's culturalist and evolutionist program in the late nineteenth century is commonly seen as a foundational step that paved the way for further controversies and alternative projects. The distinction between cultural and social anthropology, which eventually served to demarcate national traditions, identified different foci of research, each of which allowed for divergent strategies. Closer study of cultural patterns (the North American specialty) and social institutions (the Western European) could result in fleshing out the functionalist conceptions inherited from nineteenth-century thought, but it could also direct attention to concrete historical settings, and by the same token raise doubts about evolutionary models.

In theory, both cultural and social anthropology could have linked up with the notion of civilization, as developed by Durkheim and Mauss: the cultural approach would have been compatible with their concept of collective representations, and the social one with the idea of civilizations as groupings of societies. In fact, and despite Durkheim's acknowledged influence on anthropologists in the Anglophone world, there was no sustained encounter of this kind. The closest approximation was probably A. L. Kroeber's proposal to include civilizations in his survey of cultures (Kroeber 2011), but without any effort to delineate or justify a new concept. For Kroeber, culture and civilization were basically synonymous terms, although it seemed convenient to single out the more complex societies as civilizations. If there was, as has been claimed (Bidney 1968), a theoretical convergence between Kroeber and Durkheim, it was implicit and limited, related to the cultural determination of individuality. There is no evidence that Kroeber read Durkheim and Mauss on the subject, though he did take note of Spengler. His response differed from Benedict's: Kroeber was not particularly concerned with finding a more adequate empirical basis for Spengler's central concepts, but rather saw Spengler's emphasis on the aesthetic features of high cultures as a point to be taken up and cleansed of metaphysical connotations. The way to achieve that was a further elaboration of the concept of "style" (Kroeber 1963).

Obstacles to Dialogue

The differentiation of cultural and social anthropology, accompanied by divergences on each side and various cross-influences between the main currents, put its mark on the history of the discipline in the twentieth century and gave rise to intellectual attitudes strong enough to shape more recent debates. For our purposes, it seems most pertinent that certain entrenched objections to the civilizational approach go back to this phase. It is hard to find a reasoned and representative statement of the anthropological case against civilizational analysis (on the whole, anthropologists prefer to bypass the issue). That said, three invidious and interconnected preconceptions—or stereotypes—stand out as dominant themes.

For many anthropologists, the very notion of civilizations (especially if defined with reference to the Weberian themes noted above) is loaded with normative claims that make it unfit for scholarly use. It implies an a priori devaluation of societies preceding the formation of states, cities, and writing systems, or remaining outside the historical arena of such processes. To opt for this paradigm is, in other words, to perpetuate the age-old division of humanity into civilized and barbarian peoples. In our view, this objection is unwarranted. There is nothing in the civilizational approach as such that would lead us to equate the transition to state-dominated and urban-centered societies in possession of writing with unqualified progress; neither the general direction of civilizational analysis nor the concrete research programs applied by Weber and Eisenstadt are incompatible with the view that the emergence of civilizations leads to a massive increase of destructive as well as productive capacities (manifested in warfare and conquest on a new scale, and in environmental damage), and that the balance between them is subject to change. The relative merits of stateless and state-dominated societies are open to debate. Although more comparative research on cultural traditions is needed, it seems a plausible hypothesis that different civilizations develop their specific versions of an ideology best described as primitivism, the general thrust of which is to condemn civilizing processes in the name of an idealized simpler past.

A second anthropological objection to civilizational approaches is directed against the supposedly speculative and ultra-holistic constructs presented as units of inquiry. This rejection of excessively totalizing models is widely shared (not least by historians). What gives the anthropological critique its specific thrust is the assumption that anthropological efforts to make sense of social life on a small scale are the best way to open up universal perspectives. The emphasis on small social worlds, previously related to tribal societies, remains in force after anthropology's break-out from the traditional division of labor. As for the universalizing ambition, it has survived in weakened forms (a self-limiting version, aiming at global human relevance but certainly not at universal causal laws or cultural norms, is implicit in the above quotation from Clifford Geertz). This ambition was central to the history of anthropology. Durkheim's foundational work on religious life, probably the most seminal fusion of anthropological and sociological horizons, combines an intensive and carefully localized case study with strong claims to universal validity (Durkheim 1995). This direct and rapid access to universality is one of the promises built into the notion of elementary forms. But the reference to Durkheim will also help to show that the dismissal of civilizational perspectives is unfounded. As noted above, a preliminary sketch of civilizations in the plural as a field for comparative study was co-authored by Durkheim and Mauss. It belongs to the same phase of Durkheim's intellectual biography as the work on Aboriginal religion, and this enables us to contextualize both themes. The concept of civilization, defined in a way that implies plurality, is introduced as a necessary complement to the concept of society. It refers to a broader configuration of interconnected societies, characterized by specific forms of integration and differentiation. In a sense, the concept of an elementary form—meant to highlight the institutions of tribal societies at their maximum distance from the modern environment of sociology—is another such complement. Not that it suggests a pre- or infra-societal level; but it serves to put the more familiar structures of complex societies into perspective. The overall picture is one of multiple social-historical formations, with civilizations singled out as a level not to be neglected, but without any suggestion that the study of their patterns and processes should absorb or replace other established forms of social inquiry.

The third objection is closely related to the second, but it has a weight of its own. Large units of inquiry are conducive to speculative exercises of the kind that the human sciences should have left behind. The anthropological variation on this theme is based on a particular approach to empirical study: the practice of fieldwork, invented during the classical period of the discipline and later transferred beyond the tribal context. The guiding idea and the general significance of fieldwork were interpreted in widely different ways, including highly ambitious elaborations by authors whose work was in fact not particularly dependent on that background (such as Claude Lévi-Strauss). But what remains important, not least in relation to the question of civilizations, is the notion of a direct experiential—in some versions existential—access to cultural otherness. The civilizational approach can then be presented as an inferior methodological option, unduly focused on the texts of great cultural traditions (often in unsatisfactory translations). A defense can start with the point that a certain emphasis on central texts follows logically from the themes mentioned above: cultural articulations of the world and their interplay with institutional dynamics. But the next step is to note that civilizational analysts can move beyond this beginning, by comparing the relative weight of central texts in different civilizations (this is not always a question of sacred texts in the strict sense), and tracing the impact of their prescriptive contents in social-historical contexts. Marshall Hodgson's analysis of Islam (Hodgson 1974) is a model case with regard to the latter. His idea of a civilization stresses the centrality of texts, canons, and written traditions, but also the need to link their destinies to the transformations of social power.

Finally, critics of civilizational analysis should not ignore the fact that its research program is still in an early stage of formulation. So far, the most seminal ideas on civilizations have appeared or been revived in connection with broader efforts to reorient sociological thought, but failed to gain admission to mainstream developments in that field. This applies to the classical period as well as to the last decades of the twentieth century, and it is in large measure due to the particular reasons for the civilizational turn (the late-twentieth-century revival was to a very significant extent prompted by the shortcomings of modernization theory). But a sustained comparative study of civilizations cannot make significant progress without closer cooperation of the human sciences. The integration of historical and sociological approaches is obviously of key importance, but as the present book will attempt to show, anthropology also has distinctive insights and guidelines to offer. It remains to be seen whether traditional and institutional obstacles to such a synthesis can be overcome.

Toward Convergence?

A more nuanced position may, somewhat paradoxically, be emerging from a third attempt to define the scope and aims of anthropology (distinct from both social and cultural conceptions of the discipline). Claude Lévi-Strauss's reorientation of anthropological thought and research, foreshadowed in an early essay on the French sociological tradition (Lévi-Strauss 1945) and backed up by a series of major works, did not—despite recognition probably unequalled by any other anthropologist—gain general assent, but it seems to have sparked a discussion that can help to renew classical links to the civilizational field. That was, to put it mildly, not an obvious implication of the initial program. The key component of Lévi-Strauss's new paradigm was the idea of a rational unconscious, exemplified by the structures of language in light of phonological discoveries, but to be developed in more radical and general terms by anthropology. At the same time, the paradigm shift was supposed to solve problems raised by Durkheim and Mauss: the logic of cultural and social order, which they had tried to locate at the level of collective representations, had to be explained in terms of underlying and unconscious organizational principles.

The anthropological extension of this linguistics-based model involved two main steps. To begin with, the core institution of stateless societies was analyzed in a comparative perspective and shown to be a rational construct: the elementary structures of kinship (Lévi-Strauss 1969) could, on this view, be reduced to rules of matrimonial exchange, and this regulated formation of alliances beyond consanguinity was the most fundamental social bond. The second step was to apply the same analytical principles to primitive thought, now recognized as rational in its own way. For Lévi-Strauss, "savage thought," as he called it, was based on the same invariant structures of human reason as its modern scientific counterpart, but it operated through a different medium and confronted reality at a different level. This general interpretation was concretized through very extensive and detailed analyses of myths. Mythical thought appeared as an ever-varying exploration of central and constant themes, primarily the relationship between nature and culture and the alignment of social and natural order.

At first sight, this line of argument might seem very far removed from civilizational concerns. The retreat from collective representations to an invariant underlying logic of organization is, by the same token, a severing of the links that Durkheim and Mauss had established between anthropology and sociology, which had led them to consider civilizations—made up of collective representations widespread and resilient enough to constitute a shared cultural milieu for multiple societies—as a theme for both disciplines But the picture changes when we come to Lévi-Strauss's statements on the place of primitive societies in human history. Such reflections were needed to round off the program of anthropological research, and although they never amounted to a systematic argument, they do suggest ways of reconnecting to a historical sociology with civilizational perspectives. As will be seen, these hints have been taken up by later authors.

To back up his claims that *la pensée sauvage* was a distinctive but not fundamentally alien mode of thought, Lévi-Strauss adds the point that primitive societies, though not prehistorical in any literal sense, do not relate to history in the same way as the better-documented state- and class-dominated ones. The former strive to suppress the experience and minimize the impact of history, the latter embrace and activate history, thus generating a dynamism inseparable from social inequality. This thesis became known as the distinction between cold and hot societies. Since the contrasting but equally holistic approaches to history find expression in integral forms of life, we seem to be dealing with formations of the type envisaged by civilizational analysts: conceptions of the world and the human condition, embodied in patterns and directions of social practices. However, the distinction between two ways of social life—as formulated by Lévi-Strauss—is couched in much more abstract terms than the differences usually stressed in comparative studies of civilizations. The diversity of cultural worlds created by "hot societies" is bracketed out. But there is a further twist to Lévi-Strauss's philosophy of history. In his inaugural lecture at the Collège de France (Lévi-Strauss 1967), where he comes closest to claiming normative authority on behalf of anthropology, the societies singled out as representing the most balanced relationship between humanity and its environment are neolithic ones. Another reference to the neolithic transformation and its results can be found in the introductory chapter of the book on "savage thought" (Lévi-Strauss 1969b). Here, the fundamental rationality of this mindset is confirmed by the neolithic transformation, and especially by the invention of agriculture. As Lévi-Strauss saw it, such achievements could only be the outcome of systematic experimentation and cumulative learning made possible by the cognitive frameworks of the societies involved. He argues that "savage thought" is the most elementary form assumed by human reason and thus an attribute of hunting and gathering societies, but its potential is most decisively manifested in a process that takes the human species beyond that stage. The neolithic transformation (or revolution, to use a term still accepted by Lévi-Strauss but now questioned by prehistorians) seems to be the crowning practical success of primitive societies. It is a result of cumulative trends that do not amount to a radical change of the underlying relationship to history, but by creating the preconditions for such a change (permanent settlements, a division of labor, and a surplus product), this transformation undeniably relativizes the distinction between hot and cold societies.

Both these themes, the distinction between two successive and opposite societal types as well as the idea of a historical bridge between them, became important for the following generation of anthropologists and social theorists. The work of Pierre Clastres on stateless societies (Clastres 2011) added a new dimension to Lévi-Strauss's dichotomy. Clastres argued that statelessness could not be understood as the mere absence of a subsequently dominant institution; rather, the societies in question had organized themselves in ways effectively blocking the development of a separate power center. That could not be achieved without a corresponding intellectual effort. Clastres did not adopt Lévi-Strauss's conception of a rational unconscious, at least not explicitly, and his argument leaves open the possibility that the antistatist thought embodied in tribal institutions might be a habitus rooted in very early learning processes. The rejection of the state would then, in the last instance, be a reaction against primeval experiences with some kind of tyranny.

In any case, Clastres described the implicit political thought of primitive societies in ways clearly reminiscent of Lévi-Strauss's savage thought. Marcel Gauchet (2005) made the affinities more visible. For Gauchet, the focus on interconnected intellectual and political dimensions of primitive societies was a first move toward the complex synthesis developed in his work on the political history of religion (Gauchet 1999). Here, the interplay of religion and politics—both notably underdeveloped themes in Lévi-Strauss's work—takes center stage in a macrohistorical narrative, beginning with societies wholly dominated by beliefs in mythical ancestors and in a comprehensive order seen as their legacy. For Gauchet, this is not so much an elementary as an extreme and total form of religion, and its impact on the political sphere is disabling. Within this framework, autonomous and collective self-transformation is impossible, and so is the constitution of a separate power center that would set itself above society. Marcel Gauchet is primarily concerned with the logic of the trajectory that began with the emergence of sacral rulership (the *Urform* of the state) and culminated in the formation of Christianity. The point to be noted here is that his whole narrative centers on the interplay of religion and politics. The religio-political nexus, as we might call it, is a crucial theme of civilizational analysis. Although Gauchet does not use that frame of reference, we can characterize the whole line of thought leading beyond Lévi-Strauss as a substantive rapprochement with civilizational thought. This will appear more significant if another case is taken into account.

Maurice Godelier seems to have taken the same turn independently. His version of it is based on a long record of fieldwork and a sustained reflection on the relationship between Marxism and anthropology. Having abandoned the base-superstructure model (after a long effort to rescue it), he had to find an alternative answer to the question of the foundation of human societies. As he came to see it, this was not a matter of grasping absolute beginnings or ultimate determinants; the only meaningful approach was a focus on observable key factors in the formation of new societies and their collective identities. Fieldwork in New Guinea led Godelier to conclude that such processes involve a combination of several factors, and that the forces at work in tribal societies were not fundamentally different from those familiar to historians. The appropriation of a territory and its resources requires an authority of some kind, empowered to regulate the defense of the territory as well as the division of activities within it. Moreover, the legitimation of this authority involves claims beyond the experiential world: until recent times, "invisible beings, to whom humans attribute powers, have been an essential component of the sovereignty that human groups exercise over a territory" (Godelier 2007, 205). With this reference to the religious dimension of political power, Godelier moves into a field often visited by civilizational analysts; and the boundary that tends to separate their domain from tribal societies is further blurred by historical considerations. Godelier stresses the diversity of stateless societies in various places and phases, such as New Guinean tribes and the more complex cases of Polynesian islands. The result is, in short, a more historical vision of societies outside the mainstream transition to archaic civilizations.

To draw this part of the argument to a close, let us take a brief look at a very different anthropological project and its particular way of bringing civilizations in without engaging in closer examination of their patterns. It is not far-fetched to describe Clifford Geertz as a reluctant civilizationist: he unmistakably acknowledges the historical reality and the anthropological relevance of civilizations, but fails to follow this track when it comes to concrete analyses. Toward the end of his career, he described his early fieldwork in Java in terms worth quoting at length: "It was, if not the first, surely one of the earliest and most self-conscious efforts on the part of anthropologists to take on not a tribal group, an island settlement, a disappeared society, a relic people, nor even a set-off, bounded small community of herders or peasants, but a whole ancient and inhomogeneous, urbanized, literate, and politically active society—a civilization, no less" (Geertz 2000, 14). This is a claim to have pioneered anthropological approaches to civilizations, no less. But there was no effort to go beyond the verbal recognition of civilizational features; the concept is neither explicitly applied nor developed further. Another early work, the comparative study of Islam in Morocco and Indonesia, is described in an introductory remark as dealing with the "eastern and western extremities of classical Islamic civilization" (Geertz 1968, 4), but a preface written after the completion of the main text refers to "a supposedly single creed, Islam, in two quite contrasting civilizations, the Indonesian and the Moroccan" (ibid., V). The analysis that follows these divergent statements makes no attempt to mediate between them, nor is there any clarification of what it means to move from the study of religion to a civilizational context.

The ambiguity toward civilizations persists throughout Geertz's work. In one of his last major statements, a reflection on a "world in pieces," and more specifically on the declining importance of cultural cohesion and national identity, he signals the importance of civilizational perspectives: "The coexistence in most parts of the world, indeed in virtually all, of great cultural traditions, rich, distinctive, and historically deep (civilizations in the proper, not the polemical sense of the term), with an endless progression of differences within differences, divisions within divisions, jumbles within jumbles, raises questions that cannot any longer be passed off as idle or inconsequent." (Geertz 2000, 224). But again, the logical sequel to this observation is absent. Geertz could have gone on to consider the role of civilizational affinities in maintaining the "identity without unison" (ibid., 224) that prevails when nations fade and cultures split. The failure to do so is the final confirmation of a stance that can—in retrospect—also be seen in Geertz's most famous and controversial work: his analysis of the theatre state in Bali (Geertz 1980). Here, the question of variations to the relationship between culture and power, a civilizational theme par excellence, was tackled through a case study that became a classic example of thick description, but led to somewhat disconcerting results. Claude Lefort (1986, 20) distinguished between three processes involved in the cultural framing of power: interpretation (*mise en sens*), institutionalization (*mise en forme*), and representation (*mise en scène*). In that context, Geertz's Balinese theatre state appears as an extreme case of representation overshadowing the other aspects, to such an extent that the official power center rarefies into ceremonial display, whereas intensive power struggles unfold at lower levels of the social structure. We thus seem to end up with a picture of culture dissociated from power, and Geertz does not raise the question of broader implications for comparative studies. Critics found the vision of Balinese society implausible and hard to reconcile with general findings of the human sciences. Nordholt (2014) reconstructed the history of Bali in the last few centuries, with particular emphasis on the involvement of rulers in power struggles. In a more anthropological vein, Tambiah (1985) also emphasizes the rulers' pursuit of power, not least in view of the use that charismatic kings could make of their symbolic resources. More importantly for our purposes, he argues that Geertz's account of the Balinese state, properly reinterpreted, can be fitted into a general model of Southeast Asian state formation. This is the conception of the "galactic polity . . . a design that coded in a composite way cosmological, topographical and politico-economic features" (ibid., 322). The galactic polity, discussed at length in a book that combines anthropological and civilizational perspectives (Tambiah 1976), is a complex configuration of culture and power; one of its key features is the combination of a comprehensive devolution of power to subcenters with an often latent but intermittently reactivated charismatic potential of the main center. To treat this formation as a civilizational phenomenon is not to assume that it represents a separate Southeast Asian civilization; the historical record clearly suggests a composite result of Indianizing processes interacting with a regional substratum.

Eurasia

The contributions to this book deal primarily with Eurasian subjects. What we have in mind is an inclusive concept of Eurasia (Hann 2016), defined as a macroregion encompassing the conventionally (and Eurocentrically) demarcated continents of Europe and Asia, as well as the North African coastal regions (whether we need a concept of Afro-Eurasia is less clear; Sub-Saharan Africa was for a long time less closely linked to Eurasian historical destinies than Egypt and the Maghreb). The papers published below situate themselves within this Eurasian framework. The only exception is the discussion of Durkheim and Mauss's civilizational model, for which they made use of research on indigenous societies in America as well as Oceania. But further development of the concept of civilization, discontinuous as it was, drew mainly on Eurasian historical experiences. This book does not deal with the Eurasian spatial context as such, but since that question is certainly one of those we would like to see raised in anthropological and civilizational studies, a few remarks on possible approaches may be in order. Among those who have applied Eurasian perspectives (in the inclusive sense), various visions can be distinguished.

The first is a vision of Eurasia as the theatre of early globalizing processes, from the formation of the Roman and the Chinese empires to Islamic expansion (Therborn 2000). There were no comparable globalizing waves in the Americas, but the decisive turn came when the New World was integrated into Eurasian networks of power and trade. The problem with this view is that it tends to suggest a unilinear and cumulative globalizing process. In so doing, it obscures the specificity and multiplicity of Eurasian developments. Among the latter, three types of expanding intercultural—or, more emphatically, intercivilizational—formations stand out: networks of trade, imperial regimes, and transcultural religions (this is more precise than the more common "world religions"). These historical formations interact and overlap in different ways. For example, networks of trade are important for both empires and religions, and more important for some religions than others; they seem to have played a more significant role in the history of Buddhism and Islam than in the Christian case. The three fields are never coextensive. Religion and empire have sometimes been closely united, but not to the point of complete identity. The Christianization of the Roman empire coincided with the conversion of some neighboring states; the early unified Islamic empire began to disintegrate before in-depth Islamization could occur in its heartland. All three types of expansion depend on and are shaped by civilizational frameworks, but in the more important cases, such as those of world religions properly speaking, they transcend civilizational boundaries. Comparative study of this double-edged relationship is one of the key tasks on the agenda of civilizational analysis.

These Eurasian patterns have no parallel elsewhere. Trade networks and imperial states developed in the Americas, but not on a similar level; the Inca empire is rightly regarded as an astonishing achievement, in view of its archaic technological basis, but it is not in the same class as the great Eurasian empires, from the Persian onward. There were no American counterparts to the transcultural religions of Eurasia.

A further phenomenon specific to Eurasia is the formation of regions that may be described as civilizational crossroads. Commercial, imperial, and religious influences from multiple directions combine to give them a distinctive profile, not identifiable with a particular civilization. The Eastern Mediterranean and the region historically known as Bactria (roughly corresponding to Northeastern Afghanistan and neighboring areas) are familiar examples. A strong case has been made for the island of Java (Lombard 2004), and a longer list would arguably include the whole of Southeast Asia. Such cases are particularly interesting when it comes to the impact of globalization (understood as a process beginning with the European discovery and conquest of the Americas) on the Eurasian macroregion. The interaction of a vastly expanded maritime context with complex regional patterns within the Eurasian landmass is an important topic for historical anthropology.

While these approaches emphasize connectivity, an alternative vision stresses parallel lines of development in the most dynamic cultural centers. The main rationale for a broader geographical horizon is in this case the effort to tone down traditional beliefs in European exceptionalism. Both Jaspers's and Eisenstadt's conceptions of the Axial Age, mentioned above, were conceived in that spirit. The idea of Indian and Chinese (originally also Iranian) cultural transformations, comparable and roughly contemporary to Greek and Jewish ones, is (among other things) an attempt to bring Eurasian dimensions to intellectual and religious history. Jack Goody's account of multiple transitions to the Bronze Age in different parts of Eurasia belongs to the same type of interpretation (Goody 2010). It should be distinguished from the theory of alternating Eastern and Western hegemonies, proposed by the same author in the same short book (see also Goody 2015), but best understood as a third version of Eurasian views on history. This construction links up with the work of those who see the recent rise and possible predominance of East Asia as a return to earlier patterns (Jones et al. 1993); the overtaking of China by the West is an obvious case, and so is the Chinese comeback, at least up to a point, but it is more difficult to find further support for the general claim.

I am not suggesting that Goody advocates two different theories. He has certainly tried to integrate the second and the third perspective (for the most recent attempt, see Goody 2015). The point is, however, that while the idea of alternating advances or hegemonies presupposes the Bronze Age background, the latter does not entail the former. To make that connection plausible, Goody has to emphasize roughly parallel patterns of development in East and West. But a strong case can be made for significant divergences, long before the modern one brought about by European industrialization and military domination. That story begins with the enormously important crisis of the late Bronze Age in the Near East and the Eastern Mediterranean (the ancestral regions of the Occident envisioned by Weber and others), and the absence of anything comparable in the East. Events of the late thirteenth and the early twelfth century BCE, extensively discussed in recent scholarship (for an overview, see Cline 2014) led to multiple collapses of old power structures and more or less protracted new beginnings. The most momentous change was the destruction of Mycenaean Greece and the subsequent rise of polis civilization, but important shifts also took place in other parts of the region from Egypt to Mesopotamia.

In all cases, a phase of shrinkage and disintegration preceded developments along new lines. In South Asia, the centuries around the end of the second and the beginning of the first millennium BCE are very obscure; a major crisis leading to the downfall of civilizational centers in the Indus Valley and Eastern Iran seems to have occurred much earlier, and in an altogether different setting. Chinese history is much better known, and here the course of events was very different from the Near Eastern record of crisis and collapse. The rise of the Zhou dynasty around 1100 BCE (there is some disagreement on the date) led to an upgrading of the archaic state, both on the level of power structures and in regard to its ideological basis. The Zhou achievement was solid enough to ensure a long political ascendancy and a much longer cultural afterlife. Aspects of Zhou traditions, variously transfigured but clearly rooted in archaic imaginations and experiences, entered into the mainstream of Chinese thought and became a source of continuity without parallel in the West. The political crisis of the Zhou regime matured slowly but took an explosive turn after the middle of the first millennium BCE, leading to interstate competition on a scale unknown elsewhere at the time.

Another major divergence resulted from the trajectories of imperial power in East and West. The fact that the Chinese and Roman empires made their decisive breakthroughs at roughly the same time, around 200 BCE, is obviously a case of contingent parallels, and so is the roughly simultaneous crisis that crystallized around 200 CE. But the later destinies of these two power formations differed. The Roman empire was at first more successful in reforming itself and coping with the crisis than the Chinese. In the longer run, however, the Roman empire disintegrated, and the sixth-century attempt at reunification failed, whereas the contemporaneous Chinese one succeeded. Although a Buddhist vision of rulership was clearly of some importance for the restoration of imperial power, it did not lead to an exclusive identification of the empire with a transcultural religion, as in the three civilizations that divided the Roman realm between them

(Western Christendom, Byzantium, and Islam). The Chinese pattern, stabilized in the seventh century CE and adapted without any fundamental changes under later dynasties, combined a sole imperial center, endowed with sacred authority, and a plurality of religious traditions.

Islamic expansion affected both eastern and western parts of Eurasia in multiple ways. Goody is inclined to see this historical experience as one more indicator of macroregional unity, but we may note some significant contrasts between the patterns of Islamic conquest and rule. In the East, during the medieval period, expansion brought Islam into contact with Inner Eurasian societies in early stages of state formation. Their responses combined conversion with counterexpansion, and thus led to an enlargement of the Islamic religious community while increasing the number of rival political units. This process involved the Turks and—in a much more troublesome way—the Mongols. Both groups contributed to an important phase of Islamic expansion into India. On the western frontier there was no significant progress of conversion beyond the limits of early conquests. A counteroffensive of Christian powers (including the papal monarchy) gathered momentum in the first centuries of the second millennium CE, and temporarily—during the Crusades—challenged Islam in its Near Eastern heartland.

Early modern times at first sight offer more promising ground for constructions of Eurasian unity. Three great empires (Ottoman, Safavid, and Mughal) dominated the Islamic world. The Ottomans launched a new wave of expansion into Europe and absorbed the postimperial Byzantine state system that had been in the making since the thirteenth century, while the Mughals incorporated—in more variegated ways—a vast multitude of Indian states and territories. The Qing empire, centered on China and expanding into Inner Eurasia, was to some extent comparable to the Islamic formations. But alongside this undeniably cross-Eurasian pattern of continental empires, another development was to prove more decisive for the course of world history and conducive to new divergences between East and West: the creation of the first overseas empires by the states of the Atlantic seaboard.

Current historical scholarship shows a strong tendency to emphasize connections and conflicts between the societies of Inner Eurasia (largely but by no means exclusively nomadic) and their neighbors to the east, south, and west. This may be seen as the fourth Eurasian perspective. It is not easy to date the beginning of mutually formative interaction between Inner and Outer Eurasia (it was probably in the making at least as early as the second millennium BCE), but in any case, it looms particularly large in the history of states and empires from the middle of the first to the middle of the second millennium CE (Arnason 2015).

Growing interest in the Inner Eurasian side of this long entanglement has changed traditional perceptions. Inner Eurasian conquests of wealthier settled societies were sometimes extremely destructive, but they cannot be seen—as they were by serious historians just a few decades ago—as mere barbarian incursions or episodes of pure savagery. Inner Eurasian societies had their own demarcating civilizational patterns, not to be simply identified with nomadism, although the latter was of key importance. Nomads were typically the dominant force in symbiotic relationships with local settled societies or city-state cultures. Processes of state formation in Inner Eurasia reflected the specific social, ecological, and geopolitical conditions of the region (for an overview, see di Cosmo 1999, and also Kradin in, this volume). They repeatedly took an imperial turn, and a distinctive ideological vision of world domination accompanied the main ventures of that kind. Whether these recurrent features add up to a shared "civilization of the steppes" (a term occasionally used by French historians) is debatable, but a certain continuity seems evident from the rise of the sixth-century Turkic empire onward.

A better grasp of the Inner Eurasian background is only one side of the picture emerging from recent scholarship. Another is the variety and complexity of encounters with the historical civilizations of Outer Eurasia. Interactions with China were particularly close; imperial traditions in conflict across a civilizational border shaped the course of history on both sides, and the religious frameworks of imperial power may have drawn on common sources. In both cases, the claim to preeminent rulership was grounded in a privileged relationship to Heaven. The notion of a mandate of heaven was variously rationalized in the course of Chinese intellectual and political history, but its archaic version is widely believed to have been introduced toward the end of the second millennium BCE by the Zhou dynasty, whose geopolitical origins suggest an Inner Eurasian connection. As for encounters with settled civilizations farther to the south and west, the results were varied and significant. They include major Inner Eurasian influences on processes of state formation, sometimes accompanied by religious conversion of the conquerors, as in the Islamic world, sometimes across a persisting religious divide, as in Russia; adoption of marginal or persecuted religions by Inner Eurasian state builders (the conversions of the Khazars to Judaism and the Uighurs to Manichaeism are classic examples);

and the recurrent migrations of nomads into the sedentary zone, where they remained mobile, but on a new territorial and social basis. The last phenomenon, long underestimated, has recently attracted the attention of both historians and anthropologists (Khazanov and Wink 2001).

Relations between Inner and Outer Eurasia underwent a fundamental change around the middle of the second millennium CE. Sedentary empires, most notably the Russian and the Chinese ones, outdistanced all Inner Eurasian competitors and expanded into the center of the macroregion. This was one of the two great civilizational and geopolitical shifts that marked the onset of early modernity (the other being the European discovery and conquest of the Americas). The redistribution of power between Inner and Outer Eurasia was irreversible, but this did not mean that their borderlands had been removed from history. The most recent great Eurasian collapse, the disintegration of the Soviet empire, left a zone of successor states and societies in transition, from the Caucasus to Mongolia. The multilayered and cross-civilizational legacies of this reconstituted periphery make it a particularly promising terrain for historical anthropology.

Chapter Summaries

Johann P. Arnason discusses the conceptual foundations for civilizational analysis in classical French sociology, with particular emphasis on Marcel Mauss's contributions. The first text he considers is a note on the notion of civilization, published by Durkheim and Mauss jointly in 1913, but probably more directly based on Mauss's ideas. It introduces the concept of civilization as a necessary complement to the concept of society and indicates some general lines of further development. Civilizations appear as large-scale and long-term social-historical formations, characterized by an internal pluralism of societies. A later text, written by Mauss alone, defines the components, patterns, and spatiotemporal contours of civilizations in more specific terms. The result is a historical-sociological model with strong roots in anthropology. Arnason argues that this is still relevant as a corrective to the dominant approach in civilizational analysis. Two postscripts deal with civilizational themes in the works of two later French anthropologists, Claude Lévi-Strauss and Philippe Descola.

Hans Peter Hahn (chapter 2) reviews the many scholars, from Spengler and Freud to the theoreticians of the Frankfurt School, who contributed to shaping Norbert Elias's understanding of the "civilizing process," his classic work of the 1930s. Although it has been much criticized by anthropologists, and although little has been done to apply it outside Europe, Hahn argues that Elias's concept of civilization is not Eurocentric. His open-ended approach to *longue durée* history, his interest in the details of everyday life, and his ability to achieve scholarly distance, a skill nurtured in the course of a turbulent life on the margins, should all render him congenial to anthropologists. In particular, his notion of figuration is well suited to capturing the phenomenon of scale in contemporary studies of globalization.

Chapter 3 moves closer to current issues in interdisciplinary discussions. Yulia Prozorova shows that the interdisciplinary encounters between civilizational analysis and archaeology can be as rich and complex as the intercivilizational encounters studied by both. No one adheres any longer to unilinear evolutionist schemas, but Prozorova argues that archaeologists can push back the time frames and shed light on the roots of the Axial Age civilizations on which so much attention has been lavished hitherto. Those pre-axial formations deserve attention in their own right, no matter that there is no longer any unanimity concerning the necessary and sufficient criteria for what qualifies as a civilization. Cognitive archaeologists have developed theories of symbolic culture that resonate well with the focus on meaning and ideas which characterizes the sociological analysis of scholars such as Nelson, Eisenstadt, and Arnason. The idea that archaeology can function as an anthropology of the past can be traced back to Mauss. The work of Bruce Trigger exemplifies attempts to combine the two disciplines along civilizational lines. Recently, social archaeologists have drawn attention to the ecological and institutional factors that set limits to the autonomy of cultural ordering. The discipline has generated concepts that prove extremely useful in furthering the agenda of civilizational analysis, such as such as peer-polity competition, which may be a key to explaining a great deal of *intracivilizational* interaction. Prozorova concludes with an illustration of the *intercivilizational* encounter that took place in "frontier" regions north of the Black Sea between (Axial Age) Greeks and the "barbarian" Scythians, which led to a remarkable if short-lived and asymmetrical synthesis of two distinct traditions.

Anthropology returns in chapter 4, where Andre Gingrich treads a careful line. He suggests that the concept of civilization is a useful one in the ongoing revival of historical anthropology, given the need for general terms to extend analyses beyond the local or regional level. For him, a civilization is a culturally defined macroregion, distinguishable from an empire because it is only rarely congruent with an imperial state. Gingrich does, however, feel it necessary to specify the presence of cities as a condition, supplemented by the existence of writing. His reasons become clear in the second and longest part of his chapter, in which he shows how medieval South Arabia (fifth to fourteenth centuries CE) interacted with an encompassing Arab-Islamic civilization. The South Arabian record becomes particularly interesting if its various aspects are put together. This region was the only part of the Arabian peninsula where a distinctive older civilization was incorporated into the Islamic domain but not duly acknowledged in the Islamic narrative canon. South Arabia then became a refuge for groups and currents on the losing side of Islamic schisms. They remained on the sidelines of the struggle between rival centers of Islamic power. At the same time, the region became a center of maritime expansion, mostly commercial but in the very long run contributing to the rise of Islamic states in the Indonesian archipelago. Having demonstrated the value of the concept in historical analysis, in his concluding discussion Gingrich outlines why he considers the term *civilization* to be too burdened to be usable in the plural in any analysis of the contemporary world.

On the whole, Indologists and other scholars working on the South Asian subcontinent have turned more decisively against civilizational approaches than those who deal with the Islamic or the East Asian world. David Gellner reopens the case for the defense by arguing that, although earlier unitary anthropological models of Hindu civilization and a "great tradition" have been convincingly criticized, it can nonetheless be instructive to connect contemporary ethnography with long-term history and general anthropological models. He then turns to his fieldwork among the Newar of the Kathmandu valley who, despite their peripheral location and Tibeto-Burman language, can in key respects be taken to stand for a pre-Islamic India. The manner in which even the peasants participate in the ritual life of the city, the ritual center, is consistent with Sheldon Pollock's history of a "Sanskrit cosmopolis," while Clifford Geertz's analysis of Balinese politics is proffered as a comparable illustration of how sheer complexity in the politico-religious nexus can function to enable those at the bottom of the hierarchy to soften its impact, and even to "evade" the state. Gellner's paper thus makes a qualified case for the value of civilizational approaches to the Indian world.

By contrast, in chapter 6 Martin Fuchs develops a general critique of the concept of civilization and its use in comparative research, with particular reference to the Indian case. As he sees it, the notion of a civilizational dimension of human societies, introduced by Eisenstadt and presented as a move beyond classical traditions, cannot avoid the trap of essentialism. Civilizationists tend to take for granted that the various aspects of this dimension coalesce and form patterns more coherent and more stable than historical evidence suggests. This essentializing view is accentuated by association with territorial units and by the imputation of long-term processes supposedly conforming to the civilizational patterns. Some historical cases are more obviously incompatible with this model than are others, and Fuchs sees India as a paradigmatic counterexample. The roles of Buddhism and Islam in Indian history are very difficult to explain in the usual civilizational terms and too complicated to fit into a model of coexisting civilizations. Nor can civilizational analysis deal with the bhakti tradition of Indian religiosity, conspicuously neglected by Western scholars, and noteworthy not least because of its affinity with religious individualization.

Scholarship on Southeast Asia has dealt extensively with the contours of regional history, but no convincing model of a Southeast Asian civilization has yet been proposed. There are good reasons for describing the region as a multicivilizational area or crossroads, with enduring features of its own. Three contributions to this book adopt distinct anthropological perspectives. In chapter 7, Patrice Ladwig takes as his key concept Castoriadis's notion of the *imaginaire,* already used in civilizational analysis by Arnason. Whereas Fuchs argues that a more radical deconstruction is necessary, Ladwig suggests that anthropologists can be persuaded to overcome their reservations concerning the concept of civilization through adjusting the scale downward. Using Pollock's analysis of the Sanskrit case as a foil, Ladwig interprets the praxis of textual production in Southeast Asia, especially at the eastern borders of Theravada Buddhism in Laos, with particular emphasis on texts linked to statecraft and kingship He shows how a Buddhist imaginary, common to a vast region in which Pali literacy enabled considerable elite mobility, was everywhere supplemented by older and locally specific elements relevant to the politico-religious nexus. This approach throws new light on the long-standing discussion of Indianized states in Southeast Asia.

In chapter 8, Oliver Tappe undertakes a quite different localizing exercise for the same part of the world. Rejecting the familiar restriction of civilization to the Buddhist lowlands, he is also critical of James Scott's influential account of an essentially different "anarchist" frontier configuration (Zomia). Rather, upland "principalities" in the borders between present-day Laos and Vietnam have continuously borrowed from both Indian and Chinese macroregions, as well as from French colonial officials in more recent times. Ethnohistorical analysis shows that the outcomes, for example, in property relations, reflect material endowments. Contrary to the structural model of Edmund Leach, Tappe argues that these forms of civilizational encounter are highly contingent; traits typically spread through subtle, indirect means rather than through conquest or assimilation.

Joel Kahn explores anthropological objections to civilizational analysis in the light of his own research among Malay-speaking Muslim peoples in Southeast Asia, focusing on the analytic questions raised by the embedding of localized social systems in larger worlds. His earlier efforts to place this region in the larger whole of a capitalist world system came to seem unsatisfactory in the light of rapid social changes in the region after the 1970s. Kahn outlines shared characteristics of local communities across a "translocal" Malay World featuring complex parallel processes of economic development, state and nation building, ethnogenesis, and religious reform. The historical profile of the Malay world as a large-scale and long-term formation have become more visible with growing doubts about categories such as those of world system or mode of production, used by Marxist and neo-Marxist authors to place local formations in broader contexts. Kahn is hesitant to endorse civilizational analysis, partly because this Malay world is so heterogeneous, and partly because to apply this theoretical approach can itself be construed as a civilizational encounter, with ethical implications (e.g., concerning the representation of nonethnic Malays) outside the control of the investigator. But he nonetheless locates the Malay world at an analytical and historical level where the question of civilizations, their encounters, and their intermingling can be posed, and concludes with an invitation to further debate on the alternatives.

Civilizational analysts generally regard China as an exemplary case in point, and Sinologists have found the concept of civilization more congenial than many other area specialists, but such views have rarely been grounded in anthropology. Stephan Feuchtwang explores possibilities of this kind in chapter 10. He follows Mauss in deploying civilization as a moral concept. Civilization is best investigated through studying civilizations in the plural by means of a focus on embodied persons. Feuchtwang urges a concentration on the marginal and peripheral, since this is where encounters generative of renewal and of new civilizations tend to take place. He illustrates his theories with reference to the politico-religious beliefs and ritual practices of successive variations of Chinese civilization and the states that underpinned it between the Neolithic and the end of the imperial era. Imperial "cosmocracy" emerged from earlier shamanic institutions, which have persisted among neighboring Mongolian peoples. Self-cultivation was not just the prerogative of the sage-ruler but was expected of all. While the details of changes in patrilineal ancestral cults are specific to the Chinese case, Feuchtwang suggests that the sequential "steepening" of hierarchy is a phenomenon that occurs in other civilizations and deserves systematic comparative analysis.

Gonçalo Santos begins chapter 11 with details of his own experiences concerning "peeing and pooing" during his field research in a relatively poor community in rapidly modernizing rural Guangdong, China. He connects the spread of a very simple version of the interior flush-toilet to Norbert Elias's account of the "civilizing process" but the relationship between the micro materialities and societal progress toward new, more hygienic identities is full of contradictions. Toilet installation, replacing earlier reliance on external latrines and the domestic production of night soil to enhance agricultural fertility, is promoted by perceptions of backwardness and by social emulation inside the community. However, the failure to invest in public infrastructure for sewage leads to nonhygienic outcomes. More generally, adopting the Maussian approach to civilizational encounters, Santos notes the continued significance of a legacy of distinctively Chinese sanitary practices.

Shengmin Yang and Xiujie Wu provide a very different case study from China in chapter 12. Their starting point is the German-language anthropological paradigm of *Kulturkreislehre* in the first half of the twentieth century. A cultural circle is not to be confused with a civilization. Rather, these teachings offer a *method* for the reconstruction of cultural history, which should not be rejected out of hand for reasons of political correctness. After considering the impact of this approach in China in the presocialist decades via Catholic missionaries (some of whom produced work that can still be appreciated today), the authors devote the longest section of their chapter to a detailed analysis of the material culture, especially domestic architecture, of the Salar ethnic minority. While neither documents nor oral traditions are of much help in reconstructing "civilizational encounters" in their remote homeland in Qinghai, house design and technology betray nomadic links in the distant past. Economically inefficient heating arrangements have been resilient because they are consistent with the marginal character of this small minority, and in particular its kinship organization. The knowledge derived from this cultural history approach may be favorably compared with that derived from long-term, more holistic participant observation. Like Santos, but on a different scale, the authors affirm the significance of both localized, group-specific legacies, and of a more general civilizing process, which might be termed modernization.

In chapter 13, Nikolay Kradin explores civilization at two levels, both related to the historical interaction of Inner and Outer Eurasia. First, he describes the social and ecological conditions of pastoral nomads and explains why, with the notable exception of the Mongols, they have generally been considered to fall short of the criteria for civilization. Second, Kradin considers Russian scholars' interest in the concept of civilization in the aftermath of the USSR and of Marxist historical materialism. While numerous political entities inside and outside the Russian Federation nowadays abuse the concept for their nation-building purposes, Kradin is sympathetic to Lev Gumilev's long-term approach to local civilizations in the form of "super-ethnoses" in a Eurasian space corresponding roughly to the Mongol Empire at its zenith. His chapter thus represents a distinctive approach to the question of a Mongol heritage or a "post-Mongol commonwealth," debated from different angles by historians of Russia and Inner Eurasia.

Milena Benovska-Sabkova (chapter 14) addresses the invocation of "Orthodox civilization" in political rhetoric in the post-Soviet Russian Federation. The doctrines in question have antecedents in the Messianic and anti-Western discourses of presocialist centuries. They took on new, partially scientific guises in the works of the Eurasianist movement of the 1920s. The revival of Eurasianism at the end of the Soviet era has been accompanied by an efflorescence of very crude civilizational writing on the part of both secular and ecclesiastical elites. Benovska-Sabkova shows that nationalist distortions deprive these writings of any scientific plausibility while probing into the continuing power of these "ideological metatexts" for right-wing political mobilization in Russia.

References

Arnason, Johann P. 2015. "State Formation and Empire Building, 500 CE–1500 CE." In *Cambridge History of the World*, edited by Benjamin Z. Kedar and Merry Wiesner-Hanks, vol. 5: *Expanding Webs of Exchange and Conquest*. Cambridge: Cambridge University Press.

Benedict, Ruth. [1934] 1993. *Patterns of Culture*. New York: Houghton Mifflin.

Bidney, David. 1968. *Theoretical Anthropology*. New York: Transaction Publishers.

Braudel, Fernand. 1981–84. *Civilization and Capitalism, 15th–18th Century, v. 1–3.* New York: Harper Collins.

———. 1996. *The Mediterranean and the Mediterranean World in the Age of Philip II, v. 1–2.* Berkeley: University of California Press.

Clastres, Pierre. 2011. *Society against the State. Essays on Political Anthropology.* London: Zone Books; French original 1974.

Cline, Eric. 2014. *1177 B.C.: The Year Civilization Collapsed.* Princeton: Princeton University Press.

Di Cosmo, Nicola. 1999. "State Formation and Periodization in Inner Asian History." *Journal of World History* 10, no. 1: 1–40.

Durkheim, Émile. 1995. *The Elementary Forms of Religious Life.* New York: Free Press; French original 1912.

Eisenstadt, S. N., ed. 1986. *The Origins and Diversity of Axial Age Civilizations.* Stony Brook: State University of New York Press.

———. 2003. *Comparative Civilizations and Multiple Modernities, v. 1–2.* Leiden and Boston: Brill.

Elias, Norbert. 2000. *The Civilizing Process.* Malden, MA: Wiley-Blackwell; German original 1938.

———. 2012. *What Is Sociology?* Dublin: University College Dublin Press; German original 1970.

Gauchet, Marcel. 1999. *The Disenchantment of the World. A Political History of Religion.* Princeton: Princeton University Press.

———. 2005. "Politique et société. La leçon des sauvages." In *La condition politique*, 91–180. Paris: Gallimard; first published in *Textures* 10–11 and 12–13 (1975–76).

Geertz, Clifford. 1968. *Islam Observed: Religious Development in Morocco and Indonesia.* Chicago: University of Chicago Press.

———. 1980. *Negara. The Theatre State in Nineteenth-Century Bali.* Princeton: Princeton University Press.

———. 2000. *Available Light. Anthropological Reflections on Philosophical Topics.* Princeton: Princeton University Press.

Godelier, Maurice. 2007. *Au fondement des sociétés humaines. Ce que nous apprend l'anthropologie.* Paris: Albin Michel.

Goody, Jack. 2010. *The Eurasian Miracle.* Cambridge: Polity Press.

———. 2015. "Asia and Europe." *History and Anthropology* 26, no. 3: 263–307.

Hann, Chris. 2016. "A Concept of Eurasia." *Current Anthropology* 57, no. 1: 1–27.

Hodgson, Marshall S. 1974. *The Venture of Islam*, vol. 1–3. Chicago: University of Chicago Press.

Huntington, Samuel P. 1996. *The Clash of Civilizations and the Remaking of World Order*. New York: Simon and Schuster.

Jones, Eric, Colin White, and Lionel Frost. 1993. *Coming Full Circle. An Economic History of the Pacific Rim*. Boulder: Westview.

Khazanov, Anatoly M., and André Wink, eds. 2001. *Nomads in the Sedentary World*. Richmond, Surrey: Curzon Press.

Kroeber, Alfred L. 1963. *Style and Civilizations*. Los Angeles: University of California Press.

———. 2011. *Checklist of Civilizations and Culture*. New York: Aldine.

Lefort, Claude.1986. *Essais sur le politique*. Paris: Seuil.

Lévi-Strauss, Claude. 1945. "French Sociology." In *Twentieth-Century Sociology*, edited by G. Gurvitch and W. E. Moore, 503–37. New York: Philosophical Library.

———. 1967. *The Scope of Anthropology*. London: Jonathan Cape.

———. 1969a *The Elementary Structures of Kinship*. Boston: Beacon Press.

———. 1969b *The Savage Mind*. Chicago: University of Chicago Press.

Lombard, Denys. 2004. *Le carrefour javanais. Essai d'histoire globale*. Paris: Editions de l'Ecole des Hautes Etudes en Sciences Sociales.

Mann, Michael. 1986–2012. *Sources of Social Power, v. 1–4.* Cambridge: Cambridge University Press.

Nelson, Benjamin. 2011. *On the Roads to Modernity. Conscience, Science, and Civilizations. Selected Writings, with a new introduction by Toby E. Huff*. Lanham, MD: Lexington Books, Rowman and Littlefield.

Nordholt, Henk Schulte. 2014. *The Spell of Power. A History of Balinese Politics, 1650–1940*. Leiden and Boston: Brill.

Schlanger, Nathan, ed. 2006. *Marcel Mauss: Techniques, Technology, and Civilization*. Oxford and New York: Berghahn Books.

Tambiah, Stanley. 1976. *World Conqueror and World Renouncer. A Study of Buddhism and Polity in Thailand against a Historical Background*. Cambridge: Harvard University Press.

———. 1985. *Culture, Thought, and Social Action. An Anthropological Perspective*. Cambridge: Harvard University Press.

Therborn, Göran. 2000. "Globalization: Dimensions, Historical Waves, Regional Effects, Normative Governance." *International Sociology* 15, no. 2: 151–79.

1

MAUSS REVISITED

The Birth of Civilizational Analysis from the Spirit of Anthropology

Johann P. Arnason

Those who brought comparative civilizational approaches back into historical sociology after 1970 (Benjamin Nelson and S. N. Eisenstadt were the two most important pioneers) were very conscious of work done by classical forerunners. They saw themselves as revivers of a research program, prematurely abandoned and then temporarily forgotten because of the mutual estrangement of sociology and history. But they were less interested in tracing the details of classical sociological arguments in this vein, or identifying rival currents within that context. A conceptual history of civilizational themes in classical sociology has yet to be written; the present chapter will not go beyond selective prolegomena to such a discussion, and the focus will be on specific cases within a limited period of time. Classical sociology will, for present purposes, be equated with the generation of Émile Durkheim and Max Weber, active roughly between 1890 and 1920. Some later work in France will be discussed as a highly significant postscript to the classical phase proper.

Within these terms of reference, the first point to be noted is a fundamental ambiguity of the classical legacy. On the one hand, Max Weber's comparative studies of Occidental, Indian, and Chinese traditions and societies are commonly regarded as exemplars of civilizational analysis, and although nobody disputes the need for major corrections to Weber's theoretical and historical presuppositions, his overall project is still an obligatory matter of debate. However, Weber did not use the concept of civilization; in the most relevant formulations, he referred to "cultural worlds." This term is easily reconciled with the emphasis on culture in the works that later reopened the case for civilizational analysis. Even so, it must be admitted that Weber did very little to clarify the conceptual basis of his comparative analyses. He did not develop the concept of culture as a world-making pattern of interpretations and attitudes, adumbrated in an early essay (Weber 1949). At best, we can trace implicit uses of it in substantive contexts. It does not figure in the exposition of basic concepts that came to be regarded as a first chapter of the misidentified magnum opus, *Economy and Society.* On the other hand, the most important classical attempt to lay a conceptual groundwork for the study of civilizations came from the French side and was not backed up by any corresponding comparative or historical work. The key texts are a short but rich note by Émile Durkheim and Marcel Mauss, originally published in 1913 but not translated into English until much later (Durkheim and Mauss 2006), and a later reconsideration by Mauss, prompted by a debate with scholars from other disciplines (Mauss 2006). The most striking contrast with Weber's work is the effort to define civilizations with explicit reference to basic sociological concepts, and to build directly on emerging anthropological scholarship. The latter aspect was particularly alien to Weber's concerns. His comparative focus was on *Hochkulturen,* more or less synonymous with the definition later proposed by archaeologists and prehistorians who equated the "origins of civilization" with statehood, urban centers, written records, and social stratification based on wealth and power; but given the state of historical knowledge, Weber's project could only make marginal reference to the archaic civilizations that are now seen as the first instances according to this criterion.

In brief, the classical legacy of civilizational analysis consists of two separate subtraditions, with different visions of overlapping fields and without any mutual contact. The late-twentieth-century revival drew on both sources, but in a problematic and unbalanced way. Benjamin Nelson translated Durkheim and Mauss's note on the notion of civilization in 1971 and drew attention to its pioneering conceptual insights. But his own contributions to civilizational analysis were predominantly aligned with Weber's agenda; while he was well aware of the need to problematize and reformulate various aspects of the Weberian paradigm, his arguments in that vein do not suggest any links to the French classics. The primary source of substantive corrections is Nelson's historical scholarship, particularly in the area of medieval studies (Nelson 1968; 1969 [1949]; 2011, 213–29). A revised Weberian orientation is even clearer in Eisenstadt's work; his main aim—at least from the 1970s onward—was to compare the major Eurasian civilizations in a more balanced and comprehensive way than Weber had done. The core idea of this research program shifts the civilizational approach farther away from anthropology and prehistory (Eisenstadt 1986; 2003). Eisenstadt came to see the "Axial Age," the period usually defined in terms of a few centuries around the middle of the last millennium BCE, not only as a convenient entry to civilizational studies, but—above and beyond that—as a historical turning point that made the civilizational dimension of human societies fully visible for the first time. The justification for this claim is found in the intellectual and religious transformations that occurred in several centers during the period. It could be argued that the latent presence of this dimension from the beginning of history, which Eisenstadt seems to admit, calls for another kind of civilizational approach besides the axial one; but he never pursued that line of thought. His axial frame of reference led him to sideline not only prehistoric and tribal societies, but also archaic civilizations, which he tended to see as culturally continuous with the prehistoric past.

To sum up, the post-1970 return of civilizational analysis did not lead to closer examination of the French sources. The idea of civilizations in the plural was revived with explicit reference to Durkheim and Mauss (and in preference to Weber's more tentative terminology). But there was no engagement with the specific thrust of their argument, and no reappraisal of the anthropological connection. The following discussion will be based on close reading of the relevant texts, with strong emphasis on Mauss's 1929–30 publication, and aim at a critical reconstruction of the explicit as well as the underlying links between civilizational analysis and anthropology. It will, in both regards, go beyond an earlier comment on Durkheim and Mauss (Arnason 2003).

From Society to Civilization

The first point to be made about the 1913 text, the inaugural encounter of our two key authors with the civilizational field, is that the concept of civilization is introduced as a necessary complement to the concept of society that had been developed by the Durkheimian school and become central to its definition of sociology. This move is all the more interesting if we compare it to a later constellation. Late-twentieth-century social theory problematized the dominant concept of society; critical arguments along such lines were put forward by Anthony Giddens (1979), Alain Touraine (1981), and Michael Mann (1986), to mention only the most important authors. What they rejected was a conceptual decision that imposed over-integrated images of social life, articulated on various levels but ultimately derived from an idealized view of the nation-state. This model was, as the critics saw it, exemplified by Parsonian sociology and could be traced back to the Durkheimian tradition. If we read Durkheim and Mauss in light of this controversy, it seems clear that their concept of society prefigures the one that later came in for criticism, They refer to a human group "which includes within itself all the others and, in consequence, surrounds and envelops all forms of social activity," and go on to equate this higher-level society with "political society, the tribe, the people, the nation, the city, the modern state, etc." (Durkheim and Mauss 2006, 36). Politically instituted society is, in other words, society par excellence, but the quoted formulation shows that this view allows for a wide variety of institutional patterns, and since tribal societies are included, the "political organisms" (ibid., 36) in question should not be equated with states. Some kind of regulating authority over collective life within a territory is a necessary and sufficient criterion.

For Durkheim and Mauss, this concept of society is a first and fundamental step toward mapping the social realm. Civilizations are then introduced as formations presupposing societies and at the same time presupposed by them. This is another point to be contrasted with later debates: the reactivation of the civilizational approach after 1970 took place in a context marked by diffuse doubts about the dominant concept of society, but not in direct contact with the sustained critique mentioned above. Nelson presented his civilizational turn as a necessary move beyond the familiar terrain of sociology; in his post-Parsonian phase, Eisenstadt criticized a widespread tendency of contemporary sociology to misunderstand social structures as (somehow or other) naturally given. This is, first and foremost, an antievolutionistic position, but then evolutionism was at least a plausible corollary to the concept of society perfected by Parsons. Neither Nelson nor Eisenstadt intervened directly in the debate on "sociology without society," to use Touraine's formulation.

If we return to Durkheim and Mauss with these later developments in mind, that cannot mean a reendorsement of their position. Both the critical reflection on concepts of society and the theorizing of civilizations have gone beyond classical beginnings. But what can still be learned from the French classics is a way of bringing together the two lines of discussion. The social—or, in more adequate terms, social-historical—realm is a domain of multiple formations; in addition to those first noted and defined by the social sciences, there are others, less easily identifiable and in need of new conceptualizing moves. The notion of civilizations in the plural enters sociology as a necessary complement to the concept of society, and hand in hand with a reference to changing historical contents of the latter. This observation is a starting point for further differentiations on both sides, the societal and the civilizational. By the same token, the object domain of civilizational analysis is not to be thought of in isolation from other types of social-historical formations; it exists only in and through a field of interrelations with other such formations, and civilizational patterns are influenced by this broader context.

As will be seen, the French classics still have something to tell us about these matters. But every step of their argument is important, and the next one is of particular interest. It consists in the introduction of anthropological and prehistorical research as the most straightforward source of knowledge on civilizations. In fact, the notion invoked in the title is only proposed after a reference to the "immense labor" of "ethnography and prehistory in particular" (Durkheim and Mauss 2006, 36). In the given context, it seems clear that ethnography is identical with what the Anglophone world would now call anthropology, and not just with the empirical part of that discipline (it is credited with "significant theoretical results" [ibid., 36]). Anthropology and prehistory converge in the study of societies before or without writing (the term *sociétés sans écriture* was at one stage current among French anthropologists). The results achieved in this field are solid enough to constitute a primary empirical basis for a concept of civilization, and to allow a provisional definition. Civilizations "overflow frontiers" (ibid., 37); they "extend beyond the territory of any single nation, or they develop over periods of time exceeding the history of any single society" (ibid., 36). Durkheim and Mauss were obviously using the term *nation* in a way that would now be branded as unhistorical. It refers to an indefinite range of collective identities, and is thus easily coupled with the broad concept of society noted above. The transnational and transsocietal character of civilizations, evident in both spatial and temporal dimensions, can be observed in various domains of social life; the examples cited by Durkheim and Mauss range from art and language to religious and political institutions. Moreover, these different aspects are interconnected. Durkheim and

Mauss refer to an "integrated system" (ibid., 37); but here as in other cases, it would be misguided to assume that their terms carry exactly the same meaning as they mostly do today. The concept of system acquired stronger connotations in postclassical sociology.

Although this well-articulated view of civilizations is presented with direct reference to anthropological inquiry, Durkheim and Mauss resist attempts to limit the civilizational perspective (under which they include the German theory of *Kulturkreise*, cultural circles or areas) to that context. As they argue, "Ethnography has proved insufficient for the task, and history has to make the same kind of researches for historical peoples" (ibid., 38). The grounds for appealing to history are not spelled out, but a two-fold reason seems obvious: historical societies, in the sense still accepted at the time, enter into more complex and dynamic formations than those that preceded or remained outside the main current, and their destinies are known through richer and more revealing sources. Durkheim and Mauss then take the argument one step farther. The historical record highlights the social nature of civilizations: "International life is but a social life of a superior kind, which sociology should take on board" (ibid., 38); a third discipline (beyond anthropology and history) thus enters the field, in order to address this complex subject. Sociology needs the study of civilizations no less than the other way around. What the authors have in mind is obviously the kind of sociology that retains close contact with history. With this approach in mind, they take a closer look at an earlier attempt to align the idea of civilization with a sociological project. Auguste Comte is criticized for having tried to theorize civilization in general without first coming to grips with "the great collective personalities that have been formed in the course of history" (ibid., 37). The implications are clear: a viable idea of civilization in general can only—if at all—be developed on the basis of concrete analyses dealing with specific civilizations.

The interdisciplinary framework is the most clearly formulated part of Durkheim and Mauss's argument. When it comes to more specific issues, the main points to be noted have to do with a series of differentiations within the concept of civilization. It refers on the one hand to "a kind of moral milieu, within which are immersed a certain number of nations and of which each national culture is but a particular form" (ibid., 37). The term *moral* is obviously to be understood in the broad sense associated with the traditional French notion of *sciences morales,* more or less coextensive with the human sciences. We are, in other words, dealing with shared but variously developed collective representations. On the other hand, the authors emphasize inter-action and diffusion, more intensive within civilizational units than across their frontiers. Nothing more is said on the relationship between these two aspects, nor on possible changes to it, but some historical examples may be suggested. If we consider East Asia as a civilizational unit, with a regional core made up of China, Korea, and Japan (not an uncontested view, but in my opinion the most plausible one), it seems clear that the constitutive moral milieu was a complex of cultural visions, traditions, and techniques that took shape on a regional scale between the third and the seventh centuries of our era and remained dominant until the nineteenth century. By comparison, the level of interaction between the core countries seems to have varied greatly during the long period in question. Western Christendom and its modern European sequel represent a different constellation. The formative stage was characterized by a very strong set of shared representations, embodied in key institutions. The specification that Durkheim and Mauss ascribe to national cultures became particularly pronounced during later phases of European history, whereas the interaction between political units became more intensive. We may note that expanding networks of interaction can give rise to multicivilizational constellations, more integrated than their neighboring zones, but without a corresponding shift to shared collective representations. William McNeill (1963) described such formations as ecumenic zones; the first of them emerged in the Near East and the Eastern Mediterranean during the second half of the second millennium BCE, but came to an end with a great civilizational collapse (the crisis of the Late Bronze Age in the twelfth century BCE).

Another distinction concerns the ability of civilizations to cross borders: they do this "either by spreading from specific centers by their own powers of expansion, or as a result of the relationships established between different societies" (ibid., 37). Here too, we can use historical examples to clarify the range of questions implicit in the remark. There is hardly a civilization without some difference between central units (their number varies) and more peripheral ones. Byzantine civilization until 1204 (the sack of Byzantium by Western crusaders) was an extreme case of one center dominating the scene, culturally and politically; a more multicentral pattern prevailed during the following period (until 1453). The idea of Islamic civilization spreading from an original center in the Arabian peninsula has now been abandoned; its main patterns developed in the much larger geographical framework of the Near and Middle East during a few centuries after the conquest, and this process involved a shifting balance of several centers. This heartland was, in turn, central to later civilizational expansion. A particularly interesting pattern developed in ancient Greek civilization. In an early stage, a heartland with multiple centers became the hub of civilizational expansion on a large scale (known to historians as colonization). The enlarged Greek world then saw a rapid multiplication of centers. Within the new configuration, fifth-century Athens became a center of a new kind, but only in certain fields, and for a short period.

Finally, Durkheim and Mauss hint at an issue that concerns the epistemological status rather than the social-historical content of the concept of civilization. Their examples of civilizations, few in number and very briefly identified, suggest further differentiation. If there is a "Christian civilization . . . elaborated by all Christian groups" (ibid., 37), it seems logical to assume that further civilizational units (such as the Western Christian and Byzantine worlds) can be distinguished within this broadly defined one; and the same applies to "a Mediterranean civilization . . . common to all the populations bordering the Mediterranean coast" (37). Here, we can draw on Mauss's later text on civilizations, where the point is made more explicitly and in a way clearly continuous with the 1913 text. Mauss mentions "a very ancient civilization all through the coasts and islands of the Pacific," then singles out "a civilization of the South and Central Pacific" and goes on to distinguish "Malayo-Polynesian civilization, a Melanesian civilization, and a Macronesian civilization" (Mauss 2006, 63). Obviously, the choice of a broadly or more narrowly defined civilization will depend on the context of inquiry. To put it another way, a civilizational dimension (Eisenstadt 2003), consisting in the "overflowing of frontiers" mentioned above, is inherent in social-historical reality. Specific boundaries and identities within this dimension must be drawn on the basis of more or less broad interpretive projects. The concept of civilization would thus be applicable at different levels. We can, in the language of later philosophical debates, describe this position as a version of hermeneutical realism. While there is, at least for the present writer, no reason to disagree in principle, it may be useful to introduce more specific terms. For example, the medieval European world could be characterized as a civilizational constellation, within which the basic concept of civilization would be applicable to both its Western Christian and Byzantine parts. Analogously, the concept of civilizational sequence can be used to identify multicivilizational configurations across time, such as the

European trajectory from antiquity to modernity. That view seems more adequate than the construct of one continuous Western civilization.

The joint text discussed above belongs to the same period as Durkheim's *Elementary Forms of Religious Life*. It is therefore natural to ask whether civilizational concerns are reflected in the latter work. The basic framework of Durkheim's approach to Australian religions resembles the conceptual map that he laid out more or less simultaneously together with Mauss. The aboriginal Australian world is treated as a family of societies, interacting with each other and open to mutual influences. The developmental trends apparent in their religious life—indications of a supra-tribal turn—grew out of this multisocietal context. A more explicit reference can be found in the last chapter, where Durkheim outlines his conception of religion as a matrix of cultural and institutional development. In that connection, he argues that every civilization has its system of basic concepts (Durkheim 1995, 437). Given the importance of the link between religious and cognitive patterns, this claim suggests a crucial role for civilizational factors: they appear as key carriers of the metainstitutional dynamic attributed to religion. We are thus left with the impression of a privileged relationship between civilizations and religions, but without further clarification. The affinity with the 1913 text is undeniable, but limited. Considering the scope and ambition of Durkheim's last major work, he seems strangely reluctant to apply the civilizational perspective in any systematic way. This conclusion is reinforced by the reference to civilization in general at the end of the well-known essay on the dualism of human nature (Durkheim 1960). Here, we find a much more positive appreciation of Comte than in the 1913 text: his definition of sociology as a science of civilization is accepted, and Durkheim links it to his own theoretical perspective. Civilization now appears as an ongoing historical creation of human nature by society. There is no trace of the multicivilizational model proposed by Durkheim and Mauss in their "note" of 1913.

Durkheim's apparent reluctance to work with clarified systematic concept of civilization is in marked contrast to Mauss's later efforts. Mauss had already shown strong interest in spelling out the assumptions, corollaries, and possible extensions of the Durkheimian research program toward anthropology (see, e.g., the texts collected in Mauss 1968). In light of this, and of later work, it seems a plausible guess that Mauss was the main author of the "note." He was, in any case, the only one to take up its line of argument and try to develop some key points further.[1] This was done in 1929, in the context of a public discussion with scholars from other disciplines. The record of the discussion as a whole was published in the following year (Febvre et al. 1930). Mauss's contribution has been published separately and translated into English (Mauss 2006), and some comments by other participants are available in a collection of his writings (Mauss 1974, 2, 481–85). His main aim in this essay was to clarify conceptual orientations, in particular the *elements,* the *form,* and the *area* of a civilization.

Conceptual Orientations

Mauss begins with the elements, also—indeed, more frequently—described as phenomena and occasionally as facts of civilization. Here, the fundamental given is a plurality of human societies, characterized by two kinds of phenomena: those common to a larger or smaller group of societies and those demarcating a single society from the others. The former are, for Mauss, the defining components of civilizations. Both sets of phenomena presuppose contact and interaction. On the civilizational side, Mauss stresses transmission and borrowing, refers once again to the overflowing of boundaries and concludes that civilizational phenomena are "essentially international, extra-national" (Mauss 2006, 61). But societies also "develop their distinctive features" (ibid., 62) through interaction with others, and hence in the context of civilizations. To round off the picture, it must be added that both kinds of phenomena can also survive or even lead to loss of contact: societies may develop isolationist strategies in order to retain their distinctive traits, and common features can be found among societies separated by historical upheavals (Mauss's example is the enduring similarity of mutually isolated pygmy populations in Southeast Asia).

When it comes to more specific description of the elements or phenomena, Mauss emphasizes their variety, historicity, and interconnectedness. Every type of social phenomenon, from technology and institutions to art and religious beliefs, can enter into civilizational connections. It is worth noting that, although political organization is retained as the defining constitutive feature of a single society, Mauss includes principles of political life (such as the Greek idea of constitution) among the elements capable of transmission. Neither the extent nor the relative weight of these civilizational phenomena (compared to the societal ones) can be determined on any general grounds. The whole process depends on historical constellations:

some civilizations can develop particularly strong unifying patterns, while others leave more space for the differentiation of member societies. But in both cases and at any intermediate level, the phenomena that make up a civilization are integrated. Mauss continues to use the concept of system to describe these formations. He even claims that a civilization represents "a hyper-social system of social systems" (ibid., 62). But as noted above, we should not take this in the strong sense now accepted. It would seem more compatible with Mauss's general approach to allow for different forms of integration in different civilizational contexts.

In the discussion that followed Mauss's presentation, Henri Berr raised a point that Mauss seems to have left unanswered: Should we not distinguish between objects and elements of civilization? (Mauss 1974, 2, 484). All phenomena capable of migrating from one society to another can be described as civilizational objects: surely, this indeterminate category should not be conflated with the fundamental elements that constitute a civilization? The issue was not taken farther, but it can be linked to an implicit question that was not posed on this occasion. Mauss insists on the civilizational potential of all institutions and does not consider the possibility of privileged or particularly formative elements. This is most striking in regard to the role of religion. Mauss was, from early on, reserved about Durkheim's conception of religion as the original framework of all social phenomena, He did not doubt that religion was both important in its own right and exceptionally capable of influencing other domains of social life. But he seems to have preferred a model that allowed for simultaneous differentiation of religion and other institutional spheres; the broader impact of religion thus appears as transinstitutional rather than metainstitutional, and the degree of religious determination may differ from one context to another. Mauss insisted on the religious character of the early state, but he also saw its later development as a secularizing and juridifying process.

In short, the evidence shows that Mauss was moving toward a more flexible, comparative, and empirically grounded version of the Durkheimian approach to religion. It is less clear whether a theoretical alternative was in the making. Drawing on Lévi-Strauss's seminal essay on Mauss's legacy, Camille Tarot (1999, 2008) argues that Mauss was trying to formulate a novel conception of the symbolic, understood as a foundation of society and more broadly defined than was Durkheim's religious frame of reference. This new paradigm would not have abandoned the Durkheimian notion of the sacred. Rather, the task foreshadowed but left unfinished was to relocate the sacred within the symbolic. For Tarot, divergent interpretations developed around the notion of *mana* are the most conclusive proof of differences between Durkheim and Mauss. For Durkheim, *mana* is "identical with the totemic principle, the impersonal collective force of the reunited clan" (Tarot 2008: 306); for Mauss, it "associates force and representation, meaning and power" (ibid., 306), and constitutes the common ground of magic and religion. This claim is convincing, at least in the general sense that Mauss was revising the Durkheimian conception of religion in significant ways and on conceptual as well as empirical levels. But in the present context, it is also striking that arguments in that vein are not linked to the evolving ideas on civilizations (apart from one very vague allusion, to be noted below). This mutual isolation reflects a general feature of Mauss's work: he pursued several lines of inquiry and interpretation, without bringing them together in a clearly articulated project or a comprehensive work. The lack of integration does not detract from the originality of his work, but it has obstructed reception and caused some of the less prominent themes to be neglected, not least that of civilization.

The second notion to be clarified in the 1929 text is the *form* of a civilization. For Mauss, this is "the sum (the Σ) of the specific aspects taken by the ideas, practices and products which are more or less common to a certain number of given societies" (Mauss 2006, 63). The form thus seems to be more or less reducible to a collection of elements. We can easily identify both direct reasons and an enduring rationale for this approach. Mauss's emphasis on a plurality of components is closely connected to his critique of contemporary trends in anthropology. Against the search for single cultural traits, dominating whole regions and traditions, he maintains that civilizations are defined "not by one characteristic, but rather by a certain number—generally quite large—of them, and perhaps by the respective doses of these characteristics" (ibid., 65). There is no denying the relevance of this point to later debates. A certain tendency to seek common denominators for the various aspects of a civilizational pattern is still apparent (Oswald Spengler's "primal symbol" may be seen as an extreme and mostly unacknowledged precursor of such views). Against this trend, it is still appropriate to insist on the presence of multiple factors and the importance of their relative weight. That said, Mauss's definition of a civilizational form remains incomplete and fails to clarify the question of civilizational integration. The form of a civilization should not be envisaged as a separate principle beyond the components, nor as one of the latter dominating the others. Instead, it must be understood as a unity presupposing and at the same time complementing internal diversity. The sum total of civilizational elements does not, as such, amount to a unifying form. Mauss's further comments show that he was aware of the problem, but he evidently found it difficult to solve. He reiterates that "each civilization has its "aspect," and that their products have their "style, their *facies,* that can be analysed" (ibid., 66–67). The idea of style as a civilizational profile was later taken up by A. L. Kroeber, but on a more Spenglerian than Maussian note, and it never got very far. The question of the internal unity of civilizations is still subject to controversy. I have argued elsewhere (Arnason 2014) that closer examination of the varying relationships between religion and politics—the religio-political nexus, to use a convenient term—seems the most promising way to take the debate forward.

Mauss's third concept, the *area* of a civilization, is at first sight easy to grasp. It refers to "the geographic extent of the distribution of the total . . . of the common phenomena regarded as characteristic, as typical of this civilisation" (ibid., 63). Mauss adds that the "abrupt halt of an area of civilisation, is very often as sudden as the border of an established society and even of what we call a state" (ibid., 68). But this implies the possibility of less clearly marked borders or frontier areas, and thus the need for comparative perspectives on the self-demarcating practices and dynamics of different civilizations.

Another complicating factor is the notion of a civilizational *layer* (*couche*) defined as "the form which a given civilisation of a given extension takes in a given time" (ibid., 64). Mauss introduces this term only briefly, but seems to regard it as a more precise alternative to the periodizing conventions of historians. A closer look at links between layers and areas is suggested by the metaphor of a "family of societies," mentioned above and clearly meant to indicate a network of connections in time and space. If we were, for example, to take Max Weber's idea of the Occident as an example (not that Mauss ever did), it represents a complex and changing combination of areas and layers. According to Weber, the Occidental trajectory begins in the Eastern Mediterranean, with cultural innovations in ancient Greece and ancient Israel, and culminates in the Euro-American North Atlantic. The boundaries of this civilizational formation are thus highly mobile, and successive layers are associated with specific areas, but also endowed with abilities to cross their borders, and not always in the same fashion. The expansive style and capacity of ancient Greek civilization differ from those of the medieval European city or the societies most affected by the transformative potential of the Reformation. If we go on to consider the record of particular formations within this long history, selectively analyzed by Weber, the case of medieval Western Christendom (which Weber never discussed as a whole) reveals a distinctive pattern of temporal and spatial interconnections. This was a highly dynamic civilization, with successive historical layers ranging from the primary cultural and institutional crystallizations of the early Middle Ages to the multiple transformations of the late medieval phase. During the roughly millennial period in question, the emergence of new layers coincided with stages of civilizational expansion to the north and the east, giving rise to a new and more complex constellation of regions. A very different configuration can be found in East Asia. If we define this area in the way proposed above, its boundaries and its basic geopolitical structure have been remarkably constant, but successive historical layers are characterized by changing patterns of civilizational links and interactions between the societies of the region.

I have reconstructed Mauss's discussion of basic concepts, with some reference to their possible applications to the richer material now available. Having established the basic conceptual criteria, he reiterates the view that the phenomena thus circumscribed should be treated as forms of collective life, continuous though not identical with the field already subsumed under the concept of society. The elements, forms, and limits of civilizations "correspond to an inherent quality common to all social phenomena": the latter, "be they a symbol, a word, an instrument or an institution, be they even best constructed language or science: be they the instrument best adapted to the best and most numerous ends, be they the most rational possible, the most human, *they are still arbitrary*" (ibid., 67). It is here, and only here, that we can detect a link between Mauss's discovery of civilizations and his shift toward the symbolic. The list of social phenomena begins with "a symbol," but following Mauss's suggestions in other writings, as well as Tarot's interpretation of the work as a whole, it is easy to argue that this is not just one item among others; rather, it represents the medium in and through which the others exist and function. If civilizational patterns are matters of choice, however implicit and indirect, the very notion of choice only makes sense in relation to a spectrum of possibilities.

In the concluding part of his discussion, Mauss links together two themes that had already appeared in the text written with Durkheim. The idea that societies or nations develop distinctive features in the context of a larger civilization was an integral part of the argument to be developed. The notion of a universal civilization, understood either as a common ground or as an emerging union of specific civilizations, had to be confronted and put in proper perspective. Mauss now places greater emphasis on the interrelations of these two trends, the particularist and the universalist. As he notes, the Euro-American West, where the formation of nations and nation-states gives rise to highly visible boundaries and identities within a civilizational domain, also exemplifies another possibility: a "simultaneously universalist and nationalist belief" (ibid., 67), which claims privileged and paradigmatic civilizational status on behalf of particular nations. In theory, the aim is a mutual perfecting of nation and civilization, but the practical result would be a closed state where civilizational boundaries coincide with political ones. Mauss adds the somewhat cryptic comment that "some nations have realised this ideal and others, such as the United States of America, consciously pursue it" (ibid., 72). In any case, the upshot of these constructions is a subordination of universalistic pretentions to particularistic identities and interests. On a different note, we can think of "*the* human civilization in the abstract, in the future" (ibid., 72). For Mauss, this vision is open to the empirically grounded criticism that it has, time and again, proved to be an extrapolation of the Western trajectory. But he seems inclined to admit that contemporary developments—those of the early twentieth century, notwithstanding World War I—are for the first time giving real content to the idea of a universal human civilization, a "common fund of overall achievements of societies and civilizations" (ibid., 73). The first example to be mentioned is science, increasingly dominant in modern life and by definition committed to a universal language. Interestingly, Mauss then refers to the cinema as a new and tendentially universal mode of communication, description, and—less obviously—tradition. But skepticism is still in order. Mauss admits that "elements of civilization" might be transformed into "elements of national violence" (ibid., 72), and he fears that nations might still break away from humanity. Events were to prove him right.

In the discussion that followed Mauss's exposé (not included in the English translation), his cautious universalism was linked to the idea of progress. His attempt to clarify that question was summed up in a virtually untranslatable formulation: "Il y a un mouvement général vers le plus être et vers quelque chose de plus fin. Je ne dis pas vers le mieux être" (Mauss 1974, 2, 483). The upshot of arguments for and against was that a universal civilization could only be envisaged as a result a result of gradual convergence, not as a common foundation. Mauss admitted that this would have to involve a "mouvement general," not just particular achievements in specific fields, but stopped short of identifying the general trend with overall progress. Although the evidence so far seemed to support the idea of a civilizing process (in Norbert Elias's terms), transcending the borders of particular civilizations, Mauss warned against the instrumentalization of this trend by resurgent particularisms.

Mauss's anthropo-sociological conception of civilizations was not developed beyond the sketches discussed above, and it found no systematic application in his work. Echoes and allusions can be traced in his writings, but a detailed survey is not possible here. I will only mention the most interesting case. In *The Gift*, Mauss's acclaimed and widely debated masterpiece, the argument moves from close description of exemplary cases to general theoretical and moral conclusions. The last section notes in passing that societies with fully established gift practices "represent fittingly the great Neolithic civilization" (Mauss 1990 [1924], 72). This is a statement with far-reaching implications, but it has not received much attention among interpreters of *The Gift*. The reference to a neolithic civilization invokes a vast spectrum of societies and a long history, and thus recalls Mauss's demarcation of civilizations in very broad or more restrictive terms, depending on the context of inquiry. His account of the gift has, with some justification, been presented as an analysis of the social bond, more complex and adequate than the original Durkheimian version (Caillé 2007). It also proposed a corrective to the economic culture of modern capitalism and a theoretical foundation for the politics of cooperativist socialism (Dzimira 2007). If this crucially important pattern of social life is rooted in a neolithic legacy, Mauss is—by implication—arguing that a civilizational survival of the first magnitude can still be reactivated for the purposes of social reform. This might be seen as a more optimistic prefiguration of later appeals to a neolithic model (especially those of Lévi-Strauss).

There was no direct continuation of the civilizational approach outlined by Durkheim and Mauss, either within the Durkheimian school (whose influence was already declining when Mauss wrote the second text discussed here), or in broader scholarly circles. The historians who used the concept of civilization relied on their own versions of it, often intuitive rather than theoretical. Marcel Granet's work on China (Granet 1968a) is sometimes cited as an example of civilizational studies inspired by Durkheim and Mauss. But the connection is of limited importance. There is no doubt about Granet's familiarity with the ideas as well as the research of Durkheimian sociologists, and he must have been fully aware of the twist they had given to the notion of civilization. However, his discussion of Chinese civilization makes no reference to conceptual issues. The idea of a "family of societies" seems to be taken for granted when Granet analyzes the shared cultural milieu of the "warring states" that were in the end unified by an empire of conquest. He argues that it was the sentiment of a civilizational community that made the Chinese accept imperial unification. And when he writes, in a companion volume on Chinese thought, that for the Chinese "the principle of a universal harmonious agreement [*bonne entente universelle*] coincided with the principle of universal intelligibility" (Granet 1968b, 480), the Durkheimian notion of social interaction embedded in collective representations is obviously not far away. But since the work ends with the early empire and does not refer to any significant changes during later periods, there is no mention of the more complex "family of societies" that emerged in East Asia when the culture of imperial China was appropriated by other states in the region. These historical limitations are the main reasons why Granet's work, though ranked among the classics of Sinology, is now seen as an inadequate basis for long-term comparisons.

Despite the absence of direct links, later echoes of Durkheim and Mauss's thoughts on civilizational issues—briefly signaled in the introduction to this book—are strong enough to provide a bridge to current debates and a reason for reassessing the significance of the short texts discussed above. There is no doubt that, for both authors, anthropology was the primary source of civilizational themes: it was the discipline that had most directly and conclusively dealt with multisocietal formations of the kind they envisaged. History and sociology then had to be brought in to deepen our understanding of these phenomena. If other civilizational analysts opted for exclusively historical-sociological approaches, that was surely in part a matter of available sources. That choice could also be defended on more theoretical grounds, either with reference to the civilizational aspect of human societies becoming more articulate and reflexive in high cultures (Eisenstadt 2003) or to an interplay of culture and power that became possible with the emergence of the state (Arnason 2003). It can, of course, be argued that the situation has changed with the expansion of anthropology into history. More importantly, the interplay of culture and power is much older and more widespread in history than the institution of the state. In the stateless and/or prehistoric societies that were for Durkheim and Mauss the main field of anthropological research, power is unequally distributed and asymmetrically exercised, and the institutions that frame it are embedded in forms of belief, cult, and ritual. Moreover, transitions to statehood (along different paths in different situations) can only be understood as long-term processes with countercurrents, setbacks, and sometimes definitive failures. This is the lesson to be learnt from the works of Clastres, Godelier, and Gauchet, discussed in the introduction to, this volume.

In view of all this, it seems best to accept Mauss's thesis: the concept of civilization, and more specifically civilizations in the plural, is in principle applicable to all phases of human history, and the limits to its use are empirical rather than conceptual. They have to do with the sources available for the study of prehistoric societies, as well as the tribal formations that coexisted and interacted with states and empires in later history. Here, Mauss's critique of the *Kulturkreislehre* is no less valid than his defense of the civilizational approach: those who set out to demarcate cultural areas tended to extrapolate from single cultural traits, often arbitrarily chosen or accidentally noticeable. The emphasis on bringing history and sociology to the study of civilizations can be backed up by further evidence. Even if we accept the generalized concept of civilization, as introduced by Durkheim and Mauss and then defended more forcefully by the latter, a major qualification is needed. Later changes, both the rise of states, cities. and empires during the Bronze Age and the cultural innovations of the Axial Age transformed the civilizational dimension of human societies. The concept of civilization may be applicable across human history, but only with due regard to the historicity of its contents.

Postscript I: Lévi-Strauss on Civilizational Roads

As argued in the introduction, the reception of Lévi-Strauss's work has led to a certain rapprochement between anthropology and civilizational analysis, although the authors in question do not share his distinctive conception of the human sciences. The whole line of development, through structuralism and beyond, belongs to the posterity of the Durkheimian school. Lévi-Strauss is central to that story, but neither his reformulation of Durkheimian problems nor his distinctive contributions are reducible to the structuralist paradigm. To illustrate that point, we may briefly mention a text unnoticed by later authors, but highly relevant to the agenda of the present book. In a sense, it is complementary to the ideas discussed above. It is contained in the last chapters of *Tristes Tropiques* (Lévi-Strauss 1997 [1955]). They start with reflections on the task of anthropology and the existential dilemmas of its practitioners. The sequel then moves, rapidly and at first sight unexpectedly, toward a finale best described as a comparative meditation on civilizations. The text is too wide-ranging and allusive to be discussed in detail here, but an underlying argument can be reconstructed.

The journeys recalled in the final chapters took Lévi-Strauss from Brazil to the frontier between India and Buddhist Southeast Asia, but the story begins with comments on the predicament of the anthropologist, brought into stark relief by the encounter with the particularly destitute indigenous societies of Brazil. For Lévi-Strauss, the fieldworking anthropologist embodies an existential contradiction: he combines alienation from his own society with a commitment to empathic understanding of another and very different one. This is obviously a self-interpretation, and it could be objected that Lévi-Strauss overgeneralized his particular vision of anthropology; but here we are more interested in his use of this construction as a step toward civilizational perspectives. The first move makes the contradiction more manageable, but does not overcome it. Lévi-Strauss notes a "paradox of civilization," consisting in the fact that social life derives its charms from traditions and survivals which its progress inexorably destroys. The anthropologist aspires to a position that allows him to contemplate the paradox without direct involvement. But for Lévi-Strauss, this aesthetic detachment can only be a prelude to better understanding of the two sides in question: the societies that invented anthropology and those that became its first and most revealing objects. And that aim can only be achieved through broader comparison. At this point, Lévi-Strauss skips details and claims that all known societies, judged by their own norms, have been marked by shortcomings, deviations, and excesses. Not that they are all in the same category. Western societies appear as the worst culprits, without—at this stage—any particulars cited in support, but there are other extreme cases, such as the Aztecs.

But if this comparative stance no longer allows idealizing commitment to a particular society, it also opens up a new way to grasp the "unshakable basis of human society," cleansed of "abuses and crimes" (Lévi-Strauss 1997, 477). As Lévi-Strauss emphasizes, the common ground is not a state of nature: the latter notion, rejected by Rousseau and conclusively refuted by the modern human sciences, is incompatible with the basic fact that the very existence of human beings presupposes the social institution of language. The basis in question can therefore only be envisaged as a balanced relationship between natural and social dimensions of human life, and by the same token as a corrective against the imbalances that have accumulated in the course of history and taken an extreme turn in our civilization. Lévi-Strauss suggests, more explicitly than elsewhere and in line with Rousseau, that neolithic societies may have come closest to embodying such a model. This is not a return to utopian or idealizing views (neolithic societies are not exempt from the general argument about imperfections); but neolithic humanity had invented ways and means of improving the quality of life, and for a while maintained the new mode of life without lapsing into the pursuit of power, over nature and within society, that became the dominant trend of history.

The anthropological revival of this heritage cannot draw on any continuous tradition, and is thus obliged to look elsewhere for historical references. Lévi-Strauss's choice is prefigured by the following statement: "Being human signifies, for each one of us, belonging to a class, a society, a country, a continent and a civilization" (ibid., 480). It seems highly significant that civilization—one among others—is the last category on this list, obviously not synonymous with society. Although the next step is not explicitly based on civilizational premises, it is best understood in that context, and more specifically in terms of intercivilizational encounters. Civilizations are the most comprehensive subdivisions of humanity. A record of progress toward mutual understanding and recognition on that level would be particularly important for the anthropologist, whose search for a common human foundation could thus claim a strong ancestry.

Lévi-Strauss proceeds to consider two intercivilizational encounters, vastly different but both unsuccessful by his standards. A very brief comment on the European conquest of the Americas describes this event as a disaster, a destruction of the newly encountered other, and the loss of a unique opportunity. The other case is much more complicated. It is at first sight not obvious why a book with the thematic focus of *Tristes Tropiques* should end with reflections and reminiscences on India; but the civilizational angle will help to spell out the connections. Lévi-Strauss evokes the archaeological site—the former city of Taxila—where he glimpsed the traces of an encounter and the possibility of a union that would have been a counterexample to the Euro-American disaster. This is a place where several major spiritual traditions of the Old World—Hellenism, Zoroastrianism, Hinduism, and

Buddhism—coexisted for several centuries before and after the beginning of our era, and where the presence of invaders belonging to the civilization of the steppes is also well documented. In short, and to use a term foreign to Lévi-Strauss, this is one of the great Eurasian crossroads. His particular reading of the evidence is that a fusion of Mediterranean and Indian cultural worlds was in sight but failed to materialize because of the arrival of yet another civilizational actor. Lévi-Strauss sees Islamic expansion into India as the decisive turn away from an Old World ecumene. His comments on this subject have seemed overly anti-Islamic to some readers, but they should be placed in their proper context. The verdict on Islam may be negative, but it is certainly not as devastating as the judgment on the West. More importantly, Lévi-Strauss's critique of Islam as a civilization has a specific thrust that serves to define his own intellectual project. The Islamic devaluation of other traditions, even when they are tolerated as inferior versions of revealed religion, appears as a model case of exclusionary universalism, and hence as a polar opposite of the anthropological stance. Islamic believers claim privileged and self-contained possession of universal truths, whereas the mission of anthropology—as envisaged by Lévi-Strauss—is to seek universal insight through the study of cultures recognized as fundamentally equal.

There are obvious problems with this vision of history. The record and the impact of the Greeks in India are matters of debate among historians, and many aspects remain unclear. The period between the flowering of Hellenism and the arrival of Islam in India was longer and more eventful than Lévi-Strauss's account would suggest. But he did draw attention to a particularly complex instance of intercivilizational encounters, and use it to clarify his own anthropological project. Here, our main interest is in that line of argument, and there is one more point to be considered. Lévi-Strauss clearly sees Buddhism as the potentially more important force in the encounter of East and West, both because of its ability to adapt Greek art to another cultural world and with a view to its record of converting rulers. The contrasting roles of Buddhism and Islam are then explained through a very unconventional theory of religious development. History has, on this view, seen three great attempts to liberate humanity from the fear of magic, of the dead and the Beyond. In retrospect, the overall picture is one of retreat rather than any kind of evolution. Buddhism, more precisely early Buddhism, took the most radical line: "Its whole teaching can be summarized as a radical criticism of life, such as humanity would never again be capable of, leading the sage to deny all meaning to beings and things; it is a discipline which abolishes the universe, and abolishes itself as a religion" (ibid., 499). Christianity restored the Beyond, and Islam reconsolidated the subordination of this world to the other one: "politics became theology" (ibid., 499). It would be pointless to object that Lévi-Strauss is defending an obsolete view of Islam as a religion that absorbed the political sphere. He could argue that, in all three cases, his concern is with an original vision, variously modified and mitigated in later phases but also open to reactivation, though not everywhere in the same way. It seems clear that Lévi-Strauss is dealing with religions at the level where they become formative components of whole civilizational worlds (further indication of that can be found in his comments on Islamic art). Moreover, he notes the involvement of these "great collective personalities" (quoting a term used by Durkheim and Mauss) in historical encounters—such as the Hellenistic-Buddhist rapprochement—that might have led to outcomes other than those known from the record.

The civilizational angle was not expanded in Lévi-Strauss's later work. But it can be seen as a background to his conception of anthropology and its cultural mission. To clarify that point, it may be useful to link the last chapters of *Tristes Tropiques* to the concluding statements of his four-volume study of myths, where the results of that long march through the labyrinth of the "*pensée sauvage*" are integrated into a vision of history and the universe. Taken together, the two summings-up show clearly that the affinity of Buddhism and structural anthropology is no mere fancy. Lévi-Strauss's project, modeled on structural linguistics and backed up by a corresponding philosophy of science, leads to a dissolution of meaning: the underlying reality is an interplay of elements meaningless in themselves but nevertheless conducive to the appearance of meaning. It should be noted that the reduction of meaning involves several levels, and within the domain most extensively studied by Lévi-Strauss—mythical thought—we must distinguish between the manifest first-order meaning of "mythemes" (events and actors figuring in the narrative) and the more significant second-order meaning imposed by the less visible structures that Lévi-Strauss sets out to excavate. But the basic intention of circumscribing meaning as a surface phenomenon is clearly stated, and can be compared to the Buddhist destruction of illusions. The concluding passages of *Mythologies* (Lévi-Strauss 1971, 619–21), insisting on the inevitable disappearance of human beings and their worlds of meaning from the scene of a universe doomed to inertia, are akin in spirit to the Buddhist abolition of everything invoked in *Tristes*

Tropiques. And the metaphor of the sunset, already present in the earlier work, reappears as the final vision of a contemplative anthropology. In the end, the broad horizons opened up through Lévi-Strauss's civilizational intermezzo—a detour rather than a turn—thus only serve to dramatize a uniform and universal vanishing process.

Postscript II: Philippe Descola—Civilizationist Manqué or in the Making?

If Lévi-Strauss became the most influential transformer of Mauss's thought, it is now widely accepted that Philippe Descola's work represents the most significant reorientation of Lévi-Strauss's structural anthropology. With regard to civilizational themes, the results are paradoxical. On the one hand, Descola introduces the eminently civilizational idea of cultural ontologies (Benjamin Nelson seems to have been the first to use that term [Nelson 2011, 92],[2] but it corresponds closely to the patterns that Eisenstadt preferred to call ontological or cosmological visions). In Descola's case, the move from anthropological to ontological pluralism is a key part of his attempt to overcome the conflict between universalism and relativism that has troubled the human sciences in general and anthropology most of all. This epistemological issue is not as prominent in the works of civilizational analysts, but it belongs to the broader horizons of their discourse. For example, Max Weber wanted both to clarify the universality of rational patterns developed in the Occident and to link his understanding of them to specific value-orientations and interpretive perspectives of this particular cultural world; but no clear answer emerges from his unfinished project. On the other hand, Descola makes no reference at all to works representative of civilizational analysis. In his *magnum opus* (Descola 2013), he mentions Max Weber only as an example of scholarship influenced by Heinrich Rickert's distinction between natural and cultural sciences.

The following comments will focus on ways to build on Descola's affinities with civilizational analysis and bring the two lines of thought into closer contact. That requires, to begin with, a more precise grasp of Descola's relationship to structural anthropology. His critique of Lévi-Strauss is perhaps best summed up in the claim that the latter's critical reflection on nature and culture ends with a double restatement of the dualism that was to be overcome. Lévi-Strauss's fundamental commitment to naturalism is not in doubt, but when it comes to concrete analyses, the very idea of nature splits in two: on one side the specific constraints, possibilities, and resources inherent in the relationship of a society to its environment, on the other the putative general laws of the human spirit, grounded in the structure of the brain. The latter theme remains a task for the neurosciences, and is therefore beyond the practical horizons of current anthropology, whereas the former becomes, most obviously in Lévi-Strauss's study of myths, a matter of comparative inquiry into the thoughtways of different cultures, dealing with identical or analogous problems on the basis of their specific experiences and environments. The resultant picture thus differs less markedly from traditional cultural anthropology than the structuralist premises of the research program would have suggested.

Descola's response to this loss of bearings is to reformulate the structuralist project at a new level. Despite Lévi-Strauss's assumption of a rational unconscious, he did not—at least not in any sustained fashion—apply the method of structural analysis to underlying and elementary modes of thought. The contrast between the savage mind and modern scientific thought is primarily defined in terms of their different takes on reality (sensuous experience in the first case, testable abstractions in the second). Descola proposes a model that starts with the most basic and encompassing keys to categorization. He describes them as modes of identification, and in that capacity they are also ways of articulating identity and difference. In the same vein, he refers to frameworks of continuity and discontinuity; these terms are mainly used in a structural sense and in regard to the architecture of reality rather than to time or history. Regimes of temporality and historicity are not central to Descola's original formulations, and his later comments on them are inconclusive.[3]

The result of this approach is a quadripartite paradigm of ontological pluralism, now fairly well known. A short recapitulation will suffice to situate the particular civilizational angle that is to be outlined here. Descola's four ontological models are alternatives within a structural logical space, but there is no suggestion that they exhaust the possibilities given by this framework. They are the result of convergent reflections on conceptual options and available evidence. The logical and structural aspect is evident in Descola's claim that, as contrasting alternatives, the models must in principle be put on the same footing. They represent different modes of articulating, accentuating, or relativizing the distinction between nature and culture, and have a prima facie claim to be taken seriously on that level. More empirical and hermeneutical considerations come into play when Descola notes that the modern ontology that he calls naturalism has proved the most hospitable to scientific inquiry, but that the transplantation of the latter to nonnaturalist frameworks is not excluded (Descola 2011a, 98). This perspective brings to mind the arguments of authors such as Nelson and Eisenstadt, who also dealt with cases and possibilities of modern achievements—including science—integrated into civilizational contexts different from those where they originally took shape. To raise that issue is, of course, to anticipate complex problems of cultural translation, not discussed in Descola's work. Another complicating aspect stems from the particular situation of anthropology: as Descola sees it, this discipline is marked by a fundamental asymmetry between researcher and object, the former coming from a specific cultural background with corresponding intellectual orientations and trying to make sense of another cultural world whose presuppositions can only be gradually and imperfectly graasped. To cope with this problem, anthropologists have developed strategies of symmetrization, including the various models and methods recorded in the history of the discipline. Descola presents his ontological pluralism as another such strategy, with no pretensions to final answers. The symmetrizing effort is never completed, and Descola's conceptual scheme, however comprehensive, is in principle open to further innovation. His reference to "relative universalism"(Descola 2011a, 92) should be read as a general indication of direction rather than a definitive position.

Among the four ontological models, a certain hermeneutical primacy must be conceded to the one from which the anthropologist starts, which he strives to relativize, and which prefigures the choice of contrasts in other cultural worlds. This is the ontology defined as naturalism, but not to be understood as a leveling denial of differences between natural and cultural or social realities. Rather, the naturalist worldview centers on a basic articulation of identity and difference: it posits physical continuity between human and nonhuman beings (both partake in bodily existence), but discontinuity in regard to inwardness, which is attributed to humans (and may, in this context,be understood as a presupposition of social and cultural life). But this ontological division is neither a settled nor a culturally desensitized issue. According to Descola, the naturalist framework took shape in the course of a few centuries, and its development culminated in late-nineteenth-century demarcations of the natural and the cultural (or human) sciences. As he notes, this is a permanently contested field, not a final division of tasks and methods. The idea of nature, as a realm of causal laws and/or mechanisms, became predominant (although it met with enduring difficulties in the course of scientific advances into new dimensions of reality), whereas the human counterpart remained a matter of dispute between those who wanted to align the cultural sciences with models derived from the exploration of nature and those who argued for a more autonomous stance. Further distinctions can, moreover, be made on both sides. Reductionist interpretations and imitations of the natural sciences are questioned not only by culturalist thinkers, but also by those who try to reactivate an older, broader, and richer concept of nature, more or less explicitly identified with the classic notion of *natura naturans* as a creative and diversifying force. This line of thought is acknowledged in Descola's writings, but merits more emphasis. On the other side, the cultural sciences—or their philosophical advocates—are not unfailingly committed to a foundation *in interiore homine*. Proposals to remodel or eliminate "the ghost in the machine" have focused on language and culture as trans-subjective or asubjective fields; but we should also note the Durkheimian conception of human conceptual and reflective competences as products of social processes. This trend is not absent from Descola's account, but it certainly deserves a stronger profile. If all these divergent aspects are given their due, it becomes clear that we are dealing with a structured problematic, a field of mutually contested interpretations, rather than a coherent ontological scheme.

The other three alternatives do not lend themselves to the same kind of reading. The ontological framework directly opposed to naturalism is, in Descola's terms, the animistic one. Its defining feature is the attribution of "interiority" to all living beings, thus an assumption of continuity where naturalism was to draw a dividing line, but discontinuity is acknowledged on the level of bodily existence (and, by extension, ecological context), differently shaped for plants, animals, and humans. Descola's return to the widely abandoned concept of animism is a striking example of anthropologists reviving older models.

The two remaining ontologies are more interesting. The first point to note is that they represent a more abstract pair of contrasts than the first two. Interiority and physicality are specific categories, but when it comes to the schemes of totemism and analogism, the emphasis shifts to a general articulation of identity and difference. Descola's rehabilitation of totemism, after Lévi-Strauss's attempt to dissolve it into a broader conception of classificatory systems, is convincing. Totemism, as known from aboriginal societies in Australia (this is the most geographically demarcated of Descola's models), has an ontological dimension. The reference to "dreaming" as a time of world forming is particularly interesting. It seems plausible to distinguish this notion from general claims about a mythical time of origins. The dreaming is "neither a remembered past nor a retroactive present. Rather, it is an expression of the eternity confirmed in space, an invisible framework for the cosmos that guarantees the permanence of its subdivisions" (Descola 2013, 147). By the same token, it also posits a primacy of identity across secondary differences. With this interpretation, Descola has brought totemism back into the comparative study of worldviews, and to the attention of those who would—in the footsteps of Durkheim and Mauss— like to explore the openings for a civilizational approach to tribal societies.

However, it is the scheme described by Descola as analogism that seems most promising for civilizational reflections. Its basic assumption is that the world can be envisaged as a vast field of diverse phenomena, resistant to strong modes of identification, but similar enough to allow for the weaker link of analogy. The search for and systematic ordering of analogies, within human and nonhuman realms as well as between them, becomes a key intellectual activity. Descola occasionally suggests that we can define this constellation as an interplay of differences and analogies in the dimensions of physicality and interiority, but the latter part of that formulation is unconvincing. To claim that the distinction between physicality and inferiority plays a role comparable to its place in the modern configurations of naturalism, we would need extensive comparative studies. Descola's work contains nothing of the kind. That absence is even more striking when confronted with the fact that analogism is clearly the most cross-cultural of the four schemes. Descola's most detailed analysis of it is based on Mexican cultures of the pre-Columbian era, but he also refers to China, less explicitly to India, and to medieval and Renaissance Europe as well as its classical ancestors (it is worth noting that all these cases are post-tribal and premodern formations, precisely the type that has proved most amenable to civilizational analysis). There is no reason to disagree when Descola warns against unguarded speculations on China, but then this hugely important case should be recognized as a reason to avoid premature closure of ontological horizons. A note of caution is evident when Descola writes: "So my earlier definition of analogism as a combination of the differences of interiorities and the differences of physicalities should not be taken altogether literally, so indefinite do the contours of those two groups seem to be" (Descola 2013, 207).

This qualification of analogism can be taken further. It seems obvious that the construction of analogies does not serve the same purpose or carry the same meaning in contexts as different as the Chinese cosmo-anthropological notion of *dao,* Indian metaphysics of ultimate reality and mundane illusion, the polytheistic cosmologies of Meso-America, or the Hellenized Christian vision of a created cosmos. Seen in such connections, the analogistic mode of thought appears as an interpretive device, adaptable to very different settings, not as a self-contained worldview. The units of comparison are more complex constellations of meanings, and closer analysis would also have to trace their institutional ramifications. Descola takes these cultural worlds for granted, without conceptualizing their unity, and without raising the question of their difference from those of animism and totemism.

The world-making meanings central to civilizational analysis are not reducible to choices within a spectrum of logical structures. Their contents are best understood in light of a category increasingly prominent in social theory, and indispensable to civilizational analysis: the social imaginary. Descola's refusal to engage with that problematic is linked to his general rejection of phenomenological approaches, and especially of all variations on the theme of "ontology of being-in-the world" (Descola 2011a, 63–71). That notion, associated with Heidegger and Merleau-Ponty, has—as Descola sees it—served to legitimize vague claims about primordial intuition and identification. In the anthropological context, it has too often translated into spurious empathy with societies perceived as most opposed to modern ones. This uncompromising stance reflects the rationalism that Descola shares with Lévi-Strauss. His argument focuses on the logical structures through which humans divide and recompose the world. But rationalist theories of meaning, and of concept formation are not immune to criticism. The transrational aspects and sources of meaning, discussed with reference to the imagination by Cornelius Castoriadis (1987 [1975]), to metaphor by Hans Blumenberg (2010 [1997]), and to symbols by Paul Ricoeur (1959), are of particular importance for the theorizing of civilizations.

So far, I have dealt only with the most basic claims of Descola's ontological pluralism. The more complex argument built on them, especially the spectrum of possible interconnections between the subject and its others (Descola 2013, 309–35), is beyond the scope of this brief comment. But to conclude, two further indications of civilizational interest should be mentioned. One of them concerns the question of abortive moves toward naturalism. Descola's view is that this ontological framework was fully developed only in modern European culture, but that incipient trends can be found in traditions dominated by analogism. His examples are Ancient Greek atomism and the early (first century CE) Chinese philosopher Wang Chong, who is credited with materialist speculations. Scholarship on materialism in Indian thought suggests that a similar case could be made there. Apart from reinforcing the above point about the flexibility of analogism, these considerations touch upon a major theme of civilizational analysis: the varying relations between orthodoxies and heterodoxies (for comparative perspectives, see especially Eisenstadt et al. 1984).

The other line of argument is developed in the third chapter of the introductory section of *Beyond Nature and Culture* (Descola 2013, 57–88). It relates—implicitly—to the question of modernity as a new civilization. Descola analyzes the complexities, ambiguities, and multiple directions of the quest for autonomy, from the autonomy of the landscape in early modern painting to the autonomy of diverse worlds, not yet fully recognized by the human sciences. A multidimensional concept of autonomy, admittedly less than fully elaborated, is central to Eisenstadt's civilizational image of modernity, and further work on the subject can no doubt draw on Descola's interpretation. A more critical view might be appropriate when it comes to his comments on Greek and Judaic backgrounds to the modern vision of autonomy. He tends to present the genealogy of modernity as a cumulative process, a perspective that can be contested on the basis of work by other authors (such as Blumenberg, Castoriadis, and Eisenstadt), who have placed more emphasis on tensions, divergences, and discontinuities. The latter approaches gain more plausibility if we think of the process in question as a sequence of different civilizations.

Philippe Descola is not at all averse to using the term *civilization*. The trouble is that he does so without distinguishing it from the concept of culture. Neither the internal civilizational dimension, as exemplified by Eisenstadt's explorations of the interplay of culture and institutions, nor the external one that Durkheim and Mauss identified with multisocietal formations, appears as a separate aspect. The third chapter of *Beyond Nature and Culture*, devoted to the genealogy of this fundamental division, ends with a reference to "thousands of civilizations" preceding ours (Descola 2013, 88). This formulation could be rephrased in terms of cultures, with no loss of content. Similarly, in his contribution to a collection of essays on "great civilizations" (Descola 2011b) he discusses pre-Columbian America, with strong emphasis on diversity and developmental paths, but without differentiating between cultures and civilizations. He does not (as several other writers on the subject have done) use the latter term to distinguish the Aztec, Maya, and Inca formations from tribal societies. His essay contains a severe and convincing criticism of the cultural areas approach: as applied to the Americas, it tends to mix divisions of colonial or postcolonial origin with traces of older ones. But that is not a valid reason for neglecting the analytical potential of Durkheim's and Mauss's reflections on civilizations. These French pioneers did engage with the conception of cultural areas, but in a critical vein and with distinctive results.

Notes

1. In this connection, it seems appropriate to recall Mauss's close relationship to the Indologist Sylvain Lévi, whom he regarded as a mentor second only to Durkheim (Tarot 1999, 289–314). Lévi introduced Mauss to Indian studies, including Sanskrit, and prolonged contact with this field became important for comparative work. As Tarot argues, it may have been decisive for Mauss's philological and (*avant la lettre*) hermeneutical conception of language, which set him apart from the incipient structuralist turn in linguistics. But it also seems likely that Lévi's influence counted for something in Mauss's civilizational thinking. Lévi had a distinctive civilizational vision of India, probably more so than any other Indologist at the time. As he saw it, the absence of national or linguistic unity meant that India as a cultural and historical formation could only be defined in civilizational terms: there was an "Indian civilization, characterized by the predominance of an ideal, a doctrine, a language, a literature and a class" (Lévi 1928, 9). This did not exclude significant variations on local and regional scale; in fact, Lévi stressed the importance of peripheral offshoots (such as Nepal, on which he wrote a major work). They could reveal potentials less visible elsewhere. There is no doubt about the affinity of these views with those of Mauss, and some reciprocal influence is likely; but it seems clear that Lévi's idea of civilization was a logical outgrowth of his Indological research.

2. The reference to cultural ontologies is in a paper on "Civilizational complexes and intercivilizational encounters," first published in 1973. Thanks are due to Toby Huff for the information that this is the earliest documented source.

3. See Descola 2011a, 88–89. Responding to a question about temporality, he criticizes the notion of two and only two conceptions of time: the cyclical one, centered on the vision of eternal return (as described most extensively by Eliade), and the linear one culminating in modern ideas of progress. He then argues that each of the four ontologies has its distinctive regime of temporality. The notion of eternal return corresponds to analogism, whereas linear and cumulative time only make sense in the framework of naturalism. Animism is, for Descola, conducive to an impoverished sense of time, short collective memory and vague notions of mythical events in the recent past. Finally, totemic time is characterized as a mixture of eternal present and a momentary reenacting of the past.

References

Arnason, Johann P. 2003. *Civilizations in Dispute. Historical Questions and Theoretical Traditions.* Leiden and Boston: Brill.

———. 2014. "The Religio-political Nexus. Historical and Comparative Reflections." In *Religion and Politics: European and Global Perspectives*, edited by Johann P. Arnason and Ireneusz Pawel Karolewski, 8–36. Edinburgh: Edinburgh University Press.

Blumenberg, Hans. 2010 [1997]. *Paradigms for a Metaphorology.* Ithaca: Cornell University Press.

Caillé, Alain. 2007. *Anthropologie du don: Le tiers paradigme.* Paris: La Découverte.

Castoriadis, Cornelius. 1987[1975]. *The Imaginary Institution of Society.* Cambridge: Polity Press.

Descola, Philippe. 2011a. *L'écologie des autres. L'anthropologie et la question de la nature.* Versailles: Éditions Quae.

———. 2011b. "Les civilisations amérindiennes." In *Les grandes civilisations,* by Anne Cheng et al., 207–50. Montrouge: Bayard.

———. 2013. *Beyond Nature and Culture.* Chicago: University of Chicago Press.

Durkheim, Émile. 1960. "The Dualism of Human Nature and Its Social Conditions." In *Essays on Sociology and Philosophy*, edited by Kurt Wolff. 325–39. New York: Harper and Row.

———. 1995. *The Elementary Forms of Religious Life.* New York: Free Press.

———, and Marcel Mauss. [1913] 2006. "Note on the Concept of Civilisation." In *Techniques, Technology, and Civilisation,* by

Marcel Mauss, edited with an introduction by Nathan Schlanger, 35–40. New York: Berghahn Books; first published in English 1971 as "Note on the Notion of Civilization," translated and introduced by Benjamin Nelson, in *Social Research* 38, no. 4: 808–13.

Dzimira, Sylvain. 2007. *Marcel Mauss, savant et politique.* Paris: La Découverte.

Eisenstadt, S. N. 2003. "The Civilizational Dimension in Sociological Analysis." In *Comparative Civilizations and Multiple Modernities*, edited by S. N. Eisenstadt, 33–56. Leiden and Boston: Brill.

———, David Shulman, and Reuben Kahane. 1984. *Orthodoxy, Heterodoxy, and Dissent in India.* Berlin: de Gruyter.

Febvre, Lucien, et al. 1930. *Civilisation. Le mot et l'idée.* Paris: La Renaissance du Livre.

Giddens, Anthony.1979. *Central Problems in Social Theory. Action, Structure, and Contradiction in Social Analysis.* Berkeley: University of California Press.

Granet, Marcel. 1968a. *La civilisation chinoise.* Paris: Presses Universitaires de France.

———. 1968b. *La pensée chinoise.* Paris: Presses Universitaires de France.

Lévi, Sylvain. 1928. *L'Inde et le monde.* Paris: Honoré Champion.

Lévi-Strauss, Claude. 1971. *Mythologiques IV: L'homme nu.* Paris: Plon.

———. [1955] 1997. *Tristes Tropiques.* New York: Modern Library.

McNeill, William. 1963. *The Rise of the West.* Chicago: University of Chicago Press.

Mann, Michael.1986. *Sources of Social Power,* Vol. 1. Cambridge: Cambridge University Press.

Mauss, Marcel. 1968. *Essais de sociologie.* Paris: Editions de Minuit.

———. 1974. *Oeuvres, v.2: Représentations collectives et diversité des civilisations.* Paris: Éditions de Minuit.

———. [1925] 1990. *The Gift. The Form and Reason for Exchange in Archaic Societies.* London: Routledge.

———. 2006. "Civilisations. Their Elements and Forms." In *Techniques, Technology, and Civilisation*, edited by Nathan Schlanger, 57–74. New York: Berghahn Books.

Nelson, Benjamin. 1968. "Scholastic Rationales of 'Conscience', Early Modern Crises of Credibility, and the Scientific-technocultural Revolutions of the 17th and 20th Centuries," *Journal for the Scientific Study of Religion* 7, no. 2: 157–77.

———. 1969 [1949]. *The Idea of Usury. From Tribal Brotherhood to Universal Otherhood.* Chicago: Chicago University Press.

———. 2011. *On the Roads to Modernity. Conscience, Science, and Civilizations. Selected Writings, with a New Introduction by Toby E. Huff.* Lanham, MD: Lexington Books, Rowman and Littlefield.

Ricoeur, Paul. 1959. "Le symbole donne à penser," *Esprit* 27, no. 7/8: 60–76.

Tarot, Camille. 1999. *De Durkheim à Mauss: l'invention du symbolique. Sociologie et science des religions.* Paris: La Découverte.

———. 2008. *Le symbolique et le sacré. Théories de la religion.* Paris: La Découverte.

Touraine, Alain. 1981. *Une sociologie sans société.* Paris: CNRS.

Weber, Max. 1949. "Objectivity in Social Science and Social Policy." In *The Methodology of the Social Sciences,* edited by Max Weber, 50–112. Glencoe: Free Press.

2

APPROACHING CIVILIZATION FROM AN ANTHROPOLOGICAL PERSPECTIVE

The Complexities of Norbert Elias

Hans Peter Hahn

> Es ist sicherlich die Aufgabe jeder soziologischen Theorie, über die Eigentümlichkeiten Klarheit zu schaffen, die alle möglichen menschlichen Gemeinschaften miteinander gemeinsam haben.
> —Norbert Elias, *Über den Prozeß der Zivilisation*

Introduction

Is there another way—that is, beyond the public dispute between Elias and certain representatives of anthropology—to identify an approach that considers the arguments presented in *The Civilizing Process* in such a way as to enhance the conceptual framework of cultural anthropology? The primary concern of this paper is to suggest such a perspective. It will not dwell on anthropologists' popular criticisms of Elias, which, however justified, fail to provide an adequate evaluation of Elias's basic assumptions about history and power. The alternative approach presented here will highlight the specific value of an operationalization of the term *civilization,* thus making Elias's civilization theory applicable to anthropology and contributing to a substantial expansion of anthropology's conceptual framework. The method associated with civilization theory could help anthropologists move beyond the atrophy of their epistemological processes and uncover an appropriate conceptualization of globalization that places the relationship between society and cultures in a larger context.

By no means does this article seek to appropriate Norbert Elias for anthropology. Instead, it proposes that his work ought to be understood in its own right as an original and autonomous point of access to the concept of civilization. It is important to emphasize Elias's originality for several reasons. First, it is inappropriate to assess Elias as an anthropologist because he simply was not one. In fact, it is reasonable to believe that he would not have developed his conceptualization of civilization had he been an anthropologist. Second, as an author of the 1930s Elias was far more heavily influenced by early-twentieth-century sociologists and cultural historians than the current interpretation acknowledges. Accordingly, his work ought to be considered as comparative and historical and, given its focus on the human condition and the nineteenth-century understanding of the discipline, anthropological. It follows that any contextualization of Elias should attach weight to the nineteenth century for the development of his theories, instead of limiting him to the scholarship of the 1930s and the emerging ethnographic-functionalist orientations in anthropology. Third, it is justifiable to assess Elias in the context of his own self-understanding: Elias saw himself as an outsider who wanted to contribute to a new scholarly understanding of society that had not existed up to that point (Lepenies 1977).

In this last respect, a consideration of Elias's self-evaluation is justified in more than one regard. When he wrote his major work, both his personal position as an exiled and unemployed researcher and the position of his conceptual framework within the context of established sociological, historical, and anthropological fields were marginal. He was himself well aware of this challenge and later referred in more general terms to the development of scientific concepts by using the metaphor of "disciplines as tribes" (Burke 2012). He was convinced that progress in knowledge occurred through the further development of such 'tribes', and not by radical change as, for example, later argued by Thomas Kuhn. Elias was also cognizant of the fact that his concept of "historical and comparative sociology" did not resonate well with the dominant trends in sociology at his time.

Elias's distance from the dominant theories of sociology of the first half of the twentieth century—which in his opinion were far too aligned with the present and to some extent its spatial units (Goudsblom 2000; Chevalier and Privat 2004, 13)—is almost equal to the distance separating him from dominant twentieth-century anthropological approaches. While anthropologists—such as his critic Hans-Peter Dürr—considered the comparison of contemporary cultural units a plausible methodology, Elias demanded that such comparisons be embedded in the study of long-term historical processes (Maurer 1989). Stephen Mennell (2004) suggests a further explanation of Elias's intellectual distance from anthropology: the problematic nature of the idea of "development." Although anthropologists largely reject development as a concept, Elias purports that it always takes place, although this occurs not necessarily in a linear mode. For Elias, transformation and change are more important than the synchronous depiction of cultural units and the description of differences. It is thus useful at this point to scrutinize more carefully the fundamental differences between Elias's self-understanding and the positions of anthropologists in the twentieth century (Post 2016; Van Krieken 2005). Sophie Chevalier and Jean-Marie Privat (2004) correctly identify this as a "complex relationship," all the while pleading for a nuanced reception of the theory of civilization in the future. Elias did not fare much better in the historical field, where his works were generally ignored (Schwerhoff 1998). That he—even after the overwhelming resonance to his works in the 1970s—never achieved the status of a canonical classic within sociology, anthropology, or history indicated the extent of his marginalization, but also speaks for the uniqueness of his approach and the continual challenge of dealing with it appropriately. For sociologists and anthropologists, his argument focuses too heavily on history, while historians expect a more comprehensive analysis of the sources.

In order to complete the list of problematic demarcations in Elias's relationship with the "tribal" structure of the academy, it is important to mention Elias's critical remarks about the psychology of his time. With the explicit exception of psychoanalysis, Elias criticized contemporary psychologists for their attempts to measure behavior (Heerma van Voss and von Stolk 1990, 71). Social or cultural historical aspects, which were central for Elias, were not considered to be subjects worthy of attention in the discipline of psychology.

On the Concept of Civilization

What is civilization, then, according to Elias? And how could anthropology benefit from adding this term to its conceptual toolbox? The first characteristic of Elias's concept of civilization is its extraordinarily fragile character. Civilization is a process; it is not a permanent condition. Accordingly, Elias himself differentiates between culture as a description of a condition and as a set of characteristics, while he describes civilization as a concept with a constantly changing balance (Mandalios 2003). It is therefore only logical that Elias (2005 [1989], 441ff) developed the notion of the "collapse of civilization," which was later taken up by other scholars under different terminology: "barbarization," "barbarism," or "decivilization" (Keller 2009; Spier 1994).

In this sense, it is essential to understand Elias as a politically informed author. He wrote his work during a time of increasing barbarism in the form of the rise of fascism and Nazism. This is the barbarism that Elias sought to warn against, and to identify a worthy defense against. The emergence of Barbarism, he argued, was also a fragile, reversible, and absolutely political process. As an emigrant himself, Elias highlighted that the identity of every individual could be affected by politically encouraged barbarism (Elias 1977). Accordingly, it seems only natural that forced identity change combined with the dialectic of self-image and othering play an important role in his work (Guillet 2004). There is no linear process of universal development; instead Elias identified civilization as a dynamic change that can take different courses: "Den Fortschritt, an den manche unserer Väter glaubten, den universellen und automatischen Fortschritt, gibt es nicht. Aber Fortschritte, ebenso wie Rückschritte in bestimmter Hinsicht, lassen sich beobachten" (Elias 1988, 37).

It is a fundamental misconception to assume that Elias equates history with evolution. Elias reflected on the concepts of progress and development and distanced himself from the naive and optimistic "faith in progress." His opponents assumed that, for Elias, civilization is simply increased self-restraint. This is incorrect; Elias did not believe that there was less self-control in so-called 'primitive societies' (Liston and Mennell 2009). Instead, he recognized that, for example, the societies he encountered in Ghana were indeed a form of civilization in which another configuration of self-exercised and external constraints was present.

Elias understands society primarily as the presence of a mutually agreed-upon learning process (Elias 1987). Within this rather general frame, biological and psychological principles therefore play a role, for instance, in a person's ability to mimic meaningful gestures. However, in the context of this example, the specific use of a particular facial expression—or its suppression—must be learned. In general, emotions are not merely expressed, they are rehearsed. Emotions cannot be understood in isolation; instead, they require a prior contextual understanding that also considers norms and constraints. Elias's conceptualization of civilization is closely tied to Lucien Febvre's (1988) elucidation of the concept. Elias was aware of Febvre's classical text about conceptual history, published in 1929, when he was writing *The Process of Civilization* (Goudsblom 2000). Similarities can be found in the terminology that later texts by both Elias and Febvre used to describe the transformation of emotional self-control under the influence of civilization (Niestroj 1989, 146). In the context of these parallels, their recognition of the historical developments of specific emotions and more precisely, people's ability to articulate specific feelings is significant. To date, the kind of historical psychology suggested by both authors remains largely unexplored. However, if it were to become science proper, historical psychology would be anchored to Febvre's and Elias's understanding of the term *civilization.*

According to Elias, every society can be characterized by phenomena of power that mediate between the levels of action and social structure. Power thus produces structure and enforces both, decisions and control. It generates interdependencies between individuals and groups that are either planned or unplanned (Bogner 1989, 36). Artur Bogner discovered a direct parallel between Elias's concept of power to that advanced by Max Weber, insofar as power is always an attribute of action (Bogner 1989, 36). Elias suggests that power relations are expressed in the term *figuration,* a point to which I shall return later in this chapter. For the moment, however, it is important to distinguish Elias's conceptualization of the phenomena of power from others. Here, Adorno is a useful example (Elias 1977; Edström 2012). Whereas Adorno considers articulations of power in a dialectic pattern, i.e., a chain of self-contradictions, by contrast, Elias emphasized the complexity of the connections between social positions and power. The Eliasian analysis is not limited to a description of dialectics but rather to different kinds of 'figurations'. Elias also sets himself apart from Max Weber and his "implacable logic of modernity." Instead of dialectical or linear processes, the reversibility of civilizational figurations is of much greater importance for him (Goudsblom 1984).

In the light of these conceptual differentiations, the process of civilization cannot be simply understood as the enforcement of ever-increasing external pressures or complete control over individuals. This would be a rather untruthful simplification, like that presented implicitly in Johan Goudsblom's conceptualization of civilization (Goudsblom 2000). Such a simplification may lead to dangerous misinterpretations, for example, in the legitimization of the Nazi regime's constraints on individuals under the guise of civilization. In contrast, Peter Burke (2012) stresses that Elias's civilization unfolds in the individual's meaningful reproduction of norms. Here, civilization is reflected in the individual as it requires understanding and internalization.

One possible way to link civilization theory and the anthropological perspective lies in the application of Eliasian concepts to non-European societies. There are a few cases where this has already been done. For instance, Thoden Van Velzen (1984) has written about the Djuka in Surinam; and Axel Paul (2009) has addressed civilization and violence control in Africa. In the context of his case study—the Rwandan genocide—Paul concludes that elements of the Eliasian analysis are applicable, particularly in cases where state structures and an unbridled willingness to commit violent acts coincide. In contrast to Elias's expectations, however, statehood did not prevent violence.

On the Concept of Figuration

"Figurations" describe both the pattern of a particular society as a whole and the observed balance between various forms of power in any historical constellation. They relate to cultural patterns that characterize society in its entirety, while, on another level, they account for the individual at the same time. The condition of being subjected to the effects of figurations on various levels is, according to Elias, a basic characteristic of human beings. In any society, people are interdependent; their lives can only be understood within the context of these interdependencies (Elias 1969, LXVII).

In the Eliasian analysis, human beings are not conceivable as autonomous individuals. Instead, they are open beings, formed by the presence of others, inequality and social interdependencies. The concept of figuration relates to, as does the very concept of civilization, the effect of power-determined relationships. In a later epilogue to the first volume of his *Process of Civilization*, Elias clearly emphasizes how the changing balance of power can influence relationships between people and thus the figuration of a society (Bogner 1989, 36). As Annette Treibel (2008, 74ff) highlights, it is this plasticity that is the most important feature of the concept of "figuration." Changes in power relations generate new figurations, thereby creating social change. Figurations are constructed by people, while, at the same time, people are also unable to escape the effect of a particular figuration. It is not difficult to recognize that Elias's arguments are more closely related to those of Sigmund Freud than to those of Max Weber or Karl Marx. In the context of a current perspective, inspired by the debates about globalization, Elias's concept would be understood as "scaling" (Swyngedouw 2004), whereby the microlevel phenomena are directly related to those on a higher level. That is, local societies can only be interpreted with reference to the global level.

As Susanne Brandtstädter (2003) underlines, most of Elias's opponents have focused on his alleged Eurocentrism. In doing so, they have obscured some of the more important aspects of his figuration concept. The concept of "figurations" is important, as it underscores the dynamic processes associated with changes in power relations. Such long-term transformation processes depict change as the normal course of events in every society. Change in a figuration leads to new—and unplanned—patterns of power. Actors, whether they are individuals, local groups, or superpowers, do not simply follow one single telos or any specific strategic goal. Instead, they act in accordance with the necessities of the context or the configuration of power (Van Benthem van Der Bergh 2012). Furthermore, Brandtstädter (2003, 88) observes that Elias's thesis of "unplanned change" has a surprisingly high explanatory value for ethnographic observations of postsocialist transformation states, for example, in the context of the emergence of new social institutions. The benefits of applying Elias's theory are thus all the more evident, as they help to describe these processes without resorting to the dichotomies of tradition and modernity.

Against the background outlined so far, it becomes evident that Elias agreed with his Frankfurt teacher Karl Mannheim. As early as 1930, Mannheim was sharply criticized by Horkheimer and Adorno for exaggerating the significance of "thinking about the social" and "ideology" (Barboza 2010). Both Mannheim and Elias argued that social changes are the result of social constellations and are caused by shifts in power relations. Change is therefore possible even when the affected actors have no intention of bringing it about. This view is more fully developed in Elias's study of the "process of civilization," which he also identifies as an unplanned process. His emphasis on unplanned change can also be understood as a political analysis of the decade of the 1930s. In the works of both Mannheim and Elias, for example, the idiomatic expression of "a drift towards a new war" apparent throughout Europe is present (Kilminster 2007, 56). For both scholars, sociology can be understood as a form of political science, as it is concerned with mutual relationships and common cultural foundations even among conflicting groups. These more specific aspects are also of great significance for anthropology. An analysis of intentions, plans, and strategies may not be sufficient to describe how transformations unfold: the role of the actor, whether an individual or the state, can only be adequately described within the context of society in its entirety.

The *longue durée* and the Historical Comparison of Societies

As Mark Joly (2010) underlines, the Frankfurt School in its early constitutive phase is the decisive context from which Elias was able to develop his theory. As an assistant to Karl Mannheim in Frankfurt, he was familiar with the teaching and research taking place in the years before 1933. Against this background, his choice of topic for his habilitation thesis—courtly culture and society—can be considered a departure. In sharp contrast to the current practice of most Frankfurt School scholars, who have based their studies on their own society and launched a particularly critical perspective of contemporary bourgeois culture, Elias concentrates on fields that appear to lie far beyond the realm of these topics; these fields include periods that the Frankfurt School hardly took into consideration. It is possible that, to some extent, Elias intentionally sought to emplace his approach at some intellectual distance to the mainstream of the Frankfurt School. As such, he certainly had his eye on a specific goal: to realize a universalized sociological perspective while overcoming the ideologically narrow Marxist critique that dominated the Frankfurt School.

Certainly, Elias brought important elements from the Frankfurt School into his work. His contribution can, however, be distinguished further by the fact that it considers the relationship between psychoanalysis and sociology as a potential approach to understanding societies. In this context, it appears obvious that Elias describes a social field that is marked by mental changes and social dynamics that affect each other. Although it thereby becomes clear that Elias himself distanced himself from Frankfurt school mainstream, Elias's writings in exile between 1934 and 1938 were by no means disregarded by other members of the Frankfurt School (Joly 2010). The internal ramifications were complex. Another exiled member of the Frankfurt School, Walter Benjamin, did not react positively to Elias's request that he review his work (Joly 2010). As Detlev Schöttker (1988) reveals, this cleavage was a consequence of the different orientations that had emerged among the members of the School at that time. Although Horkheimer and Adorno (and subsequently Benjamin) were interested in a critique of bourgeois society, it was only Mannheim and Elias who attempted to produce a more generalized picture of social change that included psychoanalytical aspects. The basic issue that divided the approaches taken by Mannheim and Elias from the others was the degree to which cultural embeddedness matters. Mannheim and Elias stood for a more comprehensive approach than their more Marxist contemporaries.

Given the fact that Elias's research emerged from the context of the Frankfurt School while representing a significant break with its most well-established themes, it is worthwhile to extend the discussion to include studies that—in a similar mode—deal with wider historical perspectives. Here, it is useful to consider Oswald Spengler's (1919–1922) work *The Decline of the West*. Long-term perspectives are also closely related to descriptions of the extinction (or the emergence of culture), which, in addition to Spengler, are also found in Leo Frobenius's (1933) work. It is particularly relevant to relate the term *figuration* in its historical dimension to Frobenius's *Gestaltlehre* as it can be uncovered in his seminal work on the culture history of Africa (Frobenius 1933). Elias, Spengler, and Frobenius all share the common confident view that, in the sense of a broader interpretation of Gestalt Theory, the summation of phenomena provides greater insight than would have been ascertained from a single observation. Brigitte Niestroj (1989, 153) identifies Wilhelm Wundt's formulation of *Völkerpsychologie* (ethnopyschology) as an anthropologically relevant precursor to Gestalt Theory, as Wundt had contributed to some foundations of this concept a generation earlier. Karl Lamprecht, one of Wundt's most important disciples, is another nineteenth-century anthropologist who might be considered a pioneer of the anthropological approximation to Gestalt Theory. Although, to my knowledge, Elias's work does not contain any direct references to Karl Lamprecht, there are strong parallels to Lamprecht's (1912) "Introduction to Historical Thinking," which Niestroj identifies as an inspiration for Elias's concept on figuration. Both, Elias and Lamprecht, share the common belief that social transformations coincide with changes in mental abilities. A more general consideration of the analysis of long-term processes should also include the work of Arnold Toynbee (1964), whose concept of the cultural prism could have very well been inspired by Spengler's work. Finally, Eric Voegelin's (2001 [1956]) analysis of the origin of the Ancient Egyptians suggests parallels between symbolic order and displays of power, following the same principles as Elias.

One more scholar should also be mentioned in this context: Franz Borkenau, who is connected to Elias by both their shared time in Frankfurt and common interest in medieval culture. In a series of critical essays first published in the 1950s that followed the lines of argument of Toynbee and Spengler, Borkenau offered his own and independent interpretation of the specific cultural benefits of multiculturalism and transitions (Borkenau 1984). To some degree, it is justified to call Borkenau an early proponent of the idea of cultural hybridity. In contrast to Spengler and Toynbee, who tend to classify cultural change as a decline of culture and society in general, or even as a threat or a loss, Borkenau sees the potential for creativity and the emergence of new social forms in these changes. According to Árpád Szakolczai (2000, 54), the particular affinity between Elias and Borkenau derives from the fact that both scholars emphasize longer historical processes and periods of transitions. In this conceptual feature, Szakolczai recognizes a marked improvement vis-à-vis the "old" cultural historians such as Frobenius and Spengler. Elias's and Borkenau's innovations were driven by their desire to further integrate economic and cultural factors in their analyses.

Some authors have suggested a link between Elias's civilization theory and the Axial Age theory first proposed by Karl Jaspers and expanded by Shmuel Eisenstadt (Mandalios 2003). This could, however, be an unhelp-fully narrow interpretation, as Eisenstadt's theory places European-centered development in the foreground and seemingly relegates non-European civ-ilizations to the background. If, from an anthropological perspective, the concept of civilization is to play a future role as an analytic tool, it has to focus on civilizations on every continent as well as process-based changes. The global dimension and the idea of permanent change constitute the real strength of this approach. By contrast, the concept of the *longue durée,* devel-oped around the same time as Elias's early studies, seems to be less pertinent. Brett Bowden (2012) identifies the greater openness of the Eliasian con-ceptualization of civilization as networks, in contrast to Fernand Braudel's use of the term.

The Analysis of Civilization as the Study of Everyday Life

The studies identified in the last section share another feature in common: they are all based on everyday phenomena. For historians from the *Annales* School, such as Braudel and Lucien Febvre, as well as for Frobenius and no less for Elias, it was important to start with a specific understanding of society: documenting ways of life, cultural characteristics, and everyday life phenomena (Spode 1999). Following Hubertus Busche (2000, 82), this can be referred to as *Präzisionsdruck*: descriptions of societies can only be successful if they achieve a sufficient breadth and differentiation of empirical data. Elias demanded that every field of sociology—especially historical sociology—be *Materialgesättigt* (saturated with material); only specific observation and meticulous consideration of sources would enable scholars to fully describe the configuration of social groups and their power relations. Here, parallels between Elias and Huizinga become obvious (Goudsblom 1984). Apart from close thematic proximity (Elias adopted his medieval material from Huizinga), Elias made it clear that, similar to Huizinga, his study of civilization was based on observations of everyday life (Elias 1978). He was also, however, aware of the challenge his approach comprised: the study of long-term processes always extends beyond a single, definable notion of everyday life. This dilemma is of course extremely common in anthropological work.

Another aspect should also be considered, as it gives evidence of Elias's significant sensitivity toward 'observation' as a methodological tool. Elias always considered himself as an outsider. This is not only due to his background and his painful experience of exile, but even more so in the context of the aim to become an attentive observer. By standing in a marginal position, it is possible to gain a more coherent picture of the whole (Rehberg 1996). This also applies to attention to detail, as Elias was able to use his intentional self-alienation to increase his understanding (Korte 2003). The use of distancing for close observation is a trusted method in anthropology, and was also explicitly employed by Elias (Claessens 1984). It would certainly be going too far to argue that Elias used ethnographic methods, but it is important to recognize that Elias was not a naive observer, as he did not believe that it is possible to adopt the position and worldview of a member of another society. It is possible to understand the rarity of observations concerning his stay in Ghana (1962–64) as an outcome of his doubts about the very possibility of grasping a culture that was so unfamiliar to him (Van der Loyen 2012). In clear contrast to many anthropologists of that time, he did not believe that he could place himself in the world of the Ghanaian students.

This in no way diminishes his respect for the foreign cultures he embraced by, among other means, collecting art. Elias (2002) describes himself as a student in terms of African sculpture, stressing that for his own learning process on the aesthetics of African sculpture, the scrap sculptures were as valuable as the "classical" *stilechte* (genuine) pieces. His position as student of the local culture is also evident in his willingness to adapt his curriculum to the expectations of the university when he was a professor of sociology in Ghana. Consequently, he eventually inspired young Ghanaians to include their local environment as the origin for their anthropological studies.

Conclusion

In his attempt to embed Elias's thinking in the world of twentieth-century sociological theory Dennis Smith (2001, 177) provides a grim prognosis. Although he concludes his discussion with an expression of hope that, at the very least, the foundations for a civilized debate between academics are already in place, he finds that the possibility of establishing a global society based on shared values and a universal order remains far from being realized. Instead of the once-anticipated emergence of a cosmopolitan society, Smith underscores the fact that the world is moving toward new types of conflicts (for example, increased tendency toward civil war and genocide). Axel Paul's aforementioned interpretation of increasing violence in Africa, particularly the shocking example of Rwanda, confirms this skepticism. However, Elias did not expect anything better. The process of civilization is not a straight line toward greater self-control and the eradication of violence. As Elias himself learned the hard way in the course of his life, civilization is far from an automatic process. This chapter has attempted to map some of the most important connections between the cultural theorists of the late nineteenth and early twentieth centuries. On the basis of this alternative contextualization of Elias's work, emphasizing in particular the influence by the works of Spengler and Frobenius, Elias's skepticism about the imminent emergence of a global society is justified.

Sophie Chevalier's identification of a "complex relationship" between Elias and anthropology is well founded. Nevertheless, this chapter has illustrated a number of ways in which anthropology and Elias can be connected, notably through applying the notion of civilization as a plausible anthropological approach to current issues of global entanglements. Three aspects are decisive in the final assessment of civilization as an anthropological tool. First, the concept of civilization draws attention to power relations; in consequence, an anthropology that operationalizes Elias's ideas will necessarily be a political anthropology. Second, the concept of "figuration" should be considered an essential tool to explain both, (1) the tension that exists between intentional and unplanned social change, and (2) the way social structures are related to each other on different levels. Individuals and local groups no less than global phenomena are entangled in figurations; only the scale differs. This makes it possible to speak of a transnational sociology *avant la lettre* (Pries 2008). Third, Elias's emphasis on long-term historical change, apparently incompatible with twentieth-century anthropology, which increasingly resigned itself to historical amnesia, can make a valuable contribution to the analysis of contemporary global interconnections.

In contrast to other theoretical perspectives that emerged from the Frankfurt School, Elias never succumbed to the temptation to detach himself from an empirically precise observation of everyday phenomena. In combination with the advantages he sought to derive from his position, self-consciously defined as a marginal one, this inclination to empirical work should appeal to anthropologists. But let me stress again that it is not the purpose of this contribution to claim that Elias be reclassified as an anthropologist against his will. Rather, I have argued that the discipline can benefit greatly from integrating the notion of civilization through the use of Elias's concepts and tools. These have their roots in the nineteenth century, yet they remain well suited to answering twenty-first-century questions.

References

Barboza, Amalia. 2010. "Das utopische Bewusstsein in zwei Frankfurter Soziologien: Wissenssoziologie versus Kritische Theorie?" In *Soziologie in Frankfurt. Eine Zwischenbilanz,* edited by Felicia Herrschaft und Klaus Lichtblau, 161–203. Wiesbaden: VS.

Bogner, Artur. 1989. *Zivilisation und Rationalisierung: die Zivilisationstheorien Max Webers, Norbert Elias' und der Frankfurter Schule im Vergleich.* Opladen: Westdeutscher Verlag.

Borkenau, Franz. 1984. *Ende und Anfang. Von den Generationen der Hochkulturen und von der Entstehung des Abendlandes.* Klett-Cotta.

Bowden, Brett. 2012. "Politics in a World of Civilizations: Long-term Perspectives on Relations between Peoples." *Human Figurations* 1, no. 2: http://hdl.handle.net/2027/spo.11217607.0001.204.

Brandtstädter, Susanne. 2003. "With Elias in China. Civilizing Process, Local Restorations and Power in Contemporary Rural China." *Anthropological Theory* 3: 87–105.

Burke, Peter. 2012. "Norbert Elias and the Social History of Knowledge." *Human Figurations. Long-term Perspectives on the Human Condition* 1, no. 1: 7–17.

Busche, Hubertus. 2000. "Was ist Kultur? Zweiter Teil: Die dramatisierende Verknüpfung verschiedener Kulturbegriffe in Georg Simmels 'Tragödie der Kultur'." *Dialektik. Zeitschrift für Kulturphilosophie* 2000, no. 2: 5–16.

Chevalier, Sophie, and Jean-Marie Privat. 2004. "Elias pour aujourd'hui et pour demain." In *Norbert Elias et l'anthropologie: "nous sommes tous si étranges . . . ,"* edited by Sophie Chevalier and Jean-Marie Privat, 53–68. Paris: CNRS.

Claessens, Dieter. 1984. "Engagement und Distanzierung: Norbert Elias." *Merkur* 38, no. 7: 754–62.

Edström, Olle. 2012. "Elias and/or Adorno. A Short Personal Reflection and Perspective from a Musicologist." *Human Figurations. Long-term Perspectives on the Human Condition* 1, no. 1: 7–17.

Elias, Norbert. 1969. *Über den Prozeß der Zivilisation* 2 Bände. Bern: Francke; original: 1939.

———. 1977. "Adorno-Rede. Respekt und Kritik." In *Zwei Reden anlässlich der Verleihung des Theodor W.-Adorno-Preises 1977,* edited by Norbert Elias and Wolf Lepenies, 35–68. Frankfurt a.M.: Suhrkamp.

———. 1978. "Zum Begriff des Alltags." In *Materialien zur Soziologie des Alltags (Sonderheft der Kölner Zeitschrift für Soziologie und Sozialpsychologie 20)*, edited by Kurt Hammerich and Michael Klein, 22–29. Opladen: Westdeutscher Verlag.

———. 1988. "Was ich unter Zivilisation verstehe. Antwort auf Hans Peter Duerr." *Die Zeit* 25, 17/6/1988), 37–38.

———. 2002. *Ecrits sur l'art africain. Traduction de Jean-Bernard Ouédraogo et Françoise Armengaud.* Paris: Kime.

———. 2005. "Der Zusammenbruch der Zivilisation." In *Studien über die Deutschen: Machtkämpfe und Habitusentwicklung im 19. und*

20. Jahrhundert, edited by Norbert Elias and Michael Schröter, Bd. 11, 441–586. Frankfurt a.M.: Suhrkamp.

Febvre, Lucien. [1929] 1988. "Zur Entwicklung des Wortes und der Vorstellung von 'Civilisation'." In *Das Gewissen des Historikers*, edited by Lucien Febvre, 39–77. Berlin: Wagenbach.

Frobenius, Leo. 1933. *Kulturgeschichte Afrikas. Prolegomena zu einer historischen Gestaltlehre*. Zürich: Phaidon.

Goudsblom, Johan. 2000. "Norbert Elias and American Sociology." *Sociologia Internationalis* 38, no. 2: 173–81.

Goudsblom, Johan. 1984. "Zum Hintergrund der Zivilisationstheorie von Norbert Elias: Das Verhältnis zu Huizinga, Weber und Freud." In *Macht und Zivilisation. Materialien zu Norbert Elias' Zivilisationstheorie*, edited by P. Gleichmann, J. Goudsblom, H. Korte, and N. Elias, 129–47. Frankfurt a.M.: Suhrkamp.

Guillet, D. 2004. "Repenser le concept éliasien de 'configuration'." In *Norbert Elias et l'anthropologie: "nous sommes tous si étranges . . . ,"* edited by Sophie Chevalier and Jean-Marie Privat, 116–25. Paris: CNRS.

Heerma van Voss, Arend-Jan, and Abram v. Stolk. 1990. *Norbert Elias über sich selbst*. Frankfurt a.M.: Suhrkamp.

Joly, Mark. 2010. "Le projet intellectuel de Norbert Elias." *Vingtième Siècle Revue d'Histoire* 106: 81–95.

Keller, Thomas. 2009. "Deutsches Raubrittertum oder europäischer Nonkonformismus? Zur Frage der Gewalt in Norbert Elias' Doppelbiographie des Menschen und der Gesellschaft." In *Norbert Elias: "Etudes sur les allemands" lectures d'une oeuvre*, edited by Françoise Lartillot, 191–222. Paris: Harmattan.

Kilminster, Richard. 2007. "Norbert Elias: Post-Philosophical Sociology." London: Routledge.

Korte, Hermann. 2003. "Der ethnologische Blick bei Norbert Elias." In *Akzeptanz und Ignoranz. Festschrift für Jens Naumann*, edited by Rainer Jansen, 231–38. Frankfurt a.M.: IKO-Verlag für interkulturelle Kommunikation.

Lamprecht, K. 1912. *Einführung in das historische Denken*. Leipzig: R. Voigtlander.

Lepenies, Wolf. 1977. "Ein Außenseiter, voll unbefangener Einsicht." In *Zwei Reden anlässlich der Verleihung des Theodor W.-Adorno-Preises 1977*, edited by Norbert Elias, and Wolf Lepenies, 7–33. Frankfurt a.M.: Suhrkamp.

Liston, Katie, and Stephen Mennell. 2009. "Ill Met in Ghana: Jack Goody and Norbert Elias on Process and Progress in Africa." *Theory, Culture and Society* 26, no. 7–8: 52–70.

Loyen, Ulrich v. 2012. *Strände der Vernunft. Norbert Elias im inneren Afrika*. Berlin: Matthes u. Seitz.

Mandalios, John. 2003. "Civilizational Complexes and Processes: Elias, Nelson, and Eisenstadt." In *Handbook of Historical Sociology*, edited by Gerard Delanty, and Engin F. Isin, 65–80. London: Sage.

Maurer, Michael. 1989. Der Prozeß der Zivilisation—Bemerkungen eines Historikers zur Kritik des Ethnologen Hans Peter Dürr an der Theorie des Soziologen Norbert Elias. In *Geschichte in Wissenschaft und Unterricht*: 225–38.

Mennell, Stephen. 2004. "Les anthropologues et l'agnosticisme du développement." In *Norbert Elias et l'anthropologie: "nous sommes tous si étranges–,"* edited by Sophie Chevalier and Jean-Marie Privat, 7–25. Paris: CNRS.

Niestroj, Brigitte. 1989. "Norbert Elias: A Milestone in Historical Psycho-Sociology; The Making of the Social Person." *Journal of Historical Sociology* 2, no. 2: 136–60.

Paul, Axel T. 2009. "Modern Barbarism and the Prospects of Civilization. Eliasian Themes in an African Context." *Sociologia Internationalis* 47, no. 2: 133–61.

Post, Arjan. "Civilised Provocations in the Lion's Den: Norbert Elias on Racism, Assimilation and Integration: The Prinsenhof Conference, Amsterdam 1984." *Human Figurations. Long-term Perspectives on the Human Condition* 5, no 1: 1–7.

Pries, Ludger. 2008. *Die Transnationalisierung der sozialen Welt: Sozialräume jenseits von Nationalgesellschaften*. Frankfurt a.M.: Suhrkamp.

Rehberg, Karl-Siegbert. 1996. "Norbert Elias—ein etablierter Außenseiter." In *Norbert Elias und die Menschenwissenschaften. Studien zur Entstehung und Wirkungsgeschichte seines Werkes*, edited by K.-S. Rehberg, 17–39. Frankfurt a.M.: Suhrkamp.

Schöttker, Detlev. 1988. "Norbert Elias und Walter Benjamin." *Merkur* 42, no. 7: 582–95.

Schwerhoff, Gerd. 1998. "Zivilisationsprozess und Geschichtswissenschaft. Norbert Elias' Forschungsparadigma aus historischer Sicht." *Historische Zeitschrift* 266: 561–605.

Smith, Dennis. 2001. *Norbert Elias and Modern Social Theory*. London: Sage.

Spengler, Oswald. 1919. *Der Untergang des Abendlandes. Umrisse einer Morphologie der Weltgeschichte*. München: Beck.

Spier, Fred. 1994. *Norbert Elias's Theory of Civilizing Processes Again Under Discussion; An Exploration of the Sociology of Regimes*. Paper for the XIIIth World Congress of Sociology, 18–23 July 1994, Bielefeld, Germany. Amsterdam: Amsterdam School of Social Science Research.

Spode, Hasso. 1999. "Was ist Mentalitätsgeschichte?" In *Kulturunterschiede. Interdisziplinäre Konzepte zu kollektiven Identitäten und Mentalitäten*, edited by Hans Hahn, 10–57. Frankfurt a.M.: IKO-Verlag für Interkulturelle Kommunikation.

Swyngedouw, Erik. 2004. "Globalisation or 'Glocalisation'? Networks, Territories and Rescaling." *Cambridge Review of International Affairs* 17, no. 1: 25–48.

Szakolczai, Arpad. 2000. "Norbert Elias and Franz Borkenau. Intertwined Life-Works." *Theory, Culture and Society* 17, no. 2: 45–69.

Thoden Van Velzen, H. U. E. 1984. "The Djuka Civilisation." *The Netherlands Journal of Sociology* 20, no. 2: 85–97.

Toynbee, Arnold J. [1962] 1964. *Die Zukunft des Westens*. München: Nymphenburger Verlagshandlung.

Treibel, Annette. 2008. *Die Soziologie von Norbert Elias. Eine Einführung in ihre Geschichte, Systematik und Perspektiven*. Wiesbaden: VS Verlag für Sozialwissenschaften.

Van Benthem van den Bergh, Godfried. 2012. Norbert Elias and the Human Condition. *Human Figurations* 1, no. 2: http://hdl. handle.net/2027/spo.11217607.0001.202.

Van Krieken, Robert. 2005. "Occidental Self-understanding and the Elias-Duerr Dispute: 'Thick' versus 'Thin' Conceptions of Human Subjectivity and Civilization." *Modern Greek Studies* 13: 273–81.

Voegelin, Eric. [1956] 2001. "Egypt." In *Order and History. The Collected Works of Eric Voegelin, Vol 14*, edited by Eric Voegelin, and Ellis Sandoz, 91–156. Columbia: University of Missouri Press.

3

___

CIVILIZATIONAL ANALYSIS AND ARCHAEOLOGY
Prospects for Collaboration

Yulia Prozorova

Introduction

The principal purpose of this chapter is to indicate lines of collaboration between civilizational analysis and archaeology. Archaeology provides the diachronic perspective required for the analysis of long-term civilizational formations. The very concept of civilization has a long and distinctive history in archaeological discourse. V. Gordon Childe (1950) specified civilizational criteria to identify formations differing from the preceding evolutionary stages of savagery and barbarism (cf. Kradin, this volume). Colin Renfrew argued instead that civilization was best understood through a system logic, as a global response of human societies to environmental adaptive needs (Renfrew 1972, 13). In contrast to these archaeological conceptions I shall refer to "civilizational analysis" from a more sociological perspective, which has its intellectual origins in the works of Weber and of Durkheim and Mauss, and which has been intensively developed since the 1970s as a domain of comparative historical sociology. Civilizational analysis is an internally heterogeneous theoretical perspective. Its programmatic core, however, has been articulated in the works of Shmuel Eisenstadt, Benjamin Nelson, and Johann Arnason. This civilizational analysis is not evolutionist.[1] It investigates long-lasting macrohistorical formations constituted by constellations of cultural orientations, clusters of meanings and

53

institutional patterns, with a particular focus on the dynamic relationship between cultural ontologies and political and economic institutions. The stress is placed on cultural autonomy and creativity. Eisenstadt and Arnason reject the view that culture is derivative of human adaptation needs or the maintenance and reproduction of the social order, although these have been the premises of most archaeological science until recently.

Within archaeological discourse, most pertinent to the current agenda of civilizational analysis are the nature of pre-Axial trajectories and their relationship to early civilizations, and Axial civilizational complexes. I also wish to consider whether archaeology can contribute concepts and ideas relevant to the research focus of civilizational analysis, especially in studies of inter-civilizational encounters and cultural interactions. While anthropological and sociological approaches have been widely applied in archaeology, the material dimension of culture has generally been only a peripheral concern of civilizational analysis. However, when Durkheim and Mauss referred to civilization as a "family of societies," they included material complex, techniques, and tools among their criteria (Durkheim and Mauss 1971). As Mauss noted, alongside other features "archaeological facts" also help to "create the belief that these societies have been in prolonged contact and are related to each other" (Mauss 2004, 22). Material artifacts, traditions, and practices have always mediated cultural interactions and marked civilizational frontiers (see also Wengrow 2010). Material culture is an essential part of the interdependent systems that constitute "supranational" civilizational phenomena, or in Mauss's later terminology, "civilizational forms."

Chronological and Typological Approaches to Civilizations

Since the "civilizational renaissance" in sociology, much attention has been paid to the Axial Age civilizations of the middle of the first millennium BCE.[2] This epoch is of particular interest in civilizational analysis because it is seen as a period of deep cultural transformations with far-reaching consequences, even paving the way for modernity as a distinct type of civilization (Eisenstadt 2001). From the sociological perspective, all references to the past are justified if they clarify the present. Eisenstadt derived his theory of multiple modernities from his understanding of the axial civilizations. But can civilizational analysis as a general paradigm be applied to the analysis of very long-lasting historical patterns? Or is this theoretical framework better restricted to comprehending much shorter historical periods?

The Axial Age civilizations of ancient Greece and early imperial China, as well as those that emerged around Zoroastrianism, Hinduism, Buddhism, and Judaism, all crystallized around the same time (Eisenstadt 2000, 4). Christianity and Islam were initially considered to be a "secondary breakthrough," but in his later work Eisenstadt abandoned this notion and subsumed Christianity and Islam under the generalized axial type. Eisenstadt thus shifted from the analysis of Axial Age civilizations to analyzing a general type, "axial civilizations," distinguished by the new ontological vision. In the new model, the civilizations of the Axial Age were reconfigured from historical formations into an ahistorical typological framework, which decontextualizes them and disregards their direct origin from the chronological Axial Age (Arnason 2014). This shift highlights the fundamental distinction between the axial and pre-axial civilizations.

Arnason (2006; 2012; 2014) criticizes this approach, insisting that the Axial Age formations are primarily historically grounded and are not homogeneous. A variety of the early civilizations that emerged in the pre-Axial period constituted diverse backgrounds for later axial shifts. In the chronological approach, the formations of the Axial Age are seen as rooted in the pre-axial legacy (though highly transformed), while in the typological approach, the Axial Age formations are understood as a sharp rupture with the pre-axial past.[3] Consequently, the nature of the relationships between pre-axial complexes and the Axial Age civilizational formations is a crucial research theme for civilizational analysis. Efforts to resolve this question can benefit from archaeological data, our main source for preliterate societies and no less valuable in the case of archaic societies for which written sources are fragmented, provide insufficient information, and lead to distorted and ambiguous accounts of society. The deeper we go into the past, the more significant archaeological analysis becomes. Arnason is critical of Jaspers's labeling of the pre-axial civilizations as "unawakened," since it is possible to indicate a mutually constitutive and transformative dynamic of politics and religion. For this reason, "we must think of the axial breakthrough(s) as culmination(s) of long-term processes . . . .These must then be analyzed in the processual context" (Arnason 2005, 27–28). Some institutional patterns of the "non-axial" societies could be very similar to those developed in the axial ones, and pre-axial civilizations should not be seen only as "precursors" of axial civilizations or "failed axialities" (cf. Eisenstadt 2005, 532). What matters is to grasp how the "pasts" of great axial transformation relate to the new cultural horizons of the Axial formations (Arnason 2014, 185). One core topic here is the process of state formation and its reflection in material culture and rituals (Kristiansen 1996). Arnason suggests that the rise of the state is the key aspect of the emergence of civilization "as a world-historical mutation of the first order" (Arnason 2006, 235). Archaeologist Bruce Trigger (2003) distinguishes between two types of state-level political organization in the early civilizations: city-state and territorial state. These two types did not emerge in an evolutionary sequence, but rather coexisted. The trajectories of these power structures were, however, based on common premises: they involved "homologous" perceptions of the relation between the transcendental and mundane orders (Eisenstadt 2003 [1983]). Although both state types crossed the historical divide of the Axial Age, they were transformed: the pre-axial city-state of Mesopotamia differed from the axial city-state of Ancient Greece. The early states were marked by internal conflict and competitiveness between different local groups. For example, the Mesopotamian civilization (a "bricolage" as Michalowski [2005]) labeled it) is a remarkable case of a complex formation based on a number of quasi-independent city-states which hardly ever constituted a unified political whole, despite many efforts to create a centralized structure. This "cultural cluster" was far from homogenous. In Norman Yoffee's words, "a very specific and shared cultural sense of a Mesopotamian world was independent of the presence of a pan-Mesopotamian state" (2004, 53).

Early state formation was accompanied by a new ideology of the state itself. The very idea of state as "a central authority, whose leaders have privileged access to wealth and to the gods" (Yoffee 2004, 17) emerged within particular historical settings and in the context of the formation of the political center and its legitimation. The state appeared as an institutionalization of a particular ideal of authority and as a solution to the problem of order. The development of states required innovative cultural interpretations of state authority and power, and a new mode of organizing and structuring relations between different collectivities.[4] In this new ideology, the state constituted and stipulated the orderly functioning of the cosmos. It required rulers to intercede with the gods and to represent the rest of society in such intercessions. As Yoffee (2004) explains:

> States and civilizations attempt to structure the universe in different ways than do the social forms that precede them and often surround them. ... The transformations embodied in the new ideologies in and of states include the institutionalization of people's acceptance of, involvement in, and contribution towards order. (Yoffee 2004, 39–40)

The new state ideology regulated the exercise and transmission of leadership roles. It was manifest in material cultural artifacts such as decorative arts, architecture, monuments, buildings, spatial distribution, and irrigation systems. The material dimension of early states and civilizations reflects an innovative capacity to organize space and transform the living environment. It also provides the backcloth for cultural memory in the period preceding the vast distribution of literacy and text-culture.

Theoretical and methodological perspectives on state formation in archaeology have revealed a diversity of historical trajectories. There was no single model of the archaic state, and thus no unitary process of civilizational emergence (Yoffee 2004, 228). Rather, the formation of the first states brought a multiplicity of cultural meanings inherently connected with a new vision of authority and order. The accumulation of wealth in the hands of a ruler and elites was partly justified by their privileged relations with the supernatural, and by their social responsibility to reenact and reaffirm the established order through a ceremonial complex. Wealth was needed to counter fragility and chaos (Yoffee 2005).[5] Those who provided tribute to the center were thus contributing to the maintenance of order.

The other issue crucial for archaeology is the long-term relationship between advanced polities or states and their peripheries. What kind of relations did the early states and civilizations have with their less developed peripheries? An important aspect of the center-periphery issue that needs further elaboration in civilizational analysis is the dynamic which led some pre-axial civilizations to become a provincial periphery within new imperial or civilizational formations during the Axial period—for example, the Mesopotamian/Babylonian province within the Persian and then Hellenic Empire, and Egypt within the Roman Empire. Babylonian intellectuals who tried to revitalize older Mesopotamian cults constituted a peripheral heterodox movement of an anti-axial character (Michalowski 2005). The dynamic of a civilizational legacy within new civilizational or imperial boundaries is what Benjamin Nelson (1973) means by an "intra-civilizational encounter."

In this context, the study of crisis and collapse is particularly instructive (Eisenstadt 2003[1988], 243). Arnason notes that "the best-known axial transformations took place in environments shaped—in a long-term perspective—by momentous events of the Late Bronze Age: crises which weakened or destroyed civilizational centres and upset the power balance between centres and peripheries" (2005, 43). Eisenstadt (2003[1988], 242) saw collapse as a "part of a continuous process of boundary reconstruction." He saw pre-axial polities as characterized by weak distinctions between political and religious institutions and incapable of providing alternative cultural and institutional frameworks when a crisis arose. However, the correlation of collapse with the overall state political organization has not been clearly demonstrated and not all pre-axial civilizations followed the same scenario of collapse (e.g., Egypt and Mesopotamia). In the Mesopotamian case, where city-states were the principal political and sociocultural units, it is obvious that the political reforms and concomitant cultural initiatives were fostered by competition between different collectivities. Dispersed forms of authority alternated with more centralized sovereignty, and every fresh attempt to unify was predicated on a new (not necessarily successful) cultural and ideological framework with religious overtones. The city-states joined to form confederacies, which on rare occasions became regional states, but more commonly reverted to the level of the city-state, while avoiding a total collapse. In this case, archaeological analysis combined with written sources can illuminate the diverse scenarios of civilizational decline and collapse.

Early Civilizations: Backgrounds and Divergences

Archaeological investigations of early civilizations, similar to those of civilizational analysis, have focused on relationships between wealth, power, and the symbolic realms of culture and religion. According to Trigger, "each early civilization was the result of individual historical processes that produced distinctive material and institutional expressions" (Trigger 2003, 44). Cultural (especially religious) beliefs, interpretations, and concepts dynamically correlate with the institutionalization and regulation of political and economic relations and hierarchical class structure of early civilizations. As Arnason noted, "The diversity of civilizational formations can go so far that it becomes difficult to identify the shared components" (Arnason 2014, 185). Nevertheless, civilizational analysis recognizes state-level organization, urbanism, and writing as comprising a "shared core pattern" of civilizational complexes. Diversity is the result of historical variations on this combination.

Comparative analysis of early civilizations reveals some controversial cases. For example, recent studies of the Indus Valley civilization, one of the great early Eurasian civilizations, present it as having "archaic sociocultural complexity, but without the state . . . the sociocultural form that [the] Indus polity took is not known" (Possehl 2002, 5–6).[6] There are no clear signs of kingship such as palaces or sculptures, nor do we have evidence of bureaucracy or state religion in the forms of large monuments or temples. It is possible, of course, that its state structure is just hard to recover on the basis of current archaeological techniques, but it may be that we shall have to acknowledge that state organization is not an intrinsic feature of large-scale and long-term civilizational formations (Kradin 2011). The same could apply to urbanism and writing. If statehood is regarded as the necessary starting point of a singular civilizational process, alternative forms of complex society, such as nomadic empires, are overlooked (Kradin 2002; cf., this volume).

Urbanism is also an ambiguous criterion since cities differ greatly in size, structure, and function. Such literate societies as ancient Egypt and Maya do not satisfy all definitions of urbanism, even though their civilization status is undeniable (Trigger 2003, 44).

Finally, from the archaeological perspective, writing too is an equally unreliable indicator. We know of examples of nonwriting civilizations (Yoruba) and of civilizations with underdeveloped writing (e.g., khipu, the knotted writing of the Inca). In his examination of seven cases of early civilizations, (Egypt, Mesopotamia, Aztec, Inca, Maya, Shang China, and Yoruba), Trigger argues that writing is not associated with any perceptible difference in the overall degree of social, economic, and political complexity (2003, 43). It is true that recent statistical analysis of archaeological data demonstrates a unidirectional correlation between true developed writing systems and the level of political integration.[7] Links can also be demonstrated to social stratification, sedentarization, and urbanism. Overall, however, civilization seems to have no universally valid preconditions (Kradin 2006, 95–96).

These findings confirm the need to reconsider the civilizational *minimum minimorum*. If no single criterion is mandatory, we need instead to accept the notion of a flexible combination or "set of properties" (more than three in number), which are neither necessary nor sufficient (in Ludwig Wittgenstein's terms: "family resemblance"). In abandoning the "monothetic" approach to civilizations in favor of a "polythetic" perspective, we leave room for recognizing the diversity of civilizational formations.

Temporal Limits, Theories, and Concepts

Civilizational analysis is interested in the pre-axial civilizations not only in order to clarify the origins and specificities of the Axial Age but as valuable cases in their own right. But how far back can this analysis be pushed? We find complex societies with the first proto-urban settlements such as Jeriho or Catal Huyuk during the Neolithic, together with religious complexes, new forms of collective life, and a novel cognitive culture incorporated into the later ones. Let us consider the Mesopotamian case again. The formation of Mesopotamian civilization and its state structure is rooted in the Neolithic period (Yoffee 2005; Wengrow 2010). During this period, sedentary kin-based communities belonging to the different archaeologically defined cultures of the Hassuan, Samarra, and Halaf periods of the Tigris-Euphrates region, entered into long-lasting interaction. This region constituted a common cultural space, an "interaction sphere," that determined the emergence of a common belief system, the fundamental Mesopotamian supraregional cultural framework. This is presumed to have occurred in the Ubaid period. In turn, this common belief system and culture established the principal contours for the formation of the early Mesopotamian states in the Uruk period. But despite the cultural identity reflected in material commonalities of everyday life (e.g., Ubaid ceramics) and similar the temple architecture at the major sites of Eridu in the south and Gawra in the north, local differences continued to exist (Yoffee 2003, 210). What seems crucial for the Ubaid and subsequent periods of Mesopotamian history is that, despite the evolution of the common cultural boundary, the political structure persisted in a localized or networked form. The endemic Mesopotamian traditions of cultural and political localization, lasting from the pre-Ubaid Neolithic prehistory, shaped the Mesopotamian civilizational complex.

Colin Renfrew, an expert on Aegean prehistory, has suggested that Greek culture, in particular views derived from the religious complex of the Bronze Age Aegean cultures, is deeply rooted in the religious views and cult practices of the late Neolithic Age (Renfrew 2011[1972], XLVII–LI). Greek civilization, in his view, was the apogee of long-lasting transformations of cultural premises and innovations brought into the region by farmers who had migrated from Anatolia in the Neolithic. Renfrew also considers the role played by the Near Eastern civilizations in the development of the Greek city-states (and the preceding Cretan and Minoan civilizations) to be "secondary" to endogenous dynamics (Renfrew 2011[1972]). This view is opposed to conventional accounts of the relationship between the Ancient Near East and the Eastern Mediterranean, in center-periphery terms. However, it does not negate the existence of intense cultural contacts, which are easily traceable archaeologically. Imported Near Eastern objects, technologies, and artistic styles certainly contributed to the formation of the distinct civilizational framework of Hellas.

To dig deeper into the relationships between the symbolic and the material, and to uncover the processes that underlie the formation of civilizational complexes, particular branches of social and cognitive archaeology have much to offer. Analysis of material artifacts can reveal how symbols were used. According to Merlin Donald's evolutionary schema, human cognition developed through the successive stages of mimetic, linguistic-mythic, and theoretic. The last transition—from mythic to theoretic culture—is characterized by the emergence of visual symbolism and external memory as major factors in cognitive architecture (Donald 1991, 18). Although the cognitive cultures constitute sequential stages, the preceding cultures never disappear entirely but are integrated into the successive ones, as Robert Bellah (2011) has demonstrated with reference to religion in human evolution. Each stage in the development involved both a structural change in cognitive architecture and profound transformations in human culture.

What is crucial for archaeological studies is Donald's concept of *external symbolic storage* as a key feature of the theoretic stage. The highly complicated organization of complex societies demanded considerable resources of memory and more elaborate techniques for information storage and transmission. This conception of cultures was revised by Colin Renfrew (1998), who designated *symbolic material culture* as an additional foundation of the modern theoretic culture. He suggested that without artifacts and material goods, many forms of thought could not have developed, especially in the realm of religious beliefs, where representation of deities is crucial. Material culture is a constitutive force for social relations and cognitive categories, "the concept is meaningless without the actual substance . . . the material reality of the substance precedes the symbolic role which is ascribed to it when it comes to embody . . . an institutional fact" (Renfrew 2001, 130–31). Materiality precedes such concepts as "commodity," "exchange," and "value," from which in turn we derive notions such as wealth, luxury, and exclusiveness. These are closely associated with the idea and phenomenon of hierarchy—not just in social terms, but also in new hierarchies of the sacred and the political. It is only after the emergence of such concepts that material objects may function as symbols and representations of power, status, collectivity, integration, or the supernatural. Material symbolism is thus an intrinsic aspect of the institutionalization of power, religious beliefs, and sacral practices.

The physical existence of artifacts as symbols is a prerequisite for the formation of writing and the later theorization of culture and rationalization in the Axial Age. However, the transition to theoretic culture took a long time, and did not occur until after the urban revolution (fourth millennium BCE). Even after the invention of writing in the ancient civilizations (e.g., in Mesopotamia), the oral (mythic) culture remained crucial, as did the material projection of culture that served as a symbolic storage. In early civilizations where writing had limited usage, material artifacts were especially useful as cultural memory storage. Memory was preserved in collective and state architecture, monuments, and a broad range of artifacts that were significant carriers of cultural meanings, political ideology, and dominant religious views. Endeavors have been made within symbolic archaeology to treat symbolic material culture as text and to apply a structuralist approach to reveal meanings in the objects as orderly systems of signs (Hodder 2005). Since they cannot be subjected to multiple interpretations and profound exegesis, material artifacts could not provoke such a transformative impact as the writing culture, text-based forms of storage, and the "culture of interpretation" of the Axial Age (Arnason 2010, 74–75). However, they nonetheless contributed to cultural dynamics on different levels and in different forms—whether as representations of an alternating relationship between the king and the god on Mesopotamian cylinder seals in Ur III (Postgate 1994), or as a newly built capital (Akhetaton/Amarna) dedicated to the monotheistic cult of Aten as a religious reformist incentive by Akhenaten. Non–writing material artifacts are crucial external symbolic stores, especially for early civilizations in which material manifestations and narratives constituted the background for cultural memory and the anchoring of meanings and core symbols.

The study of the mental and symbolic structures of past societies in cognitive archaeology seems to be congruent with the study of historical formations of mentalities ("symbolic landscapes") as "structures of consciousness." Benjamin Nelson (1973), who introduced the concept of structures of consciousness into civilizational analysis, indicated three structures: sacro-magic, faith, and rationalized structures. These, he wrote, do not represent an evolutionary sequence, but an overlapping "cultural stratigraphy." The relationship between these cognitive and mental cultural dimensions and their material representations needs more detailed research. In any case, the introduction into civilizational analysis of the symbolic aspect of material culture, the meanings and status of materiality itself, and the later division and even opposition between material and nonmaterial are all important because externality, visuality, and external symbolic storage became core features of modern theoretic culture after the last cognitive cultural transition.

In social archaeology, the focus is placed on political and economic dimensions, including roles and status, institutions, power and economic relations, center-periphery and center-center interactions. Scholars have unambiguously confirmed the multilinearity of ancient complex societies. This perspective is common to civilizational analysis. Social archaeology is especially interested in those dynamics that lead to greater complexity at the state and civilizational level. Particular forms are analyzed as the result of many interacting endogenous and exogenous factors such as population size, density, ecological surroundings (landscape), and mode of production. This attention paid to the material factors of social organization distinguishes this archaeological approach from civilizational analysis, which, especially in the tradition of Eisenstadt, focuses more heavily on cultural-institutional complexes. The contribution of structural constraints on cultural ordering are usually ignored or downplayed even though Arnason (2004) stresses the "regional basis of civilizational distinctions" and "geographical context." Archaeological and anthropological evidence for multilinear development has turned up numerous correlations to which civilizational analysis should pay attention. For example, small-scale societies are characterized by a more active population and higher degrees of "protest," compared to the passivity that is more typical for the inhabitants of agrarian states (Kradin 2011).

Archaeologists have developed their own ad hoc concepts and theories, many of which are relevant to the research agenda of civilizational analysis. For example, the concept of *peer polity interaction* provides an explanatory model for the formation and dynamics of clusters of interrelated equivalent "peers" sharing a number of common features. Such peers are the highest-order autonomous political units that exist in a specific, delimited region; their continuous interactions form a structural homology, constituting common cultural-symbolical, religious, and social frameworks across the region. This approach aims to overcome the limitations of other modes of explaining cultural, social, and political change, usually with reference to diffusion, the influence of dominant polities from outside of the region, or endogenous processes within a single polity or territory. In peer polity interaction, the most important processes are considered to be those that take place on an intermediate level between neighboring, self-governing, and broadly equivalent polities or societies. These participate in a wide range of interactions, such as imitation and competitive emulation, competition, warfare, "symbolic entrainment," and trade and exchange of material goods, information, ideas, and symbols. The polities within a cluster demonstrate remarkable similarities in size, and share similar political institutions, governmental forms, the same system of writing (if any) and spoken language, essentially the same structure of religious beliefs (albeit with local variations, such as patron deity), customary practices, styles of material culture, and other broad cultural similarities. Continuous interactions result in structural homologies expressed in institutional arrangement, symbolic system, architectural and monumental forms, and the social structures of a region (Renfrew 1986).

As Snodgrass (1986) demonstrated, peer-polity interactions played a fundamental role in the formation of the Greek city-state system and civilization from the Archaic period (800 BCE), including the core features of the polis, warfare and the military system, the hoplite army as a symbol of polis status, codified law, and common monumental and art forms. Temples, especially great sanctuaries (e.g., Delphi), provided a "medium of rivalry between peer polities," as did Pan-Hellenic athletic festivals in Olympia. These arenas of "intracivilizational encounter," served as forums for the presentation of the "self," where the innovations and advances of one polity could be communicated to others (Snodgrass 1986). The polis system was legitimized in the context of the existence of other states that functioned along comparable lines. This model of relationship provided positive feedback for the interacting polities; as they engaged in a common symbolic universe, the actions of other agents became meaningful and significant.

Peer polities interaction is especially helpful for civilizational analysis because it explains the emergence of homological cultural and institutional patterns within the interacting independent sociopolitical units of common civilizational complexes and boundaries. Archaeological data are crucial in defining the civilizational boundaries because cultural unity and homology usually have material manifestations. The concept uncovers a specific civilizational structure and a scenario that existed in ancient Greece, Mesopotamia, Minoan and Mycenaean Greece, the Etruscan city-states, and the cities of the Mayan lowlands, among others. Along with other archaeological concepts such as *interaction sphere,* designed to explain long-distance interactions through trade and exchange, *peer polities interaction* is a valuable supplement to Benjamin Nelson's framework of inter- and intracivilizational encounters (Nelson 1973).

Intercultural and Intercivilizational Encounters

In lieu of a conclusion, I shall briefly consider one more of the central issues civilizational analysis shares with archaeology, namely, the problem of intercivilizational encounters. This term refers to far-reaching technological, ideological, and institutional changes generated by cultural interactions. These issues have been extensively studied in archaeology since the nineteenth century with reference to trade, migration, diffusion, invasion, and their role in the shaping of cultural and civilizational identities. The general premise is that "the differences were not born of isolation, but through a long process of exchange and interaction" (Wengrow 2010, 52).

I shall illustrate by examining the relationship between the Axial Age agrarian civilizations and non-axial societies of nomads or nomadic empires (e.g., China and Xiongnu, Rus' and Mongols, etc.). The region of the northern Black Sea coast in antiquity witnessed intercultural encounters between the Greek colonists and the "barbarians," Eurasian nomads. The Greek settlements were a unique frontier of the Greek *oikoumene* that were involved in intense military, trade, political, and cultural interactions with the "nomadic world" and the barbarian locals: nomadic Scythians (predominantly) and Sarmatians, together with the agrarian Maeotae and Sinds. These interactions shaped different forms of intercultural synthesis and changed both Greek and barbarian ways and forms of being, sometimes profoundly, albeit not symmetrically.

Migration and invasions of the Eurasian nomads significantly influenced the life of Greek colonies and the established relationship configurations of Hellas with the barbarians (Vinogradov 2009). Greek-barbarian interaction had been continuous in the region over several centuries, but it had remained sporadic in terms of contacts with particular ethnic groups. The pattern was not homogeneous. Intercultural influences were more perfunctory in the western Greek settlements, although here "barbarian" elements can be traced in pottery, semi-dugout dwellings, and particular cult and burial practices that indicate the coexistence of the Greeks and the barbarians. In the East, more complicated phenomena emerged as a result of intensive interaction between the Greeks and Scythians. These contacts led to a partial religious convergence. Greek symbolic and religious complexes related to art, burial practices, and the pantheon acquired new barbarian components; new deities appeared during this time and barbarian names were given to the Greek gods. At the same time, the Scythians adopted (not simply imitated) and incorporated some of the Greek sacral and artistic elements into their own cultural matrix.[8] One of the commonly recognized aspects of the latter is the growing anthropomorphism of the Scythian art objects produced for Scythian consumers, which employed the anthropomorphic style more common to Greeks. The barbarian pantheon was reconstructed according to Hellenic views (Artamonov 1961; Vakhtina 2005). Another example of the intercultural synthesis is the phenomenon of a syncretic Graeco-barbarian art tradition that integrated the nomadic animal style with Greek aesthetics.

Interactions between Greeks and "others" gave rise to the formation of a unique political macrostructure. The Bosporan Kingdom took shape as a Greek-barbarian state by the turn of the fifth and fourth centuries BCE. During the Spartocids, close relations with barbarians were established, evidenced in the king's double-title—the Bosporan *archon* and the King of the Barbarians (late fourth century BCE) (Vinogradov 2005, 266). The mixed culture of the Bosporan Kingdom manifested itself in the burial tradition of the Bosporan elite, exemplified by the remarkable aristocratic barrows of the fourth century BCE (the Kul'-Oba, the Patinioti barrow, the Kekuvatskij barrow, the Trehbratny barrow, the Snake barrow, the barrow Baksy, etc.). These *tumuli* have received ambiguous ethnic attributions (Vinogradov 2005; Butyagin 2008), but it seems safe to conclude that they "show the direction of the main political and cultural links with the steppes of the northern Black Sea area, indicating the presence of an alliance with close relations between Scythia and Bosporos" (Vinogradov 2008, 16). Intensified contacts with barbarians resulted in craft development and production oriented toward barbarian consumers. The Bosporan Kingdom became a production center for items of Graeco-barbarian art such as the famous Graeco-Scythian toreutics (Vinogradov 2005).[9] A new economic network was established connecting mainland Greece to the world of the barbarians and engaging the latter in the grain trade, an economy that opened up new horizons of profit and wealth. These new economic relations helped to promote the sedentarization of Scythians.

The trajectory of barbarianization of the Greeks in the Bosporan Kingdom started "from above." That is, barbarian influence affected first the elites and nobility and then penetrated to other social groups (Butyagin 2008). The same pattern was characteristic for the Hellenization of the barbarians. Scythian elites were more sensitive than other social groups to Greek culture, including artistic and other goods, religious views, and practices such as the consumption of wine (Khazanov et al. 1982, 36). According to Strabo, intense contacts with the Greeks negatively affected Scythian practices and mores, leading to "huckstering" and an "addiction to luxury." Barbarized Greeks and Hellenized barbarians represent the emergence of a new *habitus,* but it should be noted that the Greek civilizational complex dominated and demonstrated more resistance to the nomadic influence on different levels. The changes in the *modus vivendi* of the Scythians were evidenced by their sedentarization and borrowing of Greek tools and traditions, development of an urban mode of life, further centralization of power, active economic exchange with colonists, Hellenization of the elite, and incorporation of Greek aesthetic and religious elements (Khazanov 1975; Khazanov et al. 1982). This emergence of a new historical formation in the orbit of Greek civilization was interrupted in the late fourth–early third centuries BCE by a new wave of nomadic invasion. Great Scythia collapsed and was never restored to its former greatness. Later political and economic alliances were established with other barbarian tribes (e.g., Sarmatians, local tribes of the trans-Don and Kuban' area, etc.). However, they hardly provoked such complex cultural, social, and political transformations as the ones generated by the Greek-Scythian encounter.

Notes

I thank Johann Arnason for his insightful remarks and valuable suggestions for the improvement of this chapter. I am also grateful to all participants of the workshop in Halle for the many inspiring ideas they presented.

1. The antievolutionist stance of civilizational analysis does not imply that it ignores development. Evolutionist approaches take many forms in archaeology (Leonard 2001). The concept has long been detached from the idea of unilinear progressive development and is able to take account of diverse historical contexts, variations, and unpredictability. See, for instance, Bellah's (2011) vision of evolutionism and religion and Arnason's review of this book (2013).

2. In Jaspers's original long chronology, the Axial Age is the period from 800 to 200 BCE (Jaspers 1965). In Arnason's (2012) long chronological version, the time span is a slightly different: 800–400 BCE.

3. However, even Eisenstadt noted the importance of the study of the pre-axial civilizations for providing a better understanding of Axial innovations (2005, 544).

4. Claessen and Skalnik also mention the role of an ideology (e.g., presented in a mythical form) in the formation of the early state; however, they characterize it as having "no more than a secondary influence" (Claessen and Skalnik 1978, 628).

5. According to Eisenstadt (2003), in the pre-axial age the supernatural world was symbolically structured according to principles very similar to those of the mundane world. Trigger (2003) argues that in the early civilizations there was no clear distinction between natural, supernatural, and social realms. Deities and humans were mutually dependent. Not only humans relied on divine will, but the Gods too depended on human offerings to replenish their powers. Spectacular rituals and ceremonies were needed to improve relations with deities in order to sustain and reproduce social order. Thus, deities were not transcendental in the way they became in the later axial civilizations.

6. Here it is worth mentioning a long-standing controversy on the Greek "axial" case. Moshe Beret (2004) launched the debate on the "statelessness" of this civilization and its polis up to the fourth century BCE, the epoch of Hellenistic empires.

7. According to these results, all societies with a true developed writing system have three levels or more of political organization. However, by no means all societies with three or more political levels have writing (Kradin 2013, drawing on Peregrine 2003).

8. "Dans toute catégorie du domaine de la culture spirituelle, on observe encore plus nettement l'hellénisation. Là, elle ne se limitait plus à la simple imitation des éléments empruntés. Leur adaptation à la matrix culturelle scythe se produisit. Dans les différents domaines de la culture, cela s'effectuait diversement avec une intensité et des résultats multiples. De toute évidence, pourtant, on n'atteignit quand même pas le stade de l'intégration dans la structure" (Khazanov et al. 1982, 36).

9. Toreutics is an artistic metalwork that employs embossing and chasing to form minutely detailed reliefs or small engraved patterns.

References

Arnason, Johann P. 2004. "Civilizational Patterns and Civilizing Processes." In *Rethinking Civilizational Analysis,* edited by Said Amir Arjomand, and Edward A. Tiryakian, 103–18. London: Sage.

———. 2005. "The Axial Age and its Interpreters. Reopening a Debate." In *Axial Civilizations and World History,* edited by Jóhann Páll Árnason, S. N. Eisenstadt, Björn Wittrock, 19–50. Leiden: Brill.

———. 2006. "Civilizational Analysis, Social Theory and Comparative History." In *Handbook of Contemporary European Social Theory,* edited by Gerard Delanty, 230–41. London: Routledge.

———. 2010. "The Cultural Turn and the Civilizational Approach." *European Journal of Social Theory* 13, no. 1: 67–82.

———. 2012. "Re-Historicizing Axial Civilizations." In *The Axial Age and Its Consequences,* edited by Robert Bellah and Hans Joas, 337–65. Cambridge and London: Belknap Press of Harvard University Press.

———. 2013. "The Archaic and the Axial." Review of Robert Bellah: *Religion in Human Evolution: From the Paleolithic to the Axial Age. The Review of Politics* 75, no. 1: 143–49.

———. 2014. "Historicizing the Axial Age." In *Social Theory and Area Studies in the Global Age,* edited by Said A. Arjomand, 179–201. Albany: State University of New York Press.

Artamonov, Mikhail I. 1961. "Antropomorphnye bozhestva s skiphskoy religii". *Arkheologicheskiy sbornik Gosudarstvennogo Ermitazha,* ["Anthropomorphic Deities in the Religion of Scythes." *Archaeological Collection of the State Hermitage*] 2: 57–87.

Bellah, Robert N. 2011. *Religion in Human Evolution: From the Paleolithic to the Axial Age.* Cambridge: The Belknap Press of Harvard University Press.

Beret, Moshe. 2004. "Greece: the Stateless *Polis* (11*th*–4*th* centuries BC)." In *The Early State, Its Alternatives and Analogues,* edited by Leonid E. Grinin, Robert Carneiro, Dmitri M. Bondarenko, Nikolay N. Kradin, and Andrey V. Korotayev, 364–87. Volgograd: Uchitel.

Butyagin, Alexander. 2008. "Barrows of the Bosporan Kingdom during the 4th Century BC as a Greek-barbarian Phenomenon." *Bollettino di Archeologia on line* I 2010, Volume speciale C, C6, 3: 10–17.

Childe, V. G. 1950. "The Urban Revolution." *Town Planning Review* 21, no. 1: 3–17.

Claessen, Henry J. M., and Peter Skalnik. 1978. "Limits: Beginning and End of the Early State" In *The Early State,* edited by Henry J. M.

Claessen and Peter Skalnik, 619–36. The Hague: De Gruyter Mouton.

Donald, Merlin. 1991. *Origins of the Modern Mind: Three Stages in the Evolution of Culture and Cognition*. Cambridge: Harvard University Press.

Durkheim, Emile, and Marcel Mauss. 1971. "Note on the Notion of Civilization." Translated and introduced by B. Nelson. *Social Research* 38, no. 4: 808–13.

Eisenstadt, S. N. 2000. "The Civilizational Dimension in Sociological Analysis." *Thesis Eleven* 62: 1–21.

———. 2001. "The Civilizational Dimension of Modernity: Modernity as a Distinct Civilization." *International Sociology* 16: 320–40.

———. [1983] 2003. "The Axial Age: The Emergence of Transcendental Vision and the Rise of Clerics." In *Comparative Civilizations and Multiple Modernities*, 195–218. Leiden:

———. [1988] 2003. "Beyond Collapse." In *The Collapse of Ancient States and Civilizations*, edited by Norman Yoffee and George L. Cowgill, 236–43. Tucson: The University of Arizona Press.

———. 2005. "Axial Civilizations and the Axial Age Reconsidered." In *Axial Civilizations and World History*, edited by Jóhann Páll Árnason, S.N. Eisenstadt, Björn Wittrock, 531–64. Leiden: Brill.

Jaspers, Karl. 1965. *The Origin and Goal of History*. Translated by Michael Bullock. New Haven: Yale University Press.

Hodder, Ian. 2005. "Symbolic and Structuralist Archaeology." In *Archaeology: the Key Concepts*, edited by Colin Renfrew and Paul Bahn, 190–93. London, New York: Routledge.

Khazanov, Anatoly M. 1975. *Sotsial'naya istoriya Skiphov. Osnovnye problemy razvitiya drevnikh kochevnikov evraziyskikh stepey.* [*The Social History of the Scythians. Main Problems of Development of the Ancient Nomads of the Eurasian Steppes.*] Moscow: Nauka.

———, M. Burda, T. De Sonneville-David. 1982. "Les Scythes et la civilisation antique. Problèmes de contacts." *Dialogues d'histoire ancienne* 8: 7–51.

Kradin, Nikolay. 2002. "Nomadism, Evolution, and World-Systems: Pastoral Societies in Theories of Historical Development." *Journal of World-Systems Research* VIII, III: 368–88.

———. 2006. "Archaeological Criteria of Civilization." *Social Evolution & History* 5, no. 1: 89–108.

———. 2011. "A Panorama of Social Archaeology in Russia." In *Comparative Archaeologies: A Sociological View of the Science of the Past*, edited by Ludomir R. Lodzy, 243–71. New York: Springer Science and Business Media.

———. 2013. "Criteria of Complexity in Evolution: Cross-Cultural Studies in Archaeology of Prehistory." *Social Evolution & History* 12, no. 1: 28–50.

Kristiansen, Kristian. 1996. "Chiefdoms, States, and Systems of Social Evolution." In *Chiefdoms: Power, Economy and Ideology*, edited by Timothy Earle, 16–43. Cambridge: Cambridge University Press.

Leonard, Robert D. 2001. "Evolutionary Archaeology." In *Archaeological Theory Today*, edited by Ian Hodder, 65–97. London: Polity Press.

Mauss, Marcel. 2004. "Civilizational Forms." In *Rethinking Civilizational Analysis*, edited by Said Amir Arjomand and Edward A. Tiryakian, 21–29. London: Sage.

Michalowski, Piotr. 2005. "Mesopotamian Vistas on Axial Transformations." In *Axial Civilizations and World History*, edited by Jóhann P. Árnason, S. N. Eisenstadt, and Björn Wittrock, 157–82. Leiden: Brill.

Nelson, Benjamin. 1973. "Civilizational Complexes and Intercivilizational Encounters." *Sociological Analysis* 34, no. 2: 79–105.

Peregrine, Peter N. 2003. "Atlas of Cultural Evolution." *World Cultures* 14, no. 1: 1–89.

Possehl, Gregory. 2002. *The Indus Civilization: A Contemporary Perspective*. Walnut Creek, CA: Altamira.

Postgate, J. N. 1994. "Text and Figure in Ancient Mesopotamia: Match and Mismatch." In *The Ancient Mind: Elements of Cognitive Archaeology*, edited by Colin Renfrew and Ezra B. W. Zubrow, 176–84. Cambridge: Cambridge University Press.

Renfrew, Colin. 1972. *The Emergence of Civilisation: The Cyclades and the Aegean in the Third Millenium B.C.* London: Methuen.

———. 1986. "Introduction: Peer Polity Interaction and Socio-Political Change." In *Peer Polity Interaction and Socio-Political Change*, edited by Colin Renfrew and John F. Cherry, 1–18. Cambridge: Cambridge University Press.

———. 1998. "Mind and Matter: Cognitive Archaeology and External Symbolic Storage." In *Cognition and Material Culture: The Archaeology of Symbolic Storage*, edited by Colin Renfrew and

Chris Scarre. Cambridge: McDonald Institute for Archaeological Research, University of Cambridge.

———. 2001. "Symbol before Concept Material Engagement and the Early Development of Society." In *Archaeological Theory Today*, edited by Ian Hodder, 122–40. London: Polity Press.

———. [1972] 2011. *The Emergence of Civilization. The Cyclades and the Aegean in the Third Millennium BC*. Oxford: Oxbow Books.

Snodgrass, Anthony. 1986. "Interaction by Design: the Greek City State." In *Peer Polity Interaction and Socio-Political Change*, edited by Colin Renfrew and John F. Cherry, 47–58. Cambridge: Cambridge University Press.

Trigger, Bruce. 2003. *Understanding Early Civilizations: A Comparative Study*. Cambridge: Cambridge University Press.

Vakhtina, Maria Y. 2005. "Grecheskoe iskusstvo i iskusstvo Evropeyskoy Skiphii v VII–IV vv. do n.e." *Greki i varvary Severnogo Prichernomor'ya v skiphskuyu epokhu*, ["Greek Art and the Art of European Scythia in VII–IV Centuries BC." In *Greeks and Barbarians in the Scythian Epoch*], edited by K. K. Marchenko, 297–396. St. Petersburg: Aleteia.

Vinogradov, Yuriy A. 2005. "Bospor Kimmeriyskiy." *Greki i varvary Severnogo Prichernomor'ya v skiphskuyu epokhu*, ["Cimmerian Bosporus." In *Greeks and Barbarians in the Scythian Epoch*], edited by K. K. Marchenko, 211–96. St. Petersburg: Aleteia.

———. 2008. "Rhythms of Eurasia and the Main Historical Stages of the Kimmerian Bosporos in Pre-Roman Times." In *Meeting of Cultures in the Black Sea Region. Between Conflict and Coexistence*, edited by Pia Guldager Bilde, and Jane Hjarl Petersen, 13–27. Aarhus, Denmark, Oakville, CT: Aarhus University Press.

———. 2009. "Migratsii kochevnikov Evrazii i nekotorye osobennosti istoricheskogo razvitiya Bospora Kimmeriyskogo". Bosporskie issledovaniya, XXII "Stepi Evrazii i istoriya Bospora Kimmeriyskogo," ["Migrations of Eurasian Nomads and Some Peculiarities of the Cimmerian Bosporus Historical Development." In *Bosporus Studies* Issue XXII "Eurasian Steppes and the History of Cimmerian Bosporus"], 5–87. Kerch.

Wengrow, David. 2010. *What Makes Civilization? The Ancient Near East and the Future of the West*. Oxford: Oxford University Press.

Yoffee, Norman. [1988] 2003. "The Collapse of Ancient Mesopotamian States and Civilization." In *The Collapse of Ancient States and*

Civilizations, edited by Norman Yoffee and George L. Cowgill, 44–68. Tucson: The University of Arizona Press.

———. 2004. *Myths of the Archaic States: Evolution of the Earliest Cities, States, and Civilizations.* Cambridge: Cambridge University Press.

4

THE USE AND ABUSE
OF CIVILIZATION

An Assessment from Historical Anthropology
for South Arabia's History

Andre Gingrich

Is "civilization," in any version of the term, a useful concept for sociocultural anthropology today and for the field's inter- and transdisciplinary endeavors in the social sciences and the humanities? The present chapter offers differentiated answers to this question.[1] In the first and second sections here, I answer the question in the affirmative, with qualifications for certain fields of inquiry within historical anthropology—first on a conceptual level, and second by discussing historical examples from the southern parts of Arabia and from Southwest Arabia in particular. In the third section, I summarize these findings in support of a partially positive answer for some historical topics. That section concludes, however, with arguments that emphasize more caution and skepticism regarding other uses of the term for anthropological research in the contemporary world. In this discussion, I address themes and notions of "civilization" in a manner that paraphrases a well-known text by Marshall Sahlins (1976)—not only by referencing its title, but also by employing a core element of its orientation. Some conceptual tools and research directions—including the very term *civilization*—contain such powerful, influential, and even explosive potential that their use by social anthropologists requires special attention, care, and balance.

Conceptual Usage in Historical Anthropology

At the turn from the twentieth to the twenty-first century, historical anthropology has become reintegrated, or rather, has integrated in new ways, as one of the field's primary methodological inventories. The gradual loosening and partial dissolution of previously dominant national (or quasi-national) traditions in anthropology aided in this process, as did the simultaneous rise of transnational and global directions in the discipline. For quite some time during the twentieth century, certain of those national traditions had been reluctant to attribute any substantial relevance to historical anthropology as a legitimate methodological contribution to the field. By contrast, no one in anthropology today would seriously contest the assertion that Eric Wolf's (1982) study of the prehistory and early history of European expansion into Asia, Africa, Latin America, and the Pacific world represented a milestone in the field, and just as few would deny that Jean Comaroff and John Comaroff's (1991; 1997) inquiries into historical transformations within a South African border zone represent substantial contributions to global anthropology. Although still second in significance to studies of and in the contemporary world, historical anthropology has a newly acknowledged role to play (Gingrich 2013). But the stage and the play themselves have changed to a considerable extent, with the result that the role of historical anthropology is changing as well. Against the backdrop of a discipline that is globalizing itself, the methodological priorities of its historical subsections also tend to prioritize both "wider" and "larger" empirical fields of investigation rather than isolating the local from its wider processual contexts. At the same time, wherever the study of seemingly local historical phenomena does attain some academic or pragmatic priority, anthropological research into the past increasingly seeks to establish significant connections and comparisons with historical worlds outside and beyond the local (Gingrich and Zips 2006).

My starting point is within these new contexts of global and transnational anthropology today, with their relatively recent recognition of historical anthropology as a legitimate set of methodological endeavors and with an ensuing priority of "wider and larger" dimensions in it. *Wider and larger* implies a relational reference to size, as positioned by one's inquiry against other entities in processual and regional contexts: from the outset, then, some methodological attention to issues of scale is involved in this kind of reasoning. If one is bound to include wider contexts into one's investigation, one cannot escape the question of scale, of perspectives on comparative sizes, and of the interactions between larger and smaller entities (Gingrich and Hannerz, 2017). Along with this increased awareness of wider and larger historical dimensions, the term *civilization* may indeed deserve consideration as a potentially helpful tool in certain inquiries. In what ways, then, might *civilization* provide a useful tool for an updated historical anthropology, and for what kinds of historical themes and explorations?

Civilization seems to have some descriptive, empirical, heuristic, and medium-range comparative value for historical macrocultures, as is suggested by the co-editors of, this volume and in some of their previous work (Arnason 2010; Hann 2011). In principle, macrocultures designate larger cultural clusters that connected and intersected, internally and externally, to such an extent that an umbrella designation such as *civilization* is rendered meaningful, at least in descriptive ways. In this sense, the term *civilization* also addresses, at least partially, phenomena other than those understood by the established terms of political and historical anthropology, namely *state* and *empire*.

Anthropology's normal usage of these two terms tends to acknowledge, and even to emphasize, that their internal and external composition includes at least some degree of cultural diversity. Historical empires are conceived as more complex and differentiated versions of states in general, and by contrast to other forms of states in preindustrial eras (Pohl 2011). Along the sliding or fuzzy scale between the smaller states and empires of preindustrial times, I would tend to situate macrocultural clusters, or *civilization,* closer to the empire end of the spectrum. This has to do with some of the analytical and semantic features of the term *civilization*. Among other connotations, the Latin and Roman etymology of the term refers to "cities," a meaning that can be usefully retained on a relatively high level of abstraction for comparative purposes beyond the circum-Mediterranean region from which the concept emerged. All empires have included one or several forms of what we call "cities"; other preindustrial, smaller states may or may not have had them.

Once the close association between the terms *civilization* (macrocultural clusters) and *empire* is accepted, an additional question requires clarification. If *civilization* were largely the same as *empire,* there would be no reason to select one of these terms for specialized relevance. How, then, may the term and concept of *civilization* be differentiated and distinguished in meaningful ways from *empire?* The answer to this question is derived from our initial understanding of complex historical macrocultures: *Civilization* would designate the macrocultural flows and spheres that crosscut empires and extend beyond them, in both a temporal and a spatial sense. *Empire* refers to imperial states, including their bureaucratic, fiscal, military, and political machineries. While the emergence of empires often promotes the rise of civilizations, *civilization* is not directly dependent upon the imperial state and its maintenance. Nor does the association of macrocultures with imperial states imply that imperial states are the exclusive containers of macrocultures.

In the spatial sense, macrocultural influences may extend far beyond the fuzzy border spheres of imperial control to neighboring areas and beyond—including distant outposts, semiautonomous and independent smaller states, enclaves of a specific civilization, and a whole range of nonstate entities. In the temporal sense, shorter or longer periods of macrocultural influence—including hegemonic cultural dominance—may continue even during periods when imperial state power is nominal or has vanished altogether. Civilization's influence may continue long after political imperial power has disintegrated. The quality of both great distance and longevity, transcending temporal interruptions and spatial voids, is a necessary correlate of the term *civilization* to make it useful for historical anthropology. The "wider and larger" macrodimensions of civilization thus refer to a significant spatial and temporal expansion beyond the imperial state's immediate boundaries.

An anthropological understanding of historical civilizations will, at minimum, conceptualize them as spheres and flows of macrocultures that are associated with previous or contemporary empires but lack any necessary dependence upon their immediate imperial state machineries. Civilization thus is relatively autonomous from, albeit associated with, empire. Like empires but beyond imperial limitations, civilizations include macrocultural constellations of social heterogeneity, hierarchy, and complexity, of uneven integration, and of ethnic diversity. Still, some shared social agents and sociocultural media are required if the flexible, but relatively enduring and fairly cohesive effects of distance and longevity are to be maintained beyond the integrative stabilization of political institutions. Language, writing, and religion and their social and cognitive representatives and actors, are the most likely cultural candidates for providing some momentum across time and space for these macrocultural necessities. The activities required by these sociocognitive representatives would necessarily involve mobility (including its spatial dimensions) and learning (including its intergenerational dimensions).

The term *civilization* is thus useful as long as it remains clear that it is synonymous with specific, enduring historical macrocultural clusters that include city-like types of settlement conglomerates. These basic conceptual tools now allow for the following short examination of their usefulness for certain periods of South and Southwest Arabian history.

Examples from the History of Southwest Arabia

In historical studies of the Middle East, notions of "Islamic" or "Arab" civilization are common. Sometimes only one of these terms applies, but at times both are simultaneously in place—as in the cases discussed here, for which the designation *Arab-Islamic civilization* is used. Current highly politicized nonacademic debates in and about the Middle East in which "Islamic civilization" is contrasted with "Arab civilization" as a program for the future (with some superficial references to the past) will be discussed in the third section of this chapter. In academic research, however, these terms have not been highly contested. Historians of art, of literature, and of architecture use them, as do philologists, philosophers, geographers, and experts in religious studies, historical sociology, and the general history of what is referred to as the Middle East. Anthropologists have not invented the usage of these terms in the region; in fact, they may rely on them less frequently than do practitioners of those other disciplines because anthropologists tend to focus on micro-settings and smaller entities. Still, historical anthropologists have found few reasons to criticize or to reject terms that serve as useful common referents for most fields of expertise in this region. Like a major airport or railway station, notions of an Arab-Islamic civilization often serve as a common point of departure, arrival, or stopover for many scholars, wherever their destinations and travel purposes may otherwise lead them. I do not intend to disrupt the operations of that airport or railway station per se. On the contrary, although I discuss in the third section those cases in which it is better for anthropologists to avoid that traffic zone, I shall outline in this section why, for historical anthropologists of the region, there may be certain instances when it is useful to pass through that airport or station. I demonstrate this through historical examples from South Arabia and, more specifically, from the Yemen.

It is common opinion among experts in various disciplines that from quite early on, historical Yemen and Oman were component elements within the wider spheres of Arab-Islamic civilization. The names Yemen and Oman, which appear in early Arabic and other sources, designated the main regions of Southwest and Southeast Arabia, respectively.[2] The modalities of interaction were uneven; sometimes Yemen and Oman were more actively involved, often they were in a more peripheral position. A specific language (Arabic) and a clear belief orientation (Islam) define the kind of civilization under discussion and are therefore the first historical phenomena to be addressed here in their initial South Arabian dimensions.

Since at least the fifth century CE (Bāfaqīh 1983), Arabic had become part of the linguistic diversity that still prevailed in South Arabia. Persian, as an Indo-European language, had played a more crucial role in Oman; in the Yemen it was the minority language of small elites. Like Arabic, most of the other languages practiced in both regions were Semitic, and available in several forms of writing (Beeston 1987). In the seventh century, the version of Islam represented by the Prophet Muhammad rose to the status of prevailing faith and belief system, at least in a nominal sense, across South Arabia as throughout the entire Arab Peninsula (Brunner 2005). South Arabia's earliest and perhaps most significant contributions to the rise of Arab-Islamic empire and civilization came through demographic and social factors. Major segments in the first waves of Arab military expansion and of Arab civilians' migration into northern Arabia and North Africa were of Yemeni and Omani origin and background (Robin 1991).

The centers of the emerging Arab-Islamic empire after its rise in the second half of the seventh century, however, were always elsewhere: first in Mecca, which continued to be the main pilgrimage site of Islam; later under Umayyad rulers in Damascus, the new political center in former Roman and Byzantine territory; and finally under the rule of the Abbasids and their immediate successors in Baghdad. It is argued with some justification that the Arab-Islamic empire reached its largest spatial extension during the Umayyad period, and peaked in terms of internal coherence, political stability, and cultural achievements under certain Abbasid rulers: the so-called Islamic Golden Age, from the eighth to the mid-twelfth centuries, occurred during the Abbasid period. Military and nonmilitary encounters with European crusaders did not topple the empire, but they did promote the rise of local military leaders, among whom the Turkish Seljuks are the best known. The centrifugal force exerted by local military leaders, increasing internal rivalries, and, finally, the Mongol invasions into eastern Arabia and the establishment of Mongol rule in Iran led to the crumbling and eventual demise of the empire. After the mid-thirteenth century, the caliphate had little authority other than spiritual. The empire disintegrated into successor states of various size that were less often led by Arabic-speaking rulers, although Arabic did remain the ritual and liturgical language of Islam. A plethora of political entities of various sizes existed between Andalusia and Transoxania (Central Asia), and from North Africa to Mesopotamia, Iran, and beyond into South Asia, but some version of Arab-Islamic civilization persisted and continued to thrive at least in the core areas of the former empire: the Arab peninsula, Mesopotamia, and in northeast Africa until the late Mamluk and early Ottoman period of the fifteenth and early sixteenth centuries (Meri 2005; Sonn 2011).

Throughout these centuries, South Arabia remained an active and interactive periphery to developments elsewhere in the empire, as long as it existed. At times South Arabia may have absorbed more than it contributed, but it did give rise to creative, semiautonomous local and regional developments that were facilitated by its peripheral distance. Noteworthy advances were achieved, ranging from agricultural techniques to astronomy and mathematics, and from navigational skills to geographic expertise and philosophy. What had been an imperial periphery thereby turned into a macrocultural border zone, a threshold of civilization, and, in a sense, a melting pot. South Arabia's ports served as main points of destination for long-distance trade and, most importantly, as crucial transit zones for East African and South Asian Muslim pilgrims on their way to and from Mecca and Medina. Both before and after the empire's demise, new and important growth processes of Arab-Islamic civilization took place in southern Arabia. Out of Yemen's Hadramaut subregion, and out of the ports of Aden and Oman, merchants and craftsmen, preachers and architects, slave traders and warriors, traveled with or without their families across the Indian Ocean. Still later, they began to settle down along the Indian Ocean's other shores: from Dar es-Salaam and Madagascar to Mombasa and Kilwa, from the coasts and islands of South Asia to those of Southeast Asia's mainland and archipelagos (Freitag 2003; Heiss and Slama 2010; Ho 2006). Over time, these movements of people and cultures provided some of the context in which Vasco da Gama was given Muslim navigational help in 1498 while traveling around southern Africa.

From a South Arabian perspective, then, referring to an Arab-Islamic civilization between the seventh and the fourteenth centuries does have some descriptive and heuristic value in historical anthropology. Not surprisingly, the historical evidence addressed in this section is in line with the conceptual arguments discussed in the first part of this chapter. Yet the historical evidence is also helpful in fine-tuning and further elaborating that conceptual tool. For instance, with a focus on Arabia's history we now see that a civilization's postimperial phases may last as long as, or even longer than, the imperial political periods with which it was initially associated. This point about longevity must be further qualified by the spatial dimension. In this regard, a focus on Arab-Islamic history again reminds us of civilization's processes of territorial expansion and contraction. The establishment of Mongol rule in Iran, for example, allowed Islam to persevere but brought about the gradual demise of Arab influence in the region. Another well-known process of contraction is the vanishing of an Arab-Islamic presence in the Iberian Peninsula before, and even more so after, 1492. But prior to, simultaneous with, and after those shrinking processes, Arabic and Islamic influence expanded across the Sahara Desert and the Indian Ocean. Major and minor periods of rupture, of contraction and disappearance, and even of reemergence in the same or in different sites or regions are part and parcel of the longevity and long-distance dimensions in a historical anthropological concept of civilization—in the sense of macrocultural spheres and flows—that may become useful.

The point was made earlier that language, writing, and religion were the best candidates for providing some of the required elastic coherence to macrocultures that would merit a specialized research designation such as *civilization*. The example of Arab-Islamic civilization examined here provides a corresponding case in point, with Arabic language and text and Islamic faith as the defining features.

Prior to the advent of Islam, ancient South Arabia already had known some degree of literacy, primarily of a long-distance and elitist relevance, it seems. The state entities of Saba, Qataban, Himyar, and others, which have been fairly well documented and analyzed, communicated primarily in pre-Arabic Semitic languages, and they mostly upheld various non-monotheist belief systems (de Maigret 2002; Ryckmans 1987).[3] Yemen's integration into the rapidly emerging Arab-Islamic empire is a fascinating process that may still hold surprising discoveries for future research. The point here is that it was a long and, it seems, fairly smooth dual process of Arabization followed by Islamization; Islamization gained such a momentum that it reinforced the earlier process of Arabization. Current research indicates that in Southwest Arabia transitional periods of linguistic diversity spanned several centuries, during which Arabic was first a minority language.[4] Arabic gradually became a language of both the urban poor and elite with some aspects of a lingua franca: for the speakers of other Semitic languages in the region, it must have been comprehensible with some ease. Finally, during the sixth century at the latest, Arabic became the majority language, although minority languages seemed to have coexisted for quite some time. The kinds of Yemeni Arabic we know from medieval textual evidence, and by inference from contemporary studies of local and vernacular Arabic, obviously displayed remarkable internal differentiation by region and subregion, as well as by social and gender distinctions (Behnstedt 1985). Still, they were unmistakably Arabic, and as such it appears to have dominated as the region's primary spoken language by the sixth century and remains so to this day.

Like Arabic, Islam came to the Yemen from the outside. Building on a favorable regional constellation of acquaintance with other monotheist denominations, Islam appears to have become established rather smoothly in Southwest Arabia during the Prophet's lifetime and in the first phases of the Caliphate. Because Arabic is the language of the Qur'an and is used in the main rituals of Islam, Islamization in the Yemen also reinforced Arabic's dissemination as the main spoken language of the area. The existence of Qur'anic Arabic also helped to standardize and stabilize the emerging versions of Yemeni Arabic. Legend tends to exaggerate the speed of initial conversions to Islam, claiming that the Yemen "embraced Islam within a day"—alluding to the conversion of the Persian governor in San'a (628 CE) and several other influential leaders in the region (Brunner 2005). This interpretation is confirmed by events that followed the Prophet Muhammad's death, when elements from the Yemen played a significant role in the apostasy (*riddah*) movement from Islam. The *riddah* had to be defeated by military means where necessary. Conversion to Islam therefore had its countermovements and turns. Even so, anthropologists have argued convincingly that in the Yemen's case conversion took place primarily "from below." As elsewhere, the egalitarian concept of everyone's equality before one God provided a vision and means of mobilization that yielded a sustained impetus beyond the time of the Prophet's successors. Until the late ninth century, large parts of the Yemen remained under at least nominal sovereignty of the empire, while local and regional conflicts increased.

For Yemen's late and postimperial Islamic history before the Ottoman era, it is useful to examine briefly two periods through a discussion of the relevance of "civilization" for anthropological analyses of the region's history. These are (1) the ninth-century establishment of Zaydi rule in the highlands of northern Yemen, and (2) the thirteenth-century rise of the Rasulids in San'a, along the coast, and to the south of San'a.

The Zaydis represented a particular version of the Shiite orientation in Islam,[5] a set of minority denominations that emerged across large parts of the Arabic-speaking world after the chain of events following the battle of Kerbala (680 CE). Apart from some minor enclaves near the Caspian Sea, Zaydis also resided in their families' original homeland areas of Hijaz in northwestern and western Arabia. The establishment of Zaydi influence in the Yemen goes back to Yahya b. al-Husayn, known also as al-Hadi ila-l' Haqq ("the guide to Justice") (van Arendonk 1960; Heiss 1987), who, supported by a small group of followers, established himself in the late ninth century as the representative of Shari'a rule of law in the cities of Najran and Sa'da. From Sa'da, today the capital of Yemen's northernmost province, Zaydism established its remarkably enduring influence in the northern highlands[6]—sometimes extending to the area's other main cities as well. There is an undeniable isolationist and conservative orientation in the long-lasting periods of Zaydi leadership of northern Yemen throughout the centuries. This is understandable in view of the Zaydis' minority position within the wider Muslim world and taking into account their local alliances with tribal leadership. In many ways, for as long as it lasted, the Zaydis in Yemen represented a religious minority's conservative success story (Serjeant 1969). State rule by the Zaydi Imams (who came from one among several families that traced their genealogies to the Prophet Muhammad) was expanded gradually throughout most of the northern highlands but was rather fragile. Their success was based largely on their shifting alliances with local tribes, whose status they upgraded where it suited them, and in whose territories they often resided with their own families (of mainly Hijazi origins) in local enclaves. These processes unfolded with local opposition and internal conflicts among competing Zaydi Imams, and were further complicated by the fact that Zaydi regulations for succession before the sixteenth century prioritized the best-qualified among the Prophet's (and Ali's) descendants over direct personal descent. This began to change only when the Zaydi Imams led a successful uprising against the Yemen's first Ottoman rule during the sixteenth century (Tritton 1925). The first Ottoman presence in the Yemen had begun, in turn, as a reaction against the Portuguese advance in the Indian Ocean.

It can be argued that the successful introduction of Zaydism into northern Yemen, and the longevity of its state existence there, has some direct and even causal relationship to the peripheral yet connected adherence of that sociocultural region to Arabic-Islamic civilization (Madelung 2002). Zaydism was losing out against competing spiritual and political orientations elsewhere in the empire and its main centers of power. As a political force, Zaydism in the late ninth century was retreating to as remote an area as one could think of in those times, namely, relatively inaccessible Southwest Arabia and, inside that region, to its most remote parts in the north. Yet this "retreat to and re-emergence inside the remote periphery" would not be apparent or comprehensible *without the perspective from the wider Muslim and Arab contexts* from whence the Zaydis had retreated. Those wider contexts triggered the Zaydis' move to the Southwest in the first place, and once inside the Yemen, Zaydism's enduring minority position within the wider landscapes of Islam contributed toward its maintenance of a protective distance.

A tendency toward conservative isolationism from many unwanted influences in the wider Arab-Muslim environment was a distinctive feature of Yemeni Zaydism (although not the only one that should count). In contrast to that, innovative and inclusive networking characterized the Ayyubid rule and later Rasulid rule in San'a, in substantial areas to the south of that city, and along the Red Sea Coast. Ayyubid rule in the Yemen was ushered in by the Turkish and Kurdish troops who invaded Southwestern Arabia in 1173 from the north (Egypt), where their new rule under Saladin (as he became known to Europeans) was firmly established. Under Saladin's brother, the Ayyubids installed this new Sunni-Shafi'i dynastic and military rule in the territories to the west and south of San'a, supported at first by regular supplies from Egypt. Securing Red Sea trade and navy routes under Ayyubid control figured prominently in the original plan, and to this end the Ayyubids eventually organized a fairly coherent administrative and military rule of their Yemeni realm. The Rasulids were of Turkmen origin and had already risen as regional commanders under the Ayyubids, from whom they took over in 1228 CE by official legitimization from the Abbasid Caliph in Baghdad. Rasulid rule (until 1454 CE) was able to build on the military, administrative, and financial foundations prepared by their predecessors. Commonly, this era is described as the most productive period in late medieval Yemen, an idea promoted by the dynasty's own substantial number of scholars and writers who engaged in fields ranging from agricultural treatises and astronomy to medicine and animal husbandry (Varisco 1994). The Rasulids were able to establish themselves in San'a, conclude a truce for some time with the Zaydis in the north, and develop long-distance trade on the Red Sea and the Indian Ocean (Smith 1974). Under Sultan al-Muzaffar Yusuf (thirteenth century), their domain reached its most flourishing cultural phase and largest territorial expansion. During the fourteenth and fifteenth centuries, the Rasulid state went through gradual but repeated phases of stagnation, and it finally disintegrated in the face of Mamluk military leaders and new local dynasties in the south. In 1517, the Ottoman Sultan Selim I defeated the Mamluks in Egypt, and in 1538 the first Ottoman fleet arrived off the shores of Yemen (Smith 1996).

What I have tried to do in this second section is to summarize, as briefly as possible, four of the key turning points during a short millennium of pre-Ottoman Yemeni history: Arabization, Islamization, and the respective introduction and orientation of Zaydi and Rasulid rule. Taken on their own, these summaries present nothing new, but it is hoped that they stand as appropriate shorthand versions of the experts' primary insights, as communicated to a social science discussion of "civilization." The Yemen studies experts I have referred to would in all likelihood agree that these four processes do represent key turning-point phenomena in Southwest Arabia's history: any list of the region's ten or twelve main transformations between the fifth and the fourteenth centuries will contain references to these four.

What matters here is that *none* of these four processual phenomena can be adequately addressed, described, analyzed, and explained without outlining the very clear connections they have to the wider sociocultural environments *outside* of Southwest Arabia. For the pre-Ottoman contexts before early modern globalization, it seems necessary and useful to name those wider contexts, rather than treating them as *tabulae rasae* that might as well have included Australia or South America. The regions of South Arabia did go through historical periods that were sometimes de facto independent, or at least partially so, but Southwest and Southeast Arabia always interacted with their wider sociocultural environments. These interactions and those wider sociocultural environments can be specified and differentiated. Some of them caused key transformative processes during that millennium; others contributed few or none. And Arab-Islamic civilization as one major and much larger element among those environments rose to a position that actually resulted in inclusive and encompassing peripheral roles for South Arabia throughout the periods to come.

Now the argument resulting from these historical examples can be outlined more precisely: between the fifth and the fourteenth centuries, four of the Yemen's ten or twelve key turning-point processes were causally initiated and inspired from "elsewhere." That "elsewhere" in these four particular but significant cases was the neighboring environment that gradually encompassed Southwest Arabia. Other parts of the outside world also existed and interacted (e.g., India, Southeast Asia, East Africa), but it cannot be ignored that the rest of the Arab-Islamic world played a more relevant role for Yemeni history during these periods precisely because the Yemen was becoming (or had become) a peripheral part and threshold zone of that macrocultural sphere or civilization, encompassed within it at the periphery and contributing to its wider development. Those four key historical processes thus were initiated and inspired inside the wider realms of Arabia and of Islam, to be adopted and further elaborated in Southwest Arabia's regional contexts without losing their external connections. In this sense, the concept of "civilization" at times may attain some limited *causal* and *explanatory* value for historical anthropology. One could refer instead to "wider arenas" or "larger realms" of language, text, and religion—but in this case, at least, it seems legitimate to address the relevant sociocultural phenomenon as Arab-Islamic civilization.

Conclusion: A Concept's Potential and Limits for Anthropology

In my approach to the potentially useful qualities of a concept of "civilization" for historical anthropology, theoretical legacies from the works of three well-known authors have played their acknowledged parts—in addition to Marshall Sahlins's epistemological caveat referred to in the title and at the beginning of this piece.

My first influence was Eric Wolf's (1982) discussion of historical Asian and African social formations before their encounters with European expansion. Wolf outlined how widely connected and complex many of these precontact formations had been, preserving deep historical records of their own. Notwithstanding some of the criticism of this work, several of its main elements remain valid and inspiring. In many ways, Wolf's discussion of the precolonial histories in Asia and Africa thus opened the door for wider approaches in historical anthropology, beyond local ethnohistory and outside of evolutionist paradigms.

The second influence comes from the works of Louis Dumont (1966) and his associates (e.g., Galey 1989), with their emphasis on hierarchies and encompassment in ideological systems of complex and other societies. In spite of substantial criticism that was leveled against Dumontian approaches (Das 1994), I regard their main thrust to be helpful and productive for the present discussion. Differing in this regard from the legacy of structuralism, Dumont's reasoning helps to situate longevity and long-distance qualities in sociocultural complexity not outside of history but within its processual contexts.

Thirdly, I was influenced by my reading of an early article by Walter Dostal (1964). This piece marked Dostal's critical departure from the diffusionist legacies in German-speaking anthropology. In it, he emphasized the necessity to address interim periods of political influence in which cultural connections continued to exist, and rejected as conceptually and theoretically obsolete an orientation toward "culture circles" or *Kulturkreise.*

These sources of inspiration for the present text are mentioned because there are in fact not many earlier sources in our field that provide some guidance or point of reference when it comes to discussing *civilization*. (The respective relevance and possible dangers of works by authors from other fields are discussed by other contributors to, this volume). In this final section, I address and summarize what we may do with the term in historical anthropology, and why it should be avoided in contemporary contexts. There are several good reasons why in the history of anthropology, its various national and quasi-national traditions offer a very limited body of useful thinking with regard to concepts of *civilization*. Let me single out just three among them.

First, the narrow limitations of this conceptual heritage are related to anthropology's traditional and in many ways enduring prioritizing of small-scale networks, groups, and other microentities. Since these took priority, it follows that everything related to "macro" or "larger than" came second or was never studied at all.

A second reason why the topic of *civilization* preoccupied a mere minority of anthropologists was briefly referred to in the first section: the marginal role designed for historical anthropology by several of the old national or quasi-national traditions in this field. Engaging with notions of historical "civilization" occurred somewhat more frequently in the histories of American and German-speaking anthropology, and less frequently in the British and Francophone realms—yet even here, these sometimes were exceptional and remarkable efforts (Barth et al. 2005).

Third and most obviously for anyone sifting through anthropology's literature in this regard, the discipline's twentieth-century history of reflections about "civilization," to the extent that they occurred at all, were not infrequently loaded with pejorative terminologies and problematic theoretical implications—often with connections to colonialist, racist, or other ideological regimes. Such implications seem to adhere to the term itself: if something is classified as "larger than" or "more complex than," it is indeed tempting to combine that literal meaning with other, more metaphorical allusions, such as "more successful than" or "better than." It should be clear today how inappropriate is such a conflation of literal meaning with metaphorical messages. India, for instance, is certainly larger than, and in several ways more complex than, Singapore, but India is not necessarily by any generalized standard better or more successful than Singapore.

As clear and transparent as we may be about these distinctions today, matters were different in anthropology's past when "larger than" and "more complex than" were taken as central criteria in any of the discipline's grand theories or metanarratives. This applies in particular to some of the main works of evolutionism and neo-evolutionism in the history of American anthropology. The allegedly causal ties between criteria of greater complexity and larger size with another main metanarrative were even more dogmatically established in the history of German-speaking anthropology of a diffusionist orientation, where centers of ingenuity and superiority were seen as radiating across "cultural circles."

These are some of the main reasons why useful inspiration from anthropology's legacy is rare when it comes to critically reassessing notions of "civilization" today. The matter was not often investigated in the first place; if it was pursued, it was often done for the predetermined glory of certain grand theories that are untenable today, and not for solving a research puzzle. Still, a few useful conceptual bits and clusters remain to be retrieved, critically inspected, and perhaps also tried out in new contexts. Removed from their original evolutionist and neo-evolutionist contexts, several conceptual subtools remain interesting and promising. One is not obliged, for example, to adhere to the concept of "lower and higher stages" of development while eclectically inspecting some of these subtools. After all, any historical anthropologist should be prepared to think through the possible meanings of "rise," "crisis," "demise," "collapse," or, for that matter—as a widely discussed term across many disciplinary boundaries—"emergence."

Similarly, we should certainly remain extremely cautious and skeptical about diffusionist paradigms that presuppose "centers of human inventiveness" and about the "cultural circles" around them, through which those ingenious ideas and products are said to radiate and "diffuse" toward impoverished and immobile margins. But no one in today's anthropology could ignore that the related notions of "cultural flows" and "migration" are highly relevant terms in our discipline and beyond, and few would deny that corresponding processes also took place within those very different contexts before the advent of modernity and today's forms of globalization.

The wider requirement to distinguish between the obsolete theoretical paradigms of older metanarratives, on the one hand, and the actual research themes and problems they addressed, on the other, remains on our agenda. Within this agenda, it might also be worth rereading and reassessing some of the few classical works in sociocultural anthropology's history that did address complex sociocultural contexts in ways that seem to deserve new attention from the perspective of present-day debates on civilization in history. In British anthropology these would include, for instance, Siegfried Nadel's work (1942) that criticized the diffusionist paradigm through a focus on a "black Byzantium," and Jack Goody's writing (1990) on different scales and orientations of sociocultural complexity. In American anthropology, Alfred Kroeber's (1944) monumental late text *Configurations of Culture Growth* comes to mind, and Robert Redfield's (1956) analyses of interactions between "little" and "big" traditions. Finally, a substantial part of Stanley Tambiah's work (e.g., 1977) on historical Southeast Asia remains as relevant as it always has been. This retrospective work still needs to be done in order to further substantiate current efforts toward reconceptualizing civilization for historical anthropology.

The present text has argued for certain potential "uses" of a reconceptualized notion of "civilization" inside a historical anthropology of the more distant past. To this end, the concept of civilization was confirmed as referring to specific macrocultures: these are loosely associated with the rise and realm of empires. Being relatively autonomous from empires, civilizations may extend well beyond their ranges in terms of longevity and geographical space; they also can include small states as well as a plethora of nonstate entities. Processes of expansion and contraction are intrinsic to these factors of long distance and of longevity. Elastic continuity and some element of coherence thus have to be provided. Language, writing, and religion were identified as likely candidates in that regard, with ensuing necessities for a fair amount of long-distance mobility and intergenerational learning.

Such a conceptualization allows us to identify a relatively small but enduring opening for usefully engaging with *civilization* through a historical anthropology of the distant past. That is, the term can be used instead of the synonymous expression "spheres and flows of macrocultural life." Inside these research fields, "civilization" offers some descriptive and heuristic value, and a few explanatory notes insofar as it helps to relate to causal factors in a specified wider environment, arena, or world. In this sense, for historical anthropology's analyses of certain dimensions in the distant past, *civilization* may be a "useful" tool and a relatively "thin" concept, as Marcus Banks (1996) once formulated for another context.

When it comes to the more recent past, to contemporary history, and to the present, however, problems with almost any empirical and specified concept of *civilization* become insurmountable, and the potentials for abuse prevail. Three main sources of abuse can be identified.

One source is nonacademic, and is rooted in the contemporary potentials of ideologies of hate, hierarchical exclusion, and discrimination. In these contexts, *civilization* has too often been employed as part of inventories of mobilizing "us" against "them." Appeals to "our civilization's" heroic struggle against these intruders or those "barbarians" may or may not instrumentalize popularized versions of evolutionist imagery, but they usually serve to situate "us" in a position of superiority, and the "other" in a corresponding position of inferiority. This is typical for many arenas of the global north, as I have tried to show for cases of "frontier orientalism" in Central Europe and elsewhere (Gingrich 1998). Similar means of politicized mobilization have, however, also occurred in the global south: in Palestine, Syria, and elsewhere in the Arab world, for instance, political Islam mobilizes by reference to Islamic civilizations of the past and by envisioning its "return" in the future, while criticizing references to Arab, Ottoman, secular, or other adjectives for past civilizations (*hadara*). Acknowledging *civilization* as a legitimate anthropological term for understanding the present would render academic support and encouragement to the supporters of the ideologies in question.

A second set of reasons has to do with the applied abuses of concepts of civilization by other academic fields throughout the past decades. In short, those works that addressed *civilization* in a present-day orientation were always on the side of confrontation and of maintaining or saving existing global power relations in their advisory activities. There is no academic need to join that applied chorus. These abuses range from educational and development studies in French, where affirmative references to the "*mission civilisatrice*" were common not only before the end of colonialism, but far into the 1990s. From there, they range into recent and current quasi-academic abuses in English, such as Samuel Huntington's (1996) problematic book on the "clash of civilizations" and his related work. If anthropology were disseminating a positive argument about *civilization* as a useful tool for analyzing the present, this would unavoidably emerge in support of the "applied" abusers in other fields.

The third major reason why anthropologists should avoid the use of *civilization* in any specific contemporary sense is conceptual and logical. For historical analyses of the distant past, one may differentiate between realms of civilization, their border areas, distant outposts, and enclaves, and also classify in differentiated ways whatever is beyond that. In such a nuanced, nondualistic, and balanced manner, it is still possible to use *civilization* as a concept for distinguishing it to some extent from other entities—without ever employing any opposition between the terms *civilized* and *uncivilized*. Moreover, analyses of the distant past allow longevity as one defining feature of civilization to become visible in retrospect. By contrast, a research usage of the term *civilization* for contemporary purposes would run into a twofold barrier. First, it seems impossible to prevent the dissemination of academic notions of *civilization* in contemporary contexts into a wider public, together with the grammatically corresponding adjective *civilized,* thereby giving the antonym *uncivilized* new legitimacy and, in fact, reactivating it. This can be avoided to a certain extent for academic discourses about the distant past, by staying away from quasi-evolutionary imagery (i.e., civilization representing a higher stage of development) and from binary terminologies (civilization versus precivilization, or civilized versus uncivilized). Yet once anthropologists and their colleagues in other fields use *civilization* for present-day purposes that are already deeply contested, it is virtually impossible to avoid such a binary public understanding and usage of the term. Second, it is impossible to recognize longevity within present-day contexts. Those political and cultural empires that existed at the beginning of the twentieth century have vanished only a hundred years later. Nothing of any specific quality existing in today's sociocultural and political worlds can be safely predicted to continue over several centuries into the distant future.

For recent and contemporary purposes, to me at least, these are reasons enough why anthropologists should avoid any specific concepts of *civilization*. There is only one way in which I see a legitimate version of *civilization* for use in the present and for the future, and that is a nonspecific, general notion. This may be the case whenever we wish to address humanity's global civilization.

Notes

1. I would like to thank the editors of, this volume for their comments and for the conference that preceded, this volume. In addition, I am grateful for the thoughtful advice given by the publishing house's anonymous reviewers, as well as by readers of a first draft of this chapter at the Austrian Academy of Sciences' Institute for Social Anthropology (ISA): Marieke Brandt, Johann Heiss, and Christian Jahoda provided helpful suggestions without necessarily agreeing with the final text. I also thank Joan K. O'Donnell (Cambridge, Mass.) for her assistance in finalizing this text. The environment and time required for the present research were made available in part by the Austrian Science Fund's (FWF) grant F4203 supporting the special research realm (SFB) "Visions of Community" (VISCOM), where Christina Lutter (University of Vienna, Department of History) provided additional advice. With apologies to the experts, this text uses a simplified version of transliterating Arabic names and terms.

2. The contemporary postcolonial borders of the two countries with the same names—Yemen and Oman—are not identical with the historical extension of the two regions. The two historical regions often included more than one state in each of them, and they sometimes encompassed areas either smaller or much larger than the current state territories.

3. As in other parts of Arabia (including Medina/Yathrib at the time of the Prophet Muhammad's emigration and exile), Jewish and Christian minorities formed enclaves in Southwest Arabia. The Jewish presence remained somewhat more influential than the Christian throughout the pre-Islamic and premodern centuries. During a brief historical moment, for example, the Himyari king Dhū Nuwās embraced Judaism as the state religion. But Christian communities only came to prominence briefly in the mid-sixth century when the region was ruled by Christian governors from Ethiopia (Tobi 1999, 3–5).

4. There is some evidence that during the later period of ancient South Arabia's states, military units and mercenaries recruited from Central Arabian tribes were at the core of the early Arabic speakers in the region (al-Ansari 2010). In addition, locals engaged in commerce and transport to the north necessarily had to have some fluency in spoken and written Arabic.

5. Zaydism traces its origins to Zayd, a descendent of the Prophet's cousin and son-in-law Ali (Madelung 2002).

6. In fact, Zaydi rule in northern Yemen with a center in and around Sa'da continued for about one thousand years until the 1962 revolution in the north, and in some indirect ways is echoed in the so-called Huthi conflict of the early twenty-first century (Brandt 2012).

References

al-Ansari, Abd al-Rahman, M. 2010. "Qaryat al-Faw." In *Routes d'arabie: archéologie et histoire du royaume d'Arabie saoudite*, edited by Ali Ibrahim al-Ghabban, Béatrice André-Salvini, Françoise Demange et al., 150–62. Exhibition catalogue. Paris: Musée du Louvre.

Arnason, Johann P. 2010. "Interpreting History and Understanding Civilizations." In *The Benefit of Broad Horizons: Intellectual and Institutional Preconditions for a Global Social Science: Festschrift for Bjorn Wittrock on the Occasion of His 65th Birthday*, edited by Hans Joas, 167–84. Leiden: Brill.

Bāfaqīh, Muhammad. 1983. *Le Yémen au cours de la période des rois de Saba' et de Du Raydān*. Paris: Université de Paris IV.

Banks, Marcus. 1996. *Ethnicity: Anthropological Constructions*. London and New York: Routledge.

Barth, Fredrik, Andre Gingrich, Robert Parkin, and Sydel Silverman. 2005. *One Discipline, Four Ways: British, German, French, and American Anthropology: The Halle Lectures*. Chicago and London: University of Chicago Press.

Beeston, Alfred F. L. 1987. "Vorislamische Inschriften und vorislamische Sprachen des Jemen." In *Jemen: 3000 Jahre Kunst und Kultur des glücklichen Arabien*, edited by Werner Daum, 102–10. Innsbruck and Munich: Pinguin.

Behnstedt, Peter. 1985. *Die nordjementischen Dialekte*, 2 vols. Wiesbaden: Reichert.

Brandt, Marieke. 2012. "Friedens-Shaykh und Kriegs-Shaykh: Der Übergang von Kriegsführerschaft bei den Banū Munebbih im Hūthī-Konflikt in Nordwest-Jemen." *Anthropos* 1: 49–69.

Brunner, Ueli. 2005. "Geschichte." In *Länderkunde Jemen*, edited by Horst Kopp, 137–58. Wiesbaden: Reichert.

Comaroff, Jean, and John L. Comaroff. 1991, 1997. *Of Revelation and Revolution*, vol. 1: *Christianity, Colonialism, and Consciousness in*

South Africa; vol. 2: *The Dialectics of Modernity on a South African Frontier*. Chicago and London: University of Chicago Press.

Das, Veena. 1994. "Anthropological Discourse on India: Reason and Its Other." In *Assessing Cultural Anthropology*, edited by Robert Borofsky, 133–43. New York: McGraw-Hill.

de Maigret, Alessandro. 2002. *Arabia Felix: An Exploration of the Archaeological History of Yemen*. London: Stacey International.

Dostal, Walter. 1964. "Zur Frage der Konstanz von Kulturformen." In *Festschrift für Ad. E. Jensen*, edited by E. Haberland, M. Schuster, and H. Straube, vol. 1, 91–101. Munich: Renner.

Dumont, Louis. 1966. *Homo Hierarchicus: Essai sur le système des castes*. Paris: Gallimard, Bibliothèque des Sciences humaines.

Freitag, Ulrike. 2003. *Indian Ocean Migrants and State Formation in Hadhramaut: Reforming the Homeland*. Leiden: Brill.

Galey, Jean-Claude. 1989. "Reconsidering Kingship in India: An Ethnological Perspective." *Kingship and the Kings: History and Anthropology* 4: 123–87.

Gingrich, Andre. 1998. "Frontier Myths of Orientalism: The Muslim World in Public and Popular Cultures of Central Europe." In *Mediterranean Ethnological Summer School, Piran/Pirano Slovenia 1996*, edited by Bojan Baskar, and Borut Brumen, MESS vol. 2, 99–127. Ljubljana.

———. 2013. "Methodology." In *The Handbook of Sociocultural Anthropology*, edited by James G. Carrier and Deborah B. Gewertz, 107–24. London and New York: Bloomsbury.

———, and Ulf Hannerz. 2017. "Introduction: Exploring Small Countries." In *Small Countries: Structures and Sensibilities*, edited by Ulf Hannerz and Andre Gingrich, Philadelphia: University of Pennsylvania Press, 1–44.

———, and Werner Zips. 2006. "Ethnohistorie und Historische Anthropologie." In *Historische Anthropologie: Basistexte*, edited by Aloys Winterling, 245–63. Munich: Steiner.

Goody, Jack. 1990. *The Oriental, the Ancient, and the Primitive: Systems of Marriage and the Family in the Pre-Industrial Societies of Eurasia*. Cambridge: Cambridge University Press.

Hann, Chris. 2011. "Back to Civilization." *Anthropology Today* 27, no. 6: 1–2.

Heiss, Johann. 1987. "War and Mediation for Peace in a Tribal Society (Yemen, 9th Century)." In *Kinship, Social Change, and Evolution*.

Proceedings of a Symposium Held in Honour of Walter Dostal,
Vienna Contributions to Ethnology and Anthropology,
edited by A. Gingrich, S.M. Haas, and G. Paleczek,
vol. 5, 63–74.

———, and Martin Slama. 2010. "Genealogical Avenues, Long-Distance Flows, and Social Hierarchy: Hadhrami Migrants in the Indonesian Diaspora." *Anthropology of the Middle East* 5, no. 1: 34–52.

Ho, Engseng. 2006. *The Graves of Tarim: Genealogy and Mobility across the Indian Ocean.* Berkeley/Los Angeles/London: University of California Press.

Huntington, Samuel P. 1996. *The Clash of Civilizations and the Remaking of World Order.* New York: Simon and Schuster.

Kroeber, Alfred L. 1944. *Configurations of Culture Growth.* Berkeley: University of California Press.

Madelung, Wilferd. 2002. "Zaydiyya." In *Encyclopaedia of Islam*, 2nd ed., edited by P. J. Bearman, T. Bianquis, C. E. Bosworth, E. van Donzel, and W. P. Heinrichs, vol. 11, 477–81. Leiden: Brill.

Meri, Josef W. 2005. *Medieval Islamic Civilization: An Encyclopedia.* New York and London: Routledge.

Nadel, Siegfried. 1942. *A Black Byzantium: The Kingdom of Nupe in Nigeria.* International Institute of African Languages and Cultures, Oxford: Oxford University Press.

Pohl, Walter. 2011. "Imperium." In *Lexikon der Globalisierung*, edited by F. Kreff, E-M. Knoll, and A. Gingrich, 146–50. Bielefeld: transcript.

Redfield, Robert. 1956. *The Little Community.* Chicago: University of Chicago Press.

Robin, Christian. 1991. "L'Arabie antique de Karib'īl à Mahomet." *Revue du Monde Musulman et de la Méditerranée* 61: 71–88.

Ryckmans, Jacques. 1987. "Die Altsüdarabische Religion." In *Jemen: 3000 Jahre Kunst und Kultur des glücklichen Arabien*, edited by Werner Daum, 111–15. Innsbruck and Munich: Pingion-Umschau.

Sahlins, Marshall. 1976. *The Use and Abuse of Biology: An Anthropological Critique of Sociobiology.* Ann Arbor: University of Michigan Press.

Serjeant, Robert B. 1969. "The Zaydis." In *Religion in the Middle East: Three Religions in Concord and Conflict*, edited by Arthur J. Arberry, vol. 2, 285–301. Cambridge: Cambridge University Press.

Smith, G. Rex. 1974 [1978]. *The Ayyubids and Early Rasulids in the Yemen (567–694 / 1173–1295)*, W. Gibb Memorial, New Series 26, 2 vols. London: Trustees of the E. J. W. Gibb Memorial.

———. 1996. "Rasulids." In *The Encyclopaedia of Islam*, edited by C. E. Bosworth, E. van Donzel, W. P. Heinrichs, G. Lecomte, vol. 8, 455–57. Leiden: Brill.

Sonn, Tamara. 2011. *Islam: A Brief History*. Oxford: Wiley.

Tambiah, Stanley J. 1977. "The Galactic Polity: The Structure of Traditional Kingdoms in Southeast Asia." *Annals of the New York Academy of Sciences* 293, no. 1: 69–97.

Tobi, Yosef. 1999. *The Jews of Yemen: Studies in Their History and Culture*. Leiden: Brill.

Tritton, Arthur Stanley. 1925 [1981]. *The Rise of the Imams of Sanaa*. London and Westport: Oxford University Press-Hyperion.

van Arendonk, Cornelis. 1960. *Les Débuts de l'Imamate Zaudite au Yemen*. Publications de la Fondation de Goeje, Leiden: Brill.

Varisco, Daniel M. 1994. *Medieval Agriculture and Islamic Science: The Almanac of a Yemeni Sultan*. Seattle and London: University of Washington Press.

Wolf, Eric R. 1982. *Europe and the People without History*. Berkeley and Los Angeles: University of California Press.

5

CIVILIZATION AS A KEY GUIDING IDEA IN SOUTH ASIA

David N. Gellner

Introduction

Civilization, as recognized by Chris Hann (2011) in his call for a reintroduction of the term into anthropological analysis, is a particularly problematic concept for anthropologists. One of the classic motivations underlying the anthropological enterprise has precisely been to oppose the assumptions underlying triumphalist "civilizing mission" ideas, in whatever incarnations they appear. As Gandhi is supposed to have remarked, when asked what he thought of Western civilization, "It would be a good idea." Those who have attempted to theorize the notion and ground it anthropologically, such as Robert Redfield (1956) and, following Redfield in the Indian context, Milton Singer (1972), have not had many imitators. Redfield's terminology of Great and Little Tradition appears today as quaint and misleading, essential though the distinction undoubtedly is.[1] Singer's book, read in the light of subsequent developments in the subject, appears as epistemologically naive; his innocent and digressive reflexivity comes across as complacent and self-satisfied to those brought up on the sweeping denunciations and breast beating of Said's *Orientalism* (1978), Clifford and Marcus's *Writing Culture* (1986), and Inden's *Imagining India* (1990).

Consequently, contemporary anthropologists have tended to adopt one of three approaches to the notion of civilization: to ignore it, to deny it has any validity whatsoever, or to relativize it. (The first two responses would explain why so few anthropologists have engaged with Huntington or Ferguson, as noted by Hann.) Relativizing and multiplying concepts are natural rhetorical moves for anthropologists. Just as cosmopolitanism can become cosmopolitanisms (Pollock et al. 2002), and Christianity can be plural (Cannell 2006), so there are (and probably with greater legitimacy) numerous ideas of civilization.

As with so many concepts taken up by social science, civilization is also a notion that operates within particular traditions and cultures. My aim in this chapter is simply to confront the call for civilizational analysis with the ideas that South Asians themselves, whether learned or otherwise, have and have had about "civilization."[2] This is no easy task, because there is a long and sophisticated South Asian tradition (or more properly, traditions) of thinking about what "civilization" is. And there is also a long (though not quite so long) academic tradition of thinking about South Asian civilization. The relation between these two traditions of thought is by no means an easy one: they are neither entirely separate, nor completely dependent the one on the other. In other words, when Europeans first speculated about the nature of South Asian society, they did so drawing from the ideas of local experts as well as from their own experiences of South Asian society.[3] Yet they did more than simply generalize, or translate into European languages, what their native informants told them. They also imported plenty of their own assumptions, as postcolonial critics have delighted in pointing out.

Louis Dumont is one of those towering names who sought to capture the essence of South Asian civilization with the notion of hierarchy (Dumont 1980). He worked with, and had a very considerable knowledge of, the intellectual materials that South Asia itself provided, but at the same time his agenda came very much (as he would have seen it) from a universalizing scientific position—or (as some of his critics would put it) from an Orientalizing European perspective (Collins 1989; Dirks 2001). Critiques of Dumont are by now legion, running the gamut from brilliant and penetrating to crass and uncomprehending. In Anglophone South Asianist circles and in South Asia itself, debate, insofar as it has engaged with Dumont, has mostly moved on to other matters; even the recently renewed discussion of caste and politics is on the whole carried on independently of Dumont's influence and his terminology.[4] Evidently, in Germany, by contrast, debate with Dumont is still alive and well (Fuchs, this volume).

One of the more ethnographically and historically grounded critiques of Dumont was made by Richard Burghart (1978). He pointed out that there are at least three competing hierarchical models at play in "traditional" India, each of which, in Dumont's terms, attempts to "encompass" the others. These are the Brahmin-centered, the King-centered, and the ascetic-centered models of hierarchy. Burghart's fundamental point was that it was, of course, absurd to expect a complex civilization that had lasted thousands of years to be reducible to a single master principle. There was and is bound to be contestation, with different and competing conceptualizations having some overlap but also areas of incommensurability. In line with Burghart's insight, I certainly do not intend to claim here that "civilization," however conceived, constitutes any kind of master key. It is, rather, one guiding thread among others.

The Kathmandu Valley: A Microcosm of Classical Pre-Islamic South Asian Civilization

My original doctoral research was based on two years spent in the Kathmandu Valley, and nineteen months' fieldwork in one of the three royal cities of the valley, Lalitpur. Lalitpur (also known as Patan, and as Yala to its own Newari-speaking inhabitants) is the most Buddhist of the three cities. Bhaktapur is the most Hindu and Kathmandu is somewhere in between. Urbanization and suburbanization have grown at such a pace that the whole valley is now one large cement and brick sprawl, with patches of agricultural land in between. In the first half of the 1980s, when I was living there, this process was well under way between Kathmandu and Lalitpur, but had yet to spread beyond. The old medieval boundaries of the city of Lalitpur, though long ago breached on the west and south sides of the city, were still visible on the north and east. Rice fields came right up to where the boundary between the inside and the outside of the city was still remembered to have run; it was still of ritual significance. The culture of the Newars of the Kathmandu Valley has long been recognized to be extremely archaic in South Asian terms. It preserves the pre-Islamic civilization of north India in which Buddhism was as important as Hinduism. It was for this reason that the great French Sanskritist Sylvain Lévi visited Nepal for three months in 1898, and went on to write the history of the country in three volumes (Lévi 1905–08). Lévi famously situated Nepal (by which he meant,

as Nepalis themselves still meant in those days, the Kathmandu Valley)
as follows:

> Populated by non-Aryan races, converted and civilized by Indian
> Buddhism, conquered and absorbed by Brahmanical Hinduism,
> Nepal has already passed through the first three stages of Indian
> history. Having entered late into the process, it has yet to experi-
> ence the final phase, on which it is just embarking, but in which
> India has long been engaged: the struggle against Islam and
> European domination. This is precisely the distinguishing feature
> of Nepal's history and the reason why it is so instructive. Ceylon
> is India arrested at the stage of Buddhism and separated by the
> overwhelming force of foreign influences. Kashmir is India itself.
> Nepal is India in the making (*Le Népal, c'est l'Inde qui se fait*). In
> a territory so limited that it almost seems to have been designed
> as a laboratory, the observer can easily grasp the sequence of steps
> which from ancient India have given rise to modern India. He
> can understand by what mechanism a handful of Aryans, carried
> by a bold march into the Panjab, where they came into contact
> with a barbarous multitude, were able to subjugate, enlist, tame,
> and organize it, and to propagate their own language with such
> success that today three quarters of India speak Aryan tongues.
> (Lévi 1905, I, 28; my translation)

Several authors, myself included, have followed in Lévi's footsteps and
interpreted Newar society as in some sense representative of north India at
the end of the first millennium.[5] One of the key arguments between experts
is over whether Newar culture consists of a thin layer of Hinduization and
Buddhization—in short, superficial influence from Indic civilization—sitting over a "tribal substratum" or whether, on the contrary, Newar civilization
is classical Indic civilization, and is therefore a prime exemplar—the only
surviving evidence for—pre-Muslim India. On the whole, I, Levy, Quigley,
and Lewis have tended to argue the latter view, whereas Michael Allen and
Gérard Toffin have thought it worthwhile to seek for a tribal substratum.[6]
Among Newar intellectuals, K. P. Malla has been tempted by the tribal view
(e.g., Malla 1981; 1985), and Baldev Juju, a Newar Brahmin pundit, has
argued eloquently for it as well (without calling it tribal).[7] The view of Newar
culture as having an essential Newar core, with only superficial borrowings
from India, has, however, not generally caught on, unlike with many of the

other groups that today have received state recognition as Adivasi Janajati or "indigenous nationalities."[8] These groups—or rather the activist intellectuals who claim to speak on their behalf—seek to emphasize an original tribal and animist culture (in the case of the Rais and Limbus, who now mostly record their religion as "Kirati"), or a Buddhist identity (as in the case of Magars), or are deeply divided over whether they should be Buddhist or something else (as in the case of Gurungs). What they all have in common is their opposition to Hinduism. In this, the Newars, with their urban tradition, high levels of education, relatively high levels of representation in the Establishment, and high average standard of living, stand somewhat apart from other indigenous groups; they were somewhat controversial members of the Janajati category in the first place, with many Newars and others arguing that they should not have been included.[9]

What is the view of "civilization" embodied in the way of life of Newar cities? In the first place, it is based on a strict opposition between an urban sophisticated way of life and the *jangali* (jungly) way of life characteristic of the hills and remote areas. The more urban, the less involved in hunting, gathering, or herding. In this way, even Newar peasants inhabiting outlying villages share in this urban civilization: they do not live in isolated one- or two-story thatched homesteads scattered among their fields; on the contrary, they live in three- or four-story tiled brick terraced houses arranged around squares; their homesteads are consecrated with temples and by means of frequent ceremonial and ritual occasions. They visit their fields by day; in the evening and by night they participate in the Indic Great Traditions through ritual, singing, and festival performances.

The apogee of sophistication is reached at the center of the three large royal cities. There we find the old royal palace and in the immediate environs the houses of the highest Hindu castes, which provided the courtiers and aristocrats of the Malla kingdoms before the Parbatiya conquest of 1769.[10] In front of the palaces are temples to the high gods of Hinduism (forms of Shiva and Vishnu); incorporated into the palace itself is a temple to the goddess; one form of that goddess was the reigning monarch's tutelary deity, and her mantra provided him with special protection. The king himself was a kind of god and played the role of Vishnu, or his incarnations, in various dance dramas. The palace was conceived as the ideal center of the city (even when—as in Bhaktapur—it was markedly off-center in practice). The whole city was arranged in a kind of mandala around this center. Smaller Newar settlements, even sometimes villages, have a site—often not a building but just a point remembered through ritual—that is identified as the *layku* or palace, which acts as the mandalic and monarchical center around which festival events pivot.

The inhabitants of the city found their place in the overall polity through their relationship to the king, to the gods, and to the high-caste elite. These relationships were certainly unequal, but they also gave every group a privileged role of some sort. At the same time, each group had its own gods and shrines, from which all outsiders were excluded. At the very bottom of this socioreligious hierarchy were the Untouchables, or Dalits as it is now politically correct to call them.[11] Levy describes evocatively why the paradigmatically stigmatized group, the Sweepers (known locally as Dyahla or Pore—Po(n) in his spelling), find themselves at the bottom of the local hierarchy:

> The Po(n) have the vital function of making the city's organizing pollution system *real,* in the sense that they bring it into contact at its lowest point with a sensorially accessible world of real pollutants, and with the most dramatic of these, feces [which they are responsible for removing]. In their degraded conditions of life they also make real the penalties of bad *karma,* and thus validate the whole system of community *dharma* and help motivate people's adherence to it. Uniquely among the accumulators of pollution the Po(n)s must . . . live outside the city. . . . While people tolerate and understand and feel helpless to prevent other groups rejecting their traditional stigmatizing *thar* duties, there is widespread and passionate agreement that the Po(n)s must continue their work, and stay in their proper place. They are (as reflective citizens of the city articulate) as essential to the organized city order as are the Brahmans. (Levy 1990, 366–67; original emphasis)

As with outcastes elsewhere in the subcontinent (Fuller 1992, 139), the Sweepers are "included precisely so that they can be portrayed as excluded."[12] They are a quintessential symbol of otherness; as Levy notes (1990, 76), other Newars are unsure whether Dyahla/Po(n) belong inside or outside Newar society.

One of the key ways in which low castes—and paradigmatically the Sweepers—are thought to be different is that they are without "rules" (*niyam*), by which it is meant that they have no rituals to perform, and are therefore "without *dharma*." In this phrase, *dharma* can mean duty, religion, ritual, morality, or all of these at once. They are believed (unjustly and incorrectly) not to need to perform life-cycle rituals or *samskaras* (sacraments). (This is often cited as a reason why they are growing richer nowadays: they save money because they do not need to perform expensive rituals, especially weddings, as others do.) In this perception, they are at the opposite end of the spectrum from Brahmins, who are supposed to have the most ritualized lifestyle.

There is a classical schema of sixteen life-cycle rituals that only certain kings of the past would have been in a position to carry out in full. Newly established icons of the gods pass through all sixteen rituals in order to be infused with divinity. In practice, high castes carry out only five or six of the set as separate rituals. The degree of elaboration, and the degree to which they are observed using liturgies in Sanskrit, varies considerably according to caste background, with further degrees of elaboration depending on the wealth of the household concerned (Gellner 1992, 197–204). The term for life-cycle ritual, *samskara,* means literally something that completes, so by extension that which perfects or purifies. Someone who has been perfected (even "cooked") is *samskrta.* This word is also used for Sanskrit, which is considered the language of the gods and is used in all the most prestigious religious liturgies; it is the "perfected" language. Those people who do not pass through the purifying and molding sacraments are closer to "uncivilized" or "bare life"—as exemplified by newborn babes, Untouchables living in hovels outside the city walls, and wild tribes of the forest, none of whom need to be ritually mourned, and none of whom need to observe purity rules.

The same root and prefix that gives us *samskara* and *samskrta* also provides *samskrti,* the neologistic term today used in South Asia's languages for "culture," "customs," even "civilization." What characterizes the high caste and the civilized is that they go through a series of *samskaras* (life-cycle rituals) and have large numbers of *samskrti* (traditional customs). For many, the upholding of these traditions is one's *dharma.* That is the sum of one's religious duty. Such a view is and has always been open to challenge and reform by those who believe that a religious path involves more than simply carrying out the inherited teachings and practices of one's ancestors.[13]

One of the ways in which the city was maintained as a sacred space was through a dense calendar and network of overlapping festivals. Levy (1990) refers to this as the "civic ballet" and spends considerable space (pp. 401–576) documenting the major festivals of the city of Bhaktapur.[14]

These traditions were by no means preserved in aspic, or even *perceived* as preserved in aspic. Within a macrocosmology of world decline, the traditional view from Newar cities managed to combine a historical view of progress; it presumed that the local culture was the outcome of conscious construction and active creation sanctioned by, and frequently led by, the king. Many festivals or aspects of festivals are remembered and memorialized as having been founded by kings within the last four hundred years (often under the impulse of religious devotion to a specific god, i.e., *bhakti* of the sort discussed by Fuchs in ch. 6). The fact that a particular festival (e.g., the chariot procession of the living goddess Kumari in Kathmandu) is relatively new does not detract in any way from the fervor with which it is observed by the inhabitants of the city. A related aspect of life was the pervasiveness of ritual. As K. P. Malla puts it, in a survey of classical Newar-language literature:

> One of the most striking features of the literate culture of the Newars is their inordinate passion for the codification of . . . rituals in the form of manuals. No student of Newar society can do justice to their culture, social organization and literature without *some* acquaintance with this literature of rituals. They are, of course, not of any *intrinsic* literary merit or worth. Their significance lies mainly in the insight they provide into the society of which it is as undeniable an excrescence as poetic, narrative and dramatic literature of the more agreeable sort. (Malla 1982, 78; original emphases)

Such literature "of the more agreeable sort" was also produced in abundance, and very frequently by the Malla kings. In fact of the twenty-six dramas in classical Newari, the vast majority were composed by Malla kings between 1662 and 1757 (Malla 1982, 67–70). Dance dramas based on Hindu mythology are performed even in the most peripheral and socially stigmatized of Newar peasant villages, such as Pyangaon. As Toffin puts it, "India's cultural models, carried among other things by the Sanskrit language, by theatre, and by architecture, were not taken up only at royal courts. They penetrated even the most remote villages" (2009, 109).

Chittadhar Hridaya (1906–1982) is a great modern Newar poet, who went to prison for five years from 1940 for the simple act of publishing a poem called "Mother" in Newari. As K. P. Malla has written, the incarceration of Hridaya and other Newar literary figures was "not a curse but a blessing in disguise" (Malla 1979, 17) because of the large amount of literary production that went on during these years in jail. The greatest of these works was Hridaya's *Sugata Saurabh*, or *Life of the Buddha*. In its form and most of its content it is (and refers to itself as) an epic poem (*mahakavya*), expressing all ten of the classic *rasas* or aesthetic emotions; as such, it is an epitome of Sanskritic sensibility (Lewis and Tuladhar 2007). Though written in the vernacular, it is a lush, baroque, ornate, and highly Sanskritized form of it, self-consciously making use of more than thirty classic Sanskrit meters. At the same time, Hridaya was himself on the cusp of modernity, familiar with the notion of progress (e.g., his description of the Shakya polity where the Buddha grew up notes that child marriage was forbidden there) (ibid., 23).

The language situation was such that high-status people had command of various languages: Newari, Maithili, Sanskrit. By the twentieth century, Nepali had replaced Maithili; Hindi (earlier Persian) was the prestige language of north India. Today, English is at the top of the language hierarchy, then Hindi, then Nepali, and at the bottom (for Newars) is Newari. Other languages of Nepal, including Tamang (widely spoken by the laborers, cooks, and porters of the Kathmandu Valley), hardly register on non-Janajati people's cultural radar.

The Newar city is what Levy called "a climax community." This is what Redfield and Singer meant by an "orthogenetic city": in other words, in it all the tendencies and implications of Hindu civilization come to fruition and can be seen in their full colors. In the city, one observes the division of labor that underlies the caste system pushed to its utmost and played out to a degree of detail and differentiation that cannot be attained in the more straitened conditions of the countryside.[15] Villages simply lack the resources and the manpower. They cannot match the elaborate cultural performances and the amount of time devoted to them of the city; their festivals and rituals are bound to be a pale reflection of those in the urban center—but valued nonetheless as differentiating them from those who are still further out, who live in truly jungly conditions in the hills and forests.

The Notion of Civilization in South Asia and Beyond

There is every reason to believe, as I have indicated, that what I have described for the Kathmandu Valley was once far more widespread. The model of the "theatre state," as described by Geertz (1980), could almost have been drawn up with the small, ritual-obsessed polities of the Kathmandu Valley in mind. Tambiah's (1985) galactic polity model is more grandiose and fits better the plains of Thailand or northern India, but is evidently related. Both find their expression in the religious spatial model of the mandala, with its sacred center and series of boundaries arranged around it in geometric fashion.

The connotations of Sanskrit, both as language and as a mode of being, as found in the Kathmandu Valley, would appear to be precisely the associations made in South Asia more generally. Richard Gombrich sums them up as follows:

> It is true ... that Sanskrit is the name of a language; but the word has a more general meaning. It means "elaborated", "refined", "cultured", "civilized"; it can be used to describe anything which is adorned or otherwise prepared for some purpose. It is the contrary of Prakrit, "natural", and it is *never pejorative*. The Sanskrit language is the language of educated men, and Sanskrit is the vehicle of civilization. (Gombrich 1978, 22; original emphasis)

The hierarchy of languages in South Asia has been thoroughly explored and theorized by Sheldon Pollock in his magnum opus, *The Language of the Gods in the World of Men* (2006). This book will probably never have the influence it deserves, because it is dense, long, and spends much space considering the technical details of Sanskrit texts and inscriptions. This is a pity, as the book advances many important theses about South Asian history in the broadest sense.[16] A key point concerns the sudden appearance of Sanskrit as *the* language of royal power in about 150 CE. Before then, classical Sanskrit was confined largely to ritual contexts; from that time on, it became a part of the essential trappings of the ambitious monarch. It was also taken up by Jains and Buddhists who, for four to five hundred years, had abjured the use of Sanskrit as detrimental to their message. Exactly why this change happened may never be known precisely.

The position of the Saka dynasty, who initiated the change, was probably an important factor. The Saka were on the edge of the Vedic culture area of the time, and were therefore pretenders to Vedic respectability while not being thoroughly conservative. But it cannot be doubted that a fundamental change did occur and that what Pollock calls Sanskritic cosmopolitanism spread from India throughout Southeast Asia.

In this classical period of the Sanskrit cosmopolis a king was no mere guarantor of justice and protection. Along with the expected attributes of bravery and fearlessness in war, kings were supposed to have a deep grasp of Sanskrit grammar and an ability to compose high-flown verses. Pollock refers to "the mutually constitutive relationship of grammar and power" (2006, 168). "When the king's grammar is correct, the king's politics are correct, and his rule will be as just as his words. The king who did not command the language of the gods could command the polity no better than a drunkard" (ibid., 256). The shared language of classical Sanskrit created "a single culture-power formation" (ibid.) from Java to Cambodia to Kashmir. This Sanskrit cosmopolis was "a vast ecumene extending across a third of Eurasia over the course of a millennium or more."

> It was an immense community without factitious political unity, a community without a unique center, or, better put, one with centers everywhere—with multiple Ganga Rivers and Mount Merus—and circumferences nowhere. It was . . . primarily a symbolic network, one created by the presence of a similar kind of discourse in a similar language deploying similar idioms and styles to make similar claims about the nature and aesthetics of political rule: about kingly virtue and learning, the *dharma* of governance, and the peculiar universality of dominion in a world of plural universalities. (Pollock 2006, 257)

Around 1000 CE, a second important development took place, which Pollock calls vernacularization: the emergence of local languages as used for writing (which he calls literization) and for producing literature, including the praises of power which up to then had always been composed in Sanskrit (which he calls literarization). In most cases, there was a gap, often of hundreds of years, between these vernaculars' first appearance in writing and their first use for praise poetry. These vernaculars, which were tied to particular places as Sanskrit was not, were still heavily indebted to Sanskrit with, very often, the majority of the words being derived from Sanskrit (as in Hridaya's poem on the life of the Buddha mentioned above). Pollock admits that understanding why these processes occurred in some parts of South Asia and not in others, and why at different speeds, "remains very much a goal of future research" (2006, 423).

The emergence of these written vernaculars introduced a new hierarchy of languages and registers, all related to one another. Whereas before women and low-caste characters in dramas would have been represented speaking in various Prakrits, now they would express themselves in what was taken to be the "language of the country" (Sanskrit: *des-bhasa*). Finally, in the modern period, this hierarchy of languages was replaced with what Pollock calls "linguism," "Western linguistic monism," or the doctrine of a single mother tongue. Whereas European vernacularization led to "a correlation between people, power, and culture" (Pollock 2006, 574), the South Asian version was looser, more liberal, in short, more cosmopolitan. "Hindutva," Pollock argues, "is a perversion of India's great cosmopolitan past, while the many subnational movements (as in Assam and elsewhere) represent an entirely new, militant vernacularism, indeed, a kind of Heideggerization of Indian life" (2006, 575).

I have provided here a mini-tour through a few themes from Pollock's massive survey of the 2,500-year history of Sanskrit. My summary is intended to show that the way the Newars of the Kathmandu Valley have thought about civilization exemplifies a pattern once much more widespread throughout South Asia and beyond.[17] Pollock—to his credit—recognizes this and includes the Kathmandu Valley as a small part of his story, thereby not succumbing to the methodological nationalism of so many other scholars who read the contingent political boundaries of the present day back into history and ignore the crucial evidence that the Nepali case could bring to their arguments.[18] At the same time, Pollock's refusal to conceptualize this cosmopolis in terms of Hinduism perhaps blinds him to the specificities of the Theravada Buddhist cosmopolis of Southeast Asia as analyzed by Ladwig (ch. 7, this volume).

Evading Civilization

James Scott has recently given yet another of his calls for a bottom-up view of history, with the publication of *The Art of Not Being Governed: An Anarchist History of Upland Southeast Asia* (2009). This volume pulls together in a brilliant synthesis a vast amount of work on highland societies in Southeast Asia. Building on Willem van Schendel's (2002) concept of Zomia as a space beyond the reach of the state, Scott emphasizes the way in which the culture, ethnicity, and social organization of upland peoples can largely be explained by their state-evading behavior. Upland peoples desire escape from the control of valley-based rice-growing centralized monarchies and attempt to live in more egalitarian and freer arrangements in the hills.

There has already been much interest in Scott's book and a number of critiques.[19] Scott himself has not attempted to apply his theories beyond Southeast Asia. He has not thought to extend them farther west into the Himalayas, for example. He also generally argues that, with modern times and modern technologies of movement, the Zomia that once covered large parts of highland Asia barely exists any more. In other words, his analysis applies only to the period before 1950.

In drawing attention to state-evading behavior, and the antistate strategies of peripheral peoples, Scott has certainly given anthropologists much to think about. His overall vision ties together upland people's shifting ethnic categories, loose kinship ties, hybrid culture, religious pluralism, avoidance of writing, and shallow history—all these are interpreted as ways to avoid the gaze and control of the state.

My argument with Scott would not focus on his overall approach, which, like others, I find refreshing and exhilarating. Rather, I would like to complicate the picture somewhat by including the state-evading, or, perhaps better, state-frustrating strategies of those who cannot run away—that is, those who are tied to the sacred-royal centers and adhere to the civilizational narratives that go with them. The peasants who practice rice agriculture surely also wish to evade state arbitrariness if they can. I suggest that the solution has already been found by Geertz. Geertz is not often praised for his highly materialist analyses of state formations, so let us do so here. What he shows in *Negara* (ch. 3) is that Balinese peasants were involved in such complex and crosscutting ties that any kind of command economy, or any kind of feudalism, was impossible: "Control over land and control over people expressed themselves in distinct and uncoordinated institutions" (Geertz 1980, 66).[20] The peasantry had to be persuaded to contribute surplus through the very magnificence and attractiveness of the ritual at the center. Where Louis XIV persuaded regional nobles to give up their power base and participate in ritual at Versailles, the Balinese courts did so for an entire society.

What Geertz's material shows—and I believe it is supported also by the history of Newar civilization—is that one of the "weapons of the weak" is not just evading the state by flight, as with pastoral people or swidden agriculturalists. Evading the state can also be accomplished in a different way, through cultural complexity combined with deference (often combined with "hidden transcripts"). Finally, though Scott's emphasis on state-evading behavior and traditions is surely welcome, it should not lead us to overlook the extent to which mountain peoples accepted and made use of the political forms of lowland hierarchical states, and occasionally were able to coerce lowlanders as well (Gell 1997; Schnepel 2003; Wouters 2012).

Conclusion

I have tried to outline the notion of "civilization" as experienced and lived in classic South Asian form, as exemplified in the way of life still preserved, though today very much attenuated, in the cities of the Kathmandu Valley, Nepal. That mode of life has been interestingly described and theorized as "the Sanskrit cosmopolis" by Sheldon Pollock. He downplays radically the role of religion and ritual in this vision, but otherwise the portrait is convincing. A hierarchy of languages, with prowess in literary Sanskrit as the marker of civilization and royal supremacy, generated a particular relationship between Great and Little Traditions that was once dominant from what is now Afghanistan to as far as Bali, if not beyond. The arrival of Islam certainly made a difference, though one should be cautious about positing any kind of "clash of civilizations" between the Indic world and Islamic civilization. There were plenty of amalgams between the two, in Java, in India, and elsewhere.

The task of thinking about civilization in the abstract is probably best carried on deductively, starting from certain premises about the nature of social life, rather than as an inductive amalgam of the experiences of particular traditions. Nonetheless, a full understanding of civilization cannot be had without comparing in detail various actually existing (or actually having existed) civilizations from ancient Egypt onward. Such comparative work must be undertaken, of course, both with due deference toward the experts in the field and with full awareness of historical variability, and without falling into the various traps of essentialism, evolutionism, teleology, or Orientalism.

Notes

1. On Redfield's understanding of civilization and the political context in which he evolved it, see Sartori (1998).

2. I thank Steve Collins, Lola Martinez, and participants in the original workshop at the Max Planck Institute in Halle for comments on an earlier version.

3. A small example: the notion of "martial tribes" as used by the British to justify recruiting soldiers from some areas and some backgrounds and not from others (Caplan 1995; Streets 2004) was not a simple invention ex nihilo of the colonial authorities, as claimed by some, but drew heavily upon already existing firmly held indigenous ideas about certain groups being naturally warlike and suitable for military service.

4. An exception to this generalization—one Dumontian idea that is still regularly invoked, even if only to contest it—is his concept of "substantialization." This neologism refers to the way in which castes—formerly defined by their relations—have started to behave like solid blocs, more akin to ethnic groups (cf. Ishii 2007; Parry 2007).

5. See Allen (1975; 1982), Toffin (1984; 1993; 2007), Levy (1990), Gellner (1991; 1992; 1995a), Quigley (1995).

6. However, Toffin's monograph (2009) on the Indra Jatra festival contains plenty of evidence that can be used to support the view that Newar civilization is deeply Indic.

7. For a summary of Juju's views, see Gellner (2011).

8. For introductions to indigeneity and ethnicity in Nepal, see Gellner (2001b; 2007), Onta (2006), Hangen (2010), Whelpton et al. (2008).

9. For some of these arguments, see Gellner (2003). I had already argued, some time before the word *indigenous* was introduced into Nepal following the UN's declaration of a Year of Indigenous People in 1993, that in the South Asian context (and given the way "tribe" has come to be used there) "the Newars are the very opposite of a tribe and the epitome of a Sanskritic, caste-based society" (Gellner 1991, 107).

10. On the built environment of the cities of the Kathmandu Valley, the indispensable source, by an architect who has devoted his life to documenting and mapping it, is Gutschow (2011).

11. By an irony of recent Nepali political and cultural history, Newar untouchables are denied the official status of Dalits, because they are included in the Janajati/indigenous people's category as Newars. This is doubly ironic because the first Dalit activist in Nepal was a Newar untouchable, a Kapali.

12. Fuller is here summarizing the work of Srinivas, Moffatt, and Beck on south Indian villages: "The unity of the south Indian village is, in an important sense, ritually predicated on the Harijans' exclusion . . . the division of ritual labor requires Harijans to participate. In that way, the hierarchical design of the village community is forcefully displayed. Harijans must also be present as symbolic denizens of the exterior in opposition to which the village is represented as a civilized center" (Fuller 1992, 138–39).

13. See LeVine and Gellner (2005) for the story of those who sought (and to a considerable extent succeeded) in reforming the traditional Tantric Buddhism of the Kathmandu Valley; see pp. 107–108 for a critique of those who take *samskara* (life-cycle rituals) and *samskrti* (customs) to be *dharma*.

14. See Gellner (1997) for a summary and analysis.

15. I was interested to discover that this principle of maximal elaboration applies as much to the low castes within the city as to the high. This is contrary to the high-caste stereotype of them as being "without rules" or "without ritual elaboration." In fact, in one particular case (i.e., the distinction between auspicious and inauspicious occasions for ritual barbering and toenail cutting) the low castes are actually *more* elaborate in that they recognize more distinctions than the high castes. See Gellner (1995b, especially 271–72).

16. One element of Pollock's theorizing, namely his allergy to what he calls "legitimation theory," seems to be quite detachable from his other conceptualizations (and in fact, far from being contradicted by them, it would seem to be highly compatible with his arguments in many places). I am not the only one to find his aversion to Weber, and his refusal to engage with religion, as the least convincing parts of his book (Gellner 2008; 2017; Nemec 2007).

17. This was a point I argued in my very first ethnographic article (Gellner 1986): despite their Tibeto-Burman language the Newars are fully a part of Indic culture and civilization.

18. I have protested at precisely this absence in Ronald Davidson's social history of medieval Tantric Buddhism (Gellner 2004; Davidson 2002).

19. See the special issue of *Global History* (2010), and, for the Nepal context, Shneiderman (2010). See also Wouters (2012) on Assam.

20. "There was no unitary government, weak or powerful, over the whole realm at all. There was merely a knotted web of specific claims usually acknowledged" (Geertz 1990, 68).

References

Allen, Michael. 1975. *The Cult of Kumari: Virgin Worship in Nepal.* Kathmandu: INAS; Reissued 1987, Mandala Book Point, Kathmandu.

———. 1982. "Girls' Pre-Puberty Rites among the Newars of the Kathmandu Valley." In *Women in India and Nepal,* edited by M. Allen and S.N. Mukherjee, 211–51. ANU Monographs.

Burghart, Richard. 1978. "Hierarchical Models of the Hindu Social System." *Man* 13, no. 4: 519–36; reissued in R. Burghart (1996) *The Conditions of Listening: Essays on Religion, History and Politics in South Asia*. Delhi: Oxford University Press.

Cannell, Fenella. 2006. "Introduction." In *The Anthropology of Christianity*, edited by F. Cannell, 1–50. Durham: Duke University Press.

Caplan, Lionel. 1995. *Warrior Gentlemen: "Gurkhas" in the Western Imagination*. Oxford: Berghahn.

Clifford, James, and George E. Marcus, eds. 1986. *Writing Culture: The Poetics and Politics of Ethnography*. Berkeley: University of California Press.

Collins, Steven. 1989. "Louis Dumont and the Study of Religions." *Religious Studies Review* 15, no. 1: 14–20.

Davidson, Ronald M. 2002. *Indian Esoteric Buddhism: A Social History of the Tantric Movement*. New York: Columbia University Press.

Dirks, Nicholas. 2001. *Castes of Mind: Colonialism and the Making of Modern India*. Princeton: Princeton University Press.

Dumont, Louis. 1980. *Homo Hierarchicus: The Caste System and its Implications*. Chicago: The University of Chicago Press.

Fuller, C. J. 1992. *The Camphor Flame: Popular Hinduism and Society in India*. Princeton: Princeton University Press.

Geertz, Clifford. 1980. *Negara: The Theatre State in Nineteenth-Century Bali*. Princeton: Princeton University Press.

Gell, Alfred. 1997. "Exhalting the King and Obstructing the State: A Political Interpretation of Royal Ritual in Bastar State, Central India." *Journal of the Royal Anthropological Institute* (N.S.) 3: 433–50.

Gellner, David N. 1986. "Language, Caste, Religion, and Territory: Newar Identity Ancient and Modern." *European Journal of Sociology* 27, no. 1: 102–48.

———. 1991. "Hinduism, Tribalism, and the Position of Women: The Problem of Newar Identity" *Man* (N.S.) 26: 105–25; Reprinted as ch. 11 in D. N. Gellner (2001a).

———. 1992. *Monk, Householder, and Tantric Priest: Newar Buddhism and its Hierarchy of Ritual*. Cambridge: Cambridge University Press.

———. 1995a. "Introduction." In *Contested Hierarchies: A Collaborative Ethnography of Caste among the Newars of the Kathmandu Valley, Nepal*, edited by D. N. Gellner and D. Quigley, 1–37. Oxford: Clarendon.

———. 1995b. "Low Castes in Lalitpur." In *Contested Hierarchies: A Collaborative Ethnography of Caste among the Newars of the Kathmandu Valley, Nepal*, edited by D. N. Gellner and D. Quigley, 264–97. Oxford: Clarendon.

———. 1997. "Does Symbolism 'construct an urban mesocosm'? Robert Levy's *Mesocosm* and the Question of Value Consensus in Bhaktapur." *Journal of Hindu Studies* 1, no. 3: 541–64; Republished as ch. 13 in Gellner 2001a.

———. 2001a. *The Anthropology of Buddhism and Hinduism: Weberian Themes*. Delhi: Oxford University Press.

———. 2001b. "From Group Rights to Individual Rights and Back: Nepalese Struggles with Culture and Equality." In *Culture and the Anthropology of Rights*, edited by J. Cowan, M. Dembour, and R. Wilson, 177–200. Cambridge: Cambridge University Press.

———. 2003. "From Cultural Hierarchies to a Hierarchy of Multiculturalisms: The Case of the Newars of Nepal." In *Ethnic Revival and Religious Turmoil in the Himalayas*, edited by M. Lecomte-Tilouine and P. Dolfuss, 73–131. Delhi: Oxford University Press.

———. 2004. "Himalayan Conundrum? A Puzzling Absence in Ronald M. Davidson's Indian Esoteric Buddhism." *Journal of the International Association of Buddhist Studies* 27, no. 2: 411–17.

———. 2007. "Caste, Ethnicity and Inequality in Nepal." *Economic and Political Weekly* 42, no. 20: 1823–28.

———. 2008. "Review of Pollock (2006)." *JRAI* 14, no. 2: 443–45.

———. 2011. "Belonging, Indigeneity, Rights, and Rites: The Newar Case." In *The Politics of Belonging in the Himalayas: Local Attachments and Boundary Dynamics*, edited by J. Pfaff-Czarnecka, and G. Toffin, 45–76. Delhi: Sage.

———. 2017. "Sheldon Pollock and Max Weber: Why Pollock is more Weberian than he Thinks." *Max Weber Studies* 17, no. 2: 212–234

Gombrich, Richard F. 1978. *On Being Sanskritic: A Plea for Civilized Study and the Study of Civilization* (inaugural lecture). Oxford: Clarendon Press.

Gutschow, Niels 2011. *Architecture of the Newars: A History of Building Typologies and Details in Nepal*. 3 vols. Chicago: Serindia.

Hangen, Susan I. 2010. *The Rise of Ethnic Politics in Nepal: Democracy in the Margins*. London: Routledge.

Hann, Chris. 2011. 'Back to Civilization' (Guest Editorial) *Anthropology Today* 27, no. 6: 1–2.

Inden, Ronald B. 1990. *Imagining India*. Oxford: Blackwell.

Ishii, Hiroshi. 2007. "The Transformation of Caste Relationships in Nepal: Rethinking 'Substantialization.'" In *Political and Social Transformations in North India and Nepal*, edited by H. Ishii, D. N. Gellner, and K. Nawa, 91–129. Delhi: Manohar.

Lévi, Sylvain. 1905–08. *Étude historique d'un royaume hindou: le Népal*. 3 vols. Paris: Leroux.

LeVine, Sarah and David N. Gellner. 2005. *Rebuilding Buddhism: The Theravada Movement in Twentieth-Century Nepal*. Cambridge: Harvard University Press.

Levy, Robert I., and Kedar R. Rajopadhyaya. 1990. *Mesocosm: Hinduism and the Organization of a Traditional Newar City in Nepal*. Berkeley: University of California Press.

Lewis, Todd T., and Subarna Man Tuladhar. 2007. *Sugata Saurabha: An Epic Poem from Nepal on the Life of the Buddha by Chittadhar Hrdaya*. Cambridge: Dept of Sanskrit and Indian Studies, Harvard University. (Harvard Oriental Series 67.)

Malla, K. P. 1979. *Nepal Bhasaya dhwana saphuya dhalah (Bibliography of Nepal Bhasa): N.S. 1020–1097*. Kathmandu: Layta Dabu.

———. 1981. "Linguistic Archaeology of the Nepal Valley: Preliminary Report." *Kailash* 8, no. 1–2: 5–23.

———. 1982. *Classical Newari Literature: A Sketch*. Kathmandu: Educational Enterprise.

———. 1985. "Epigraphy and Society in Ancient Nepal: A Critique of Regmi, 1983." *Contributions to Nepalese Studies* 13: 57–94.

Nemec, John. 2007. "Review of Pollock 2006." *Journal of the American Academy of Religion* 75, no. 1: 207–11.

Onta, Pratyoush. 2006. "The Growth of the *Adivasi Janajati* Movement in Nepal after 1990: The Non-Political Institutional Agents." *Studies in Nepali History and Society* 11, no. 2: 303–54.

Parry, Jonathan. 2007. "A Note on the 'Substantialization' of Caste and its 'Hegemony.'" In *Political and Social Transformations in North India and Nepal*, edited by H. Ishii, D. N. Gellner, and K. Nawa, 479–95. Delhi: Manohar.

Pollock, Sheldon, Homi K. Bhabha, Carol A. Breckenridge, and Dipesh Chakrabarty 2002. "Cosmopolitanisms." In *Cosmopolitanism,* edited by C. A. Breckenridge, S. Pollock, H. K. Bhabha, and D. Chakrabarty, 1–14. Durham: Duke University Press.

Pollock, Sheldon 2006. *The Language of the Gods in the World of Men: Sanskrit, Culture, and Power in Premodern India*. Berkeley: University of California Press.

Quigley, Declan. 1995. "Conclusion: Caste Organization and the Ancient City." In *Contested Hierarchies: A Collaborative Ethnography of Caste among the Newars of the Kathmandu Valley, Nepal*, edited by D. N. Gellner and D. Quigley, 298–327. Oxford: Clarendon.

Redfield, Robert. 1956. *Peasant Society and Culture: An Anthropological Approach to Civilization*. Chicago: University of Chicago Press.

Said, Edward W. 1978. *Orientalism*. London: Routledge and Kegan Paul.

Sartori, Andrew. 1998. "Redfield's Comparative Civilizations Project and the Political Imagination of Postwar America." *Positions* 6, no. 1: 33–65.

Shneiderman, Sara. 2010. "Are the Central Himalayas in Zomia? Some Scholarly and Political Considerations across Time and Space." *Journal of Global History* (Special Issue entitled *Zomia and the Southeast Asian Massif*, ed. Jean Michaud) 5, no. 2: 289–312.

Schnepel, Burkhard. 2003. *The Jungle Kings: Ethnohistorical Aspects of Politics and Ritual in Orissa*. Delhi: Manohar.

Scott, James C. 2009. *The Art of Not Being Governed: An Anarchist History of Upland Southeast Asia*. New Haven: Yale University Press.

Singer, Milton. 1972. *When a Great Tradition Modernizes: An Anthropological Approach to Indian Civilization*. London: Pall Mall.

Streets, Heather. 2004. *Martial Races: The Military, Race and Masculinity in British Imperial Culture, 1857–1914*, Manchester: Manchester University Press.

Tambiah, Stanley J. 1985 (1977). "The Galactic Polity: The Structure of Traditional Kingdoms in Southeast Asia." In *Culture, Thought, and Social Action*, 252–86. Cambridge: Harvard University Press.

Toffin, Gérard. 1984. *Religion et société chez les Néwar du Népal*. Paris: CNRS.

———. 1993. *Le palais et le temple: La function royale dans la vallée du Népal*. Paris: CNRS.

———. 2007. *Newar Society: City, Village and Periphery*. Lalitpur: Social Science Baha.

———. 2009. *La fête-spectacle: Théâtre et rite au Népal.* Paris: Editions de la Maison des Sciences de l'Homme.

Van Schendel, Willem. 2002. "Geographies of Knowing, Geographies of Ignorance: Jumping Scale in Southeast Asia." *Environment and Planning D: Society and Space* 20: 647–68.

Whelpton, John, David N. Gellner, and Joanna Pfaff-Czarnecka 2008. "New Nepal, New Ethnicities: Changes since the mid 1990s." In *Nationalism and Ethnicity in Nepal,* edited by D. N. Gellner, J. Pfaff-Czarnecka, and J. Whelpton, i–xxxii. Kathmandu: Vajra Books.

Wouters, Jelle. 2012. " 'Keeping the Hill Tribes at Bay': A Critique from India's Northeast of James C. Scott's Paradigm of State Evasion." *European Bulletin of Himalayan Research* 39: 41–65.

6

INDIAN IMBROGLIOS

Bhakti Neglected; Or,
The Missed Opportunities for a New Approach to
a Comparative Analysis of Civilizational Diversity

Martin Fuchs

Are civilizations complexes we can observe, or are they aggregates that we create? Can we observe continuities and commonalities in distinct world regions—unbroken lines of identity, recurrent patterns of cultural practices of pivotal significance, or core social *problématiques*—across long expanses of time among variegated social and cultural formations? Can we, in this context, think of a strategy that avoids cultural generalizations and does not overstate cultural boundaries? Or are civilizations rather to be seen as an invention of global historical comparison that now has to be revised? In this chapter, I suggest we need to perceive "civilizational dimensions" as elements of multifaceted sociocultural constellations, not as the common or core characteristics of whole civilizational complexes. In my usage, civilizational dimensions are aspects or strands of sociocultural formations that are of wider, transcontextual significance and connect with other formations, but they cannot stand for any such configuration in its entirety.

The traditional concept of civilization has been criticized for conveying a notion of "self-contained worlds" (Arnason 2003, 217).[1] This critique refers especially to the supra-historical character associated with "civilizations," to the propensity for cultural determinism, and to the search for origins. This is based on the image of civilizational seedbeds from which all later developments germinate, and which are invoked to explain the geopolitical arrangements that we encounter in the world today. To the allegation of "essentialization" and the attempt to read contemporary ideas and the contemporary situation back into history, I would add the charge of a penchant for elitism. With anthropology as one of my disciplinary backgrounds and being wedded to a praxeological-pragmatist-interactionist and hermeneutical approach to social theory, I share the skepticism of many regarding such a concept of "civilization." And yet, we have to concede that "civilization" and related concepts such as "world religions" are tenacious and have experienced a strong revival in recent scholarship.[2] The idea of civilizations *in the plural* seems to provide a kind of natural frame for the historical reconstruction of developmental processes in various world regions, if not always explicitly then at least implicitly.

In some instances, the delineations of civilizations overlap with the territorial and cultural boundaries established by the new paradigm of Area Studies after 1945. In certain cases, world religions are seen as representing the civilizational core; in others, lineages of empires or certain forms of sociopolitical order are seen to form the core. The cases of India and China seem to present relatively clear-cut civilizational exemplars, at least at first glance, ostensibly comprising their whole known histories. The same, it appears, applies to the Orthodox Christian world, to the pastoral-nomadic empires of Inner Eurasia, and to the Latin-Christian civilization that is usually taken as defining the core of what we somewhat vaguely refer to as "the West." Less easy to demarcate are an Arabic and/or Islamic civilization or a Southeast Asian civilization (see Kahn, Ladwig, this volume).

Even the seemingly clear-cut example of India raises the problem of how to integrate the Islamic and Buddhist elements. Islam and Buddhism both transcend cultural and regional boundaries, moving in opposite directions (into and out of India respectively), yet they simultaneously denote core components of what is considered to be "Indian culture."[3] Each of the two stands for a different epoch, thus denoting historical change as much as civilizational continuity. Thus the term *civilization,* examined more closely, raises the question of what scholars of civilizational studies want to distinguish. Are they looking for formations that stretch across regions (and may even have a universalist dimension), like these two religious formations? Or, are they looking for territorially grounded constellations comprising a plurality of social dimensions? If we take the first option, only certain dimensions of any particular sociocultural constellation—in this case, those connected to religion—will be designated as "civilizational," while other dimensions will be considered merely local. If we take the second, continuities and commonalities between regions and between historical periods will be greatly reduced and civilization would be identified according to the principle of family resemblances (where context A shares elements with context B, while B shares different elements with context C). In this latter case we would remain haunted by the problem of how to pin down core elements or *problématiques* of the family and how to evaluate the multiple ingredients that show up in different (historical) contexts.

Deployment of the term *civilization,* even after so much sociological debate, remains socially selective and partly normative. It is most commonly applied to elite configurations and cultures, which in many contexts differ, sometimes radically, from the (themselves varied) ideas and practices of other people. If we want to save the concept of civilization, I argue that we should pay much more attention to the reception of ideas and concepts on the everyday level.

Process Categories

The idea of civilization shares some of its analytical problems with macrosociology and global comparison more generally. The interpretive frame of civilizational comparison and analysis, as we know it, has been defined by the double question of the road to modernity (assuming that there is something that can be delineated as "modernity") and of the universality or universal significance of the processes that made up that road. Progressive process categories, encapsulating the idea of the directedness of societal development, have played a hegemonic role in sociological scholarship. Some civilizations are seen as more conducive to such processes than others. The bias has been to privilege those that were seen as part of, or as geared toward, the modernization process as it emanated from the West, because this alone was perceived to be of global significance. Not only has comparison thus been confined to the search for "progressive" elements, but analysis for a long time has also taken those very processes being studied as given. Prominent process categories of this kind would include "secularization," "individualization," and "rationalization." Problematic is both the inbuilt sociocentrism and, more significantly, the explicit or implicit notions of path-dependency.[4] Doubts have been voiced regarding the scope, directionality, and unambiguity of such processes. Even more important, however, is the assumption that certain constitutive determinations, made at an early stage of a civilization's development, act as "switchgears" that determine if and where such processes could or could not occur. The problem of historical contingency needs to be addressed more carefully.

Much debate in recent years has concerned the idea of progressive secularization, and the idea has lost a lot of its persuasiveness as a result. While we can *contextually* observe certain kinds of developments or trends of secularization (be it in the narrower sense of a "decline of religious beliefs and practices among *individuals*" or in the broader sense of the "diminution of the *social* significance of religion" and the "emancipation of the secular spheres," as distinguished by José Casanova [2003, 17]), hardly any contemporary scholars would argue the case for a general, expanding secularization process. We encounter very different forms and conceptualizations of secularization in different cultural contexts, including cases of secularization in what we have called "premodern" times. As for rationalization, Max Weber (whose name for many still stands for the most prominent classical sociological formulation of an overall [*universalgeschichtlichen*] process of rationalization) himself expressed doubts, both concerning the nature of the assumed progress and its unidirectionality. His early death prevented him from following up his recognition of nonmodern and noncapitalist forms of rationalization of various kind in different civilizational contexts.[5] With respect to individualization, scholars have only recently started seriously to explore its roots long before modernity in different cultural contexts, very often, but not exclusively, in religious guise. The very fact that individualization is nonlinear and exhibits enormous cultural and historical diversity demonstrates the bias of the modern Gestalt of individualization. We have to return to exploring the specific actor combinations and the contexts of interaction, as well as the frames of thought and social imaginaries that facilitate specific forms of individualization. Only in this way can we hope to grasp the contingencies of these developments.[6]

Unidirectional process categories appear less and less convincing as their correlation with specific civilizations and their role as the driving forces of human progress become less and less straightforward. As a result, attempts at sorting civilizations in a hierarchical or juxtapositional classificatory order lose their basic credibility. If process categories no longer lend themselves to contrasting whole cultures, how can we take cultural developments as civilizational paths? Should we not, instead, rather explore the diversity of developments within different regions and cultural contexts, look for resemblances and differences, and leave the question of cumulative processes, involving intercultural or intercivilizational exchange, an open question to be researched in the future? It seems we have to accept much more diversity within continuities, and we have to put much more thought into the question of how continuities come about. Do contemporary social actors and scholars construct them retrospectively? We need to take account of all those facts and trends that represent other options and alternative paths if we are to conceive of continuities without sacrificing historical contingency.

In what follows, I will concentrate on certain religious aspects, since religious articulations of the world have provided one main ingredient in the standard theories of civilization. I acknowledge the force of Johann Arnason's suggestion that, to overcome cultural determinism, we need to pay more attention to political arrangements, especially empires (2003, 247ff; 2005). This does not exempt us from the need to consider *what it is* that is being reproduced. Is it always *one* ethical model or one religious worldview that plays the defining role throughout a civilization's history? This would make the duration of a civilization dependent on the continuing dominance of one worldview or sociocultural *problématique,* as defining the civilizational core.[7] The flaw of much civilizational analysis is not only cultural determinism as such, but the reductionist and unitary depiction of religions and ethical codes. Moreover, let us not forget that not all (postulated) civilizations have depended on empires as a prominent or continuous feature. Some have instead experimented with variant and shifting political arrangements. This is certainly true of India, my case here (cf. Kradin and Prozorova, this volume). The religious linkages of political entities—empires and others—in India have been of diverse kinds, in accordance with the pluralism of the religious landscape itself.

For the sake of space, I shall deconstruct the classical model of Indian civilization with reference to the neglect, or rather, the lopsided treatment of one major dimension of Indian religiosity: bhakti. I will then ask if we can construct a different, more adequate model of Indian religious civilization, or whether it might be preferable to dispense with the concept of civilization altogether. The religious strand of bhakti represents a phenomenon (or a chain of phenomena) that has intrigued modern scholars and others engaged with the cultures and belief systems of the Indian subcontinent since the early phase of the consolidation of British territorial rule and the beginnings of the Protestant missions in India. Bhakti also provides privileged spaces for studying processes of individualization, partially different from, partially similar to, but anyhow occurring before modern individualization. Bhakti is thus an example of individualization that is not the property of the (modern) West, nor restricted to the familiar notion of the renouncer who stands "outside" the world, or society.

A Missed Opportunity:
Bhakti as Neglected Civilizational Dimension

Bhakti—"participation in God" (Prentiss 1999, 23)—refers to forms of "active self-involvement" with, and personal devotion to, either a personal God or an abstract Supreme Being. The term, as it is being used today, indexes something of a strand or an attitude of religion that is different in principle from ritualism, the path of knowledge, or asceticism, although empirically there have been many ways in which these four strands have interacted, intersected, or interlaced. Bhakti appears in the textual records first in the Bhagavadgita some two thousand years ago. It appears in an already developed form and in Sanskrit, a language not spoken by the majority of people. We then encounter waves of emergence, or textual appearance, of various religious forms (and shapes) in different Indian regions from the sixth century CE, which have been assembled under the label of bhakti. The way history is accessible to us today, it looks as if bhakti as a publicly available format of religious modalities using spoken languages (the "vernaculars") has been moving northward across the subcontinent over the following centuries. (The usual depiction is that of a move from the Southeast, Tamil Nadu, over the West, Karnataka and Maharashtra, toward the North, Northwest and Northeast, Punjab, the Ganges plain and Bengal.) While this may suffice as a general introductory picture, we have to be aware that the modalities we club together under the term *bhakti* are quite diverse, as are their combinations with other religious attitudes and dimensions. Still, what seems common to all forms that are called bhakti is the possibility of direct access to God, or the direct personal experience of God (or of the Absolute or of the Highest Self). Today, some form or other of bhakti represents a prominent element in many varieties of "popular Hinduism," to use Chris Fuller's phrase (Fuller 1992). We should also be cognizant of the fact that modes of bhakti are also found in Jainism and Buddhism (e.g., Cort 2002), developments that I will not discuss here.

Max Weber and Louis Dumont are the preeminent names that stand for the conventional model of construction of an Indian "civilization," representing as they do the major attempts of classical civilizational analysis of the Indian case by Western social science scholarship. Both had major difficulties to satisfactorily appreciate bhakti. To these approaches I will add Chris Fuller's depiction of Hinduism as an example from more recent anthropology that partly perpetuates the conventional model. Fuller writes about Hinduism only, but for him Hinduism represents the core of Indian civilization (even though he avoids the term *civilization* itself), as it does for Weber, Dumont, and most other scholars.

The starting point of my deliberations is the baffling observation that the two most influential civilizational representations of India within the social sciences—Weber's geared more toward sociology and Dumont's toward anthropology—have not been able to find an adequate place for bhakti in their respective theoretical schemes. This is the case not so much for contingent reasons, like the oft-critiqued moral Puritanism of the time that is reflected in Weber's writings on India, but has, I would argue, systematic reasons. Thus, Weber acknowledges that the belief in a "supreme, personal, merciful Lord of creation,"[8] articulated in bhakti, represents a new relationship to God that includes emphasis on the concept of grace. Weber also recognizes the universalization of the chances of salvation, when he mentions the "religious equality of all human beings, also of women" in bhakti (referring especially to the Lingayats) and the fact that caste differences have been questioned or relativized by several bhakti sects.[9] All these remain momentary insights, however. They do not fit into Weber's basic scheme of an Indian worldview dominated by the urge "to escape from the world," or at least to attain an attitude of "indifference" to the world and one's actions in the world, as proposed by the Gita, even though such aspirations, in his eyes, could properly be pursued only by the intellectual milieus of Indian society.[10] Weber does not make any attempt to discuss the attitudes toward the world expressed in the later and more widespread forms of bhakti. His depiction of later bhakti is dominated by his attempt to show that it represents decline, the "plebeisation" of Indian soteriology, an adaptation to the emotional needs of the "masses." Weber sees the "masses" or "lay people" as ruled by magic, beliefs in saviors, the worship of other humans ("anthropolatry"), "orgiastic" practices, and determined by the fear of karma and karmic retribution (Weber 1978 [1921], 255, 332–34, 336–341, 351, 357, 359; Weber 1958, 237, 302–304, 306–11, 319, 324, 325); they are people without independent ideas or capabilities of reflection and little inclination to object to their fate.[11] Weber, through this attitude to popular religion, forfeits the great chance to extend his approach and analytics to the culturally most widespread forms of Indian religiosity. Thus, he was unable to see what others later described as an attitude of world affirmation in at least some of the most prominent forms of bhakti (Hardy 1983, 233f, 314, 447; Prentiss 1999, 18f),[12] the acceptance of humans as "full human being(s) with body, soul, and emotions" (Hardy 1983, 449). Weber instead regards the perspective of a restrictively conceived cultural as well as social elite as dominating and determining the overall Indian worldview and through this Indian civilization (or the Indian *Kulturkreis*). He considers the intellectual Brahmanical elite as the "carriers" (*Träger*; Weber 1978 [1921], 134), and the only carriers at that, of Indian civilization.[13]

Whereas Weber had little regard for the beliefs and practices of ordinary people in India, thus contradicting and overwriting his own insights regarding the significance of bhakti, Dumont saw it as a challenge and threat to his model of India and his contrast of India and Europe. Dumont applies a dualistic scheme to the analysis of Indian civilization that adapts Weber's model to the more recent scholarly trend of structuralism.[14] On the one side are society and its members, determined by the caste order, religiously underpinned by hierarchical values, and closed to even an inkling of individual subjecthood. On the other side is the renouncer, or the individual, who lives "outside the world." However, Dumont too is forced, when confronted with the bhakti phenomenon, to acknowledge that bhakti shows the possibility of individualization and salvation without renunciation within society. It shows the possibility that "one can leave the world *from within*": "Renunciation is transcended by being internalized . . . *everybody* can become free individuals" (1980, 282f; emphasis added). Dumont even acknowledges that the authority of his dichotomous model is undermined.[15] However, having made these concessions Dumont then puts bhakti aside and makes no attempt whatsoever to integrate it into his model of Indian society and civilization. Bhakti for him remains derivative of *samnayasi*-hood. He is the proponent of a theory of Indian civilization that puts a contradiction at its core—that between the Brahminical model of social hierarchy and the individual "outside the world"—which integrates society, but he refuses to entertain the tension between the hierarchical model and social imaginaries or models that oppose hierarchy and its religious legitimation.[16]

Both theories briefly discussed in this section work within a set frame of sociological comparison. India and Indian religions are being used to prove a case—for Weber: that India's endogenous development, in contrast to that of Europe, ended in an impasse; for Dumont: that India represents the perfect mirror image of Western social life and social ideas, and can be used for a critical, anti-egalitarian reconsideration of the state of modern Western society.[17] Weber, as well as Dumont, takes religious worldviews and ideologies as overarching, unifying, and on the level of principles, unitary; and both work with the concept of "carriers" of a civilization. They both consider that it is the elites who lay down what can and cannot be thought in a society. The views and orientations of the rest, the majority of the populace, are considered either immaterial or predetermined in a culturalist manner by the ideas initially inscribed into a belief system once and for all by the original intellectual elite. For both, beliefs are always considered to appear in the form of systems. On this background, trying to give bhakti its due could thus be understood as a call to rewrite core sociological assumptions of Indian society and of civilizational comparison. Weber and Dumont brushed aside or locked away their own insights from the beginning, as they did not fit their basic analytical agendas.

One would expect later anthropology to have made amendments to these civilizational conceptualizations. Chris Fuller (1992, 5) does acknowledge the importance of "devotionalist movements" in Hinduism, and even states that these are "antithetical to much in Hindu religion and society"; devotionalist Hinduism "owes much . . . to *resistance*" against hierarchical values (1992, 158; emphasis added). However, Fuller, himself pursuing an explicitly structuralist-synchronist, non- or supra-historical approach,[18] also remains stuck in a holistic civilizational framework and keeps emphasizing the unity of Hinduism and India respectively. Some casual qualifiers notwithstanding (1992, 7), Fuller too wants to make Hinduism stand for India.[19] The "structure" of Hinduism, he writes, "is adequately—although not totally—consistent with the structure of society as a whole" (ibid.). Fuller is even more upfront than Dumont, and definitely Weber, about the claim that India's civilizational unity is an observer's claim. Not unlike Dumont before him, he challenges the emphasis many Hindus, and especially Brahmins, place on dividing lines within Hinduism:[20] it is they, the social actors, who are "reifying" difference in Fuller's view.[21] While thus from the natives' point of view a "sharp distinction"[22] is being made between "shastric or scriptural" and "laukik or popular" Hinduism, in Fuller's eyes no "real separation between Sanskritic and non-Sanskritic Hinduism" exists (1992, 27)!

It seems that for all three authors there is more to a civilization than is allowed by their analyses, which have been so overwhelmingly influential. Both Dumont and Weber discovered with bhakti something new, something that did not fit the alleged civilizational pattern, a new type of religiosity, which changed the equation. But they were unwilling or unable to integrate these insights into their designs of Indian civilization or redesign their models of India. Weber and Dumont not only had difficulties acknowledging and doing justice to the subjectivity and agentive capabilities, and to the scope of individualization of people other than the privileged intellectual few. What is more, there seems to be no place for contingencies, innovations, or alternative paths in their models. Fuller is able to see the "counterpoint" that bhakti represents to the more dominant strands of Indian religion and society (1992, 203), but he fails to take the next step of breaking Hinduism into its diverse strands and trends in order to do full justice to each of them and to their mutual tensions.

Although he has not particularly focused on India, considering the significance of his work for the field of comparative civilizational studies I might add a short remark regarding Shmuel Eisenstadt's treatment of bhakti. He tends to bracket it together with Buddhism and Jainism, all three propagating "more universalistic definitions of the religious communities"; greater equality within; principled social openness irrespective of caste; and "pure unmediated devotion to the Absolute" (2003, 597).[23] Taking all three as "movements of heterodoxy and dissent" in his early writings (1984, 7), Eisenstadt later prefers the less precise label "sectarianism" (2003, 597). Following Weber and Dumont, even rigidifying their diagnosis further, he sees all three religious strands as derivative of, and bound to, what he regards as the central vision of Indian civilization, its "other-worldliness," embodied by the figure of the "renouncer."[24] What he misses is the very difference in character of bhakti religiosity compared to ritualism, renunciation, and metaphysical and philosophical speculation and theoreticization (see below); he also misses the world-affirmative aspects of many forms of bhakti. Eisenstadt emphatically holds to Weber's, and in a way also Dumont's, strict opposition between *Weltverneinung* and *Weltbejahung* (world-rejection and a positive attitude toward the world); to the wholesale attribution of these attitudes to entire civilizational traditions; and to the fundamental difference of civilizations, at least in this respect. Eisenstadt equates "transcendental" and "other-worldly" in the Indian context (e.g., Eisenstadt 1984, 6f) while the transcendent and the "mundane" principally occupy separate spheres for him; it does not seem to occur to him that the transcendent can be considered a presence within immanence.[25]

Let me end this section by pointing to a reverse position, one in which for once bhakti becomes a core dimension of Indian civilization, or at least of Hinduism as the national religion of India. John Hawley has shown how "Orientalists" of Protestant persuasion, like George Grierson, historians of Hindi literature such as Ramchandra Shukla and Hazariprasad Dvivedi, and propagators of bhakti in Bengal like Kshitimohan Sen and Bipin Chandra Pal during the first half of the twentieth century together contributed to the construction of the notion of a trans-Indian bhakti movement (*andolan*) that came from the South and, after a breakthrough in the fifteenth and sixteenth centuries, culminated in the North—the "vision of the historical progress of bhakti as a single, powerful flood—never old, never new, but constantly throbbing with energy over the course of centuries" (Hawley 2009, 9, 12–15, et passim; Hawley 2015, esp. ch. 1 and 6). It is the telos of this construction that is of special interest here: the telos of national integration through the northward movement of bhakti, toward the Hindi-speaking area as modern India's hub (Hawley 2009, 18; 2015, 58). Again, however in a way opposite to Weber and Dumont or Eisenstadt, bhakti is not taken here on its own terms.[26]

Understanding and Analyzing Bhakti

As indicated above, bhakti represents a multiple challenge to dominant positions: socially and historically, it is a challenge to an emphasis on ritualism, and thereby also a challenge to the position of Brahmin priesthood and the social and religious pervasiveness of hierarchies, as it is a challenge to the soteriological exclusivity of the search for redemption and liberty enshrined in the model of *samnyasin*-hood. Epistemologically, it is a challenge to prevalent and exclusively elite-centered constructions of civilizational patterns, and especially to elitist worldviews and views of religion. Bhakti cuts across social segments, demarcations, and distinctions. In particular, it threatens the idea of a unitary character of "Hinduism," even if we accept an attenuated version of "unity in diversity." At the same time, bakhti weakens the distinctions between Hinduism and other religions, as it develops into a thread that infiltrates ever-wider circles of Indian religion. The consecutive establishment of bhakti throughout Indian history signified an acknowledgement of "popular" religion and thus of the diversity of religious patterns and religious attitudes, as it indicated continuing conflicts about core values guiding human action.

Bringing bhakti into the foreground is more than the (re)discovery of a strand of Indian religion neglected or underrated and miscalculated in civilizational comparison. While it is right that bhakti is connected with opposition to Brahmanical ritualism and to the attempted exclusion of large sections of the population from access to the Divine, it would be too simplistic to interpret it as a social movement of resistance. What is at least equally important is that bhakti refers to a different religious modality. Bhakti relates to a level of *individual experiences* and contextual expressions of *active participation* in God—expressions and experiences, that is, of religious transcendence as well as of immanence and experiences of congregational community. It is against this background that bhakti then provides spaces for social critique and the exploration of new possibilities. This experiential modality escapes models that are based on rigorous intellectual-metaphysical conceptualizations and structural rigidity, or that define the individual, as Dumont does, in purely formal sociological terms. And here lies another reason why a civilizational approach of the kind pursued especially by Weber and Dumont cannot accommodate bhakti. What is important methodologically, and what makes the analysis of bhakti itself an analytical challenge, is that it cannot be grasped by deducing its worldview from dogmatic and prescriptive texts. Bhakti, before all else, stands for interactive practices and for an experiential mode or range of modes. Theological arguments and philosophical systematizations are secondary reflections; this also applies to the Bhagavadgita.[27] Cultural-historical and civilizational analysis would have to thus change their approach. We need different analytical tools: a change of focus first of religious analysis, secondly of sociohistorical analysis—and we need time.

As an experiential modality, bhakti has sedimented in diverse forms, and the label has been meanwhile attached to a wide range of beliefs and practices. Scholarship is faced with the difficulty of reconstructing experiences and practices from the historical material available—mainly anthologies of originally oral poems, hagiographies, and theological treatises—and it is faced with a large linguistic variety. Here, I shall suggest one possible analytical perspective as a way of approaching this field. This will allow me to draw some conclusions regarding the possibilities of a civilizational analysis of the Indian context, without thereby proposing a new unitary concept of Indian civilization.

Bhakti in general perception stands for personal devotion to the Divine—God being either understood as supreme personal Being or as impersonally conceived ultimate reality, the Supreme "without attributes" (i.e., as *saguna* or as *nirguna*). God or the Supreme denotes a real presence for those who practice bhakti (*bhaktas*). I suggest conceiving of bhakti as a triangular interactive relationship of a *bhakta,* the formless or personal Supreme, and the community of other *bhaktas* or adherents of an exemplary *bhakta.*[28] While *bhaktas* seek some form of transcendental experience of God, one central aspect of their experience, if we phrase this in sociological terms, is that of mutual recognition: by and through God, people experience a form of direct, personal, intersubjective acknowledgment. This may be understood and expressed differently: as love, as grace, as surrender, and also (and this is important for those who experience systematic humiliation through others in society) simply and basically as recognition of one's personhood, subjectivity, and humanness. The underlying assumption is that human subjects can relate to themselves in a positive manner, and assure themselves of their identity, only when they experience themselves as fully accepted by others. Equally important as the recognition by and through God is the sharing of one's experience with others, and thus one's recognition by one's peers. The meaning of the relationship to other humans is that of confirming the individual's experience of interaction with the Divine, as it prepares the other *bhaktas* for their personal experience of God. And, as some forms of bhakti contend, God too requires recognition by humans who love or worship him or her.[29] Other than the concepts of social recognition as currently discussed in Western sociophilosophical contexts, which conceive of these as binary relationships, recognition in bhakti is a triangular constellation.[30]

Karen Pechilis Prentiss's interpretation of bhakti seems to best fit the triangular model. She takes bhakti, following in the steps of Charles Hallisey,[31] as meaning "participation in God." Her analysis rests on etymology: the root *bhaj* means "partake (of)," "engage in," "participate," "turn and resort to," "serve and honour," "love and adore" (Prentiss 1999, 24; Sharma 1987, 40; Hardy 1983, 28). It is the notion of "I am involved" that Hallisey and Pechilis Prentiss regard as "the core of devotion." They object to an understanding of devotion as mere mysticism, or to a notion of devotionalism in the loose sense of religious zeal or "dedication" (Prentiss 1999, 22f). Instead, they take bhakti as a religious "strategy" and emphasize the "conscious activity" of religious agents, or the *bhaktas'* "active self-involvement" (ibid., 23). As "committed engagement," bhakti "encourages a critical distance" to worldly matters (ibid., 20); at the same time, bhakti insists on the human embodiment of the divine relationship. Pechilis Prentiss emphasizes the tensions that inhere in bhakti between a (yogic renunciatory) critical stance toward the world and world affirmation, and between emotion and "intellection" (ibid., 19, 20).[32]

The congregational dimension of bhakti has often been pointed out. It has been a regular feature that *bhaktas* meet more or less informally for congregational worship and the singing of *kirtans* or other *bhajans*. Often the people who thus assemble hail from different social or caste backgrounds. The possibility is that people with different social affiliations can come together. Such congregations can consolidate into, or can accompany, longer-lasting sectarian or denominational arrangements (e.g., in the form of *sampradayas*). In the case of some marginalized groups they served as the nucleus of some kind of local counterpublic (and later sometimes formed the basis of local or regional social movements). The other communitarian aspect, especially foregrounded in some northern *nirguna sampradayas,* including Sikhism, now considered a religion of its own, is the daily offering and sharing of free food in a joint meal at the temple (*langar*), served to all visitors regardless of their social background.[33] New scholarship has enlarged the view on bhakti's congregational and public side. Thus, Christian Novetzke has argued that bhakti (and especially that of *Namdev*) could best be understood as performance practices that reflect the conditions in which they occur, and through which publics and public memories are created (Novetzke 2007; 2008).

The potentiality of bhakti, or of certain of its forms, shows in particular ways with respect to the possibilities of women as well as low caste people, and with regard to its expressive force that allows the mobilization of and inspires social movements among marginalized people. Even if only few women may have actually realized the full potential of bhakti, their example played a large role in social imaginaries, especially within *saguna* traditions. Eminent women *bhaktas,* some partly mythologized, include Karaikkal Ammaiyar (ca. 550 CE), Antal (tenth century), Mahadeviyakka (twelfth century), Mirabai (ca. 1498–1546), and Soyrabai and Nirmala (late thirteenth, early fourteenth century) as well as Bahinabai (seventeenth century) in the Varkari tradition. For these women, bhakti offered an imaginary and sometimes real possibility of opting out of constraining social relationships. They experienced their relationship to God as liberation, and many decided against marriage and family dependency to devote their lives to worship and the search for God. Several of them have been seen as examples capable of leaving their husbands or abandoning their prospective husbands—a major social scandal in each case. This they did without giving up their female identity "constructed by the female body," experiencing God as a confident (Chakravarty 1989, 28).[34]

Even though the cases who have officially been put "on record" in anthologies and hagiographies are limited in numbers, most bhakti traditions did acknowledge (and felt forced to acknowledge), examples of Dalit ("Untouchable") saint-poets, including those whose poems express anger and critique regarding their exclusion and their treatment. Prominent names include Nandanar (betweeen 660–842 CE), Tiruppan-Alvar (perhaps eighth to ninth century), Cokhamela (between second half of the thirteenth century and 1338), and Ravidas (fifteenth century). Among others from lower caste (but not "untouchable") background would be names such as Namdev (ca. 1270–1350), Kabir (ca. 1440–1518), or Tukaram (1608–1649). While bhakti *sampradayas,* once they became established and dominated by members of higher caste origin, tended to marginalize Dalit *bhaktas* (and often also female *bhaktas*), the memories of the Dalit *bhaktas* were never wiped out. Several Dalit *bhaktas* served as inspirations and icons of Dalit religious and social movements, already in "premodern" times, such as the Kabir Panthis, who eventually turned into a *sampradaya*; the Shiv Narainis, a much neglected *sampradaya* with its center in Eastern Uttar Pradesh/Western Bihar; and perhaps, though institutionally weaker, the Raidasis. Many others, better recorded, emanated during colonial times (while having earlier roots), like the Satnami Panth or the Ad Dharm movement. The incidence of "untouchable" saints was more than a sting in the flesh of social and religious hierarchy, it was of theological importance for at least parts of the bhakti traditions. Taking the example of Tiruppan-Alvar, Friedhelm Hardy has argued that the Untouchable, the exemplar of the humiliated person, appears as the exemplary human in need of redemption: "[M]etaphorically the untouchable symbolizes the unliberated man's distance from Visnu in *samsara*" (Hardy 1991, 149).[35]

The expressive force of bhakti shows in the poetic literature that it initiated. This literature is of a wide range and exhibits regionally and chronologically different forms, but in all cases it was originally oral. The poems and songs bring out the very different modes of the *bhaktas'* experiences of God and allow for articulating alternative (social) imaginaries. The most renowned example is that of *nirguna bhakta* or *sant* Kabir (ca. 1440–1518) whose fame has spread, and endured until today, over at least the whole of Northern India. He has been considered one of India's most outspoken religious and social critics. Scholars have emphasized the satirical and abrasive character of his poems, which make fun of scholars, ascetics, and cult idols; oppose the authority of the Vedas and Brahmins, as well as that of Mullahs; slate and lambast the notion of "untouchability"; and play with common sense perceptions, often using a particular paradoxical "upside-down language" (*ulatbamsi*). More than other saints, Kabir directly addresses his audience, whom he challenges time and again (Hess 1983).

Implications

Bhakti traditions put heavy emphasis on "exemplary" individuals who, epitomizing the presence of God or the Supreme, can also themselves become an object of worship. Their followers, again, can experience the Divine in their own specific ways. Bhakti provides a high potential for religious individualization, and this even for those who are socially marginalized or excluded; it also provides a high potential for experiences of recognition that then also allow *bhaktas* to stand up in or against society, a potential that, however infrequently, has again and again been realized. The contiguity between experiential openness, individual access, and sharing with others is constitutive. What one has to emphasize is that the attitude toward the Supreme enshrined in bhakti, the spiritual path of personal participation and devotion, signifies a possibility that can be clearly distinguished from the paths of knowledge and ritualism, and from the bodily, microcosmic experience of divine energy by means of certain techniques (*tantra, yoga* or bodily practices, meditation, alternative forms of ritual). In practical terms, however, this potential often appears diluted, and bhakti has been combined and intermixed in various ways with elements of the other strands within mainstream (Puranic and contemporary) Hinduism.

What, then, is the civilizational relevance of bhakti? What would be the consequences of a new approach to bhakti for civilizational analysis?

1. Bhakti exemplifies the diversity of elements and of attitudes, including attitudes "toward the world," available under the generic label "Hinduism." Bhakti provides just one example of alternative, sometimes antinomian, forms of religiosity in India. If bhakti were to be included in civilizational analysis, we would have also to include the Nath Yogis; to some extent other forms of tantra, Sufism, and shapes of Buddhism; and perhaps further varieties of religion (see esp. Vaudeville 1974). While some forms

of bhakti have retained streaks of their independent and partly antinomian origins, other forms have moved into the mainstream and coalesced with other practices, especially those of (temple) ritual and asceticism; or they were arrogated by Brahmanical discourses and Puranic traditions.[36] Even in these cases, tensions did not totally disappear; bhakti both influenced the development of the religion of the temple and allowed expressions of distance to temple worship.[37] But there is another factor that we should take into account, again concerning the institutional aspect (and thus, indirectly, also the question of power). Even though bhakti, especially the *saguna* forms,[38] became a major font of temple worship, many forms of bhakti seem largely to have spread through own channels among wider sections of the *nonelite* population, especially through *itinerant networks* of mendicants, preachers and teachers, and of exemplary saints (e.g., Vaudeville 1974, 81ff). This mode of dissemination, which at least in the North *bhaktas* and *sants* shared with Nath Yogis and Sufis, has not received sufficient attention, particularly in sociological analysis. Practices of bhakti crystallized in ever-new forms in ever-new places, and in new congregations; and in many cases, new *sampradaya*s were established.

2. Taken together, the various facets of bhakti show that Indian religions, or even Hinduism alone, do not follow one pattern or represent one continuous *problématique*. We can see continuities as well as conjunctions of elements of different background and different character, but if we take a long-term perspective they do not add up to a structural whole nor to a final conclusive agreement about the balance of the elements. One can even state, and this finds support in India's scriptural traditions, that Indian religions are made up of different strands or "paths," *margas,* that have existed and interacted over long periods, but these represent very different religious modalities and very different relationships "to the world."[39] One can go farther and depict elite and subaltern levels, relatively speaking, of networks and religious articulation (including, in certain cases, distinct *sampradaya*s of nonelite people), but the model of relation between the levels would be of exchange and interaction; the relation between the levels is not one of derivation.[40] Attempts at defining one or two strands

as core dimensions of Indian or Hindu religion, or as the site of core *problématiques,* privileges some dimensions or strands over the others. Obvious candidates are Brahmanical ritualism plus renunciation and their respective relationships with the king; or simply otherworldliness, mysticism, or a nonpersonal concept of the Supreme. This privileging leaves out the experiences and perspectives of larger sections of the nonprivileged, but also of the better-off who lead a "worldly" life. To actually see Hinduism from the metaphysical perspective declared dominant, in particular the perspective of monism (Advaita Vedanta), means to construct a genealogy based on those values that over a long process won the upper hand, and whose prevalence over other options had again and again to be corroborated. Indeed this dominance was confirmed only relatively recently, in the nineteenth and twentieth centuries, thanks to the combined efforts of Indology, colonialism, and (Hindu) nationalism. Ironically enough, this very construction of a dominant Indian civilizational worldview thus involves contributions from the side of what is considered another civilization, and one that is thought to represent a supposedly oppositional worldview.[41]

3. One has to be aware that strands are also constructions. At least some, like bhakti, have taken on very diverse forms. There is no phenomenological "unity" of any strand, let alone of Hinduism or Indian religion more broadly. This applies even if we abstain from including the inputs from, and interactions with, other religious strands found in India.

Indian culture and society appear as much more diverse than the classical civilizational formulas would allow. What the case of bhakti demonstrates is the danger of simplification, of reducing India to some simple structural principle or formula—one "attitude toward the world." Even if bhakti did not lead to establishing a new social order, the recurrent practices that are summarized under this term show the continuous (even if demoted) existence of social counterimaginaries that not only accompanied the dominant order of hierarchy and social as well as religious exclusion, but which also enforced certain changes. More importantly even, the different religious approaches were built on different premises regarding humans and humanness, the human relationship to the Divine, and sociality.[42]

What I have laid out here represents only one possibility of structuring Indian religious diversity without falling back into the language of patterns and path-dependencies, and without denying contingency. Where to go from here? As a form of conclusion I would like to just indicate two different directions: one regarding the reconceptualization of Indian culture and society, the other regarding comparison and, in particular, the confrontation with "the West" and its modernity.

1. The first direction regards the question of how, for now, we should conceive of civilizational dimensions in the Indian context, covering a period of 3,500 years (if we leave out the Indus and proto-Indus cultures) and extending over the breadth of a subcontinent. I see two options. Taking into account India's (cultural, religious, social, political, economic) *diversity*; the multiple, criss-crossing *interactions* (articulations, combinations, modes of overruling); and the shifting, alternative as well as parallel, *continuities* (including ruptures and discontinuities) of practices and ideas on various levels of social and intellectual life—the first option would be to take this diversity and the continuous struggle for its integration as *the* Indian characteristic. While diverse, everything seems to hang together with everything else. (Or, alternatively, as has often been stated, in Indian history nothing is ever lost.)

   That diversity and the struggle for its integration should be seen as the primary characteristics of Indian civilization would be further supported by the fact that from early on we encounter transregional and sometimes transsubcontinental cultural imaginaries. Before all else, religious people representing different religious traditions traveled across the subcontinent, and made attempts to include faraway regions and ever-new meanings and even competing versions of events in their mythologies as they created replicas in other parts of the country of the religious landscapes that had been established in one region (Eck 2012).[43] The most appropriate image at the moment, then, seems to be that of India as a network of networks with family resemblances, but also with strong discrepancies between and across components and (collective as well as individual) social actors. This would be a network of parallel civilizational dimensions and strands that partially interact, but do not fully integrate and dissolve into each other. Or, to put it a little differently: the image of India thus evoked would be that of a space of communication of a wide range, with shifting centers, changing modes and different levels of communication, and shifting boundaries at all points. The space of communication also includes the continuing antinomies between a hegemonizing agenda that is itself changing (i.e., ever adapting to shifting circumstances) and a range of alternative agendas; subsuming or clubbing these together under one heading of "heterodoxy or dissent" would mean reducing their range and their independent sources.

This model of civilization takes the territorial reference as a given, and takes civilization as a container (within which everything seems possible). The distinctiveness of this civilization—as a general trait—would be nothing specific and nothing in particular; not even "otherwordliness" can still be considered a uniting factor. Insofar as the civilization conceived thus forms a whole, or a "family of societies" in Durkheim's and Mauss's sense (1971), spanning over extended periods of time, guided by some common trait or common idea, it is one only on the level of certain elite discourses and practices (including those of world renunciation); or on the level of coalescing and compromising constructions that this would hold; or with respect to various religious and/or political networks (very few of which, however, have ever covered larger parts of the subcontinent). Such a construction of an "Indian civilization" might be handy for a certain kind of "comparative" approach, which at the end does no more than confirm the otherness of the other; or it might be handy for a unitary, essentializing nationalist project. It is telling, however, that even today many members of the nonelite sections do not feel included in these coalescing "mainstream" constructions.

We can look at the fact of religious diversity in India and the problem of its integration also in another way. Since the days of the Bhagavadgita, we encounter attempts to envisage the different margas, with their different approaches to life and to liberation, in formulas of compromise. It is significant that the compromise character is never lost and each religious mode keeps its specific rationale. This does not mean, however, that each marga has substantially remained the same throughout history, rather "marga" has provided a handy format or a formula to identify and classify similar, but discrepant elements.

Perhaps, in this context, we should then, as our second option, think of introducing the concept of civilizational ruptures into the comparative civilizational analysis of India. This would not so much have to be understood in a chronological (and even territorial) sense, as regarding the ruptures between the Greek, Roman, Latin-Christian, Byzantine, and Islamic civilizations in Europe and West Asia, but rather more particularly in a "synchronic" sense as ruptures between different civilizational complexes or modes or principles. The image of synchronic ruptures contends that the respective civilizational complexes and principles coexist in tension and that they interlace at the same time by way of the interactions of the agents and agencies involved. These interactions, spanning long periods of time, sometimes exhibiting a certain temporal sequence, however, vary in density and intensity.

Conceiving of Indian civilization in this way would allow us to transcend the territorial concept of civilization. It would also make it easier to conceive of intercultural and intercivilizational "encounters" (to take Benjamin Nelson's term). If we are interested in a meaningful distinction of civilizational dimensions, an understanding of the variances of intercivilizational engagement, and an understanding of the variant forms of local articulation and appropriation of civilizational dimensions—the way to go would be to identify cultural and/or sociopolitical ideational as well as institutional continuities of some extent, duration, and significance. Instead of clubbing everything encountered in a specific constellation together as one unit occupying one contiguous space, we could then see the individual dynamics of each of these dimensions or strands—at the Indian end: Brahmanical ritualism, renunciation, the path of knowledge (*jnana*), tantra, bhakti, various Buddhisms as well as Jainisms, various forms of Islam, folk and tribal religions, etc.—and equally of the different modes of hierarchization. And we would also be able to appropriately acknowledge the variant local traditions and institutions and their contributions to a social or cultural formation. We could then under this perspective be more specific when looking into intercultural and intercivilizational "encounters": it is not

"India" that meets "China" or "the West," but it is in each case the encounter of elements of specific strands, specific complexes, specific institutions and specific actors and mediators. It would be the strands and institutions that seem more significant and more enduring—keeping some continuity (reconstructed identities) from one moment to the other—and that manage to reach beyond one context that would then qualify as "civilizational."

The attractiveness of a model of synchronic civilizational ruptures would be that it would allow doing justice to the notion of cosmopolitanisms, as recently and forcefully proposed by Sheldon Pollock (2000, 2005; cf. Gellner in, this volume) in his comparison of the first millennium Sanskrit and Roman-Latin cosmopolitanisms. Cosmopolitanism in this sense refers to concepts, ideas, and modes of practice that can be delinked from their context of origin and can travel, becoming newly appropriated elsewhere. Instead of thinking in terms of expansion of entire civilizations, we would focus on the meeting, the extension and the adaptation of certain strands. In addition, this allows better taking recognizance of such concepts and ideas that carry universalistic messages or values. The various forms and discourses of Islam and Buddhism as well as of bhakti and other practices as well as concepts of the Self in Indian traditions or of Christianity and of the later European Enlightenment would be obvious candidates of this kind.

2. If there is some value in this suggestion, then what we need is to further explore new ways of undertaking comparative research of the *longue durée*. These explorations go beyond the minutiae of ethnographic and historical case studies that explain how the different strands have been contextually articulated, combined, changed, or overruled. The new comparative research would need to be structured, not with respect to imagined social or cultural wholes, but with respect to meaningful dimensions and segments. This in itself requires a self-reflective hermeneutics, which, while acknowledging one's own knowledge interests, would involve permanently reconsidering one's conceptual frame and research questions. In the course of research, such a hermeneutics would also require adapting one's concepts to what has been encountered elsewhere; it would involve turning around the

newly gained perspectives to revisit and reframe one's own still largely Western contexts.

To indicate what this may imply with respect to my depiction of the Indian religious scene, with a view to comparison, it might be that specific aspects seem worthwhile—or meaningful—taking up: types of processes such as Western and Indian forms of individualization; forms of interaction between and across religious and political dimensions on the different social levels in India, in the West, and elsewhere (including a comparison of the different ways in which secularization has become an issue); elite and nonelite translocal forms of learned communication and interaction (recognizing that both sides integrate aspects of the other);[44] modes of intersubjectivity and social recognition in different life forms; metaphysical-theological concepts of Self, humanness, and the Absolute in various traditions; or the different mysticisms. Such comparison would have to avoid falling back into a binary and dichotomous mode; it rather would have to show, beyond similarity and difference, the selectivity of each path or line, and the selectivity of each form of universalization.

In Place of an Afterword

Thinking of the conceptualization of civilizational dimensions on a more general and comparative level, we require greater clarity regarding their theoretical status. Following the argument made here, it seems most promising to start from Johann Arnason's "ways of articulating the world and the human condition" (2003, 221) to conceptualize civilizational dimensions. Referring to ideas of Maurice Merleau-Ponty, Arnason thus wants to foreground the interpretive, praxeological, and agentive aspect of human existence—the various ways of appropriating and experiencing the world. Alternatively, in the same book, he suggests the notion of "ways of worldmaking" (Goodman 1978; see Arnason 2003, 199). Compared to other hermeneutical agendas, including Weber's, this allows for a more comprehensive approach regarding the content as well as the form of civilizational dimensions. If, for the sake of simplification, we take those "sets or bodies of practices and ideas (including values where appropriate)"[45] that infuse social imaginaries and are widely shared by or underlie the positions of groups of social actors as a more manageable shortcut for practical, objectifying research, we would thus deal with cultural continuities that via their rearticulation by social actors, in a manner of speaking, "have got a life of their own." We would deal with articulations that are relevant not just for individuals, but for larger groups of people and that by way of such transmission have a *longue durée*. Bodies of practices and ideas come with particular institutional arrangements: monasteries, priesthoods, networks of itinerant mendicants, individual saint-poets, self-instituted congregations, theater states, and various others, which often seem particularly congenial to specific kinds of ideas and practices (and vice versa), although none of these exhaust the possibilities for the institutionalization of practices and ideas in any case. On a second level of analysis, these sets of practices and ideas, and the accompanying institutionalizations, may be seen supported and kept alive through respective political structures, especially but not exclusively those encapsulated in states.

Civilization in its core meaning would then refer to certain social and cultural components that have some broader appeal and a longer-term endurance. Such civilizational components may dominate a particular social and political constellation over some time, just as they may stretch beyond and cross the confines of such constellations and larger regions. We would no longer be stuck with a narrowly conceived, territorially grounded concept of civilization and its inherent danger of generalization.

The approach suggested here would suggest searching for developmental processes that are contextual and time- as well as region-specific (e.g., diverse and specific processes of individualization as a singular or plural process; or processes of rationalization). We would have to research anew if, and then how, these developmental processes, and especially those with a cumulative dimension, link up with particular civilizational articulations and continuities as I have outlined here. We would definitely have to avoid enshrining them in notions of larger cultural entities or civilizations in the territorial container-sense of the term.

Notes

1. See also Charles Tilly (1997, 46) who questions the a priori "presumption that distinctive, autonomous, coherent, self-sustaining civilizations, societies, cultures, and/or great events not only exist but possess their own logics *sui generis*" (cf. Knöbl 2007, 61).

2. For example, in the writings of Shmuel Eisenstadt and Johann Arnason, and in the recent Axial Age discussions. See Arnason's Introduction to, this volume.

3. While the contributions of Islam originate "outside" the subcontinent and are therefore being disowned by Hindu nationalists, those of Buddhism are an example of the influence of cultural elements originating in India, though they too have been misrepresented in a hegemonic sense in Indian nationalism.

4. In the field of macrosociology, Wolfgang Knöbl has been pushing this issue recently (e.g., 2007; 2011).

5. Fuchs 1988, 160f, 166f. Weber never retracted his notion of an exemplary rationalization laid out for humankind in general. In the 1970s and 80s, several prominent sociologists, in their different ways, rehearsed the idea of progressive rationalization. Among these neo-Weberians, Eisenstadt's notion of the "antinomies of modernity" questioned the progressive character of the process of rationalization most forcefully (Eisenstadt 1998, 1999; the German version of the book reflects the critique in its title). On the other hand, Eisenstadt's notion of a multiple modernity, or multiple modernities, tackles the diversity of rationalizations only with regard to modernity and leaves out those rationalizations that pointed in other directions or cannot be subsumed under the modernity paradigm (Eisenstadt 2003).

6. Research on this has over recent years been undertaken at the Max-Weber-Kolleg, Erfurt, in the form of a collaborative project under the title "Religious Individualization in Historical Perspective." For overviews see Joas and Rüpke 2013; Fuchs and Rüpke 2015; and Fuchs 2015.

7. Even the caste order in its strict form had first to develop; even before the colonial period, the caste principle did not have the same depth or hold over society in all areas throughout India.

8. Weber 1978 (1921), 173; transl. MF; comp. Weber 1958, 168; German original: "Glaube an einen höchsten gütigen Schöpfergott."

9. Weber 1978 (1921), 334; Weber 1958, 304. In his references to other shapes of bhakti, he mentions "indifference toward caste distinctions" (Tenkalai branch of Sri Vaisnavism), or the "permission of the lower castes to achieve *guru* status" (Kabir and Raidas) (Weber 1978 (1921), 342; 343f; Weber 1958, 311; 312; transl. adapted).

10. "World-rejection," according to Weber, takes different forms in India. That of orthodox contemplative Brahmanical Hinduism is "absolute flight from the world" (Weber 1978 [1921], 359; Weber 1958, 326); that is,

"withdrawal, not only from everyday life but from the world in general" (Weber 1978 [1921], 171f; Weber 1958, 166). The intellectualist context in which bhakti, and with it the idea of devotion to God and the concept of a "redeemer," appears in the Bhagavadgita exhibits for Weber an attitude of "world-indifference," which means to act "without regard to results and without personal interests" in one's acts; he regards this as the "crown of classical ethics of Indian intellectuals" (Weber 1978 [1921], 194–200; Weber 1958, 185–89).

11. That the concept of karma, its working and consequences were variously interpreted, and that karmic ideas were never all-pervasive in India, has been widely discussed. For a summary of these positions see Fuchs 1988, 64–81; see also Fuchs 2016.

12. Hardy, in his work on (Tamil) Krishna bhakti and Shrivaishnavism, uses phrases such as "positive attitude to the world" (1983, 234), "this-worldly attitude" (314), "world-positive" (447). Prentiss, in her work on Tamil Shaiva Siddhanta, talks of "(b)hakti's positive valuation of action in the world" as "a constitutive premise of bhakti's thesis on embodiment" and of "two competing world views in bhakti: the perspective of renunciation and that of affirming life in the world" (1999, 18f).

13. A detailed critique of Weber's treatment of bhakti can be found in Fuchs 1988, 199–224.

14. Foremost in Dumont are the separation between priesthood and renunciation, and, regarding caste, the shift from emphasis on karma, as found with Weber, to an emphasis on purity-pollution and hierarchy.

15. "At the end of the movement—achieved very early, with *bhakti*—the renouncer is in fact absorbed, whether he invents a religion of love open to all, whether he becomes the spiritual head of worldly people, rich or poor, or whether he remains a Brahmin while becoming a *sanyasi,* as with Ramanuja. At this point, if to everyone the path of spiritual adventure is as open as ever, socially the circle is closed. The two kinds of thought, the two ideal types I set out to distinguish, mingle at the mercy of various milieux and temperaments, and some men who in spirit are sanyasis live in the world" (Dumont 1980, 285). To derive bhakti in toto from renunciation, as this quote implies, shows that Dumont's revised position still has unsatisfactory limits.

16. Dumont entertains another opposition, that between worldly religion or Brahmins and the political sphere or Kshatriyas, whereby the latter are hierarchically "encompassed" by the former. For further critique of this analysis see Fuchs 1988.

17. How much this is forced can be seen in Dumont's case. While taking Indian society as the prime example of a hierarchical society in which individual humans have "no substance," "no Being" (1980, 272), and from which the modern West should learn, he also discovers India as the birthplace of the idea of individuality in the shape of the "renouncer" and speculates about how this idea then reached the West (1975, 168; see Fuchs 1988, 517f). While putting him "outside" the world, he saw the figure of the renouncer at the same time as the preeminent historical agent of innovation and change in Indian society (ibid., 509ff).

18. While objecting to "the myth of timeless India," he insists on doing "a mainly synchronic" analysis (Fuller 1992, 6).

19. He sees "enduring structures within Hindu religion and Indian society" (Fuller 1992, 6), referring primarily to "hierarchical inequality" as "one of the most fundamental principles in Indian society."

20. Often in conjunction with the emphasis laid on social divides and distinctions.

21. "[A]mong Hindus themselves, especially Brahmans and others keen to assert their own superiority, there is a marked disposition to reify the putatively separate strata" (Fuller 1992, 28).

22. A quote Fuller takes from Jonathan Parry (1985, 204f.).

23. Eisenstadt's application of the term *the Absolute* to (classical) Buddhism and Jainism here is problematic.

24. "The most important of these sects—Bhakti, Jainism, originally Buddhism itself—all closely connected with the traditions and orientations of the renouncer—emphasized the pristine other-worldly orientations" (Eisenstadt 2003, 597). He again reduces all of Indian soteriologies to one type, that of world-renunciation. Beyond that his further claim is that none of the three "sects" triggered any decisive changes in political structures.

25. Amending Eisenstadt, Johann Arnason has been arguing against identifying the opposition of "transcendental" and "mundane" with the divide between "other-worldly" and "this-worldly" domains (2003, 163).

26. The construction of this religious narrative is of interest as an alternative to the construction of Advaita Vedanta as the central theology of Hinduism. I will not go here into the claims of Grierson and others of parallels between Christianity and bhakti, nor into Krishna Sharma's (1987) critique that the construction of a bhakti movement has been biased toward Vaisnavism and neglects *nirguna* bhakti as well as Saivism.

27. The later historical forms of lived bhakti cannot be deduced from the intellectualist conceptualization as found in the Bhagavadgita (see, among

others, Hardy 1983), nor are they necessarily in conformity with the Gita's insistence on fulfillment of one's karmic duties.

28. Earlier references to the triangular character of bhakti communication and the rhetorical structure of bhakti hymns and poems are found with Norman Cutler (1987, 22) and Karen Pechilis Prentiss (1999, 20; also 2012, 16).

29. A particularly telling, in some sense extreme illustration of the relational and interactional character of bhakti can be found depicted in the *Gitagovinda* (composed by Jayadeva in the twelfth century) concerning the love between Radha and Krishna. Not only does this poem dwell in the pleasures of love and in depictions of the longing of Radha for Krishna, it also shows that the Supreme God, in his personal form, *requires* the *recognition* of Radha, the cowherd woman. The poem goes even further and depicts God in some scenes as submitting himself to Radha's will. Although she thus is in a way superhuman, she is also a human *bhakta*. The aspect of *mutuality*, characteristic of recognition in the full sense of the term, could not be expressed more forcefully.

30. I take the emphasis on recognition from modern social philosophical literature. Based on the ideas of G. W. F. Hegel and George Herbert Mead, Axel Honneth brought this issue back onto the agenda with his book *The Struggle for Recognition* (1996; German original: *Kampf um Anerkennung*, 1992). The underlying assumption is that human subjects can relate to themselves in a positive manner, and assure themselves of their identity, only when they experience themselves as fully accepted by others. This model is of particular significance for me here not only with respect to bhakti, but with respect as well to the situation of Dalits, whose struggles symbolize the difficulty of combining recognition as equals and recognition of difference (Fuchs 1999, 271, 282, 317–27). Regarding bhakti, however, the aspect that has to be added to this Western conceptual model, whose design conforms to a dyadic type of relationship, is that of a triangular constellation, or the inclusion of a third party. This triangle is the invention of bhakti and it lays the ground for a concept of sociality that includes reference to something transcendent.

31. Charles Hallisey, "Devotion in the Buddhist Literature of Medieval Sri Lanka," PhD thesis, University of Chicago 1988.

32. Or, as Friedhelm Hardy (1983, 449) had said, humans are being accepted as "full human beings," which includes mind and soul, as well as emotions and the erotic side.

33. Weber's deprecation of bhakti led him to miss its potential for "fraternization." Weber regarded *Verbrüderung* across social demarcations as a decisive element of Western development toward universalization (universal brotherhood) and saw this exemplified first in the cultic and commensal community of the medieval European city. He took India as an embodiment of the contrary principle, and saw no possibility that ritual boundaries between groups could be overcome in India (Weber 1978 [1921], 36–41).

34. On women *bhaktas* see among others Chakravarty 1989 as well as the other contributions to Manushi (1989); Tharu and Lalita 1993; Hawley 2005; Pechilis Prentiss 2012.

35. On Dalit and low caste bhaktas see, among others, Zelliot and Mokashi-Punekar 2005; Novetzke 2008; and Omvedt and Patankar 2012; on Kabir in particular Vaudeville 1974; Hess 1983; Agrawal 2009; Wakankar 2010.

36. For Tamil Nadu this has been illustrated by R. Champakalakshmi. She argues that *bhakti* in the Tamil region started as an "instrument of protest or dissent," developed into an "ethical and moral principle capable of evolving new values systems," and was then integrated into a "dominant ideology that was to ultimately become the ruling ideology"; however in her view, bhakti even then kept the capacity to "sustain and revitalize itself during situations of crisis" (Champakalakshmi 2011, 53, cf. 19).

37. Scholarship has not reached full consensus on this. See Hardy 1991 for a position that emphasizes the tensions and antagonisms between bhakti and temple worship.

38. I stick here to the *saguna-nirguna* distinction, well aware that both aspects of the divine are interdependent and that dichotomizing them was partially the result of sectarian politics since the sixteenth century. Even then there were anthologies, which did not observe this distinction (Hawley 1995).

39. One should, however, not get caught in the exteriority of individual and world that this image purveys.

40. This refers to the suggestion that bhakti is to be seen as derivative of *samnayasi*-hood, as it refers to the use of elements of established philosophy and mythology at the stage of secondary theological or philosophical interpretation of experiences and practices among subaltern *sampradaya*s. The once very fashionable paradigm of "great" versus "little traditions" in Indian religions has been a clear expression of what I refer to here as a relationship of exchange and interaction. However, this image still takes both

the sides involved as internally homogenous and assumes a bifurcation of society into two, and only two, branches.

41. It has to be underlined that I here refer to the emergence of the claim of preeminence of one metaphysical perspective, monism of the Advaitic variant, as that which allegedly overshadows and embraces all others. This has to be distinguished from the debate about the process of unification of what came to be called Hinduism, which, with regard to the commonalities among philosophical systems, apparently got some impetus during the late medieval period (esp. Nicholson 2011).

42. I have discussed this in more detail in a paper presented at the conference "Moral Imaginaries—Emerging Normative Regimes in India, China and the West," University of Bergen, 22–24 November 2012. See also Fuchs 2015 and Patrice Ladwig in, this volume. The concept of social imaginary goes back to Cornelius Castoriadis (1987) and Charles Taylor (2002). However, there are problems in applying the latter's concept of social imaginary to "nonmodern" constellations.

43. To a large extent, the same logic applies in the social field concerning the regional and local replicas of caste hierarchy.

44. Learning can be based on texts or on oral transmission. The primacy of orality (not only) in bhakti does not exclude secondary textualization of bhakti experiences and subsequent engagement in philosophical debate that interacts with the textual scholarly traditions. In India there has always been a strong emphasis on, and respect for, oral transmission of knowledge, and much space has been granted for oral (and public) disputation.

45. To paraphrase Taylor 2002.

References

Agrawāla, Purūṣhottama. 2009. *Akatha kahānī prema kī: Kabīra kī kavitā aura unakā samaya.* Naī Dillī: Rājakamala Prakāśana.

Arnason, Johann P. 2003. *Civilizations in Dispute. Historical Questions and Theoretical Traditions.* Leiden: Brill.

———. 2005. "The Axial Age and its Interpreters. Reopening a Debate." In *Axial Civilizations in World History*, edited by Johann P. Arnason, Shmuel N. Eisenstadt, and Björn Wittrock, 19–49. Leiden: Brill.

Casanova, José. 2003. "Beyond European and American Exceptionalisms: Towards a Global Perspective." In *Predicting Religion. Christian,*

Secular, and Alternative Futures, edited by Grace Davie, Paul Heelas, and Linda Woodhead, 17–29. Aldershot (Hampshire): Ashgate.

Castoriadis, Cornelius. 1987. *The Imaginary Institution of Society*. Cambridge: Polity.

Chakravarty, Uma. 1989. "The World of the Bhaktin in South Indian Traditions: The Body and Beyond." *Manushi* no. 50–52: 18–29.

Champakalakshmi, R. 2011. *Religion, Tradition, and Ideology. Pre-colonial South India*. New Delhi: Oxford University Press.

Cort, John. 2002. "Bhakti in the Early Jain Tradition: Understanding Devotional Religion in South Asia." *History of Religions* 42, no. 1: 59–86.

Cutler, Norman J. 1987. *Songs of Experience. The Poetics of Tamil Devotion*. Bloomington: Indiana University Press.

Dumont, Louis. 1975. "On the Comparative Understanding of Non-Modern Civilizations." *Daedalus* 104: 153–72.

———. 1980. "World Renunciation in Indian Religions." In *Homo Hierarchicus. The Caste System and Its Implications*, 267–86, 425–39. Chicago and London: University of Chicago Press.

Durkheim, Émile, and Marcel Mauss. 1971. "Note on the Notion of Civilization." Translated and introduced by Benjamin Nelson. *Social Research* 38, no. 4: 808–13.

Eck, Diana L. 2012. *India: A Sacred Geography*. New York: Harmony.

Eisenstadt, Shmuel N. 1984. "Dissent, Heterodoxy, and Civilizational Dynamics: Some Analytical and Comparative Indications." In *Orthodoxy, Heterodoxy, and Dissent in India*, edited by Shmuel N. Eisenstadt, Reuven Kahane, and David Shulman, 1–9. Berlin: Mouton.

———. 1998. *Die Antinomien der Moderne. Die jakobinischen Grundzüge der Moderne und des Fundamentalismus. Heterodoxien, Utopismus und Jakobinismus in der Konstitution fundamentalistischer Bewegungen*. Frankfurt (Main): Suhrkamp.

———. 1999. *Fundamentalism, Sectarianism, and Revolution. The Jacobin Dimension of Modernity*. Cambridge: Cambridge University Press.

———. 2003. *Comparative Civilizations and Multiple Modernities*. 2 vols. Leiden: Brill.

Fuchs, Martin. 1988. *Theorie und Verfremdung. Max Weber, Louis Dumont und die Analyse der indischen Gesellschaft*. Frankfurt/Main: Peter Lang.

———. 1999. *Kampf um Differenz. Repräsentation, Subjektivität und soziale Bewegungen—Das Beispiel Indien*. Frankfurt am Main: Suhrkamp.

———. 2012. "Indian Counter-Imaginaries: Struggles for Social Recognition and the Conundrum of Shared Universals." Paper presented at the conference "Moral Imaginaries—Emerging Normative Regimes in India, China and the West," University of Bergen (manuscript).

———. 2015. "Processes of Religious Individualization: Stocktaking and Issues for the Future." *Religion* 45, no. 1, forthcoming.

———, and Jörg Rüpke, eds. 2015. "Religious Individualization." Special issue of *Religion*, 45, no. 1, forthcoming.

Fuller, Chris J. 1992. *The Camphor Flame. Popular Hinduism and Society in India*. New Delhi: Viking.

Goodman, Nelson. 1978. *Ways of Worldmaking*. Hassocks (Sussex): Harvester.

Hardy, Friedhelm. 1983. *Viraha-bhakti. The Early History of Krsna Devotion in South India*. Delhi: Oxford University Press.

———. 1991. "TirupPāṇ-Ālvār, The Untouchable Who Rode Piggy-Back on the Brahmin." In *Devotion Divine. Bhakti Traditions from the Regions of India*, edited by Diana L. Eck and Fançoise Mallison, 129–54. Groningen / Paris: Egbert Forsten / Ècole Française d'Extrême-Orient.

Hawley, John Stratton. 1995. "The Nirguṇ/Saguṇ Distinction in Early Manuscript Anthologies of Hindu Devotion." In *Bhakti Religion in North India. Community Identity and Political Action*, edited by David Lorenzen, 160–81. New Delhi: Manohar.

———. 2005. *Three Bhakti Voices. Mirabai, Surdas, and Kabir in Their Time and Ours*. New Delhi: Oxford University Press.

———. 2009. *The Bhakti Movement—From Where? Since When?* Occasional Publication 10, New Delhi: India International Centre.

———. 2015. *A Storm of Songs. India and the Idea of the Bhakti Movement*. Cambridge: Harvard University Press.

Hess, Linda. 1983. "Introduction." In *The Bījak of Kabir*, edited by Linda Hess and Shukdev Singh (translators), 3–37. Delhi: Motilal Banarsidass.

Honneth, Axel. 1996. *The Struggle for Recognition: The Moral Grammar of Social Conflicts*. Cambridge: Polity.

Joas, Hans, and Jörg Rüpke, eds. 2013. Bericht über die erste Förderperiode der Kolleg-Forschergruppe 'Religiöse Individualisierung in historischer Perspektive' (2008–12), Erfurt: Max-Weber-Kolleg der Universität Erfurt.

Knöbl, Wolfgang. 2007. *Die Kontingenz der Moderne. Wege in Europa, Asien und Amerika.* Frankfurt (Main): Campus.

———. 2011. "Contingency and Modernity in the Thought of J. P. Arnason." *European Journal of Social Theory* 14, no.1: 9–22.

Manushi. 1989. "*Women Bhakta Poets.*" Special issue of *Manushi* no. 50–52.

Nicholson, Andrew J. 2011. *Unifying Hinduism. Philosophy and Identity in Indian Intellectual History.* Ranikhet: Permanent Black.

Novetzke, Christian Lee. 2007. "Bhakti and Its Public." *International Journal of Hindu Studies* 11, no. 3: 255–72.

Novetzke, Christian Lee. 2008. *Religion and Public Memory. A Cultural History of Saint Namdev in India.* New York: Columbia University Press.

Omvedt, Gail, and Bharat Patankar. 2012. *The Songs of Tukoba.* New Delhi: Manohar.

Parry, Jonathan. 1985. "The Brahmanical Tradition and the Technology of the Intellect." In *Reason and Morality*, edited by Joanna Overing, 200–24. London: Tavistock.

Pechilis, Karen. 2012. *Interpreting Devotion. The Poetry and Legacy of a Female Bhakti Saint of India.* London: Routledge.

Pollock, Sheldon. 2000. "Cosmopolitan and Vernacular in History." *Public Culture* 12, no. 3: 591–625.

———. 2005. "Axialism and Empire." In *Axial Civilizations and World History*, edited by Johann P. Arnason, S. N. Eisenstadt. and Björn Wittrock, 397–450. Leiden: Brill.

Prentiss, Karen Pechilis. 1999. *The Embodiment of Bhakti.* New York: Oxford University Press.

Sharma, Krishna. 1987. *Bhakti and the Bhakti Movement. A New Perspective. A Study in the History of Ideas.* New Delhi: Munshiram Manoharlal.

Taylor, Charles. 2002. "Modern Social Imaginaries." *Public Culture* 14, no. 1: 91–124.

Tharu, Susie, and K. Lalita, eds. 1993. *Women Writing in India 600 B.C. to the Present, Vol. I: 600 B.C. to the Early Twentieth Century.* Delhi: Oxford University Press.

Tilly, Charles. 1997. "Means and Ends of Comparison in Macrosociology." In *Methodological Issues in Comparative Social Science. Comparative Social Research* 16, edited by Lars Mjøset, 43–53. Greenwich, CT: JAI Press.

Vaudeville, Charlotte. 1974. *Kabir.* Vol. 1. Oxford: Clarendon Press.

Wakankar, Milind. 2010. *Subalternity and Religion. The Prehistory of Dalit Empowerment in South Asia,* Abingdon: Routledge.

Weber, Max. 1958. *The Religion of India. The Sociology of Hinduism and Buddhism.* Translated and edited by Hans H. Gerth and Don Martindale. Glencoe, IL: Free Press.

———. 1978 [1921]. *Gesammelte Aufsätze zur Religionssoziologie, Bd. 2. Hinduismus und Buddhismus.* Tübingen: Mohr.

Zelliot, Eleanor, and Rohini Mokashi-Punekar, eds. 2005. *Untouchable Saints. An Indian Phenomenon.* New Delhi: Manohar.

7

THE INDIANIZATION AND LOCALIZATION OF TEXTUAL IMAGINARIES

Theravada Buddhist Statecraft in Mainland Southeast Asia and Laos in the Context of Civilizational Analysis

Patrice Ladwig

Introduction

Many of the diverging views of large-scale civilizational analysis and historical sociology, on the one hand, and anthropological microanalysis on the other hand, are based on different approaches and perspectives regarding time frames and units of spatial analysis. While for Arnason "civilizations appear as emergent overall patterns . . . which shape the texture of social life and the course of historical events on a large scale and over a long span of time" (2003, 59–60), it seems that for many anthropologists this approach can lead to a level of "generalization" that erases the significance of the particular. By pointing to local ethnography and specific histories, the implicit argument of many anthropologists is that larger patterns are hardly visible at all. Chris Hann (2012, 114) remarked that "Arnason's synthetic, meta-theoretical panorama of civilizational analysis is liable to leave anthropologists gasping for breath and wondering how they might possibly operationalize the concept." I understand this as a problem of *scaling*. Here, the different levels of analysis—the panoramic *longue dureé* bird's-eye view of historical sociology and anthropology's local microperspective—seem

155

hard to fuse. Many proponents of anthropology seem to be unhappy with the grand perspective advanced by civilizational analysis, and demand to switch to another level of analysis, focusing on a smaller scale and processes of localization.[1]

The problem of scaling and switching between different levels of analysis also arises in relation to specific concepts and notions that are employed in the research process. Although it figures in few other approaches in historical sociology and civilizational analysis, the notion of the imaginary has had a crucial influence on Arnason's conceptualization of civilization (Arnason 1989; Adams 2011). This notion (and its French forerunner *imaginaire*) has recently gained wider popularity in the social sciences thanks to the works of Benedict Anderson (1983), Charles Taylor (2002), and others (Strauss 2006, see also Fuchs's discussion of the notion in, this volume).[2] However, these works seldom refer to the most sophisticated deployment of this concept, by Cornelius Castoriadis (2005; 1997). The aversion to Castoriadis's work might be linked to its philosophical and classicist orientation, but it could also come from the emphasis he places on large-scale formations, which makes it a difficult concept for anthropologists to operationalize (Strauss 2006, 324).

This essay explores localization and vernacularization as processes of scaling down larger civilizational patterns that in previous research have often been linked to debates on the "Indianization" of cultures outside of India. The implications of these processes are connected to the notion of the imaginary by examining the development of the textual basis of the Theravada Buddhist political thought in mainland Southeast Asia between the fifteenth and nineteenth centuries.[3] This extended time frame and the large regional perspective, will oblige me to be "drastically schematic and shamelessly reductive," as Sheldon Pollock (2000, 595) has put it in his writing on Sanskrit as a cosmopolitan language.[4] By referring to larger models of political organization and Buddhist kingship that have been described as *mandalas* or galactic polities, I want to shift my level of analysis to a smaller scale and explore how these larger notions of statecraft enter local life-worlds through the transformation of texts. With reference to Steven Collins's (1998) definitions of the Pali *imaginaire,* and a brief excursion into Castoriadis's and Arnason's explications of the imaginary, this chapter specifically focuses on how imaginaries become localized and vernacularized in the premodern Tai kingdoms of Laos and Northern Thailand.[5] The emphasis will be on the textual production and articulations of imaginaries as exemplified in Indian and Buddhist texts linked to statecraft, law, and kingship. Although we typically know little about the transmission of these texts, their history, or practical application, premodern ways of composing these texts show how Theravada Buddhist political imaginaries become part of local ideas of kingship, politics, and law. For readers not acquainted with discussions on Indianization and the transmission processes that brought Buddhism and Brahmanism to Southeast Asia, I start with a rather lengthy overview of this topic. I then argue (on a somewhat speculative level) that the way scribes and monks composed works on law and kingship in vernacular languages is a form of praxis that connects larger civilizational imaginaries to more localized ones. I exemplify this with reference to Southeast Asian Theravada Buddhist manuscript culture, which is based on techniques of textual bricolage and improvisation (McDaniel 2008) that radically alter Indian and Buddhist conceptions on the local level, but nevertheless take up certain motifs that reflect larger civilizational imaginaries. The process of localizing larger civilizational imaginaries does not lead us to a "true to scale" replication on a lower level, but to innovative reworkings that echo Castoriadis's and Arnason's understandings of the imaginary as an articulation of creativity and innovation.

Theravada Buddhist Political Imaginaries

What Georges Coedès (1968) has labeled the "Indianized states of Southeast Asia" comprises a complex, imperfectly understood flow and transformation of elements of Brahmanism, Hinduism, and Buddhism to mainland and insular Southeast Asia. As Arnason (1997, 108) remarks, the process of Indianization has not been discussed extensively by civilizational theorists, but nevertheless "may be seen as one of the most representative accounts of intercivilizational encounters." Initial contact between Southeast Asia and India began around 300 BCE. The slow spread of Buddhism as a world religion in the region contributed to the historical complexity of the developing contacts. Peter Skilling (2009, 47) mentions that among the "unmapped territories . . . the blanks in the historical geography of Buddhism. One of the biggest blanks is Southeast Asia." We also know very little about the transfer of Buddhism in the region which today is called Laos, as "the conditions surrounding this penetration remain very imprecise, due to the long duration of this process" (Lorrillard 2006, 144).

Buddhism, as an urban religion, primarily traveled with Indian merchants, and thereby transmitted ideas as well as commodities to the various regions of South and Southeast Asia (Neelis 2010). This fueled a process of political centralization. It also brought script, a class of religious professionals, and new systems of supra-local training and instruction. But such transmission narratives oversimplify a complex process and reflect hegemonic ways of writing the history of mainland Southeast Asia that overlook the significance of numerous ethnic minorities that were not, or only partially, Buddhicized (Ladwig 2016; 2017: 277f.).[6]

Focusing only on the lowlands of mainland Southeast Asia, another crucial process was the adoption of Pali and Sanskrit as languages. Buddhism, its literary works, and its technical-ritual treatises connected people to larger (today one would say transnational) cultural and political entities, and also contributed to the rise of a rich vernacular literature. This migration of peoples, ideas, and concepts created continuous translocal patterns and interactions, which are still visible today and continue to exercise their influence. However, Juliana Schober and Steven Collins (2012, 159) rightly ask: "What is (or is imagined to be) trans-local in Theravada civilization?" They refer to examples that involve the travels and establishment of images, relics, texts, and monastic initiation traditions. There is abundant evidence for an interaction of Northern Thai and Sri Lankan Buddhism (Frankfurter 1907). For example, the Pali *Jinakālamālīpakaraṇa* (also *Jinakalamani*; *The Sheaf of Garlands of the Epochs of the Conqueror*), a chronicle written in Chiang Mai around 1520, describes in detail the Buddhist exchanges between Sri Lanka and Southeast Asia.[7] In narratives and popular belief, important palladia of Laos such as the Phabang statue are still today linked to Sri Lanka, which is imagined as the heartland of Theravada Buddhism.[8] Indeed, there is an abundance of stories that refer to the travels and origins of relics, statues, texts, and monks between Sri Lanka and Southeast Asia. This portable imaginary Buddhicized the landscape and its inhabitants, making Hindu-Buddhist cosmology universally transplantable.[9]

The circulation of texts and the introduction of monastic manuscript culture are the main evidence for what could be labeled a "Pali cosmopolis" (cf. Pollock 2006, 12) in the sense of a transregional social and political imagination.[10] Most chronicles report that with the introduction of Buddhism to Burma, Laos, Thailand, and Cambodia, the Pali Buddhist canon (*tipitaka*) was brought by monks, kings, and scribes. The *Jinakalamani* chronicle from Chiang Mai from 1527 states that the King of

Lan Na has sent a sixty-volume *tipitaka* to Luang Prabang in northern Laos together with knowledgeable monks (Lorrillard 2009, 42). Although this has to be understood as more symbolic than real (the canon did not come as a finalized package),[11] Pali thereby became the transregional language of a religious and political elite:

> Pali was a sign of trans-locality in both space and time.... [T]exts in Pali had ipso facto trans-local and trans-temporal reference, linking the here-and-now spatially to the broader world of Buddhism as a contemporary whole, and temporally to the past Gotama Buddha... and on a deeper and further temporal horizon of past and future Buddhas. (Collins 1998, 53)

Despite the important differences between Sanskrit and Pali as metalanguages that connected huge areas and empires,[12] Collins asserts that "when there is in this part of the premodern world an isomorphism between a single language and a unitary ideology... it is Pali and Theravada Buddhism." The writing of history was modeled on the Sri Lanka chronicle tradition (*vaṃsa*), and extended as visible in its Thai and Lao versions.[13] As in South Asia (Pollock 2006, 15; see also Gellner and Fuchs, this volume), rulers, lords, and kings supported an ideological link between language and politics; at their courts they sponsored monks, writers, and astrologers who composed works in Pali, Sanskrit, and vernacular languages. The fact that the education of Southeast Asian kings (even today) often entailed temporary ordination as a monk, and at least some very basic learning of Sanskrit or Pali, shows the continuing relevance of language for the display and enactment of power. Moreover, the presence of Brahmins at the courts of larger Tai imperial formations such as Sukhothai (1238–1438) or Ayuthaya (1351–1767) also attests to their role as advisors, ritual experts, and poets who composed and extrapolated technical manuals (*śāstra*) dealing with statecraft and political economy (Andaya 1978, 13).

In his reading of Theravada Buddhism as a civilization, Collins refers to what he calls the Pali imaginaire. Taking his inspiration from Jacques Le Goff, he proposes that the imaginaire is "a non-material, imaginative world constituted by texts, especially works of art and literature" (Collins 1998, 73) as opposed to the material-historical world.[14] In this more philological approach to civilization, "the Pali imaginaire is a mental universe created by and within Pali texts, which remained remarkably stable in content throughout the traditional period, but which moved, as a developing whole, through various times and places within the premodern material-historical world" (Collins 1998, 41). Most important for my endeavor here is Collins's reference to politics, in which "the Pali imaginaire, was, among other things, a shared belief and symbol-system among elites ruling trans-local political formations, paradigmatically in a *mandala* of client-kings around a central monarch, which naturalized the hierarchy of tribute-givers and tribute-takers" (Collins 1998, 566). Since in the processes of localization and vernacularization non-Pali inspirations also became crucial, I shall argue that this consciously limited notion of the imaginary is somewhat insufficient for the discussions presented in this paper.[15]

What was at the basis of this textual continuity, and how did these relate to other features of the historical-material world outside of texts? Taking a very general perspective, Buddhism introduced a new relationship of politics and religion through its ideology of Buddhist kingship and the intertwinement of monastic order (*saṅgha*), state, and the population:

> This interdependence has assumed the form of reciprocal and interlocking relationships within the state: that is, the king, the sangha and the people. The state, represented by the ruler, upholds Buddhism by providing support and protection for the sangha, in effect acts as a law enforcement officer with regard to the monastic code of discipline, the vinaya. The sangha, in co-operation with the ruler and sometimes advising him, provides a symbol of morality, integrity and legitimacy for the state. In their relationship with the people, sangha members act as teachers, religious guides, and mentors, and provide the model of moral conduct which the people regard as an ideal to be striven for. (Suksamran 1993, 103)

I have argued elsewhere (Ladwig 2013) that monks constituted a kind of intelligentsia, or, when speaking of rural Buddhism in Laos, can be seen as "peasant intellectuals." Eisenstadt (1973) and Arnason, in their versions of civilizational analysis, both build on Weber with regard to these "intellectuals of a new type" (Arnason 2003, 165) who emerged with the rise of civilizations and during the axial age. I do not find the notion of the axial age very useful for the case I describe in this chapter.[16] I largely agree, however, with Arnason's point that these "thinkers without a clear-cut religious identity ... made their most decisive mark in alliance with rulers in search of new legitimizing sources to match their evolving strategies" (2003, 165). This alliance is well documented for Theravada Southeast Asia, where local leaders from early on saw the usefulness of associating themselves with asceticism in order to draw on its powers. The association of the monk as an ascetic with rulers has been a constant feature of the overlap of the religious order (*sāsanacakra*) and the secular order (*ānācakra*) in Theravada Southeast Asia. Ferguson speaks of the "fascination" of Burmese rulers with severe ascetics (Ferguson 1978, 66).

However, this association, for example for the case of northern Thailand, took on a variety of forms including cooption, adaptation, and resistance.[17] Monks were not only part of the strategies of ruling elites; they also had active roles in politics, as shown for the case of northern Laos in the eighteenth century.[18] This strong association of the religious and the political fields contributed significantly to the development of larger principalities or "states." Monasteries became important institutions that enabled local rulers to boost their forms of representation, but also exercise a higher degree of control over the population through what could be understood as premodern forms of Buddhist governmentality[19] Tambiah neatly sums up this development of Buddhism into a world religion:

> It is precisely the development and far-flung situating of monastic communities—in cities, towns, and along overland trade routes, combined with the "corporate" living of the monks in small-scale communities which enables them to constitute "fields of merit" for donors ranging from royal courts, merchant guilds, trading caravans, and peasant communities that enabled early Buddhism to successfully missionize and develop into a "world religion." (Tambiah 1986, 466)

The works of Anthony Reid (1990) and Victor Liebermann (2003) place these developments in mainland Southeast Asia in a *longue dureé* perspective. They see Theravada Buddhism in the forms in which it spread from the fourteenth century onward as one major force that fueled political centralization and state formation. Lieberman (2003, 58), however, also points to the fact that this was a hesitant, fragmentary, and slow process, which only contributed incrementally to a significant cultural integration though Buddhism in mainland Southeast Asia.

The rise of new forms of knowledge transmission through script and the connection to new ideologies of rule and power were crucial elements. How these ideas flowed and what impact they had on real political practice is often nebulous, but on a very general level one can attest that in comparison to Hinduism, Theravada Buddhism reordered the link between the political and the religious fields. Buddhism, through its rejection of the caste system, developed a new relationship between politics and religion. In Southeast Asia, we witness, according to Arnason (1997, 110–11), a "de-differentiation of the Indian model" and that the "framework that in India served to maintain some distance between the two spheres was correspondingly less developed." From the perspective of civilizational analysis, Eisenstadt (2003, 324) attests that "Theravada Buddhism had a much more positive orientation towards the political arena than Hinduism did. Political activity was not seen just as secondary to ritual and religious activity; it was defined as a reflection or representation of basic cosmic conception".[20] This positive orientation is grounded in the constitutive narratives of Buddhist kingship contained in the Pali imaginaire: The ideological blueprint for Buddhist statecraft and its basic cosmic conceptions is the Mauryan King Aśoka, who ruled over large parts of India around 250 BCE. Aśoka is said to have fervently promoted Buddhism, and in this model of statecraft the ruler was considered a wheel-turning king and universal monarch (Pali: *cakkavattin*) standing at the apex of social organization. He grants the monastic order protection and supports it, while the *saṅgha* spreads the *dhamma*, which gives the leader legitimacy for his rule and can also have significant political influence. Strong's remark that "throughout Buddhist Asia, the figure of Asoka has played a major role in concretizing conceptions of kingship and general attitudes towards rulers and government" (1983, 39) is also valid for the kingdoms that developed in mainland Southeast Asia. The *Aśokāvadāna* (*The Legend of Aśoka*) is referred to in numerous Lao and Thai chronicles associated with Buddhist relics, temples and statues, and lineages of rulers. In the Pali imaginaire, mainly two narratives have served as enduring references to this conception of kingship. Both in the story of King Mahasammata described in the Buddhist *Story of Creation* (*Aggañña Sutta*) and in the *Cakkavatti Sīhanāda-Sutta*, the world slips from the condition of social harmony and equal distribution of property into increasing chaos and lawlessness.[21] Kingship evolves as a social contract—the righteous rule of a king can ensure stability, prosperity, and the spreading of the Buddhist *dhamma*. Although allusions to these narratives and Aśoka are found in many law texts from Southeast Asia and other works, they mainly function as foundation narratives with little concrete content regarding the workings of Theravada kingship.

On a conceptual level of this new understanding of politics and statecraft lies the idea of the *mandala* (circle; circle of states). *Mandala* is a model of political and economic organization that centers on the court of an overlord. Tambiah (1977), taking his inspiration from Wolters (1992, 126f.), understands *mandala* as a "galactic polity." A *mandala* model of sociopolitical organization as described in the first Indian political manual, the *Arthaśāstra*,[22] stipulates that these polities do not have fixed boundaries and a fluid territory, but its rulers tries to attract other, smaller dependencies and extract revenue from them. There have been extensive discussions about the validity and applicability of the *mandala* model in Southeast Asia (see Reynolds 1995). Whereas in the early discussions about Indianization it was assumed that Buddhist kingship and the *mandala* organization of the political field were almost exclusively based on the introduction of Indian models of rule, later research has emphasized the localization and indigenization of Indian influences—an important point to which I shall return.[23] This critical view of the influence of an Indian conception of statecraft is also connected to a new evaluation of the administrative and bureaucratic strength of the kingdoms of premodern Southeast Asia. Arnason (1997, 109) mentions the "tendency to exaggerate the strength of early states" and Chutintaranond (1990, 92) remarks that "in the case of Ayudhya, like in medieval South India, the terms 'centralized' or 'bureaucratized' are widely and inappropriately applied."[24] Even for the case of Aśoka's own Indian polity, some researchers seriously question the form of the Mauryan Empire as a large and organized state (cf. Chutintaranond 1990, 89). Moreover, in recent research on Aśoka according to Pollock (2005, 419), it "is even unclear whether the Mauryan emperor even had a religious plan to spread the dharma." The ideology of the *Cakkavatti* stresses a universal world ruler and a universal imperial form, but very often these remained aspirations of transregional imperial rule. Pollock (2005, 413) states that there was never any proper Buddhist empire after Aśoka and "indeed even in Southeast Asia . . . the belief system never provided the basis for transregional political unity." We deal here with very different forms of the early state in a continuum of various capacities of governance and administration.[25]

The power of some of the kingdoms of mainland Southeast Asia was limited to river basins and the lowlands, only marginally integrating the non-Buddhist populations in the hills (see also Tappe's contribution in, this volume). Assavavirulhakarn (2010, 19) remarks on the location of *mandalas*: "The areas that sustained these mandalas can be described as mainly riverine and lowland. They were situated at strategic points, mostly at nodes of intra- or extraregional trading centres, and usually located at the controlling point of a river valley that acted as a gateway to the hinterland beyond." This is certainly true for the earlier kingdoms that evolved in the area of the current Lao nation-state. Until today, Laos remains the country with the lowest population quota (about 60 percent) of Buddhists in mainland Southeast Asia. Historical research has shown that the expansion of Lao kingdoms was mainly limited to the valleys of the Mekong and other rivers, and hardly ever reached into the mountains occupied by a plethora of ethnic minorities (Scott 2009) Many modern maps depicting these polities have led to the rather distorted views that these kingdoms "covered" a homogeneous terrain.[26]

The political imaginary of kingship, the rise of monastic institutions and clerical intellectuals, a shared language expressing political and ascetic power, and the mandala organization of these polities show that for mainland Southeast Asia "civilizational formations take the shape of regional configurations" (Arnason 2001, 1916). These configurations doubtless contributed to political centralization, even if it was a hesitant and evolving process with great variation, and not necessarily a historical breakthrough of the axial age. However, despite the insistence of civilizational analysis on the "plurality of fundamental and comprehensive socio-cultural patterns, seen as sufficiently different from each other" (Arnason 2001, 1910), the features I have described so far are widely shared. Outside of the Pali imaginary, how were these concepts of kingship localized? How did this imaginary enter into local forms of political organization? Staying largely in the realm of texts, I turn now to explore how the larger imaginary of Buddhist kingship and rule enters into local and vernacular forms of social and political organization.

Localizations of Theravada Statecraft in Laos and Northern Thailand

The Indianization of mainland Southeast Asia—as a meeting of civilizations—has in earlier research been described as a unidirectional process, especially by Georges Coèdes (1968). What was largely left out was the receptiveness of certain societies to these concepts, and the subsequent transformations for making them work in specific localities. Indeed, one could also suggest that an indigenization happened. Pollock (2006, 528–37) has also discerned two phases of theorizing the Indianization/indigenization of Southeast Asia, each one giving more emphasis to either Indian or autochthonous pre-Indian elements. He doubts the usefulness of these two approaches, but also rejects hybridization, suggesting instead that we deal with a process of "transculturation" (ibid.). Although I agree with the conceptual framework, I think it might still be useful to discern certain elements according to their genealogy, and analyze how they were worked into local life-worlds.

Despite the wealth of theorizing on the ideologies of Buddhist statecraft and the Pali imaginary, Pollock remains skeptical and states that "precious little that can be identified as 'Buddhist' can be found in their actual practices of governance. . . . [I]f there is any determining religious dimension to rulership it seems to have been Brahmanical ritualism" (Pollock 2005, 415). Pollock admits in the footnote that "Buddhist inflections of political theory are found elsewhere," such as Sri Lanka and Thailand, but he insists that Brahmanistic elements are easier to identify than Buddhist ones. Other researchers also suggest (with reference to Thailand) that the picture presented above is much more complicated, and involves a multitude of actors from different religious traditions (Skilling 2008). Beyond the question of whether there was anything "Buddhist" in these conceptions of statecraft at all, or if it was the presence of Brahmins that enhanced the administrative capacity of these polities, I think that even these more complex views do not take into account further processes of localization and vernacularization. The transfer of this generalized view of Hindu-Buddhist political organization to mainland Southeast Asia has to be broken down farther. Although the Pali imaginary delivered models and narratives, Buddhist concepts of rule and statecraft were heavily localized and often far away from what in Lao and Thai chronicles (*phonsavadan)* and local histories (*tamnan*) were presented as an ideal. What in previous research on the political and social organization of the whole premodern phase has been described as *mandala* is perhaps a useful generalization, but misses out the specificity of how this particular Indian concept was localized. Stuart-Fox (1998, 15) states that the Lao and Thai administrative unit of *monthon* derives from *mandala.* To my knowledge, the term *mandala,* or *monthon,* rarely occurs in Lao sources dealing with the organization of polities, except for Lao regions that were under Siamese control for longer periods of time.

Some studies on Laos, especially by Reynolds (1969) and Archaimbault (1973), have advanced an approach that takes Lao local concepts of rule into consideration beyond general references to Buddhist statecraft. The case of Laos in general is well suited for exploring these localizations in more depth: The small kingdoms that evolved around the fifteenth century in the area that now marks the socialist nation-state of Laos represent the eastern limit of the expansion of Theravada Buddhism in mainland Southeast Asia.

Compared to the larger polities such as Ayuthaya or Sukhotai, extended *mandalas* covering a large terrain with dense networks could hardly evolve in this area. The area is mainly composed of rugged and hilly terrain which does not allow the establishment of permanent temple-centers or wet-rice cultivation. Even the first large Lao kingdom of Lan Xang probably has to be restricted to the Mekong valley.[27] A sentence ascribed to the archaeologist D. G. Hogarth in relation to India states that "the Sanskrit tongue was chilled to silence at 500 meters" (cited in Wheatley 1975, 251). This might be a crude generalization, and is certainly not true, for example, for the Tibetan regions, but with a few important exceptions it can be applied to mainland Southeast Asia and Laos.[28]

So how do we have to conceptualize these localizations of the political imaginary? Early polities in the region of Laos and northern Thailand were based on the organization of *mueang*. This system of supra-village organization dates from the pre-Indianization era and can also be found among (partially nonliterate) Tai groups that have not been Buddhicized, such as the Tai Dam and Tai Daeng in northern Laos and the highlands of Vietnam. Some of the basic features of the social and political structure of Tai groups was already established before the influx of Buddhism, (Raendchen and Raendchen 1998) and was regulated by a code that is still known as *hit khong* (traditions and rules). These rules were applied to a variety of fields including irrigation, kinship, and property. Important is here that villages (*baan*) were subordinated to larger political units or principalities (*muang*). Condominas (1990) has called this the hierarchically ordered "system of emboxment" of Tai political organization. Richard O'Connor (1990) and Christian Taillard (1977) also refer to *muang* as principality or statelet. Askew summarizes these views:

> The muang was a system of relationships between superior and subordinate rulers, extending from village (ban) level through minor rulers to more powerful chiefs. The muang itself was thus a socio-spatial system of relationships between its component elements. Notably, muang is an entirely indigenous Tai word, used by the various subgroups of this large ethnolinguistic family. . . . It refers to local collectives of villages (ban) or to more transcendent entities, such as principalities or large states (sometimes referred to as ban muang). (Askew 2009, 207)

Some glimpses of the pre-Buddhist political organization of *ban-muang* can be seen in a category of manuscripts subsumed under *hitsipsong khong sipsi* (twelve rites and fourteen rules). Here, the organization of the *muang* is classified according to metaphors of the body or a house: a diplomat is the ear of the *muang* (*hu mueang*); the head of ritual affairs is the heart of the *mueang* (*cai mueang*). One finds little Sanskrit vocabulary in some of these documents; an exception is the term for the position responsible for economic affairs which is called the *sati muang* (the consciousness of the *muang*). The term *mandala* is not mentioned at all. This pre-Buddhist stratification has led Condominas to examine the process of Tai-ization without Buddhism (cf. Evans 2000, 267).[29] O'Connor (1983) argues that *muang* is a specific form of early Tai social organization and urbanism based on the values of community and hierarchy. Community refers to locality-specific reciprocal relations between leaders and followers that were embedded in a language that emphasized kinship ties and mutual obligations. Hierarchy refers to the social ranking and symbolic precedence, which was also embodied in the *muang*.

Although Grabowsky (2004, 4–14) differentiates between *muang* and *mandala* according to their different cultural backgrounds, most research does not make take such trouble. Stuart-Fox (1998), for example, in his history of the first Lao Buddhist kingdom seems to treat *mandala* and *muang* as interchangeable. Probably the idea "that there was an indigenous pattern into which these newcomers were integrated" (Hall 1976, 3) in the process of Indianization and indigenization has to be taken seriously. Due to their interpenetration, these concepts of rule now seem to overlap, both referencing loosely structured and fluctuating polities, dependency, and decreasing power of the center at the margins. But some features of the *hit khong* code are obviously not imported from Buddhist statecraft or the Pali imaginary. Interestingly, even the researchers who insist on the indigenization aspect of Indianization, mostly refer to *mandala* and other "Indian" elements of statecraft.

However, what in my opinion can be ascertained is that Pali political imaginaries such as those of the *cakkavattin* and *mandala* were embedded and transformed, allowing for the enhancement of local ideologies of leadership and the creation of larger social spaces. Local leaders, as men of prowess, were already installed before the reception of Buddhism, and Tai societies already had a hierarchically ordered system of social organization. Wolters (1992, 10) mentions that Indianization "brought ancient and persistent indigenous beliefs into sharper focus." Jana Raendchen comments on the meeting of this indigenous Tai social organization and Buddhism:

With their ban-muang system the Lao, like almost all Tai, had developed a special "technology of state building" with great continuity in administration and external relations that could explain the sudden increase in power when additionally having taken over Indian concepts of the centralized state during the 13th/14th century. (Raendchen 2004, 417)

The Indic-derived values further assigned honor and precedence to rulers and thereby supplemented an already stratified political organization. Buddhism and Hinduism lend crucial support to the symbolic self-representation of the *muang* and its leaders. The early Lao kingdoms display the first clear signs of the Buddhicization of royal power around the middle of the fourteenth century when kings were labeled *cakkavatti*.[30] With the idea of rule linked to the *cakkavattin,* the Tai polities of mainland Southeast Asia's polities began to adopt prefix and suffix terms derived from Sanskrit and Pali that denote centralization and urbanity, including *phura, nágara* (Thai and Lao: *nakhon*), or *buli* (Thai: *buri*) "which accord civilized status to such centers" (Askew 2009, 209).

Although titles of local leaders and the naming of cities show an Indian influence, these localized and pre-Buddhist forms of social organization of Lao and Tai polities only partially drew on the Pali imaginary of Buddhist kingship. I think it is here crucial to take Durkheim and Mauss seriously by reflecting on "the transformation of civilization by the borrowing of elements, by migrations, by mixtures of the peoples bearing these elements, or by autonomous activity on the part of these peoples" (2006, 59). Besides drawing on pre-Buddhist Tai sources of political organization as shown by the *ban-muang* system, concepts of political rule also drew on sources outside the Pali imaginary.

Knowledge and manuscripts did not travel in "package form" when coming with Buddhist monks and Brahmins. How these ideas flowed and what impact they had on real political practice is still somewhat nebulous, but a look at technical manuals (*śāstra*) that traveled with Buddhism and Brahmanism might at least give a clue about what was depicted as an ideal state reigned by a Buddhist king. Most importantly, the method of translating and composing these works gives important hints about how the political imaginary was localized through vernacularization, defined by Pollock as "as the historical process of choosing to create a written literature, along with its complement, a political discourse, in local languages according to models supplied by a superordinate, usually cosmopolitan, literary culture" (Pollock 2006, 23).[31] Significantly, it does not seem to be Pali imaginary that gave these rulers the new administrative vocabulary and concepts for organizing these kingdoms, but Brahmanism. Robert Lingat (1989, 152), looking at the organization of Buddhist kingdoms in Sri Lanka, mentions that Buddhist rulers and their employees at the court did not look into the Buddhist canon regarding questions of political organization, but at an independent literature, namely, that of Sanskrit works such as the *dharmaśāstra* or *arthaśāstra* that explicitly dealt with these issues. According to Bronkhorst (2011, 61) the "reason in this case is not the need for legitimation, but the absence of a workable alternative." Buddhism's vision of the political sphere already provided legitimacy via its notions of kingship, but its canonical scriptures contained little of what was of *direct practical use* for organizing bureaucracies. It was not only at the Hindu courts of the Khmer Empire where Brahmins functioned as ministers and counselors alongside Buddhist monks. Although Theravada Buddhism was already well established at the courts, Brahmins and the study of Sanskrit remained crucial for certain sciences such as medicine or astrology (Bechert 2005, 35; Quatrich-Wales 1931, 54f.). So the Pali imaginary and local concepts deriving from the *ban-muang* system were further supplemented with Sanskrit concepts.

Although Tambiah (1976, 32) states that the Buddhist tradition of kingship rejects "that brand of arthasastric thought that recommends the objective of maximum advantage to the ruler and his polity," it seems that the *arthaśāstra* (treatise in statecraft, economics, rule), the *nītiśāstra* (general maxims on right conduct), and the *dharmaśāstra* (general legal-religious duties) delivered for the most part the new concepts and vocabulary for administration and politics.[32] Finot (1917, 137) states that *śāstra*—denoting a technical manual or knowledge in a defined area—is a rather rare category of manuscript in Laos. We do not find full versions of Kautilya's *arthaśāstra*—the first Indian treatise on statecraft, economy, and military strategy—in mainland Southeast Asia. Some of its elements traveled with Buddhist kingship to Southeast Asia and were vernacularized. The Lao *nītiśāstra,* for example, is a collection of verses that explicate good ethical conduct in all areas of life, but also give directions for the political conduct of the king (Viravong 1962). The Lao version lists several persons necessary for the good management of the state (the king, the rich man, the wise man, lords of water, and the healer) and the ethical qualities a king should have (e.g., generosity, mercy) (Raendchen 2004, 411). These are also to be found in the ten *pāramī* (perfections) of the king. The *thammasat luang* (the great law) depicts the tenfold royal code by which a king should govern, and thereby ethicizes statecraft. In a section labeled "laws of the civil hierarchy," the Thai *thammasat*—very similar in form and content to the Lao one mentioned above—also contains sections on the king, bureaucracy, administration, and on the mechanisms through which smaller tribute-paying principalities were supposed to be governed (Ishi 1986b, 159f.). This text has a "bureaucratic character" (Hooker 1986, 18). Documents such as *anachak lae thammachak* (the wheel of the king and the wheel of the dhamma) (Buasisavat 1995) and *rasasad* (the science of kings) (Buasisavat 1997) contain further guidelines for governance and sections on the norms and duties of kings.

Other law texts display a stronger influence of the Pali imaginary and do not rely on *śāstras*. Texts that draw on the *vinaya-pitaka* (the basket of discipline), which regulates life inside monastic order, also crossed the monastery walls into society. The local Lao law *khadi look khadi tam*[33] is believed to have been brought from Lanna to Luang Prabang in 1546. Here, law cases for monks are compared with those of laypeople, thereby comparing laws of the religious and the secular order. Therefore, the rules of behavior taken from the monastic *vinaya* are in less strict form also promoted as ideals for the life of laypeople. Temporary ordination of large parts of the male population, and the gradual and not absolute difference between layperson and monk, enhanced the spread of ideas and practices initially reserved for monks into society.

As became clear from the last section, concepts of kingship, politics, and administration derive from a multiplicity of sources that are at times hard to locate. Many Pali sources are informed by Sanskrit texts; *mandala* concepts are fused with pre-Buddhist notions of *ban-muang* and law texts carry names that invoke Indic origins, although their content and language has nothing to do with *dharmaśāstras*.

Improvising and Localizing the Imaginary: The Example of Text Composition

How can we imagine the impact of these works, and how were they translated and made operational in the region today covering Laos and northern Thailand? The *dharmaśāstras* and the *arthaśāstra* were composed for an Indian society marked by the caste system, and many of the rules presented there would make no sense at all in the Southeast Asian context. Huxley (1995) gives us some statistics concerning the Burmese *dharmaśāstras*, which are also valid for the Lao and Thai legal codes:

> 90% of this Sanskrit text concerns matters of caste, pollution, ritual and penance that are meaningless in a society unconcerned with caste and uninterested in pollution. Where Southeast Asian Buddhists have borrowed from the remaining 10% of the text, they more often than not adapt the material to their own ends. . . . I estimate Sanskrit influence at between 4% and 5% of the whole. (Huxley 1995, 61)

"Remixed" and transformed parts of *Śāstra* can be found throughout the region of Burma, Thailand, Laos, and Cambodia. We also have evidence that the *arthaśāstra* was used by kings in Sri Lanka (Lingat 1950) and Burma (Bechert 1970). Coming back to documents on statecraft and legal codes as depicted in the Lao *thammasat luang,* we can observe how these documents entered local life-worlds. Significant here is how writers invoke the Hindu *dharmaśāstra* as a source, but relate the origin of law to Mahasammata, the first king who brought social order as depicted in the *cakkavattin*-ideal of the Pali canon (Tambiah 1989, 116). In the *thammasat luang* one can at the same time observe a de-brahmanization, as the five Buddhist precepts are used as juridical categories or the ten royal virtues of the Buddhist kings (*pharami*) which in turn are based on the stories of the previous lives of the Buddha (*jātaka*) (Ishi 1986b, 199).

In addition to the double reference to Hinduism and Buddhist kingship, the way the works were translated from Sanskrit and Pali into vernacular Lao and Thai is of prime significance. How were these works localized and put into vernacular languages and form? In his classical work on Southeast Asian law, Lingat (1950) portrays a process of composing these works as a system in the making. Drawing on the Burmese example (the best researched case), he shows how Mon monks in the Pagan epoch (849–1297) composed works locally in Pali that were based on the Sanskrit *dharmaśāstras*. The authors picked certain key words and concepts from these sources, translated them, and localized the teachings so they became relevant for everyday life. Hereby, the Mon jurists successfully de-brahmanized the Hindu code of Manu by adopting only very few elements and changing these "in such a way that it be palatable to the Theravada Buddhist community" (Ishi 1986b, 196).[34] So a kind of mix evolved that kept the holy reference to the Veda but also localized it (Tambiah 1989,

116). Neither in form nor content did they have much in common with the Indian *dharmaśāstras,* although their name and mythic reference always goes back to them as a "source." This might be just the opposite of the process for which David Wengrow (2010, 19ff.) has used the term *camouflage borrowing.* This describes the exchange between civilizations, in which apparently "foreign" influences are presented as "indigenous" elements. In linguistics this is referred to as phono-semantic matching (Zuckermann 2003): a foreign word is matched with a phonetically and semantically similar native word. In the case of *śāstra* we seem to have it the other way around: the foreign form is kept (the title of the documents, the reference to the Veda), but the content of the borrowing has very little, if nothing to do with the Sanskrit source. This also echoes Chris Hann's point that the core of civilizations is "affected by dynamic expansion and contraction at the periphery. The whole system is in flux, though the core is *imagined* to be immutable" (2011, 2; my emphasis).

This process is also congruent with the localizations of other classical texts with origins either in Pali or Sanskrit. Two of the most important works of Lao literature are also vernacularizations of works composed originally in Sanskrit or Pali. The Indian epos *Ramayana* and its Lao version—the *Phra Lak Phra Lam*—share the basic framework of the story, but the places are now to be found along the Mekong (Sahai 1973). The same can be said for the Lao *Vessantara Jātaka*—perhaps the most important Buddhist story in mainland Southeast Asia (Ladwig 2009). They both transplant Indian geography to Laos and thereby localize Indian places in Southeast Asia by giving them names deriving from Sanskrit, but they also Indianize local places by relating local places to a metalanguage from the Sanskrit cosmopolis. The analysis of a Pali work that deals with the use of politics, the *Lokaneyyappakaranam* (treatise on the guidance of the world) reveals another mechanism of invoking sources.

> [It] combines two canonical jataka, and tales from the pannasa jataka with niti verses from non-Buddhist materials in the Sanskrit language. While the Lokaneyya borrows some of its tales from Pannasa Jataka, its contents reveal a wide knowledge of both Pali and Sanskrit texts. The term niti refers to secular wisdom, the duties of the king, his court, and the other regulations that make good government and a prosperous state possible. (Wilson 2009, 111)

We can here already see how even works composed in Pali were aggregated by their writers. In order to explore the process of localization and vernacularization further, the concrete methods of composition are instructive. These techniques have been well documented for other manuscripts. Justin McDaniel has described how the "lifting of words" (Lao: *nyok sab*) functions in the case for a variety of composition styles:

> The authors of these pedagogical texts took Pali source texts (although occasionally the source is locally produced), either physically present or in mind, and drew words and passages from the source for glossing. Sometimes these glosses were expansive, and the author comments on the grammar and secondary and tertiary meanings of terms and compares them to other known Pali terms. (McDaniel 2008, 125)

These comments, glosses, and the whole exegesis of texts shows that "Lao and Northern Thai teachers were not primarily concerned with transmitting whole canonical Pali Buddhist texts; rather, they drew on Pali terms and phrases from a wide selection of canonical and extra-canonical texts in order to teach their own idea of Buddhism" (McDaniel 2008, 212). Another practice which I have observed when monks in the current period compose modern books from older manuscripts is also relevant here. The modification of texts in Thai labeled *chamra* (cleansing or purification) not only refers to the correction of errors of a given text, but can also lead to more profound changes. Authors invent new phrases where they think a manuscript is not complete and sometimes perform a rewriting of the manuscript. Wilson notes that this method of composition is to be understood as an updating of texts because "as ideas change so does the need for cleansing . . . the process of chamra is never finished" (Wilson 1983, 4). It is also reported that kings intervened in discussions and writing processes. This may be mythical, but given the fact that some of these rulers ordained as monks and learned Pali and Sanskrit, there may be some truth to such narratives. Reporting on the Lao king Suriyavongsa (1638–1695) and his administration, the Portuguese traveler De Marini reports from the court that the king himself during his interactions with writers and administrators "corrects their faults, explains theological problems, resolves disputes, regulates rituals" (De Marini cited in Krieken-Peters 2010, 91).

This process of taking Sanskrit and Pali texts that deal with administration and law shows how vernacularization works in practice and how these texts become locally "standardized," mostly departing quite radically from their sources, but always invoking them with names derived from "ancient" Sanskrit or Pali. McDaniel states that these "lifted words, removed from their original source context, take on the adapted meaning assigned to them by the original 'lifters' and subsequent 'citers'. These lifted words, if repeated enough and incorporated into vernacular syntax slowly, become part of the vernacular vocabulary." (McDaniel 2008, 188).

I think that this reference to composition techniques provides us with an excellent example of how larger imaginaries (such as the Pali imaginary, or those provided by *śāstra* texts) become the subject of creativity for a variety of writers. By taking specific phrases or key terms, and then commenting upon these in vernacular languages, parts of the larger imaginary become selectively integrated into local life-worlds. We might now also understand why, for example, the concept of *mandala* is actually not invoked in the sources relating to administration. Some terms were lifted from *śāstra*s, while others were not or were glossed in Lao terms such as *baan-muang*. Although the idea of the *mandala* from the *arthaśāstra* is still visible in Lao sources, the vocabulary chosen to describe the administrative system also draws on pre-Buddhist localized sources that in the process of writing are remixed. How can we apply this theoretically to the idea of political imaginary and its localization and vernacularization? I think that here the notion of the imaginary as a form of cultural praxis is of prime importance. According to Suzie Adams, Castoriadis proposed a notion of the imaginary that is grounded in the "interplay of *signification* and *doing*" (Adams 2013, 29).[35] However, she also attests that the doing or practice aspect of his work did not keep pace with his development of the notion. In line with the critique aired by Strauss (2006), Adams states that in Castoriadis's theory we witness "a persistent ambiguity that vacillated between a conception of history instituted by the collective anonymous, and an image of history as the product of particular agencies" (Adams 2013, 30). Interestingly, Habermas (1985, 386) mentions in his critique of Castoriadis that the original emphasis on practice and politics cannot be "localized" any more through the lack of intersubjectivity, thereby echoing Adams's point about particular agencies.

When taking the shaping of the Theravada political imaginary in the world of texts as a production process that is subject to creative techniques of text composition and thereby giving room to the particular agencies of writers and premodern intellectuals, we arrive at a notion of the imaginary that is more open and less deterministic than that of Castoriadis. Arnason pleas for such an openness that unfolds in the interplay of "background" (horizon) and explicit articulation:

> The new interest in imaginary dimensions of meaning goes together with other ways of highlighting openness and indeterminacy. Imaginary significations constitute a background or a substratum to more structura; and definite modes of interpretation, and a varying range of such modes may emerge against a shared background. The distinction between underlying constellations and explicit articulations of meaning is crucial to the project of civilizational theory. (Arnason 2003, 205)

The shared background and underlying constellations—in my case the Pali *imaginaire,* sastric texts, and local Tai forms of social organization—thereby get articulated by local writers and scribes in vernacular languages. These writers drew on what Collins labels Pali *imaginaire,* but on other sources as well. For Castoriadis, these articulations would probably represent "the peripheral imaginary" (1997, 131) and the "successive layers and sedimentations" of symbolization: "An icon is a symbolic object of an imaginary—but is invested with another imaginary signification when the faithful scrape off the paint and drink it as a medication" (ibid.). I think that the composition strategies of Buddhist monks, Brahmins, and other scribes are similar. They took splinters or words from Pali and Sanskrit texts, and invested them with other imaginary significations that nevertheless kept their connection to the source, even if only invoked for reasons of justification. According to Pollock (2006, 6), this vernacularization was for the case of Sanskrit a conscious choice: "The creation of vernacular literature, for example, was intimately related to new conceptions of communities and places, which in turn correlated with a new kind of vernacular political order." One might also add that in the case of Southeast Asia these writers had little choice, as practical texts related to law had to be localized because they only worked in local political orders that were radically different from those in India.

Conclusion

Limiting my analysis largely to the realm of texts, in this chapter I have argued that, from the standpoint of civilizational analysis, it makes sense to speak of a common Theravada Buddhist political imaginary in mainland Southeast Asia. By connecting the figure of the king to its various enunciations in the Pali imaginary (as a *cakkavattin* ruling a *mandala*) and by linking the origins of kingship to a myth of a social contract, this imaginary indeed seems to suggest a great continuity in terms of time and patterns that is deemed characteristic for larger civilizational complexes. However, I have also argued that behind this imaginary stands a very localized version of Buddhist statecraft that textually comes into being through combining pre-Buddhist Tai-conceptions of political organization (the *ban-muang* system) and selective appropriations of Brahmanistic concepts deriving from various *śāstras*. This process of composition heavily draws on selection, improvisation, and techniques of bricolage. I have understood techniques of text composition as a way of localizing larger imaginaries and presented them essentially as forms of *praxis*; as ways of interacting with, and transforming an imaginary articulated in texts.

Coming back to my point of departure of this essay—the problem of scaling the perspectives of civilizational analysis and anthropology—I think that in textual production we find a potential point of contact. Religious intellectuals, writers, scribes, and monks consciously select and localize elements from larger imaginaries, thereby scaling the imaginary down to a local level. This selection and improvisation is not random or simply a production of hybrids, but a conscious and practical process that looks for correspondences of larger patterns provided by civilizations and features that can be operationalized in local contexts. Looking at the *production of imaginaries* might be one way of combining the creative aspect of the imaginary originally emphasized by Castoriadis and taken up by Arnason. We are not dealing with ex nihilo creations, or linear and causal writings of history. Rather, we are witnessing creative appropriations of new horizons (and ontologies) in the political realm.

Concerning the heterogeneity of forms of political organization of the premodern Buddhist polities of Theravada Southeast Asia, one could also advance a gradual distinction of form and content regarding civilizational patterns. Although all Buddhist principalities and empires of mainland Southeast Asia invoked Asoka and relevant parts of the Pali imaginary for legitimizing Buddhist kingship, the actual forms of organizing these polities were quite different. Sheldon Pollock states that "an exercise in comparative vernacularization would show us that, while the new polities brought into being across much of Eurasia as a result of the breakthrough of the classical ecumenes may look formally similar, their political and cultural contents are radically different" (Pollock 2005, 447). Here we again come back to the problem of scaling and localization: from a larger perspective, systems of Buddhist kingship may look strikingly similar with their references to Aśoka, the power of the *saṅgha,* and so on. However, when one zooms in and scales the imaginary down to specific locales, these larger patterns begin to blur quickly. But the "radical difference" postulated by Pollock becomes especially problematic when one chooses a very large scale. I think that for the case of Theravada Buddhism in the limited area of mainland Southeast Asia there are enough points of comparison to switch between larger and more localized forms of the imaginary.

Notes

1. Despite the growth of global history, *longue dureé* and large-scale history still might suffer from the current trend to focus on small-scale processes. The reactions of the majority of anthropologists to civilizational analysis could be described as following: "The almost immediate discovery of countercases . . . induce(s) a powerful resistance to generalization and large-scale interpretation" (Pollock 2006, 11).

2. Throughout this chapter I use the term *imaginary,* except when discussing the works of particular authors who have used the French version.

3. I build on the substantial work that has been done on the connections between politics and religion in the Theravada Buddhist countries of Southeast Asia (Bechert 1966; Mendelsohn 1975; Tambiah 1976; Ishi 1986a). Two recent volumes attest to the continuing relevance of the topic in modern nation-states (Harris 2008; Brac de la Perrière and Reiniche 2007). Theravada Buddhism also features in some works of civilizational analysis (Eisenstadt 2003; Tambiah 1986). Because of their assumed relative homogeneity in the religious realm, Theravada societies appear as sharing "social phenomena which are common to several societies, more or less related to each other" (Durkheim and Mauss 2006, 61) or as a "family of societies" (ibid., 62).

4. The trend in Buddhist Studies has moved away from grand models of Buddhism as civilization, putting more emphasis on localized forms of Buddhism beyond the great languages and dynasties. This applies also to the notion of Theravada Buddhism itself as an assumed "family" of Buddhism

(Skilling and Carbine 2011). The work of Steven Collins (1998), to be discussed later, is the most significant exception.

5. Tai (not Thai) is a branch of the Tai-Kadai language family. Tai speakers are found in Laos, Thailand, northern Burma (Shan), northern Vietnam, and in the southern parts of Yunnan (Sipsongpanna). Due to the comparative perspective of the essay, I sometimes refer to "Tai-polities." The majority of Tai speakers are Buddhists.

6. For alternative histories of the region see the recent work of James Scott (2009), who focuses on the uplands that, for him, represent a mirror image of the lowland. He postulates (2009, 10) that "civilization held little attraction" for these groups, and that they therefore "actively resist incorporation into the state" (ibid., 19). See also Tappe's contribution in, this volume. For a critical view of dominant ways of writing Southeast Asian and Thai history, see Craig Reynolds (2006).

7. Although Buddhism was already present in the region hundreds of years before the events described, the text gives ample evidence for the introduction of specific ordination lines from Sri Lanka. It refers to a group of thirty-nine monks from Chiang Mai, Lopburi, and lower Burma that traveled to Sri Lanka in 1423. There they learned a new script, studied, and visited important shrines such as the Buddha's tooth relic in Kandy. They were finally reordained in the Sri Lanka Mahāvihāra order (*sinhala nikāya*) in 1424. After their return to Northern Thailand, this sect (*nikāya*) was promoted by the king (Jayawickrama 1968). Chronicles and archaeological evidence suggest that through the patronage of this sect Buddhism grew extensively in Northern Thailand (Swearer and Premchit 1978, 27–28).

8. This marking of the landscape with relics and statues (and associated temples) is of prime importance for the spread of Buddhism (Schober 2004). For the Lao Phabang and another important statue called Pha Keo see Lingat (1934). There are also many popular Lao books on these statues to be found on the market in Vientiane (e.g., Vannacid 2005; Luangphasi 2006).

9. As part of the Sankrit cosmopolis, "in their own geographical imagination the imperial polities of Southeast Asia . . . made themselves part of a cosmopolitan order by wholesale appropriation of its toponomy. With Mount Meru and River Ganga locatable everywhere, there was no spatial centre from which one could be excluded; the Sanskrit cosmopolis was everywhere" (Pollock 2006, 16).

10. For further discussion of Pollock's theories in the context of South Asia see David Gellner's and Martin Fuchs's contributions to, this volume.

I thank David Gellner for some illuminating discussions concerning Pollock's rather complicated, but nevertheless novel readings of the link between language and power, and Martin Fuchs for further suggestions for thinking with and against Pollock in the context of civilizational analysis.

11. See Collins's (1990) useful conceptualization of the Pali canon.

12. Whereas Sanskrit emerged in South Asia as the "public literary expression of political will" (Pollock 1998, 11), Pali was rarely used for inscriptions. The connection between Pali and Buddhism was closer than that between Sanskrit and any religious tradition. According to Collins (1998, 74), "in the Indic model, the use of Sanskrit as the language of translocalism implied nothing about the content of the dominant ideologies—kings would normally support Sivaites, Jains, Buddhists, and others." In the Indic model, Sanskrit provided an aesthetics of power (Pollock 2005, 424) and a single medium of expression, but not necessarily a unified system of belief such as Theravada.

13. In general, chronicles in Southeast Asia model themselves on Sri Lankan ones, but are sometimes also extended. See Bechert (1979) on Buddhism's historiography and *vaṃsa*. Northern Thailand has its own *Mahāvaṃsa,* which is even longer than the Sri Lanka one (Skilling 2009, 55). See for comparison the Lao manuscript *Lam mahavangsa,* Vat Comcaeng, Savannakhet Province, National Library of Laos, PLMP Code: 13010107010_00.

14. In this sense, Collins (1998, 73) means a nonmaterial, imaginative world constituted by texts, especially works of art and literature. For him "such worlds are by definition not the same as the material world, but in so far as the material world is thought and experienced in part through them" (ibid.), they are still regarded as efficacious. Recently, he has added, "To be very brief, Pali imaginaire means any and every text written (or translated) into Pali" (Collins 2010, 4).

15. This essay does not offer the space to review Castoriadis's complex notion of the imaginary. See Adams (2013) and Castoriadis himself (1997) for further elaborations, and Arnason (2012) for the links to civilizational analysis.

16. Eisenstadt's distinction between mundane and transmundane postulates a "radical ontological difference . . . unknown to earlier modes of thought . . . constructed between a higher or more fundamental and a less authentic level of reality" (Arnason 2003, 164). This might be applicable when we construct Buddhism from specific early texts, but this would be

to ignore the whole social history of Buddhism. Novel readings of Buddhist texts such as, for example, those advanced by Schopen (2004) do not support this. See also Collins (1998, 20–23), who finds this distinction of limited use for Theravada. Moreover, I think that it is hard to speak of an axial breakthrough in the case of the spread of Theravada in Southeast Asia. These breakthroughs "often appear through a clearer lens of specialist historiography to be, not so much sudden irruptions of the new, but rather spikes on a timeline of more continuous intellectual history reaching far into the past and future" (Pollock 2005, 397).

17. Sweaerer and Premchit (1978) have convincingly shown that in northern Thailand over the course of 150 years (1360–ca. 1500) and various rulers a variety of models subsumed under "symbiosis" can be made out.

18. High-ranking monks often acted as advisors of kings and might take over in case of the death of the king. Grabowsky (2007) describes such a situation for premodern Laos, where the *mahasanghalad* (head of the *sangha*) often was consulted on political questions. Some monks temporarily took political power, and some monks in Luang Prabang also held political offices, or were at least heavily involved in local politics. This is also attested for the southern Laos Champassak Kingdom in the eighteenth century (Archaimbault 1961).

19. Kulke (1993, 292) attests for Burma that "monastic institutions . . . provided imperial kings and their courts with an additional infrastructure. . . . It allowed the imperial courts, perhaps for the first time, a permanent and in some cases even a direct access to the sphere of local matters even outside the limited nuclear area which was under their direct political control." This was perhaps not given in Laos to such a high degree as in Burma (cf. Lorrillard 2003).

20. In India, according to Louis Dumont's (1980) theory of values, the relationship of Brahmin and king was marked by a hierarchy in which worldly power and politics (*artha*) is always marked by impurity and is considered to be subordinated to the dharma of the Brahmin. Although in specific contexts this relationship can be reversed, the king is dependent on Brahmanism's ritual purity and power. Purity is a matter of status, and power cannot avoid contamination by impurity, leading to a separation and division of labor between priest and king in India (Arnason 2003, 239).

21. See Tambiah (1989) and Strong (1983, 44–49) for more details on this conception of kingship. For a translation of these parts of the Pali *imaginaire* see Collins (1991; 1998, 480–96).

22. Sanskrit *artha* denotes "motive, notion, wealth, economy or gain," and *śāstra* is a kind of manual of specific knowledge. *Arthaśāstra* has been translated as "treatise on polity" or "science of political economy." The literature on the *Arthaśāstra* is vast, but its supposed author Kautilya is often called the "first political realist" (Boesche 2003). Max Weber (1978, 220) referred to the book as "truly radical 'Machiavellianism' . . . compared to it, Machiavelli's *The Prince* is harmless." On the link of Buddhist statecraft and Aśoka see, for example, and Basham (1982). See below for the significance of *śāstra*.

23. In his earlier work, Wolters (1968, 172–77) sticks to Kautilya's idea of the *mandala* for analyzing the imperial kingdom of Ayuthaya. In his later work (Wolters 1992, 25f.), he assumes that *mandala* has its origins in the sociopolitical cultures of pre-Indianized Southeast Asia long before the emergence of developed polities and the arrival of Hindu culture. Local cults around "men of prowess" were the basic structure on which Indianization was built.

24. These polities were mainly based on personal networks which, however, collapsed with the death of the ruler. The whole system was much more dependent on the person of the king. Leach (1960, 56) summarizes this problem of succession: "Every monarch has a successor . . . but the successor must create a new state from his own personal endeavours." However, also see Gesick (1976) on the provincial administration in larger kingdoms such as Ayuthaya.

25. Kulke (1993) suggests that the process of state formation runs through three phases: the local or chieftain phase; the regional and early kingdom phase; and finally the imperial phase. The empire is based on forced unification of former independent kingdoms in which the smaller galactic polities become absorbed into larger ones. Superregional powers such as Angkor or Ayuthaya are the third level of development: "It was no longer a subordination of the former regional leaders of these annexed areas, but their complete extinction as autonomous authorities" (Kulke 1993, 276; see also Chutintaranond 1990, 91). Usually, the elites were replaced by members of the central polity.

26. For a preliminary overview for Laos see Lorrillard (2008). Lorrillard is in the course of publishing a monumental volume on all inscriptions found in Laos. In fact, if we look at the epigraphic evidence for Laos what comes to the fore is that Buddhist polities, as already mentioned, were limited to the valleys. They certainly had trade relations with the hinterland, and

at times might have received tribute, but these relations were of minimal importance to these principalities because the mountainous areas were and are still populated by groups who have only been marginally integrated.

27. The first hard evidence for the development of Buddhism in Laos and the kingdom of Lan Xang (1354–1707) are the steles dating from the second quarter of the sixteenth century. These are primarily steles marking the foundation of temples (Lorrillard 2009, 42).

28. A number of Tibeto-Burman and Mon-Khmer groups have been Buddhicized and built temples in the highlands. See, for example, Bouté (2011) for an excellent analysis regarding the Phu Neuy, a highland group in Northern Laos.

29. Condominas argues that the Tai-ization of non-Tai peoples in northern Indochina was a key element in the expansion of Tai peoples into Southeast Asia: "Where they succeeded in consolidating their power, the Tai were able to strengthen their position through a thorough policy of Tai-ization of the subjugated population" (Condominas 1990, 45).

30. The first royal inscriptions to be found in Laos were commissioned by King Photisarat and King Setthatilat. These are the first hard historical evidence in Laos. They bear a strong mark of northern Thai (Lanna) Buddhism. A first wave of Buddhism coming from North Thailand reached North Laos in the fifteenth century; a second more orthodox wave arrived in the sixteenth century. See Lorrillard (2006).

31. The following texts that draw on *śāstra*s and other sources are all written in Lao *tham* script. They contain single sentences in Pali or Sanskrit, but are overwhelmingly written in vernacular scripts and languages.

32. For a basic overview of Lao law and literature on administration see Ishi (1986b, 198f.), and for a wider regional comparison, Huxley (1996).

33. The literal translation could be "worldy cases and dhamma cases," but Ishi (1986b, 200) rightly sees this as a whole class of documents that he labels "comparison of the secular and religious order."

34. Tambiah (1989, 117) attests that two processes of composing law and documents on statecraft are present. The first process involves giving the old *dharmaśāstra*s a Buddhist validation. The second process gives an update to new customary practices and lends Buddhist doctrinal support to their becoming integrated into the law code.

35. I thank Suzie Adams for sending me the draft of the paper, which has since been published.

References

Adams, Suzi 2011. "Arnasons and Castoriadis' Unfinished Dialogue: Articulating the World." *European Journal of Social Theory* 14, no. 1: 71–88.

———. 2013. "Castoriadis and the Non-Subjective Field: Social Doing, Instituting Society and Political Imaginaries." *Critical Horizons* 13, no. 1: 29–51.

Andaya, Barbara. 1978. "Statecraft in the Reign of Lue Tai of Sukhodaya (ca. 1347–1374)." In *Religion and Legitimation of Power in Thailand, Laos and Burma*, edited by Bardwell Smith. Chambesburgh: Anima Books.

Anderson, Benedict. 1983. *Imagined Communities. Reflections on the Origin and Spread of Nationalism*. London: Verso.

Archaimbault, Charles. 1961. L'histoire de Champassak. *Journal Asiatique* 249, no. 4: 519–95.

———. 1973. *Structures religieuses lao (rites et mythes)*. Vithagna: Vientiane.

Arnason, Johann P. 1989. "Culture and Imaginary Significations." *Thesis Eleven* 22: 26–45.

———. 1997. "The Southeast Asian Labyrinth: Historical and Comparative Perspectives." *Thesis Eleven* 50: 90–122.

———. 2001. Civilizational Analysis, History of. In *International Encyclopedia of Social & Behavioral Sciences*, edited by Neil Smelser, and Paul Baltes, 1909–15. Oxford: Elsevier.

———. 2003. *Civilizations in Dispute. Historical Questions and Theoretical Traditions*. Leiden: Brill.

———. 2012. "Castoriadis as a Civilizational Analyst: Sense and Nonsense in Ancient Greece." *European Journal of Social Theory* 15, no. 3: 295–311.

Askew, Marc. 2009. "Urbanism and the Lao Culture Region. An Interpretation of the Significance of the Pre-modern Lao Urban Landscape." In *The Middle Mekong River Basin. Studies in Tai History and Culture*. Edited by Constance Wilson. DeKalb, IL: Center for Southeast Asian Studies.

Assavavirulhakarn, Prapod. 2010. *The Ascendancy of Theravada Buddhism in Southeast Asia*. Chiang Mai: Silkworm Books.

Basham, Arthur L. 1982. "Asoka and Buddhism: A Reexamination." *Journal of the International Association for Buddhist Studies* 5: 131–43.

Bechert, Heinz. 1966. *Buddhismus, Staat und Gesellschaft in den Ländern des Theravāda-Buddhismus.* (2 vol.). Frankfurt a.M.: Metzner-Verlag.

———. 1970. "Theravada Buddhist Sangha: Some General Observations on Historical and Political Factors in its Development." *Journal of Asian Studies* 29, no. 4: 761–78.

———. 1979. "The Beginnings of Buddhist Historiography: *Mahavamsa* and Political Thinking." In *Religion and the Legitimation of Power in Sri Lanka*, edited by Bardwell L. Smith. Chambersburg: Anima Books.

Bechert, Heinz. 2005. *Eine regionale hochsprachliche Tradition in Südasien: Sanskrit-Literatur bei den buddhistischen Singhalesen.* Wien: Österreichische Akademie der Wissenschaften.

Boesche, Roger. 2003. *The First Great Realist: Kautilya and his Arthashastra.* Lanham, MD: Lexington Books.

Bouté, Vanina. 2011. *En miroir du pouvoir. Les Phounoy du Nord-Laos: ethnogenèse et dynamiques d'intégration.* Paris: EFEO.

Brac de la Perrière, Bénédicte, and Marie Louise Reiniche, eds. 2007. *Les apparences du monde: Royautés hindoues et bouddhiques de l'Asie du Sud et du Sud-Est.* Paris: EFEO.

Bronkhorst, Johannes. 2011. *Buddhism in the Shadow of Brahmanism.* Leiden: Brill.

Buasisavat, Samlit. 1995. *Khamphii raasasaat. Kotmaai buhaan Lao.* Vientiane: Toyota Foundation [in Lao].

———. 1997. *Khamphii aanaachak lae thammachak haeng thammasaat. Kotmaai buhaan Lao.* Vientiane: Toyota Foundation [in Lao].

Castoriadis, Cornelius. 1997. *World in Fragments. Writings on Politics, Society, Psychoanalysis, and the Imagination.* Stanford: Stanford University Press.

———. 2005. *The Imaginary Institution of Society.* Cambridge: Polity Press.

Chutintaranond, Sunait. 1990. "Mandala, Segmentary State, and Politics of Centralization in Medieval Ayudhya." *Journal of the Siam Society* 78, no. 1: 89–100.

Coedès, George. 1968. *The Indianized States of Southeast Asia.* Honolulu: Hawai'i University Press.

Collins, Steven. 1990. "On the Very Idea of the Pali Canon." *Journal of the Pali Text Society* XV: 89–126.

———. 1991. *The Discourse on What Is Primary (Agganna Sutta): An Annotated Translation.* New Delhi: Sahitya Akademi.

———. 1998. *Nirvana and Other Buddhist Felicities. Utopias of the Pali Imaginaire.* Cambridge: Cambridge University Press.

———. 2010. *Nirvana: Concept, Imagery, Narrative.* Cambridge: Cambridge University Press.

Condominas, Georges. 1990. *From Lawa to Mon, from Saa' to Thai: Historical and Anthropological Aspects of Southeast Asian Social Spaces.* Canberra: Department of Anthropology.

Dumont, Louis. 1980. *Homo Hierarchicus. The Caste System and Its Implications.* Chicago: University of Chicago Press.

Durkheim. Emile, and Marcel Mauss. 2006. "Note on the Concept of Civilisation." In *Techniques, Technology, Civilization*, edited and introduced by Nathan Schlanger. New York/Oxford: Berghahn.

Eisenstadt, Shmuel E.. 2003. "A Short Comparative Excurse on the (Theravada) Buddhist Civilizational Format and Historical Experience." In *Comparative Civilizations and Multiple Modernities*, edited by Shmuel N. Eisenstadt. Leiden/Boston: Brill.

Evans, Grant. 2000. "Tai-Ization: Ethnic Change in Northern Indo-China." In *Civility and Savagery: Social Identity in Tai States*, edited by Andrew Turton. Richmond, Surrey: Curzon Press.

Ferguson, John. P. 1978. "The *Quest for Legitimacy* by Burmese Monks and Kings: The Case of the Shwegyin Sect (18th–19th century)." In *Religion and Legitimation of Power in Thailand, Laos and Burma*, edited by Bardwell Smith. Chambersburgh: Anima Books.

Finot, Louis. 1917. "Recherches sur la littérature laotienne." *Bulletin de l'Ecole Francaise d'Extreme-Orient* 17, no. 5: 1–219.

Frankfurter, Oskar. 1907 "Siamese Missions to Ceylon in the 18*th* Century." *Journal of the Siam Society* 4, no. 1: 23–25.

Gesick, Lorraine. 1976. "Kingship and Political Integration in Traditional Siam 1767–1824." PhD diss. Cornell University.

Grabowsky, Volker. 2004. *Bevoelkerung und Staat in Lanna. Ein Beitrag zur Bevoelkerungsgeschichte in Suedostasien.* Wiesbaden: Harrassowitz.

———. 2007. "Buddhism and Political Order in Pre–Twentieth Century Laos." In *Buddhism, Power, and Political Order in*

Theravada Buddhist Asia, edited by Ian Harris. London: Routledge/Curzon.

Habermas, Jürgen. 1985. *Der philosophische Diskurs der Moderne.* Frankfurt: Suhrkamp.

Hall, Kenneth. R. 1976. "*An Introductory Essay on Southeast Asian Statecraft in the Classical Period.*" In *Explorations in Early Southeast Asian History: The Origins of Southeast Asian Statecraft*, edited by Kenneth R. Hall, and John K. Whitmore. Ann Arbor: University of Michigan Center for South and Southeast Asian Studies.

Hann, Chris. 2011. "Back to Civilization." *Anthropology Today* 27, no. 6: 1–2.

———. 2012. "Civilizational Analysis for Beginners." *Focaal. Journal of Global and Historical Anthropology* 62, no. 1: 113–21.

Harris, Ian. ed. 2008. *Buddhism, Power and Political Order.* London: Routledge.

Hooker, M. Barry. 1986. "Introduction. The Southeast Asian Law Texts. Materials and Definitions." In *Laws of Southeast Asia. Volume 1. The Pre-modern Texts*, edited by M. B. Hooker. Singapore: Butterworth.

Huxley, Andrew. 1995. "Buddhism and Law. The View from Mandalay." *Journal of the International Association of Buddhist Studies* 18, no. 1: 47–97.

———, ed. 1996. *Thai Law, Buddhist Law: Essays on the Legal History of Thailand, Laos and Burma.* Bangkok: White Orchid Press.

Ishi, Yoneo. 1986a: *Sangha, State, and Society: Thai Buddhism in History.* Honolulu: University of Hawaii Press.

———. 1986b. "The Thai thammsat (with a note on the Lap thammasat)." In *Laws of Southeast Asia. Volume 1. The Pre-modern Texts*, edited by M. B. Hooker. Singapore: Butterworth.

Jayawickrama, N. A., trans. 1968. *The Sheaf of Garlands of the Epochs of the Conqueror, Being a Translation of the Jinakālamālipakaraṇam of* Ratanapañña Thera *of Thailand.* London: Pali Text Society.

Krieken-Peters, Juliette. 2010. "Van Wuysthoff's Journal in Perspective." In *Van Wuysthoff and the Lane Xang Kingdom. A Dutch Merchant's Visit to Laos*, edited by Juliette Krieken-Peters. Leiden: Gingko Publishers.

Kulke, Hermann. 1993. *Kings and Cults—State Formation and Legitimation in India and Southeast Asia.* Delhi: Manohar Publishers.

Ladwig, Patrice. 2009. "Narrative Ethics: The Excess of Giving and Moral Ambiguity in the Lao Vessantara-Jataka." In *The Anthropology of Moralities*, edited by Monica. Heintz. Oxford/ New York: Berghahn.

———. 2013. "Schools, Ritual Economies and the Expanding State. The Changing Roles of Lao Buddhist Monks as 'Traditional Intellectuals.'" In *Buddhism, Modernity, and the State in Asia. Forms of Engagement*, edited by P. Kitiarsa, and J. Whalen-Bridge. London: Palgrave.

———. 2016. "Religious Place Making. Civilized Modernity and the Spread of Buddhism among the Cheng, a Mon-Khmer Minority in Southern Laos." In *Religion, Place, and Modernity. Spatial Articulations in Southeast Asia and East Asia*, edited by Michael. Dickhardt and Andrea. Lauser. Leiden: Brill.

———. 2017 "Contemporary Lao Buddhism. Ruptured Histories." In *The Oxford Handbook of Contemporary Buddhism*, edited by Michael Jerryson. New York: Oxford University Press.

Leach, Edmund. 1960. "The Frontiers of Burma." *Comparative Studies in Culture and Society* 3, no. 1: 49–68.

Lieberman, Victor. 2003. *Strange Parallels: Southeast Asia in Global Context. c. 800–1830, Volume I: Integration on the Mainland.* Cambridge: Cambridge University Press.

Lingat, Robert. 1934. "Le culte du Bouddha d'émeraude." *Journal of the Siam Society* 27, no. 1: 9–38.

———. 1950. "Evolution of the Conception of Law in Burma and Siam." *Journal of the Siam Society* 38, no. 1: 13–24.

———. 1989. *Royautés bouddhiques: Asoka. La fonction royale à Ceylan.* Paris: Editions de E.H.E.S.S.

Lorrillard, Michel. 2003. "The Earliest Lao Buddhist Monasteries According to Philological and Epigraphic Sources." In *The Buddhist Monastery: A Cross-cultural Survey*, edited by Pierre Pichard, and François Lagirarde. Paris: École Française d'Extrême-Orient

———. 2006. "Lao History Revisited: Paradoxes and Problems in Current Research." *South East Asia Research* 14, no. 3: 87–10.

———. 2008. "Pour une géographie historique du bouddhisme au Laos." In *Recherches nouvelles sur le Laos,* edited by Yves Goudineau, and Michel Lorrillard. Bangkok: EFEO.

———. 2009. "Scripts and History: the Case of Laos." In *Written Cultures in Mainland Southeast Asia*, edited by Masao Kashinaga, Osaka: Senri Ethnological Studies 74.

Luangphasi, Duangsai. 2006. *tamnan phra keo moradok*. Vientiane: Mitkhanpim Publishers [in Lao].

Mabbett, Ian. 1977. "The 'Indianization' of Southeast Asia: Reflections on the Historical Sources." *Journal of Southeast Asian Studies* 8, no. 2: 143–61.

McDaniel, Justin. 2008. *Gathering Leaves and Lifting Words. Histories of Monastic Education in Laos and Thailand.* London and Seattle: University of Washington Press.

Mendelson, Michael. 1975. *Sangha and State in Burma: A Study of Monastic Sectarianism and Leadership.* Ithaca and New York: Cornell University Press.

Neelis, Jason. 2010. *Early Buddhist Transmission and Trade Networks: Mobility and Exchange within and beyond the Northwestern Borderlands of South Asia.* Leiden: Brill.

O'Connor, Richard. 1983. *A Theory of Indigenous Southeast Asian Urbanism.* Singapore: Institute for Southeast Asian Studies.

———. 1990. "Siamese Tai in Tai Context: The Impact of a Ruling Center." *Crossroads* 5, no. 1: 1–21.

Pollock, Sheldon. 2000. "Cosmopolitan and Vernacular in History." *Public Culture* 12, no. 3: 561–625.

———. 2005. "Axialism and Empire." In *Axial Civlizations and World History*, edited by Björn Wittrock, Johann P. Arnason, and Shmuel N. Eisenstadt. Leiden/Boston: Brill.

———. 2006. *The Language of the Gods in the World of Men. Sanskrit, Culture, and Power in Premodern India.* Berkeley/Los Angeles: University of California Press.

Quatrich-Wales, Horace. 1931. *Siamese State Ceremonies: Their History and Function.* Hertford: Stephen Austin and Sons.

Raendchen, Jana, and Oliver Raendchen. 1998. "Present State, Problems, and Purpose of baan-müang Studies." *Tai Culture* 3, no. 2: 5–11.

———. 2004. *The Socio-political and Administrative Organisation of müang in the Light of Lao Historical Manuscripts.* Paper presented at the conference "The Literary Heritage of Laos," Vientiane.

Reid, Anthony. 1990. *Southeast Asia in the Age of Commerce I, 1450–1680: The Lands Below the Winds.* New Haven: Yale University Press.

Reynolds, Craig. 1995. "A New Look at Old Southeast Asia." *Journal of Asian Studies* 54, no. 2: 419–46.

———. 2006. *Seditious Histories: Contesting Thai and Southeast Asian Pasts.* Seattle: University of Washington Press.

———. 1969. "Ritual and Social Hierarchy: An Aspect of Traditional Religion in Buddhist Laos." *History of Religions* 9, no. 1: 81–101.

Sahai, Sanchidanan. 1973. *The Ramayana in Laos: A Study in the Gvay Dvorahbi.* Dehli: D.K. Publishers.

Schober, Juliane, and Steven Collins. 2012. "The Theravada Civilizations Project: Future Directions in the Study of Buddhism in Southeast Asia." *Contemporary Buddhism* 13, no. 1: 157–66.

———. 2004. "Mapping the Sacred in Theravada Buddhist Southeast Asia." In *Sacred Places and Modern Landscapes: Sacred Geography and Social-Religious Transformations in South and Southeast Asia*, edited by Ronald A. Lukens-Bull. Tucson: Arizona State University.

Schopen, Gregory. 2004. *Buddhist Monks and Business Matters.* Honolulu: University of Hawai'i Press.

Scott, James. 2009. *On the Art of Not Being Governed. An Anarchist History of Upland Southeast Asia.* New Haven: Yale University Press.

Skilling, Peter. 2008. "King, Sangha, and Brahmans: Ideology, Ritual, and Power in Pre-modern Siam." In *Buddhism, Power and Political Order*, edited by Ian Harris, 182–215. London: Routledge.

———. 2009. *Buddhism and Buddhist Literature of Southeast Asia. Selected Papers.* Edited by Claudio Cicuzza. Bangkok: Lumbuni International Research Centre.

———, *and J. Carbine, eds. 2011. How Theravāda is Theravāda? Exploring Buddhist Identities. Bangkok/Taipeh: Dharma Drum.*

Strauss, Claudia. 2006. "The Imaginary." *Anthropological Theory* 6, no. 3: 322–34.

Strong, John. 1983. *The Legend of King Asoka.* Princeton: Princeton University Press.

Stuart-Fox, Martin. 1998. *The Lao Kingdom of Lan Xang: Rise and Decline.* Bangkok: White Lotus Press.

Suksamran, Somboon. 1993. "Buddhism, Political Authority, and Legitimacy in Thailand and Cambodia." In *Buddhist Trends in Southeast Asia*, edited by Trevor Ling. Singapore: ISEAS.

Swearer, Donald, and Somnai Premchit. 1978. "The Relationship between the Religious and Political Orders in Northern Thailand (14*th*–16th Centuries)." In *Religion and Legitimation of Power in Thailand, Laos and Burma*, edited by Bardwell Smith. Chambesburgh: Anima Books.

Taillard, Christian. 1977. "L'espace social: quelques réflexions à partir de deux exemples au Laos, *in* Espace social et analyse des sociétés en Asie du Sud-Est." *ASEMI* 8, no. 2: 81–102, 179–82.

Tambiah, Stanley. 1976. *World Conqueror and World Renouncer. A Study of Buddhism and Polity in Thailand against a Historical Background.* Cambridge: Cambridge University Press.

———. *1977.* "The *Galactic Polity*: The Structure of Traditional Kingdoms in Southeast Asia." *Annals of the New York Academy of Sciences* 293: 69–97.

———. 1986. "The Reflexive and Institutional Achievements of Early Buddhism." In *The Origins and Diversity of Axial Age Civilizations*, edited by Shmuel N. Eisenstadt. Albany: State University of New York Press.

———. 1989. "King Mahasammata: The First King in the Buddhist Story of Creation, and His Persisting Relevance." *Journal, Anthropological Society of Oxford* 20, no. 2: 227–34.

Taylor, Charles. 2002. "Modern Social Imaginaries." *Public Culture* 14, no. 1: 91–124.

Vannacid, C. 2005. *phavad phrabang*. Vientiane: Thavisay Publishing [in Lao].

Viravong, Mahasila. 1962. *Lokaniti*. Vientiane: State Printing [in Lao].

Weber, Max. 1978. "Politics as a Vocation." In *Selections in Translation*, edited by Walter G. Runciman, translated by Eric Matthews. Cambridge: Cambridge University Press.

Wengrow, David. 2010. *What Makes Civilization? The Ancient Near East and the Future of the West.* Oxford: Oxford University Press.

Wheatley, Paul. 1975. "Satyanr.ta in Suvarnadvi-pa: From Reciprocity to Redistribution in Ancient Southeast Asia." In *Ancient Civilization and Trade*, edited by Jeremy Sabloff, and C. C. Lamberg-Karlovsky. Albuquerque: University of New Mexico Press.

Wilson, Constance. 1983. "Cultural Values and Record Keeping in Thailand." *Cormosea Bulletin* 10, no. 2: 2–17.

———. 2009. "The Jataka in Laos. Le Syvsat (Sieo Savat)." In *The Middle Mekong River Basis. Studies in Tai History and Culture,* edited by Constance Wilson. DeKalb, IL: Centre for Southeast Asian Studies.

Wolters, Oliver. 1968. "Ayudhya and the Rearward part of the Word." *Journal of the Royal Asiatic Society of Great Britain & Ireland* 3–4: 166–78.

———. 1992. *History, Culture, and Region in Southeast Asian Perspectives*. Singapore: Institute of Southeast Asian Studies.

Zuckermann, Ghil'ad. 2003. "Language Contact and Globalisation: The Camouflaged Influence of English on the World's Languages—With Special Attention to Israeli [*sic*] and Mandarin." *Cambridge Review of International Affairs* 16, no. 2: 287–307.

8

—————————

FRONTIER AS CIVILIZATION?

Sociocultural Dynamics in the Uplands of Southeast Asia

Oliver Tappe

Introduction

In 1887, when Auguste Pavie (1847–1925), one of the eminent figures of French colonization in Southeast Asia, explored the mountainous areas of what are now the Lao-Vietnamese borderlands on a mission to settle the border between Siam and the new French protectorate of Tonkin (northern Vietnam), he found himself in the crossfire of regional political conflicts, which appeared as a struggle between lowland imperial civilization and upland "barbarians." In the same year, the Siamese had taken hostage some family members of the White Tai ruler Deo Van Tri from the upland valleys in present-day NW Vietnam. Bangkok had attempted to claim the region— known as Sipsong Chau Tai—but had underestimated the flow of weapons that were brought from China by diverse remnants of the rebellions that had unsettled the Qing Empire in the mid-nineteenth century.

In retaliation, Deo Van Tri attacked and looted Bangkok's Lao vassal kingdom of Luang Prabang, located at the edge of the vast mountains that separated the Siamese from the Vietnamese realm. While the Lao king of Luang Prabang sought French protection instead of submission to Bangkok, Pavie managed to forge an alliance with the upland Tai leader by negotiating the return of Deo Van Tri's relatives from Bangkok. The upshot was that former tributary relations between the upland Tai and the Vietnamese

193

court in Hué were transformed into a colonial political relationship, with the White Tai controlling territory and trade in this frontier region between Vietnam, Siam/Laos, and China (see Pavie 1901, 1967; Le Failler 2011, 2014; Davis 2016).[1]

This episode exemplifies the dynamics of the upland frontier and its relation to lowland imperial formations. For the French, it was clear where to locate "civilization," namely in the lowland imperial centers which were characterized by the interplay between religion (Buddhism, Confucianism) and state administration. In contrast, the upland frontier in between these centers appeared as inaccessible and unruly hinterland. Yet the French identified civilizational features within upland societies, such as the "feudal" structures of the Tai that made their leaders suitable subjects for colonial cooptation—to the disadvantage of other allegedly "less civilized" ethnic groups such as the Khmu or the Hmong. On the one hand, therefore, the French distinguished between civilizational cores and less civilized peripheries. Yet, on the other hand, they recognized at least semi-civilizations in the uplands—often considered as products of "state mimicry" (Scott 2009, 37) that imitated lowland kingdoms by replicating certain features or structures. Upland Tai polities (*müang*) were considered to be unstable petty kingdoms lacking proper bureaucratic administration. This obvious blurring of the upland-lowland dichotomy hints at economic, political, and cultural processes of exchange and interpenetration, which affected both lowland civilizations and upland frontier societies.

In this chapter, the concept of the "frontier" will be used as a heuristic tool to comprehend the various civilizational processes and sociocultural entanglements within the Southeast Asian massif. Of course, it is necessary first to identify some problematic ideological connotations of this concept and to develop appropriate working definitions. Case studies from the Lao-Vietnamese borderlands will illuminate the significance of the interplay of geographical conditions, local interethnic exchange and conflict, and external civilizational influences for the emergence of specific sociocultural configurations located along upland frontier spaces. The main question to be discussed is whether the internal upland frontier of Southeast Asia—constituting the geographical center of this variegated civilizational complex—can be treated analytically as a frontier *of* civilization or *as* civilization per se. I will therefore investigate how specific frontier dynamics shaped upland sociocultural configurations, and discuss whether the social spaces of frontier regions should be considered anticivilizations, civilizational peripheries, or civilizational formations in their own right. I will also ask if—in spite of shifting social and cultural configurations—durable patterns of migration, exchange, and cultural encounters and transformations constitute a *longue durée* of upland civilization in the sense of Johann Arnason's definition of civilizations as "units of larger dimensions and longer duration than the single societies that they encompass" (Arnason 2001, 1910). My material comes from the period just before and at the beginning of the French *mission civilisatrice* at the end of the nineteenth century, yet I try to avoid the specific imperialist connotations of the term *civilization* by focusing on cultural encounters and entanglements.

Since Frederick Jackson Turner (1921, 1) proclaimed his romantic vision of the moving frontier of civilization, as "the outer edge of the wave—the meeting point between savagery and civilization," both concepts—frontier and civilization—have entertained an ambivalent relationship. The frontier appears as the limit of civilization or as civilization-to-come—a perspective subverted by James Scott (2009) with his idea of a deliberately anticivilizational upland frontier in mainland Southeast Asia. To avoid this intransigent dichotomy, I consider the upland frontier as "a liminal space where cultural identities merged and shifted" (Perdue 2005, 41), where "cultures interpenetrate in a dynamic manner" (Leach 1960, 50). In the case of the upland frontier of the Lao-Vietnamese borderlands, there is a complex pattern of different ethnic groups and their variant relationships as well as multilayered external civilizational influences, emanating from the Chinese and Indian worlds (Tappe 2015; cf. Gellner, Ladwig, this volume).

Although the internal diversity of Southeast Asia makes the region difficult to compare with China and India as a civilizational complex, it is exactly this diversity of social, political, and cultural formations and their historical internal and external interconnections that makes Southeast Asia a fruitful field for ethnohistorical investigations. We can identify this frontier zone as an extremely heterogeneous "unit of larger dimensions" (Arnason 2001; Durkheim and Mauss 1971; Arnason et al. 2005), which shares certain elements and can be explored through civilizational analysis. Southeast Asia is a macroregion of the Eurasian landmass. Our job is to examine the "entanglements and continuous osmosis across the membranes which temporarily divide societies and civilizations" (Hann 2012, 90) within the macroregion, as well as links to India and China. The significance of external cultural influence was emphasized by scholars such as George Coedès (1968) who distinguished the "Indianized" states of Southeast Asia (i.e., the Buddhist kingdoms of Siam, Laos, and Burma) from the "Sinicized" parts (i.e., Vietnam).

This perspective ignored indigenous civilizational processes, in particular at the upland margins of the "classical" lowland kingdoms of the Khmer, Thai, Lao, and Vietnamese. Such ignorance was later given a new twist when area studies focused on the nation-states and their respective hegemonic cultures. It inspired the geographer Willem van Schendel (2005) to create the neologism "Zomia" in order to bring the upland periphery into the focus of research: "Zomia lacked a strong lobby of colonial experts. Nor had it developed a powerful civilisational persona in Northern universities because it also lay at the margins or beyond the 'civilisational' impact of India, China and Islam. And therefore it had few civilisational specialists to fend for it" (van Schendel 2005, 286).

This perspective inspired discussions about what, exactly, the delineations of the new area could be (Michaud 2010). James Scott (2009) took the concept as a label for upland Southeast Asia in general and moved the mountainous imperial fringes into the center of scientific debate. By stressing upland-lowland antagonism and downplaying the dynamics of the *longue durée* of trade, exchange, and cultural borrowings across the lowland empires and their upland margins, however, Scott perpetuated an essentialized dichotomy between exploitative states and more egalitarian peripheries and neglected the fluidity and ambiguity of imperial and/or ethnic boundaries as well as the dynamics of upland-lowland interactions must be highlighted (see Lieberman 2010 and Jonsson 2014 for thorough historical critiques of Scott's main arguments).

While this chapter focuses on colonial and precolonial transformations, it should be mentioned that even in the 2000s, cultural exchanges, appropriations, and mimetic processes cut across ethnic and national boundaries. This is so even though the patterns of political organization and power relations have changed considerably since the establishment of nation-states in Southeast Asia. Today, upland ethnic groups have minority status and are subject to different ideas of national integration and development. In the case of socialist Laos and Vietnam, they are considered "little brothers" who must be educated and motivated to climb the ladder of development defined by Marxist historical materialism (Hardy 2003; Pelley 2002; Pholsena 2006; Schlemmer 2017). In Thailand's current national discourse, the upland periphery is rendered the civilizational Other or "Dark Twin" (Scott 2009) of the lowland empire. The conflation of the lowland empires with "civilization" is thus problematic, even today, because dominant lowland groups such as the Thai and Lao use this concept to exclude upland minorities as "uncivilized" and "backward" (Winichakul 2000).[2]

The Southeast Asian Uplands: A Historical Contextualization

In precolonial Southeast Asia, ethnic boundaries did not mean strict exclusion. Rather, empires were characterized by the interplay of inclusion and difference through permeable boundaries. This was clearly demonstrated by Edmund Leach (1954) with the example of the Kachin switching between three systems: the *gumlao* egalitarian, the *gumsa* hierarchical, and the "feudal" system of the Buddhist Shan (a group of the Tai language family). Leach was criticized because of his ahistorical focus on social structure and his ignorance of historical changes in the regional political economy as a factor of social change (Robinne and Sadan 2007). Yet his analysis of Shan/Tai cultural and political influence among highlanders is still relevant. According to Olivier Evrard (2007, 128), Leach was one of the first authors to identify the "duality" of Taiization processes: "[T]he cultural influence of the lowlands resonates within highland groups, but the latter use their own cultural resources and systems of values to transform this lowland culture into practices, behaviours and/or ideologies." Thus, civilizational processes do not lead unidirectionally toward assimilation, but leave room for mutual cultural interactions and appropriations (for a theoretical discussion of cultural appropriation see Hahn 2011). The site where this happens is the upland frontier, in regions such as the Lao-Vietnamese borderlands where more or less "chance contact" takes place.

According to Owen Lattimore (1962, 469), "[A] frontier is created when a community occupies a territory. From then on the frontier is changed and shaped by the activity and growth of the community, or by the impact on it of another community."[3] Scott (2009) sharpens the argument and suggests that upland social systems have emerged as a response to state oppression and thus as products of state-evasion. As Jonsson (2014) alerts us, Scott overemphasizes upland autonomy and downplays social interaction and entanglements, thereby producing an ideal of nonstate "freedom." However, there is a grain of truth in Scott's simplistic dichotomy since political centralization and inclination to expansion is inherent to many civilizations. Lowland civilizational complexes appear to be characterized by social stratification, political centralization, a transcendental religion, and the corresponding transformation or emergence of social institutions (see Arnason et al. 2005; Hann 2012). Their margins are much less defined in comparison. Yet, the different societies and cultures in the mountains should not be prematurely configured as refugees from the state or empire. As archaeological findings in the Lao uplands suggest, early megalithic "civilizations" preceded the emergence of the famous lowland empires (Colani 1935; Heine-Geldern 1928). It appears doubtful that, to use the idiom of Braudel and Scott, "civilizations cannot climb hills." At least certain elements have done so.

What exactly happens at the frontier where the impact of civilization fades? To answer such questions, one should avoid Scott's essentialization of the mountains as upland anticivilization marked by negation of the "state." Scott's understanding of anarchy refers to the idea that some people actively resist state structures and that even their respective forms of social organization function as a strategy of state-avoidance (cf. Clastres 1987; Graeber 2006). However, often this emphasis on autonomy does not exclude cases of submission to an authority or risky contacts with traders, which makes the term *anarchy* questionable (Walker 2012). Even people stereotypically characterized as free and rebellious highlanders, such as the Hmong, have a history of close relations—albeit mainly through trading—with lowland civilizations (Culas and Michaud 1997). Therefore, even if mountainous hinterlands may be regarded as zones of refuge and rebellion, they are not anarchic but characterized by more or less interpenetration by civilization or selective appropriation of certain elements of lowland civilization by uplanders. This should not be regarded as a first step in submission toward the "state" and acculturation, but as one option in negotiating external influences and maintaining cultural autonomy in a changing political environment (Lee 2015).

Frontier regions as civilization have "a collective life of a special genre, the substratum of which is a plurality of interrelated political bodies acting upon one another" (Durkheim and Mauss 1971, 813). The Lao-Vietnamese border region is a typical upland frontier of lowland empires. It constitutes a contact zone where different civilizational spheres overlap, but it can equally be conceptualized as a center in itself "where exchange, mixing, contestation and negotiation take place" (Rajkai and Bellér-Hann 2012, 3). If one considers Southeast Asia as a variegated civilizational complex, Zomia is the core and dramatization of this kaleidoscopic pattern. I argue that sociocultural entanglements and interpenetrations—of course including lowland civilizational influences—produce a shifting multisocietal configuration that, from an ethnohistorical perspective, enables us to analyze civilizational processes *en miniature*. Upland sociocultural configurations are shaped both by lowland civilizations and by the geography, flexible livelihoods, and cultural heterogeneity of the hills (Bruneau 2001; Badenoch and Shinsuke 2013; Ladwig 2016).

Houaphan and Sipsong Chau Tai: Political and Cultural Trajectories of the Lao-Vietnamese Upland Frontier

The mountainous regions that today constitute northwestern Vietnam and northeastern Laos historically formed a natural frontier between the "Indianized" and the "Sinicized" cultural worlds of Southeast Asia (see Arnason 1997; Scott 2009; Ladwig, this volume). Northwestern Vietnam is often considered the cradle of the Tai-speaking peoples. Among the Lao, an origin myth tells that the legendary king Khun Borom descended from heaven at Müang Theng (Dien Bien Phu) (Stuart-Fox 1997). Another myth describes how the different ethnic groups of the region emerged from a holy gourd, and recounts the hierarchical relations between the Tai and the Mon-Khmer speaking people. The Mon-Khmer are considered autochthonous to the region yet are politically subordinated to the Tai, for whom they deliver taxes and *corvée*. Yet the valleys of the Red and Black Rivers and their tributaries are home to many different Tai groups who entertain tributary relations to upland peoples such as the Khmu of the Mon-Khmer language family and the Hmong who migrated from China in the nineteenth century. In particular, the Tai of upland river valleys acted as intermediaries between the upland populations and, for example, Chinese merchants (Le Failler 2014).

The jagged, densely forested, and ethnically heterogeneous uplands were more often than not remote from the imperial lowland centers both in a geographic and an administrative sense. Direct conquest was the exception. Rather, the Vietnamese and Lao rulers relied on tributary and trade relations with local elites to achieve at least a certain economic control of their resource-rich hinterlands. While the Vietnamese reduced their presence to a minimum and almost fully relied on local alliances, the Lao constituted a politically dominant minority in the upland valleys. However, the upland

Lao principalities were small and isolated and entertained only loose tributary relations with the respective Lao imperial centers by the Mekong River (Luang Prabang and Vientiane). According to the Southeast Asian model of the *mandala* or "galactic polity" (Tambiah 1977; Wolters 1982), the political influence of lowland centers often waned and peripheral polities entertained shifting tributary relations with different centers.

For example, the six Lao *müang* of Houaphan (Houaphan Tang Hok in old chronicles), established tributary relations with the Vietnamese court of Hué to balance Siamese pressure during the eighteenth and nineteenth centuries (Foropon 1927; Tappe 2015). It is therefore problematic to include Houaphan into a unified territorial body of a Lao state, as historical maps in Lao history books attempt to do (Tappe 2008). The Sipsong Chau Tai (Twelve Tai counties), a loose alliance of twelve to sixteen upland Tai *müang,* provide a similar case. The White, Black, and Red Tai (subgroups of the Tai-Kadai language family which also includes the Lao, Central Thai, and Shan) enjoyed certain autonomy from lowland empires, even if they were considered tributary vassals and were subject to occasional military attacks from China, Vietnam, and Siam. The Sipsong Chau Tai entertained tributary relations with Chinese, Vietnamese, Lao, Siamese, and Burmese centers, and constituted a regional power that was only fully integrated into the Vietnamese state after the French defeat of 1954. Both Houaphan and Sipsong Chau Tai are characterized by the scarcity of suitable land for wet rice cultivation, considered as essential for enabling population growth and concentration (cf. Lieberman 2003). The main form of agricultural cultivation was shifting or swidden cultivation that was practiced by the various ethnic groups living in the region. Besides the Tai-speaking groups, members of the Mon-Khmer, Sino-Tibetan, and Hmong-Mien language families settled in the region—contributing to specific frontier characteristics to be explored below.

To better assess the sociopolitical peculiarity of these upland polities in comparison with the more unified lowland kingdoms, a linguistic excursion appears fruitful (cf. Tappe forthc.). Houaphan means "head of a thousand" which probably refers to the population of each of the "six Houaphan" principalities (*müang*) (Bourlet 1906). The "twelve Tai counties" of the Sipsong Chau Tai clearly refer to the loose structure of the alliance with its independent local rulers who were related through kinship, trade relations, and occasional conflict. Another similarly structured polity, the Sipsong Panna in contemporary Yunnan, can be similarly translated as "twelve principalities," with *pan na* literally meaning "1,000 rice fields" (Rispaud 1937, 78). This designation hints at a political organization based on cultivable land, a principle that will be discussed further below. In many Tai languages the word *phan/pan* also refers to enclosure in the sense of a delimited area of settlement (ibid., 115). Accordingly, Houaphan Tang Hok can be translated as "six chiefs of delimited settlements." To be more precise, these settlements refer to ethnic Lao settlements that were initiated by the king of Luang Prabang in the sixteenth century. From that time forward, Buddhist Lao rulers dominated the region through control of the most fertile lands and strategic, hierarchic alliances with other ethnic groups such as the Khmu—similar to the relation between Shan and Kachin in Upper Burma that was famously described by Leach (1954).

In the nineteenth century, the six *müang* of Houaphan constituted a field of tension between different civilizational influences. They entertained direct tributary relations to the precolonial Lao and Vietnamese kingdoms and indirect relations with the Siamese and Chinese. Siam—which had subjugated the Lao principalities in the beginning of the eighteenth century—competed with Vietnam for political control of the frontier regions. The six principalities of Houaphan were different from neighboring Sipsong Chau Tai because they were dominated since the sixteenth century by a small Buddhist Lao elite who considered themselves to be civilized lowlanders. In contrast, the Vietnamese never bothered to assume direct control in any upland areas. The upland areas were considered "unhealthy" before World War II, and the Vietnamese preferred indirect cooperation with local elites (Poisson 2009; Gourou 1953). However, the Lao principalities in the upland valleys resembled more closely the upland Tai principalities of the Sipsong Chau Tai than the lowland Lao kingdoms, not least because of geographic and demographic constraints. Sipsong Chau Tai and Houaphan (together with the southern neighbor Xieng Khouang, former kingdom of the Tai-speaking Phuan) constituted a contested space between the expanding Vietnamese and Siamese kingdoms until the French established their colonial administration in the region at the end of the nineteenth century (Goscha 2012; Tappe forthc.).

Under pressure in these ways, the sociopolitical configurations of the northern frontier region were further disrupted by invasions of the Ho Chinese, in fact ethnically heterogeneous remnants of the Taiping Rebellion who had unsettled the Qing Empire since the mid-nineteenth century. In 1867, the first Vietnamese reports about so-called Qing rebels informed the Vietnamese emperor at Hué about the increasing political chaos in the northwestern mountains (Davis 2009, 26; 2016). Different local Tai rulers of the Sipsong Chau Tai either fought against the intruders or sided with them against the increased Vietnamese military presence. With the appearance of the French, the general political situation including local power struggles changed considerably. During his 1888 explorations of the upland regions along the Black River, which was still under the influence of Chinese bands, Auguste Pavie was accompanied by a Vietnamese-Tai *métis* who had received from the colonial authorities the title of *quan phong* (head of district; *quan* meaning "mandarin"; see below). Yet it became clear soon that this local power broker was not the kind of bureaucratic administrator that the French had expected; he was mainly interested in controlling trade and collecting tributes from other upland groups (Pavie 1967, 205; Le Failler 2014, 140–43). In addition, the *quan phong* tried to prevent any negotiations between the French and another local Tai leader, Deo Van Tri, who had attacked Luang Prabang one year before in response to Siamese aggressions that were perceived by the French as a hostile act against their Lao protégées-to-be. The French thus intervened in these local power struggles when they later chose the diplomatic and efficient Deo Van Tri as their main local ally, to the disadvantage of other Tai rulers of the Sipsong Chau Tai.

Deo Van Tri became the most important colonial collaborator in the Black River Basin. He embodied Tai dominance in the region, with the French perpetuating the traditional Vietnamese entitlements (Le Failler 2011; 2014). Deo Van Tri's offspring remained loyal to the French while other upland Tai joined the Vietnamese anticolonial struggle. The Sipsong Chau Tai enjoyed certain autonomy as pro-French "Thai federation" between 1948 and 1953. The Vietnamese pursued unprecedented control of the region after the end of colonial rule—marked by the battle of Dien Bien Phu close to the Lao-Vietnamese border, where the Tai groups found themselves on different sides of the conflict as a reflection of previous power struggles—and incorporated the Tai regions into Vietnamese proper (Lentz 2011). Also during the First Indochina War (1946–1954), Houaphan became the stronghold of the Lao revolutionary movement that was backed mainly by the non-Lao ethnic groups of the uplands, and supported and sustained by the Viet Minh (Stuart-Fox 1997; Goscha 2003).

It can thus be seen that the emergence of the present socialist states of Laos and Vietnam owes a great deal to social and political upheavals in the upland frontier regions (Pholsena 2012). The preceding decades that were characterized by Lao-Siamese and Vietnamese competition and additional disruptions through the Ho factor created the conditions for later developments. The various transformations during the colonial period marked the shift from empire to the modern state with its spatial regulations and administrative centralization. The expansive tendency of lowland civilizational formations was now transformed into a spatial entity, and was rendered sovereign by both political boundary making and civilizational discourses during and after the creation of French Indochina.

Tai versus Kha: Interethnic Relations in the Southeast Asian Uplands

When the French entered the upland regions of Laos in the late nineteenth century, they perceived numerous differences among the ethnically heterogeneous populations. Many of the differences were related to the multiple forms of political organization, which contrasted with the more centralized and hierarchized forms that were more familiar and visible to the colonial administrative gaze. In the river deltas, the French promoted plantation agriculture, but in the uplands they were mainly concerned with the extraction of resources. Of particular interest were local tributary relations since they could be translated into a system of taxation.

The fundamental opposition in precolonial Laos and Northwestern Vietnam was between the Tai-Lao and the so-called Kha, a pejorative name for the autochthonous Mon-Khmer-speaking people meaning "serf" or "slave" (Condominas 1990; Turton 2000).[4] Since many upland groups paid tribute and *corvée* to the Lao and other Tai groups such as Deo Van Tri's White Tai, the French considered the latter to be mandarins and co-opted them for the lowest level of colonial administration. In doing so—and in contradiction to their recurrent complaints about "the excessive subordination of the Kha to the Laotians" (Lefèvre-Pontalis 2000, 373)—the French aggravated interethnic hierarchies and encouraged many local rulers to exploit the Kha (Le Failler 2011; Davis 2011).

However, the concept of Kha masked the uplanders' important socioeconomic positions. At certain times in history Kha and Tai even had "a symbiotic relationship based on both ritual and economic exchanges" (Grabowsky and Wichasin 2008, 11). As autochthonous people, the Kha were considered lords of territorial guardian spirits. Moreover, they provided valuable forest products such as incense, opium, and ivory, which were in high esteem at lowland royal courts (ibid.). An English traveler in the nineteenth century wrote: "Without the Khas, their lazy, pleasure-loving, opium-smoking masters would have to work, or die of hunger" (Hallet 1988 [1890], 22). The Lamet (Rmeet) in Northwestern Laos, for example, were providers of upland rice and forest products for their Tai neighbors (e.g., in the Northern Thai kingdom of Nan) (Izikowitz 2001). Yet these subtleties in exchange patterns have been ignored by many, including James Scott (2009), who can also be criticized for ignoring some forms of rebellions. In fact there was a large-scale Khmu rebellion against Lao domination in the 1870s and 1880s in Houaphan that Scott does not mention (see Foropon 1927; Jonsson 2014). This rebellion did not emerge from an inherent "antistate" sentiment but had more complex demographic and political-economic motivations. During the Siamese-Vietnamese power struggle in the Lao territories, Bangkok carried out immense resettlement campaigns directed mainly toward the Lao and other Tai-speaking groups. Many Lao fled into already established settlements in the uplands, thus changing the local demographic and economic situation. The Chinese Ho bands added to the tension of local livelihoods, triggering millenarian movements that gained momentum over the years—anarchic in appearance but in the end aimed at establishing a new relation between Kha and Tai.

Peoples such as the Khmu did not reject lowland civilization as such but rather attempted to renegotiate their relation with the Lao. The Khmu resented the increased pressure from the Lao—who were backed by Siamese military presence—and responded with the so-called Kha Cheuang rebellions when the Ho unsettled the local power structures (Proschan 1998; Jonsson 2014). However, the movement remained dispersed and local, and after a few years of violent excesses ebbed down to a negligible factor when many Khmu communities returned to their village life (ibid.). As a French colonial observer stated, the Khmu apparently "lost any hope of freedom and took on the yoke again" (Boutin 1937, 96). In addition, they were pushed aside economically by the Hmong who despite their reputation as savage mountain people found a lucrative way of interacting with the colonial state in the opium trade (Lee 2015; Le Failler 2014). On the other hand, some dispersed Khmu communities had established new and prosperous settlements in Vietnam and were finally sedentarized (Cupet 1900). This can be interpreted as a general inclination to appropriate elements of lowland civilization if the conditions allow it. Consequently, such outcomes of upland rebellions do not fit into Scott's (2009) model of the state-repellant uplander.[5]

The Kha Cheuang rebellion coincided in the 1880s–'90s with the anti-French *cần vương* movement incited by rebellious members of the Vietnamese royal elite (Fourniau 2002). The result was a jumble of shifting local alliances and power struggles that included Lao and Tai notables, Khmu village heads, Vietnamese and Chinese "pirates" (as the French used to call them), and French colonial administrators (Tappe 2015). Instead of resenting lowland state representatives as such, some Khmu leaders approached the French in order to balance Lao and Tai dominance—only after previously having been attracted by the military power of the Vietnamese rebels. In 1895, for example, the French solved a dispute between Lao and Khmu in the upland *müang* of Sam Tai. The *lasa quan* of Sam Tai,[6] a Khmu notable incorporated into the local transethnic sociopolitical hierarchy, promised peaceful coexistence in exchange for French guarantees to restrict Lao political and economic hegemony.[7]

Transformations of the Tai-Kha relation—Shan versus Kachin in Leach's (1954) famous case study of highland Burma—characterize the history of interethnic relations at the Lao-Vietnamese upland frontier. As already mentioned, the migration of Lao lowlanders to Houaphan was a kind of frontier colonization initiated by the Lao king of Luang Prabang. In the upland river valleys, the local Lao rulers created lowland-type social spaces based on—albeit small-scale due to environmental constraints—wet rice cultivation, Buddhist religion, and *müang* organization. However, the geographical distance from the Mekong basin implied minimal contact and only long-distance economic relations. Instead, close relations with neighboring Tai- and Mon-Khmer-speaking groups—entailing processes of cultural approximation or even assimilation—over the centuries resulted in sociocultural and linguistic changes.

Linguistic evidence and French colonial sources suggest considerable processes of cultural interaction and transfer that resulted in a certain differentiation of the Lao in Houaphan from other Lao. French sources, for example, note that the Lao from Luang Prabang considered the Lao from Houaphan as Tai Neua (Tai from the North) who had different religious customs (Raquez 1902) and may have been opium-smoking monks (Anonymous 1898, 225). In the course of Lao nation building, however, the Tai Neua became firmly integrated into the Lao cultural mainstream. Today, no one considers the Lao from Houaphan as different—even though there is a notion of a specific northeastern dialect closely related to the language of the Red and Black Tai. The reintegration of the colonial Tai Neua in the ethnic category of Lao was probably a pragmatic decision since it enabled the Lao to exceed the symbolic mark of 50 percent in the national census.[8]

The Lao of Houaphan—the Tai Neua/Northern Tai of French colonial sources—have incorporated certain elements usually associated with upland cultures. Still claiming to be "Lao of the Lowlands," they have adopted livelihood patterns typical for other mountain-dwelling groups such as the Khmu or the Hmong—in particular swidden agriculture due to scarcity of land suitable for wet rice cultivation. Such interethnic or intercivilizational dynamics can be historically identified as well in the field of property relations, as I shall now demonstrate.

Land Tenure and Property Relations: Intercivilizational Dynamics and Cultural Borrowings

In an early issue of the journal *Anthropos*, the French missionary Antoine Bourlet claimed to have observed a strange form of "socialism" in Houaphan: "une manière de communisme, mais un communisme qui ressemble fort à de la féodalité" (Bourlet 1906, 525). Every couple of years the village land was redistributed according to household size. In addition, anyone who cleared a tract of new land for cultivation could claim proprietary rights as long as he cultivated it. This reflects Scott's (2009) assumption of a "common property frontier" in upland Southeast Asia. However, land conflicts occurred even if there appeared to be no scarcity of land in the sparsely populated uplands. Following the French pacification campaigns in the Lao-Vietnamese uplands, some Lao refugees returned to their former settlements in Houaphan to find that their rice fields had been occupied by land-seeking Red Tai from Vietnam. The resulting conflict was one of the first challenges for the fledgling French administration in the region (Foropon 1927; Tappe 2015).

Land scarcity can alter local land tenure organization even within an ethnic group. According to Izikowitz (2001), the Lamet (a Mon-Khmer speaking group) know the system of cultivator-proprietor as described by Bourlet for the Tai groups in Houaphan. Yet there is a difference between upper Lamet who have bounded territory and the lower Lamet whose territory is not determined because of the availability of cultivable land (Izikowitz

2001, 294). Bourlet's observation of a dual system of land tenure suggests a certain adaptability of Tai-Lao land tenure systems to environmental conditions. In the uplands, the scarce plains suitable for productive wet rice cultivation had to be cultivated intensively, and thus the village community usually controlled the redistribution of such land according to available manpower. Large individual landholding patterns were unknown in the uplands, which led to misleading interpretations of upland communities as egalitarian; the non-Buddhist Tai, for example, did have hierarchical structures, but outsiders found them difficult to identify. Notably, the abundance of farmland in the Mekong plain corresponded with a hierarchized system of tributary flows and the accumulation of wealth among an aristocratic elite. In this respect, lowland social structures seem to alter under upland frontier conditions, as in the case of the Lao of Houaphan.

Bourlet (1906, 526) appears to have been struck by the "socialist" appearance of the feudal structures in Houaphan, both among the Lao and the Red Tai. On the one hand, he noticed a clear hierarchy from the *phanya* of each *hua pan* (ruling on behalf of the *chao sivit* or king of Luang Prabang) over different levels of mandarins to the village headman. On the other hand, he found minimal differences of status and wealth and a communal system of land tenure. One can only speculate about whether upland livelihoods and interethnic encounters transformed an original hierarchical system that was modeled in the lowland Lao kingdoms after Siamese examples and brought to Houaphan by Lao settlers as early as the sixteenth century. The local concepts of *hua pan* and *hua hoi* (hundred) are reminiscent of the system of *nai sip*/*hua sip* (head of ten households or villages) as described by Grabowsky and Wichasin (2008) according to old Tai Lü chronicles. Rispaud (1937, 116) argues that *hua sip* "indique donc un rapport entre un foyer et la parcelle de rizières d'où celui-ci tire sa subsistance." The principle of a headman over a certain number of households in steps of ten has possibly diffused from Burma and the Northern Thai kingdoms to the Lao-Vietnamese frontier region. For example, the administrative language of the Tai Lü of Northwestern Laos is characterized by Burmese loanwords since the Tai groups east of the Salween used to entertain tributary relations with the court of Ava (Grabowsky and Wichasin 2008, 18). The origins of the concept *nai* can be traced back to the Mongol word *noyan*, which also designates a leader of a military unit in China (Lemoine 1997, 189; Grabowsky 2010, 223). It is still used today in the Lao expression for village headman: *nai ban*.

Among the Tai in Vietnam, the equivalent expression is *quan ban,* *quan* being a Chinese/Vietnamese loanword meaning mandarin (Robert 1941, 23). The appropriation of the Vietnamese title *quan* by Tai groups hints at an inclination to mimetically adapt to the Confucian bureaucratic system. The idea of mimesis refers here to local processes of appropriation (see Jonsson 2010), which have to be distinguished from systems imposed locally by a dominant civilization. When the White Tai leader Deo Van Tri received the title Quan Dao (Uplands Patrol Commissioner) from the French colonial administration in 1893 (Le Failler 2011, 49), it served his strategy of self-empowerment through superficial incorporation into the French-Vietnamese colonial state—only one example of how key concepts of lowland civilization enter the uplands (for a more detailed discussion of mimetic processes in the Lao-Vietnamese borderlands, see Tappe forthc.).

Nai (and *quan*) can be considered as social phenomena according to Durkheim and Mauss, extending "into areas that reach beyond the national territory or [developing] over periods of time that exceed the history of a single society" (Durkheim and Mauss 1971, 810). The *nai sip* system reaches from Shan states in Burma and the Northern Thai, over the Lü, and to the different Tai people of Houaphan. Interethnic exchanges and borrowings transformed the system further. Under Vietnamese influence, some Red Tai—who have a history of migration different from that of the Lao—translated Vietnamese bureaucratic principles into their local political organization or just borrowed Vietnamese terms to be intelligible in a mimetic fashion within the wider Vietnamese civilizational complex.

The idea of proprietary rights according to ongoing cultivation of land is more pronounced in the lowlands (Condominas 1961). The idea of redistribution according to available workforce of the households is typical for the uplands where the scarce amounts of land suitable for productive wet rice cultivation have to be managed more efficiently. In the case of the Lao who settled in the uplands of Houaphan, the hybrid form of land tenure as regarded by the French missionary as a mixture of communism and feudalism can the interpreted as an adaption to the new environment. Interestingly, the property relations in contemporary Houaphan are even more complex. There are still traces of the customary law systems observed by Bourlet, even though there are some restrictions concerning the clearance of new land for "uncivilized" swidden cultivation. Systems of redistribution are still known while the few attempts of collective farms initiated in the late 1970s are gradually disappearing. Instead, a land titling program directed by the World Bank and the Asian Development Bank (see Lestrelin 2011) is being implemented which will transform local property relations in Houaphan, as has happened already in Northwestern Vietnam—albeit to different degrees in different regions (Sikor 2004).

Conclusion

As Joel Kahn (this volume) has observed for the Malay World, economic, political, and social interaction and flexible boundaries between ethnic groups are characteristic features of mainland Southeast Asia. This is also true for the upland regions. The uplands of the Sipsong Chau Tai and Houaphan constitute a frontier of different civilizational spheres, a region of translocal and transcultural entanglements, exchanges, and borrowings. The economic relations are crucial and precede political alliances, recalling Peter Perdue's definition of the frontier: "The frontier zone was a liminal space where cultural identities merged and shifted, as peoples of different ethnic and linguistic roots interacted for common economic purposes" (Perdue 2005, 41). Civilizational analysis can be a useful tool, provided that it focuses not on empire or state, but on the *longue durée* of cultural encounters and entanglements in their economic and political contexts—sometimes hierarchical and conflictual, sometimes less so, and even egalitarian in appearance.

Lao migrants to Houaphan were refashioned by the lowland Lao into cultural Others from the North—Tai Neua—with allegedly "uncivilized" practices such as swidden agriculture and smoking monks. At the beginning of the twentieth century, bureaucratic and administrative patterns among upland Tai groups attested to both Vietnamese and French influences. Administrative concepts from different origins were adapted locally and experienced shifts of signification. Long-distance trade networks and their local components implied potential political relationships, hierarchies, and conflicts. External economic and political influences affected local sociopolitical configurations and sometimes aggravated interethnic tensions.

Even if we can identify coherent socioeconomic patterns and common forms of symbolic communication in the Lao-Vietnamese upland frontier region, it seems misleading to talk about a distinctive upland frontier civilization in the sense in which that concept is used in civilizational analysis (Arnason et al. 2005). The heterogeneity and decentralization of this region make it difficult to identify a "congealed core" (Hann 2011). One might regard the lack of a core as key element of Zomian civilization, but since such a proposition leads to a dead end, historical anthropologists have little choice but to focus on the dynamics of cultural encounters. Civilizational influences in this frontier region triggered sociocultural creativity (Arnason 2001: 1912). Such creativity occurred through apparently arbitrary and situated collective choices under the temporally and spatially varying influences of contingent civilizational patterns (e.g., in mimetic appropriations of lowland lifestyles). The examples given above have illustrated how certain sociocultural patterns emanate from powerful civilizational centers and become localized. At the same time, it has been shown that this dynamic is not unidirectional but consists of mutual influences and borrowings.

According to Durkheim and Mauss (1971, 812) "[N]ot all social phenomena are equally apt to internationalize themselves." They distinguish between political and juridical institutions forming "part of the specific character of each people" (ibid.), and other elements such as myths, commerce, arts, techniques, and language—elements that supposedly travel and are borrowed. However, institutions, too, can be subject to external influences, as the examples of land tenure and political administration have demonstrated. The influence does not manifest itself strictly as acculturation, but as hybrid forms and appropriations that contribute to the complexity of specific sociocultural configurations. As Lowie (1920, 441) once put it: "Cultures develop mainly through the borrowings due to chance contact." The same can be said for civilizations. The overlaps of civilizations at their frontiers produce civilizational effects such as the emergence of hybrid forms of sociocultural phenomena, ritual innovation, various materializations, and economic specializations.

In order to distinguish the concept of civilization from the concepts of culture and society, one might stress the potential power inequalities, an acceptance of cultural difference, and even the existence of an internal essential other for the self-legitimation of a specific civilizational core. Aspects of political economy play an important role, in particular when the periphery nourishes the core. The myths of frontier people as well as their property relations and political systems reflect the amalgamation of different historical civilizational influences and corresponding local responses. A specific phenomenon is the incorporation of "barbarian" elements into the allegedly civilized societies inhabiting the frontier. Thus, there is no essential dichotomy pitting lowland civilization against savage mountains, but a dynamic civilizational complex of gradual interpenetrations and entanglements.

When focusing on the upland frontier of Southeast Asia, it is thus crucial to consider "the wider political, social, or economic context of even the apparently most isolated people" (Evans 2000, 265; see Wolf 1982).

By analogy to Upper Burma and Leach's idea of taking ethnic groups as different "sectors" of a common social structure, we may conclude that the culturally heterogeneous population of the Sipsong Chau Tai and Houaphan constitutes a frontier society shaped by specific environmental conditions, interethnic exchange dynamics, and varying external civilizational influences. The emergence of this specific upland sociocultural configuration beyond local ethnic (or even village) identities is thus a consequence of the interplay between political, social, cultural, and economic aspects of civilizational process in the uplands. These are not isolated groups, the life-worlds of which are largely determined by environmental constraints. Rather, different societies engage actively with both nature and other human settlements to secure their social reproduction. Upland societies are not conservative in the sense that they avoid social and cultural change, but are characterized by a dialectic of adaptability and resilience that allows for flexible responses to external conditions while maintaining a sense of cultural intactness.

Even if it seems difficult to analyze Zomia as civilization in its own right, the Southeast Asian uplands definitely form part of a civilizational continuum linking lowland royal centers such as Luang Prabang or Hué with even the remotest mountain settlement. This continuum or process is characterized by the interplay between sociocultural difference and tentative rapprochement, by different levels of civilizational interpenetration, by transfers of knowledge and ideas, by political frictions and hierarchies, and by permanent movements of people. It is not helpful to overemphasize an antagonistic upland-lowland dichotomy, as James Scott seems to. Rather, recognition of the multilayered entanglements within the sociocultural diversity of mainland Southeast Asia provide the key to a better understanding of regional history. The upland frontier forms part and parcel of lowland civilizations. Civilizational analysis thus provides a suitable analytical tool to explore the allegedly "savage" fringes.

Notes

1. Further archival research on this topic was discussed during a workshop "Frontier Frictions: Cultural Encounters, Exchange, and Emergence

in Asian Uplands" at the Max Planck Institute for Social Anthropology (14–15 Nov. 2013), which resulted in a special issue of *The Asia Pacific Journal of Anthropology* (4/2015; see Tappe 2015). An in-depth discussion of recent works on upland SEA history and sociocultural dynamics (see, e.g., Le Failler 2014, Jonsson 2014, Lee 2015, Davis 2016) is beyond the scope of the present paper (see Tappe forthc.).

2. Fiskesjö (2012, 171) remarks that both Roman and Chinese empire builders shaped the idea of their own civilizational superiority against barbarian frontier people.

3. Lattimore (1962, 469) continues: "History being composed of records of growth, it is the changing of frontiers by the social growth of communities that is of primary importance for the historian."

4. Under French colonialism the alternative term *phu thoeng* ("upland people") gained prominence and later the concept of *lao thoeng* ("upland Lao") came to be used emphasizing common Laotian nationality. In a similar vein, uplanders such as the Hmong, pejoratively called *maeo* ("savages") by lowland societies, came to be known as *lao sung* ("Lao of the mountain tops") (Pholsena 2006).

5. Millenarian movements occasionally flared up under French colonial administration as well. Yet, as Salemink (1994) points out, more violent forms of millenarian movements were rather reactions to hypersensitive French officials than an expression of specifically political intentions. The colonial administration could not accept rebellion as a way of negotiating "state" influence, and were in fact ignorant of other forms of transethnic communication apart from the hierarchical tributary relations.

6. This title combines a Lao honorific title (*lasa,* derived from Sanskrit *rājā*) and the Chinese/Vietnamese word for mandarin (*quan*); a good example of how elements from the Indianized and Sinicized worlds were combined (Coedès 1968). Given the fact that this title was given to a local Kha notable, it represents the entanglements of different civilizational influences and appropriations at the upland frontier.

7. Archives Nationales d'Outre-Mer, Aix-en-Provence, "Rapport Vacle à Gouverneur Général, 12 April 1895," Gouvernement Général d'Indochine 20749 (for a more detailed account of this historical episode, see Tappe 2015; forthc.).

8. After the Mekong became the boundary between Siam and French Indochina (in 1893), the majority of Lao found themselves subjects of Bangkok while 80 percent of the territory of the later Lao nation-state consisted of the ethnically heterogeneous uplands (Stuart-Fox 1997).

References

Anonymous 1898. "Notice sur le territoire des Hua Phans Thang Hoc." *Bulletin Économique de l'Indochine Francaise*: 222–35.

Arnason, Johann. 1997. "The Southeast Asian Labyrinth: Historical and Comparative Perspectives." *Thesis Eleven* 50: 99–122.

———. 2001. "Civilizational Analysis." In *International Encyclopedia of the Social & Behavioral Sciences*, edited by Neil J. Smelser and Paul B. Baltes, 1909–15. Amsterdam: Elsevier.

———, S. N. Eisenstadt, and B. Wittrock, eds. 2005. *Axial Civilizations and World History*. Leiden: Brill.

Badenoch, Nathan, and Tomita Shinsuke. 2013. "Mountain People in the Muang: Creation and Governance of a Tai Polity in Northern Laos." *Southeast Asian Studies* 2, no. 1: 29–67.

Bourlet, Antoine. 1906. "Socialisme dans les hŭa phăn (Laos, Indo-Chine)." *Anthropos* 1, no. 3: 521–28.

Boutin, Andre. 1937. "Monographie de la province des Houa-Phan." *Bulletin des Amis de Laos* 1: 69–119.

Bruneau, Michel. 2001. "La notion de frontière et sa signification dans la péninsule indochinoise." *Moussons* 3: 33–55.

Clastres, Pierre. 1987. *Society against the State: Essays in Political Anthropology*. New York: Zone Books.

Coedès, George. 1968. *The Indianized States of Southeast Asia*. Honolulu: East-West Center Press.

Colani, Madeleine. 1935. *Megaliths du Haut Laos*. Paris: EFEO.

Condominas, Georges. 1961. "Notes sur le droit foncier lao en milieu rural dans la plaine de Vientiane." *Artibus Asiae* 24, no. 3–4: 255–62.

———. 1990. *From Lawa to Mon, from Saa' to Thai: Historical and Anthropological Aspects of Southeast Asian Social Spaces*. Canberra: ANU, Research School of Pacific Studies.

Culas, Christian, and Jean Michaud. 1997. "A Contribution to the Study of Hmong (Miao) Migrations and History." *Bijdragen* 153, no. 2: 211–43.

Cupet, Pierre-Paul. 2000 [1900]. *Travels in Laos and Among the Tribes of Southeast Indochina. The Pavie Mission Indochina Papers*, Vol. 6. Bangkok: White Lotus.

Davis, Bradley. 2009. "Post-Taiping Fallout: Nguyen-Qing Collaboration in the Pursuit of Bandits on the Border." In *On the Borders of*

State Power: Frontiers in the Greater Mekong Sub-region, edited by Martin Gainsborough, 25–34. London: Routledge.

———. 2011. "Black Flag Rumors and the Black River Basin: Powerbrokers and the State in the Tonkin-China Borderlands." *Journal of Vietnamese Studies* 6, no. 2: 16–41.

———. 2016. *Imperial Bandits: Outlaws and Rebels in the China-Vietnam Borderlands*. Seattle: University of Washington Press.

Durkheim, Emile, and Marcel Mauss. 1971. "Note on the Notion of Civilization." *Social Research* 38, no. 4: 808–13.

Evans, Grant. 2000. "Tai-ization: Ethnic Change in Northern Indo-China." In *Civility and Savagery: Social Identity in Tai States*, edited by Andrew Turton, 263–90. Richmond: Curzon.

Evrard, Olivier. 2007. "Interethnic Systems and Localized Identities: The Khmu Subgroups (tmoy) in North-West Laos." In *Social Dynamics in the Highlands of Southeast Asia: Reconsidering Political Systems of Highland Burma by E. R. Leach*, edited by Francois Robinne and Mandy Sadan, 127–59. Leiden: Brill.

Fiskesjö, Magnus. 2012. "Outlaws, Barbarians, Slaves: Critical Reflections on Agamben's homo sacer." *HAU: Journal of Ethnographic Theory* 2, no. 1: 161–80.

Foropon, Jean. 1927. "La province des Hua-Phan (Laos)." *Extrême-Asie* 14: 93–106.

Fourniau, Charles. 2002. *Vietnam: domination coloniale et résistance nationale*. Paris: Les Indes Savantes.

Goscha, Christopher E. 2003. "Une guerre pour l'Indochine? Le Laos et le Cambodge dans le conflit franco-vietnamien (1948–1954)." *Guerres mondiales et conflits contemporains* 3, no. 211: 29–58.

———. 2012. *Going Indochinese: Contesting Concepts of Space and Place in French Indochina*. Copenhagen: NIAS Press.

Gourou, Pierre 1953. *L'Asie*. Paris: Hachette.

Grabowsky, Volker, and Renoo Wichasin. 2008. *Chronicles of Chiang Khaeng: a Tai Lü Principality of the Upper Mekong*. Honolulu: University of Hawaii Press.

———. 2010. "The Northern Tai Polity of Lan Na (Ba-bai Da-dian) in the 14*th* and 15*th* Centuries: The Ming Factor." In *Southeast Asia in the Fifteenth Century: The China Factor*, edited by Geoff Wade, 197–245. Singapore: NUS Press.

Graeber, David. 2006. *Fragments on an Anarchist Anthropology*. Chicago: Prickly Paradigm Press.

Hahn, Hans Peter. 2011. "Antinomien kultureller Aneignung: Einführung." *Zeitschrift für Ethnologie* 136: 11–26.

Hallet, Holt. [1890] 1988. *A Thousand Miles on an Elephant in the Shan States*. Bangkok: White Lotus.

Hann, Chris. 2011. "Back to Civilization." *Anthropology Today* 27, no. 6: 1–2.

———. 2012. "Europe in Eurasia." In *A Companion to the Anthropology of Europe*, edited by Ullrich Kockel et al., 88–102. Chichester: Wiley-Blackwell.

Hardy, Andrew. 2003. *Red Hills: Migrants and the State in the Highlands of Vietnam*. Honolulu: University of Hawaii Press.

Heine-Geldern, Robert. 1928. "Die Megalithen Südostasiens und ihre Bedeutung für die Klärung der Megalithenfrage in Europa und Polynesien." *Anthropos* 23: 276–315.

Izikowitz, Karl G. 2001. *Lamet—Hill Peasants of French Indochina*. Bangkok: White Lotus.

Jonsson, Hjorleifur. 2010. "Mimetic Minorities: National Identity and Desire on Thailand's Fringe." *Identities* 17: 108–30.

———. 2014. *Slow Anthropology: Negotiating Difference with the Iu Mien*. Ithaca: Cornell University Press.

Ladwig, Patrice. 2016. "Religious Place Making: Civilized Modernity and the Spread of Buddhism among the Cheng, a Mon-Khmer Minority in Southern Laos." In *Religion, Place and Modernity: Spatial Articulations in Southeast Asia and East Asia*, edited by Michael Dickhardt and Andrea Lauser, 95–124. Leiden: Brill.

Lattimore, Owen. 1962. *Studies in Frontier History. Collected Papers 1928–1958*. London: Oxford University Press.

Le Failler, Philippe. 2011. "The Dèo Family of Lai Châu: Traditional Power and Unconventional Practices." *Journal of Vietnamese Studies* 6, no. 2: 42–67.

———. 2014. *La rivière Noire. L'intégration d'une marche frontière au Vietnam*. Paris: Editions CNRS.

Leach, Edmund. 1954. *Political Systems of Highland Burma*. London: Athlone.

———. 1960. "The Frontiers of Burma." *Comparative Studies in Society and History* 3, no. 1: 49–68.

Lee, Mai Na M. 2015. *Dreams of the Hmong Kingdom: The Quest for Legitimation in French Indochina, 1850–1960*. Madison: University of Wisconsin Press.

Lefèvre-Pontalis, Pierre. 2000. *Travels in Upper Laos and on the Borders of Yunnan and Burma*. Bangkok: White Lotus.

Lemoine, Jacques. 1997. "Féodalité Taï chez les Lü des Sipsong Panna et les Taï Blancs, Noirs et Rouges du Nord-Ouest du Viêt-Nam." *Péninsule* 35, no. 2: 171–217.

Lentz, Christian. 2011. "Making the Northwest Vietnamese." *Journal of Vietnamese Studies* 6, no. 2: 68–105.

Lestrelin, Guillaume. 2011. "Rethinking State–ethnic Minority Relations in Laos: Internal Resettlement, Land Reform and Counter-territorialization." *Political Geography* 30: 311–19.

Lieberman, Victor. 2003. *Strange Parallels: Southeast Asia in Global Context, c. 800–1830. Vol. 1: Integration of the Mainland*. Cambridge: Cambridge University Press.

———. 2010. "A Zone of Refuge in Southeast Asia? Reconceptualizing Interior Spaces." Journal of Global History 5: 333–46.

Lowie, Robert H. 1920. *Primitive Society*. New York: Liveright.

Mauss, Marcel. 1930. "Les civilisations: Éléments et formes. Exposé présenté à la Première Semaine Internationale de Synthèse." In *Civilisation. Le mot et l'idée*, 81–106. Paris: La Renaissance du livre.

Michaud, Jean. 2010. "Editorial—Zomia and Beyond." *Journal of Global History* 5: 187–214.

Pavie, Auguste. 1901. *Mission Pavie Indo-Chine, 1879–1895. Géographie et Voyages*. Paris: Leroux.

———. 1967. *Eine friedliche Eroberung: Indochina 1888*. Tübingen: Erdmann.

Pelley, Patricia M. 2002. *Postcolonial Vietnam: New Histories of the National Past*. Durham: Duke University Press.

Perdue, Peter. 2005. *China Marches West—The Qing Conquest of Central Eurasia*. Cambridge: Harvard University Press.

Pholsena, Vatthana. 2006. *Post-War Laos: The Politics of Culture, History, and Identity*. Ithaca: Cornell University Press.

———. 2012. "The (Transformative) Impacts of the Vietnam War and the Communist Revolution in a Border Region in Southeastern Laos." *War and Society* 31, no. 2: 163–83.

Poisson, Emmanuel. 2009. "Unhealthy Air of the Mountains: Kinh and Ethnic Minority Rule on the Sino-Vietnamese Frontier from the Fifteenth to the Twentieth Century." In *On the Borders of*

State Power: Frontiers in the Greater Mekong Sub-region, edited by Martin Gainsborough, 12–24. London: Routledge.

Proschan, Frank. 1998. "Cheuang in Kmhmu Folklore, History, and Memory." In *Tamnan keokap thao hung thao chuang: miti thang prawattisat lae wattanatham* [Proceedings of the First International Conference on the Literary, Historical, and Cultural Aspects of Thao Hung Thao Cheuang], edited by Sumitr Pitiphat, 174–209. Bangkok: Thammasat University, Thai Khadi Research Institute.

Rajkai, Zsombor, and Ildikó Bellér-Hann, eds. 2012. *Frontiers and Boundaries: Encounters on China's Margins*. Wiesbaden: Harrassowitz.

Raquez, Alfred. 1902. *Pages laotiennes*. Hanoi: F. H. Schneider.

Rispaud, Jean. 1937. "Les noms à éléments numéraux des principautés Tai." *Journal of the Siam Society* 22: 77–122.

Robert, René 1941. *Notes sur les Tay Dèng de Lang Chánh (Thanh-hoá—Annam)*. Hanoi: Imprimerie d'Extrême-Orient.

Robinne, Francois, and Mandy Sadan, eds. 2007. *Social Dynamics in the Highlands of Southeast Asia: Reconsidering Political Systems of Highland Burma by E. R. Leach*. Leiden: Brill.

Salemink, Oscar. 1994. "The Return of the Python God: Multiple Interpretations of a Millenarian Movement in Colonial Vietnam." *History and Anthropology* 8: 129–64.

Schendel, Willem van. 2005. "Geographies of Knowing, Geographies of Ignorance: Jumping Scale in Southeast Asia." In *Locating Southeast Asia: Geographies of Knowledge and Politics of Space*, edited by Paul Kratoska, 275–307. Leiden: KITLV Press.

Schlemmer, Grégoire. 2017. "Ethnic Belonging in Laos: A Politico-Historical Perspective." In *Changing Lives in Laos: Society, Politics, and Culture in a Post-Socialist State*, edited by Vanina Bouté and Vatthana Pholsena, 251–80. Singapore: NUS Press.

Scott, James C. 2009. *The Art of Not Being Governed. An Anarchist History of Upland Southeast Asia*. New Haven: Yale University Press.

Sikor, Thomas. 2004. "Conflicting Concepts: Contested Land Relations in North-western Vietnam." *Conservation and Society* 2, no. 1: 59–79.

Stuart-Fox, Martin. 1997. *A History of Laos*. Cambridge: Cambridge University Press.

Tambiah, Stanley. 1977. *World Conqueror and World Renouncer: A Study of Buddhism and Polity in Thailand against a Historical Background.* Cambridge: Cambridge University Press.

Tappe, Oliver. 2008. *Geschichte, Nationsbildung und Legitimationspolitik in Laos. Untersuchungen zur laotischen nationalen Historiographie und Ikonographie.* Berlin: Lit.

———. 2015. "A Frontier in the Frontier: Sociopolitical Dynamics and Colonial Administration in the Lao-Vietnamese Borderlands." *The Asia Pacific Journal of Anthropology* 16, no. 4: 368–87.

———. Forthcoming "Variants of Frontier Mimesis: Colonial Encounter and Intercultural Interaction in the Lao-Vietnamese Uplands." *Social Analysis*, 62/2 (2018).

Turner, Frederick Jackson. 1921. *The Frontier in American History.* New York: Holt.

Turton, Andrew, ed. 2000. *Civility and Savagery: Social Identity in Tai States.* Richmond: Curzon Press.

Walker, Harry. 2012. On Anarchist Anthropology. *Anthropology of this Century* 3. http://aotcpress.com/articles/anarchist-anthropology/.

Winichakul, Thongchai. 2000. "The Quest for 'Siwilai': A Geographical Discourse of Civilizational Thinking in the Late Nineteenth and Early Twentieth-Century Siam." *Journal of Asian Studies* 59, no. 3: 528–49.

Wolf, Eric. R. 1982. *Europe and the People without History.* Berkeley: University of California Press.

Wolters, Oliver W. 1982. *History, Culture, and Region in Southeast Asian Perspectives.* Singapore: ISEAS.

9

ANTHROPOLOGY, CIVILIZATIONAL ANALYSIS, AND THE MALAY WORLD

Joel S. Kahn

Introduction. Anthropology, Ethnography, Locality, Society

Like many of my contemporaries, I began my anthropological career in the 1970s by conducting localized fieldwork in rural communities, firstly in the Indonesian province of West Sumatra, and then in the Malaysian state of Negeri Sembilan. Influenced by the kinds of social anthropology being practiced in Britain at the time, however, I had never intended to restrict the analysis to two or three local communities. Rather, my PhD supervisors, and the authors of much of the anthropological literature to which I had been exposed, encouraged me to think of my task as that of documenting and analyzing the distinctive social structure of the Minangkabau "peoples" who inhabited these regions, peoples who, as it happened, already occupied an important place in the anthropological canon.[1] To be sure, the villages in which I had chosen to work would inevitably be atypical in certain respects. But this did not stop me from setting out to produce, or more accurately to refine, generalized models of Minangkabau social structure.

However, at the precise time that I was undertaking this research, developments both internal and external to the discipline were generating significant changes in our understanding of the goals of anthropological analysis, resulting, among other things, in a shift of focus from relatively homogeneous "societies" to the more heterogeneous "macroformations" within which these societies seemed to be embedded. At the same time, there was a general move away from synchronic models of societies toward a concern with the conditions of their appearance (and disappearance) in history (see for example Godelier 1977).

It is important to note that the problem was not that classical anthropology's methodological commitment to ethnography prevented us from dealing with macroformations per se, that is, with translocal sociocultural worlds dispersed across political boundaries (including those of nation-states and colonial empires).[2] Contra at least some of the critics of classical anthropology, Radcliffe-Brown's claim that anthropology could build models of social structure on the basis of ethnographic research "in any convenient locality of a suitable size" (Radcliffe-Brown 1963, 193) did not depend on a conceptualization of social worlds as necessarily localized (Werbner 2008).[3] Rather, as Robert Redfield, one of the pioneers of peasant studies in anthropology, asked as long ago as 1955—drawing our attention to a problem with a discipline that had focused almost exclusively on homogeneous social and cultural forms—"What forms of thought are available to us for conceiving and describing a whole that is both inclosed [*sic*] within other wholes and is also in part permeated by them?" (Redfield 1955, 114). In other words, the problem arises when anthropology seeks to tackle social worlds that are heterogeneous, that is when the relatively homogeneous "societies" they set out to study turn out to be embedded in more complex social "wholes." In such cases the commitment to ethnography makes the comparative analysis of social "wholes," which Radcliffe-Brown saw as anthropology's main theoretical task, particularly problematic.

A World Capitalist System?

The social wholes that seemed most relevant to us in the 1970s were not so much Redfield's peasantries per se—another American anthropologist having pointed out much earlier that peasantries were themselves in any case only "part-societies, part-cultures"[4]—but the colonial and "neocolonial" social formations within which the societies we were studying were "enclosed," which in turn "permeated" them, and from which derived the very conditions of their historical appearance (and possible disappearance).

From the perspective of the study of the linkages between global capitalism and local social and economic systems, the theory of what some called the "articulation of modes of production" seemed particularly relevant. Drawing on the theoretical work of Louis Althusser, Étienne Balibar, and Maurice Godelier, anthropologists and others with an interest in so-called political economy produced analyses of the relations between the local and the global understood in terms of the articulation of capitalist and precapitalist modes of production (see especially Rey 1973). For rather similar reasons, others were looking instead to dependency and world system theory as a way of "conceiving and describing" the particular macroformation within which "our" peoples seemed so clearly to be embedded, the formation that Wallerstein (1974) called the "modern world system."

However, with the benefit of hindsight, it is relatively easy to identify at least some of the reasons why these paradigms fell out of favor, at least among anthropologists. Their categories came to seem static and ahistorical; their analyses were always economistic and functionalist (everything served the "needs of capitalism"); they failed to anticipate the "development" and industrialization of supposedly "underdeveloped" regions in Asia and Latin America; they focused almost entirely on flows of commodities, finance, and surplus; they failed to anticipate the growing significance of global flows of people/labor from (and in some cases subsequently also to) the places we were studying; they appeared to significantly underplay the power of at least some "peripheral" states to affect the terms on which nations take part in the global system; they failed to anticipate the depth of attachment to cultural, gendered, and sexual identities; and they almost completely ignored the revitalization of religion in the so-called third world. Overall, their perspective seemed unduly Eurocentric—theirs was a world in which all power and influence flowed from a Euro-American "core" to a third world "periphery," ignoring flows of culture, people, and finance in other directions; and they failed what might be called the challenge of reflexivity. In particular, categories such as core, periphery, and semiperiphery seemed inadequate for the task of conceptualizing the religious, cultural, and economic specificity of the places we were studying, as well as the transformations that they were undergoing.

To be sure, before the implementation of Malaysia's so-called New Economic Policy in 1970 and the significant social transformations that followed, the Malay "community" was overwhelmingly rural and agricultural, with relatively high levels of poverty, economic marginality, and commercial "backwardness." Although some Malays—the political elite together with small numbers of Malay civil servants and aristocrats—lived in cities and towns, and while there was a scattering of Malay entrepreneurs, the main locus of economic, social, cultural, and religious life for the great majority of Malays was the territorial unit known as the *kampong*, where the main occupation was (small-scale) agricultural production. Apparently, the lives of Malay peasants differed little from those of the rural poor in large parts of the "third world."

However, after 1970 all this began to change fairly rapidly. Industrialization, the development of a dynamic service sector and the accompanying exponential growth of both "working-" and "middle-class" employment opportunities, together with the implementation of systematic preferences for ethnic Malays in employment, credit, urban housing, and tertiary education markets were all working to erode the older regime, which was characterized by the spatial segregation of Malaysia's main ethnic groups, the economic viability of peasant agriculture, and the peripheral status of the Malaysian economy. The result of these broad socioeconomic transformations was a decline, and in many cases (including some of the places where I had conducted fieldwork in the mid-1970s) the effective disappearance of the "traditional" Malay *kampong* altogether. Alongside these developments, the period saw a decline of an older nationalist narrative of Malay ethnic awakening.

This was not merely a repetition of a Western trajectory of societal modernization or of a familiar "transition" to capitalism. Rather, Malaysian "modernity" seems distinctive in a number of key respects: institutionally in the persistence of a separation between economic and political power; culturally in the thematization of Malay cultural distinctiveness and Malay rights, and in the strengthening of a kind of Malayo-Islamic civilizational imaginary as a means of making sense of the experience and destiny of Malays in the modern world. All this confirms the judgment that Malaysia in general, and Malay society in particular, could not be fully described in terms derived either from so-called modernization theory or from the categories of political economy.

An interest in the distinctive characteristics of this alternative "Malaysian modernity," therefore, took me away from the concerns of the so-called political economists, as well as mainstream anthropology. It was not until I began to think again about the historical background to Malaysia's post-1970 trajectory of social and political "modernization," and to the transformations that had occurred in the lifetimes of many of the people among whom I had worked, that I found myself returning to the problem of the anthropology of the Malays in general, and to questions about the appropriate objects of anthropological analysis in particular. What is Malay culture and society? And how are they to be conceptualized and studied in context of the increasing virtualization of modern Malayness? In asking questions such as these I claim no originality. As I was thinking about the changes in the nature and meanings of Malayness in the last decades of the twentieth century, there was renewed interest among anthropologists in the erosion of the links between cultures and territories. And it is fair to say that most were coming to the conclusion that one of the key characteristics of the latest phase of global modernization was that an earlier close connection between the two was being dissolved through a process of "deterritorialization." Correspondingly, much of the new literature focuses, then, on new kinds of translocal formations: transnational migrant "communities," diasporas, and the like.

However, when I began to look more closely at the period before the 1970s, I found the periodization implied in the theory of sociocultural deterritorialization—and along with this the idea of a uniquely, Malay(si)an-inflected form of modernity—less and less persuasive. This is because a closer look at the history of the Malays from the latter decades of the nineteenth century through the late 1960s suggested two things. Firstly, far from being the spatial locus of traditional indigenous Malay social and cultural life rooted in territorially based communities, the Malay *kampong* (along with many of the Malay ways of life associated with *kampong* existence) were themselves precipitates of earlier processes of Malayan modernization that had their roots in the colonial period. This is not to say that the category "Malay" was in any simple sense an invented tradition or a mere product of colonialism. But certainly ideas about Malay indigeneity, ethnic or racial distinctiveness, and, importantly, many of the actual ways of life associated with the "traditional" Malay *kampong,* the supposed *locus classicus* of Malay culture, turned out to have been a product of historical processes that were played out in the period when Malaya was a British colony. These ways of life were not survivals from some timeless premodern past. Specifically, indigenous Malay-ness as it came to be understood during the course of the early twentieth century was in some sense a creation of nationalist discourse and nation-building projects that began with the imposition of modern forms of colonial rule and the reshaping of discursive, but also physical, landscapes in the period from the early 1920s to the early 1950s (see Kahn 2006, 134–57). Secondly, prior to the "ethnogenetic" process that had given rise to the modern meanings of Malayness, the peoples (and territories) whose descendants came to be labeled ethnic Malays (*Bangsa Melayu*)[5] were part of a broad and extremely heterogeneous "Malay World" in which Malay-ness had very different meanings. What kind of world was this, and, to address the theme of, this volume, might we be justified in thinking of it in civilizational terms?

A Malay World

Although to speak of the existence of a discrete Malay World (*Dunia Melayu*) is problematic, the term is commonly used to refer to both the peoples and territories of insular and peninsular Southeast Asia (Malaya and northern Borneo; Kalimantan; Sumatra, along with parts of Java and what is now eastern Indonesia; southern Thailand; southern Vietnam; and the southern Philippines). Despite an internal diversity of lands and peoples, this world manifested—and frequently still does—a number of shared characteristics that mark it off both from East and South Asia, as well as from the cultural/civilizational heartlands of mainland Southeast Asia and even parts of island Southeast Asia, such as central Java and Bali, where territorially based states held sway.

The patterns of political, economic, cultural, and religious life in the classical Malay World have been described in greater detail elsewhere.[6] Many analysts have focused in particular on the distinctive nature of precolonial states in the region, which—unlike the nearby inland and island areas mentioned above (see, e.g., Lieberman 1997)—were rather small, located on coasts and river mouths, and derived their revenues mainly from participating in, or by levying taxes on, the trade that flowed between upland and interior regions and the outside world. As many observers have noted, land-based states elsewhere in Asia exercised power through their control over territory. In contrast, insofar as they can be said to have had it, the power of Malay rulers derived from their control over people. Moreover, given the links between Islam and trade, it is no accident that when Islam spread to Southeast Asia it did so mainly following the conversion of the rulers of precolonial Malay states, leading to a concentration of religious authority in the person of the ruler or Sultan and of personalized ties of dependency between "ruler" and "ruled," a system that Milner (1992) calls *kerajaan*.

There has been less discussion of the patterns of social, cultural, and economic life of the majority of the peoples who inhabited the uplands and interior regions of the Malay World who, although the dependents of particular rulers, particularly when it came to formalities of religious teaching and observance, did not seem unduly burdened by demands emanating from their rulers. Indeed, it seems that in certain circumstances demands for their labor or other kinds of extraction could be evaded if and when they became burdensome (cf. Tagliacozzo 2003).

Despite the ethnolinguistic diversity of the Malay World, its people do appear to have shared a number of other characteristics. These include relatively "loose" social structures (to borrow the term from students of rural Thailand) in which community membership was relatively fluid; systems of gender relations that, if not egalitarian, were at least less rigidly hierarchical than elsewhere; and patterns of inequality in which something like class- rather than status-based systems of social differentiation prevailed. Moreover, most of the regions that make up the Malay World were sparsely, even very sparsely populated at least at the beginning of the "modern" period. Their inhabitants were much more mobile than were those of the heartlands. Although there were pockets of sedentary, subsistence agriculture—including the inland valleys of peninsular Malaya and the central Sumatran highlands—swidden cultivation was also widely practiced, yielding produce for markets as well as for subsistence. Contrary to the stereotype of isolated tribal peoples, those who live in these marginal regions have a long history of involvement in trade and commerce. And contrary to the image of more or less homogeneous and stable village communities, the ancestors of many of today's *kampong* dwellers actually came from elsewhere. Local communities were relatively unstable and rates of geographical mobility were on the whole very high. People moved largely in response to new commercial opportunities, sometimes individually or in small groups as temporary migrants (a pattern of migration that the Minangkabau call *marantau*), sometimes as whole kin groups or village communities. And, as noted, the Malay World was ethnically and linguistically extremely diverse.

Colonialism, the State, Modernization, and Development in the Malay World

Although it certainly had significant implications for economy, polity, and society in the Southeast Asian heartlands, the coming of Europeans did not at first drastically alter the situation in much of the Malay World. It was only sometime around the middle of the nineteenth century that qualitative changes began to manifest themselves with a significant increase in the levels of commercialization and immigration into the frontiers and borderlands. These shifts set in motion a distinctive process of economic "development" and societal modernization that also marks these regions off from other parts of Asia. Typically this development has been attributed to fact that these regions were the main sites of large-scale Western, multinational, and/ or transnational enterprise in plantation agriculture; agribusiness; banking, finance, processing, and marketing of agricultural commodities; logging and timber processing; and mining. However, very significant numbers of smaller-scale (and even some larger-scale) Asian entrepreneurs, including cash croppers, miners, traders, retail and wholesale merchants, artisans and manufacturers, transport owners and operators, land speculators, and money lenders—many of them also involved in transnational commercial networks (Chinese, Indian, Hadhrami, and Muslim)—were active participants in, and beneficiaries of, the rapid emergence of "capitalist" economy on the margins and borderlands of the Netherlands East Indies, British Malaya, the Philippines, and colonial Indochina.

All this took place in regions that were peripheral to the centers of modern (colonial and "para-colonial") state formation, at least in the early phases of economic development. This accounts for the fact that, from the perspective of the region's states, their peoples were viewed as relatively wild and uncivilized. Modern state and nation building in these regions did not really begin to gain traction until the late colonial period. Prior to that, the regions were subjected to relatively loose or informal systems of economic and political control. And in some cases, these regions have remained politically marginal because they continue to be underrepresented in political centers. Because these regions were nonetheless sites of rapid commercial development—indeed, they are or have often been the main centers of economic modernization in Southeast Asia—the result has been the above-noted disjuncture between economic and formal political power that seems to prevail in much of modern Southeast Asia.

This somewhat schematic account of the Malay World should be sufficient to give a sense of the sort of macroformation within which localized Malay communities were formed, and in which they were, and in a certain sense still are, embedded. What sort of entity is this Malay World? How is it best studied and analyzed? And specifically, given the focus of, this volume, is it a (proper) object for civilizational analysis?

The Malay World and Civilizational Analysis

What some have called the Malay World constituted a sociocultural world that was (and in some sense still is): (1) translocal, in that it transcended the boundaries of local communities as well as the territorial spheres of influence of what were typically relatively small states, principalities, and sultanates that constituted the main forms of political organization above the level of the local community before the consolidation of modern bureaucratic rule; (2) a place in which certain shared patterns of social, cultural, economic, and political life had "congealed," to borrow a term from the editors of the volume, over a relatively long period of time; (3) relatively distinctive vis-à-vis other sociocultural worlds; and (4) particularly receptive to processes of economic development and societal modernization, generating a rather specific pattern of development that might lead one to speak of an alternative, Malay modernity.[7]

All this suggests the pertinence of some recent developments in civilizational analysis to the case of the Malay World and to the shared patterns of economic, political, social, and cultural life within it.[8] There are those, of course, who reject civilizational analysis on the grounds of its supposed elitism. "Little Traditions," to borrow another of Robert Redfield's conceptual contributions to the study of complex macroformations, may resist assimilation by civilizational "Great Traditions."[9] However, upland (or, more typically, upstream) peoples in insular and peninsular Southeast Asia are not typically best thought of as wholly autonomous from Malay religio-political elites, or from larger merchant elites of Chinese, Indian, or Hadhrami extraction. Upstream peoples, such as the Minangkabau, operate within broader civilizational imaginaries even as they resist their control.

However, instead of becoming embroiled in a semantic debate over whether or not the Malay World is properly labeled a civilization, I will conclude by raising two matters which any such determination must take into account. Firstly, there is the issue of the heterogeneity of this entity. Among the defining features of the Malay World is that it was characterized precisely by the absence of any single, overarching cultural, religious, or civilizational imaginary; the Malay world was characterized by a diversity of such imaginaries. Secondly, there is what might be called the problem of reflexivity. I am referring here not to civilizational reflexivity in the manner of Eisenstadt (2000), but to reflection on the very role of the civilizational analyst. I want to ask, in other words, what it is at stake in the current debate over the concept of civilization, and more particularly what would be at stake in any attempt to speak of a Malay Civilization.

A Heterogeneous Malay World

As the above discussion suggests, the Malay World has been a site of a great diversity of languages, cultures, and religions. Moreover, given the high rates of population mobility both within insular and peninsular Southeast Asia and between Southeast Asia and other parts of the world—notably southern China, parts of South Asia, parts of the Middle East (particularly the Hadhramaut) and, from the sixteenth century onward, Portugal, Spain, the Netherlands, France, and Britain—categories such as insider and outsider, native and latecomer, are highly misleading. Contrary to the claims of nationalists, few peoples in the Malay World are accurately conceived as indigenous; most of the "indigenous" inhabitants of places like peninsular Malaya, large swathes of "Outer Island Indonesia," or the Mekong Delta were either born elsewhere or are descended from sojourners or immigrants. At the very least, it can be said that considerable numbers of those labeled Bumiputera in Malaysia or Pribumi in Indonesia are no more indigenous to the places they currently inhabit than are their "nonindigenous" ethnically Chinese, Indian, and Arab compatriots.

Moreover, it would be misleading to think of the Malay World as a patchwork of timeless and discrete cultures and societies. High levels of economic, political, and social interaction and flexible boundaries between ethnic groups and local communities have been defining features of these regions since well before the colonial period. This high degree of flexibility resulted not only in religious, cultural, and linguistic diversity, but also in processes of ethnogenesis and of cultural and linguistic hybridization that are unique to the region. A clear example is the continually evolving pattern of linguistic usage and linguistic hybridization, which has facilitated communication across the linguistic divides within it.

If the Malay World is to be thought of in civilizational terms, therefore, it cannot be thought of as the project of any single civilizational framework. Rather it was both the site and outgrowth of a diversity of such frameworks—Hindu, Buddhist, Confucian, Islamic, and even Western—often at the same time. All have contributed to the formation of the Malay

World, as have the so-called traditional ontologies of a variety of groups in the region. In other words, the Malay World has been multicultural and multireligious—even multicivilizational—from the outset. If this world is to be labeled Malay, it cannot be Malay in an ethnic, cultural, or religious sense. Malay can only have an inter- or trans-ethnic, -cultural, or -religious sense. It is an open question, therefore, whether the concept of civilization is sufficiently flexible to be pertinent to the case of the Malay World, or whether this world might be thought of as an intercivilizational arena. Even this possibility must be questioned because it would imply that civilizations are really culturally and religiously homogeneous. It may be that civilizations only appear homogenous because certain groups within them have a stake in presenting them as if they were.

In my view, it is important to take some time to think about the implications of adopting any particular analytic language, or framework to the context of contemporary Southeast Asia. Clearly, there is a desire to escape the normative implications of the older language of civilization in more recent contributions to civilizational analysis. However, even if it were possible to escape earlier connotations of Western superiority, the use of the term still runs the risk of playing into the hands of Malay ultranationalists who continue to work to exclude or marginalize non-Malays as well as non-Muslims in contemporary Malaysia. Such talk would also provide an ideological platform for the push by certain members of the Malay elite for regional political and economic hegemony. Nonethnic Malays have already raised strong objections that my work on the "modern Malay World" could facilitate ethnocentric ideologies, even when I have made it perfectly clear that I use Malay in a nonethnic sense. These objections by nonethnic Malays make me extremely hesitant to use a term such as *Malay Civilization*.

On the other hand, equally in need of attention are questions about the role of Western analysts themselves in the Malay World. What are the ultimate goals of civilizational analysis? Is our goal to produce accurate and authentic accounts of other civilizations? If so, how can we study Asian civilizational imaginaries without at the same time altering them through translation, interpretation, and negotiation? Or do we study other civilizations for us? What is the place of civilizational analysis in "our" civilization? In my view, none of these questions can be answered unless we treat civilizational analysis itself as a particular form of intercivilizational encounter.

Notes

1. In fact, the Malays of Negeri Sembilan are said to be descended from migrants from West Sumatra (although the precise connection is lost in time), and the two groups have typically been lumped together by anthropologists due to similarities of social structure (see for example Josselin de Jong 1951).

2. I use the term *translocal* rather than *transnational* because in many cases such worlds predate processes of modern state and nation building.

3. As Johann Arnason points out in his Introduction to, this volume, Marcel Mauss's concept of civilization was broad enough also to include such more or less homogeneous, but territorially dispersed macroformations, while American anthropologists worked with a parallel notion of "culture area."

4. See Kroeber (1948).

5. The Malay term *Bangsa* was, in fact, more commonly glossed by the English word *race*. For a discussion of the relevance of the term in the Malaysian context, see Kahn (2008).

6. See for example the work of J. M. Gullick (1958), Anthony Reid (1988, 1993; Reid and Castles 1975), and Anthony Milner (1982, 1995, 2008) on the nature of the precolonial Malay polity; Michael Laffan (2003), among others, on the coming of Islam and the links between island Southeast Asia and the Middle East; and my own work on economic development in the frontiers and borderlands of the Malay World and the impact of modern state and nation building on community formation, ethnicity, and identity (Kahn 2006, 2012).

7. Even today, the leading sites of Southeast Asia's "modern" economic and capitalist development are located in what are, or used to be, "frontier" regions. Such cases include Malaysia's Klang Valley, Indonesia's Riau Archipelago, and even Singapore, which became perhaps the most important cultural and commercial center of the Malay World in the early nineteenth century.

8. My understanding of these debates comes particularly from the work of Arnason (2003; 2006).

9. Most recently, James Scott has analyzed Southeast Asia's "upland" peoples in anticivilizational terms (2009), maintaining that "civilizations cannot climb hills."

References

Arnason, Johann P. 2003. *Civilizations in Dispute: Historical Questions and Theoretical Traditions*. Leiden and Boston: Brill.

———. 2006. "Civilizational Analysis, Social Theory and Comparative History." In *Handbook of Contemporary Social Theory*, edited by Gerard Delanty. Oxford and New York: Taylor and Francis e-Library.

Eisenstadt, Shmuel N. 2000. "Multiple Modernities." *Daedulus* 129, no. 1: 119–35.

Godelier, Maurice. [1973] 1977. *Marxist Perspectives in Anthropology*. Cambridge: Cambridge University Press.

Gullick, J. M. 1958. *Indigenous Political Systems of Western Malaya*. London School of Economics Monographs on Social Anthropology no. 17, London: Athlone Press.

Josselin de Jong, P. E. de 1951. *Minangkabau and Negri Sembilan*. Leiden: Ijdo.

Kahn, Joel S. 2006. *Other Malays: Nationalism and Cosmopolitanism in the Modern Malay World*. Asian Studies Association of Australia in association with Singapore University Press (Singapore) and NIAS Press (Copenhagen) [published in the United States by University of Hawaii Press].

———. 2008. "Culture and Modernities." In *The Sage Handbook of Cultural Analysis*, edited by Tony Bennett and John Frow, 338–58. Los Angeles, London, New Delhi, Singapore: Sage.

———. 2012. "Islam and Capitalism in the Frontiers and Borderlands of the Modern Malay World." In *Modernity in Question: Southeast Asian Perspectives*, edited by Wendy Mee and Joel S. Kahn. Kyoto: Kyoto University Press.

Kroeber, A. L. 1948. *Anthropology*. New York: Harcourt, Brace.

Laffan, Michael F. 2003. *Islamic Nationhood and Colonial Indonesia: The Umma below the Winds*. London and New York: Routledge Curzon.

Lieberman, Victor 1997. "Transcending East-West Dichotomies: State and Culture Formation in Six Ostensibly Disparate Areas." *Modern Asian Studies* 31, no. 3: 463–546.

Milner, Anthony. 1992. *Kerajaan: Malay Political Culture on the Eve of Colonial Rule*. Tucson: University of Arizona Press.

———. 1995. *The Invention of Politics in Colonial Malaya*. Cambridge and New York: Cambridge University Press.

———. 2008. *The Malays*. Malden, MA, and Oxford: Wiley-Blackwell.

Redfield, Robert. 1955. *The Little Community*. Chicago: Chicago University Press.

Radcliffe-Brown, A. R. 1963. *Structure and Function in Primitive Society*. London: Cohen and West.

Reid, Anthony. 1988. *Southeast Asia in the Age of Commerce, 1450–1680. Vol. I: The Lands below the Winds*. New Haven: Yale University Press.

———. 1993. *Southeast Asia in the Age of Commerce, 1450–1680. Vol. II: Expansion and Crisis*. New Haven: Yale University Press.

———, and Lance Castles, eds. 1975. *Precolonial States Systems in Southeast Asia*. Kuala Lumpur: Malaysian Branch of the Royal Asiatic Society.

Rey, Pierre-Philippe. 1973. *Les alliances des classes*. Paris: Maspero.

Scott, James C. 2009. *The Art of Not Being Governed: An Anarchist History of Upland Southeast Asia*. New Haven: Yale University Press.

Tagliacozzo, Eric. 2003. "Finding Captivity among the Peasantry: The Malay/Indonesian World 1850–1925." *South East Asia Research* 11, no. 2: 203–32.

Wallerstein, Immanuel. 1974. *The Modern World System*. Vol 1. New York: Academic Press.

Werbner, Pnina. 2008. "The Cosmopolitan Encounter: Social Anthropology and the Kindness of Strangers." In *Anthropology and the New Cosmopolitanism: Rooted, Feminist, and Vernacular Perspectives*, edited by Pnina Werbner, 47–68. Oxford and New York: Berg.

10

CHINESE CIVILIZATION IN COMPARATIVE PERSPECTIVE
Some Markers

Stephan Feuchtwang

Introduction

I shall start from a concept, based on Mauss, of civilizations as multicentered hierarchies of aspiration and exclusion.[1] It is a concept to be used to compare and to critically describe each civilization's criteria of human being, its outsides and lower reaches, and as a way of learning and adapting to what is absorbed into its centers from great peripheral regions and other centers of civilization. On this basis, I will provide a sketch of moments of irreversible change in the history of civilization in China, in which I will select certain themes, in particular that of hierarchy, by which comparison with other civilizations will be suggested.

In a late solo essay published in 1929, Marcel Mauss considered how a civilization spreads from an origin. For him, it was important not only to trace the evolution of any one civilization over time and in any one location but also to trace the evolution of a people who distinguish themselves and are politically, customarily, linguistically, or religiously distinct (Schlanger 2006, 59). As Mauss defined it, a civilization consists of "those social phenomena which are common to several societies," and "more or less related to each other" by lasting contact "through some permanent intermediaries, or through relationships from common descent" (ibid., 61). A civilization is, then, "a family of societies" (ibid., 62). We can imagine what these permanent intermediaries are when we think of tributary or diplomatic, trading or marital relations. In the technical terms of Mauss's and Durkheim's sociology, a civilization is the spread of collective representations and practices, which are the social aspect of the materials of civilization. Mauss says they are "arbitrary," by which he means that they are not universal but preferred modes of making and doing things. In other civilizations, the same things are done in different ways.

In the actual order of analysis, to say that a set of shared phenomena belong together as a civilization is to infer from archaeological and historical evidence a common set of practices and meanings, not one dominant characteristic, design, or thing but the way they all hang together and evolve over time and space. Note that these inferences mark boundaries of civilizational spread, which should be treated as broad frontier regions. Beyond them are the further spreads of bartered or marketed goods that are accepted for their strangeness, or exoticism, rather than the symbolic meaning or the practice and conduct that goes with them within the civilization from which and within which they are produced. But this raises difficulties of distinguishing regions of trade and commerce from civilizational spreads: Where do the latter end and the former continue?[2] This is an empirical issue, but it can never be resolved into a hard and fast border.

Within a civilizational spread there are other boundaries of more coherent social and cultural structures and their centers. These singularities enclose and differentiate themselves from others in similar ways that characterize a civilization. In this sense, the civilization, as a way of defining inside and outside, logically precedes and gives societies and cultures a mode of self-definition and internal coherence. Insides are defined by denying borrowing from similar but differentiated outsides.

Civilization Singular and Plural

Mauss, like Durkheim, was, of course, committed to a social science that was also a moral project—a way of knowing what they called a moral milieu as a way of knowing how to reform a world lacking moral sense. Mauss's concept of civilization is no less part of this project than any of his other writings. Like the rest of his and Durkheim's work, "civilization" is both an analytic and a critical concept.

It is normal to use the word *civilization* and even more its adjectival versions, *civilized* and *uncivilized,* as moral evaluations. And it is possible to use all the different civilizations that have been identifiable in various definitions as a common fund of human morality, philosophically combining them or extracting from them a concept of humanity as a contrast to what is identifiable as science-based modern civilization. This would be a similar move to that made by Lévi-Strauss in his reflection on the unity of what he had demonstrated: the common human classificatory science of the concrete and its basis in close empirical observation. From this classification, argued Lévi-Strauss, all civilizations have emerged, including that governed by modern abstract and experimental science and its destructive and exploitative as well productive propensities (1962: 22, 291, 294). However we distill it, what it is to be human could become a criterion of what a particular civilization does and harms, its particular forms of violence, and what other possibilities its practices and patterns provide. The point of the exercise would be to raise hopes of less harm, which is basically the harm of oppression, and in closing off raised hopes and expectations.

Contrary to those who treat civilization as a singular, general, normative standard, Michael Rowlands and I have been working on a project of comparative civilizations in which we tease out analytically and conceptually both the common themes that exercise the creativity and tensions that produce civilizations and their distinctiveness (i.e., what Mauss called their arbitrariness). In other words, what might be common to humanity in the sequences of civilizations' emerging and diminishing, their evolution through contingent and endogenous processes of transformation, and the themes we can see at play in them, are all open questions (Feuchtwang and Rowlands 2010). Universals have empirically to be demonstrated. While we share with Johann Arnason (1988) and Mauss the centrality of moral aspirations as formations of humanity, we do not stress the higher reaches of civilizations. We reject the idea that those who are at the bottom or at the margins of the hierarchy created in every civilization are any less part of those civilizations and any less human than those who have the accomplishments that each civilization ranks high. Indeed, it is among the heterodox, at the margins, and at the lower reaches of a civilization where we often find within civilizations critical disputes to the claim of being civilized or human. Further, those who retreat from civilizational empires cannot be understood except by reference to what they seek to escape and indeed to some extent still aspire (see Scott 2009; Tappe, this volume).

While we follow Arnason's high regard for the work of Durkheim and Mauss (Arnason, this volume), we seek to take it in a different direction by stressing spread, mix, and variation. New civilizations emerge and are transformed out of borrowings and fusions at the margins, and at their lower reaches, where the hopes and aspirations raised by the criteria of civilization are dashed or denied.

The Moral Person at the Heart of Civilization

At the center of Durkheim and Mauss's sociology and anthropology is the concept of the person. The person is a body of experience that learns and acts as a moral being. All humans are moral beings, which is to say social persons acting in and with or against their roles, making everyday practical judgments and decisions, mainly habitually but to some extent consciously. Moral behaviors are made through and affect human physical and other capacities. We contain representations of self and others that we imagine automatically, as second nature, because we have learned of and from their presence through infancy and onward. These representations inform our habitual actions and are modified by the habitual actions of others constantly in practice and in experiencing the ambivalent feelings they arouse as guides to action and judgment.

Endorsing this element of Maussian sociology, but emphasizing the activity of the moral person rather than treating it simply as a result, a subject of passive reception of a social milieu, we start our study of civilization from the person's embodiment, habitual and experienced; from morality learned as norms of conduct, principally through everyday and more formal and extended rituals of eating together, of feeding or offering, of polite address, greeting and hospitality, not only to other living humans but also to ancestors, ghosts, gods, demons, and spirits of the environment, animate and inanimate. Another way of saying the same thing is that each civilization has its own anthropology, a learned sense of what it is to be a human among other things and beings in the world, and a way of knowing them, framing the results of cognitive and sensory experience.

A civilization is a number of ways of learning to be human that bear, as Mauss puts it, a family resemblance. The activity of moral persons must be assumed behind the material evidence of rituals, buildings, settlements, burials, middens, ways of cooking, things eaten and excreted, and whatever else can be gleaned from the archaeological record. What follows is a sketch of civilization in China over a long duration of several millennia, including both archaeological, written, and observational source materials. It is necessarily provisional, a selection of what seems from the perspective of long-term history to have been significant both comparatively and thematically. The evidence, largely secondary, upon which I base this sketch suggests a sequence that might be repeated elsewhere, in part or with different outcomes at any one point, but that took place in a distinctive way in China.

What I select are senses of being in the world, of hierarchy and aspiration, as the key elements of any civilization. "Hierarchy" is here understood as a ranked scheme of accomplishment encompassed by a "world" or a "cosmology." This is not the same as a class system, though it is affected by and itself affects class formation and the history of states in the political economy of what became the Chinese Empire. There is great overlap, particularly in China, between the centering of a cosmology and the formation of an empire from multiple states; many of the civilizational transformations I shall recount occurred because of political and economic causes in what became a politically centered cosmocracy.

Mark 1: Steepening of Hierarchy and Centralizing Hegemony from the Stone to the Iron Age in China

Pottery vessels of the Middle Neolithic (Yangshao) period, 5000–3000 BCE, found in sites stretching across the north China plains and the loess land to the west, included vessels such as the tripod for heating offerings, probably to ancestors and spirits that could influence the weather. Remains of grain—millet in all sites, wheat and rice in some—and of domesticated and hunted animals show that all these must have been included in sacrificial offerings. In the same period and the same sites, unprepared oracle bones, ready to be fired to produce cracks for divination have been found. These bones come from the shoulder blades of the same animals that were sacrificed: pigs, dogs, sheep, goats, cattle, and deer. Houses and tombs in these settlements were not markedly differentiated. Most settlements were centers of territories for hunting, fishing, and extensive agriculture, but the main site at Yangshao was defended by a moat, indicating that it was a center for a number of neighboring settlements. Hierarchy is indicated in the encompassing world of spirits and ancestors more than among living humans.

In later Neolithic sites (4000–3000 BCE) that form a belt down the eastern coast of China from present-day Liaoning to Guangzhou, spirits and ancestors come together in the jades that were buried around the burned bodies in the most elaborate tombs—in other words, in a hierarchical order. Some of the jades, particularly those that were much later called *cong,* are carved with semihuman, zoo-anthropological monsters, possible successors to similar but earlier figures on pots. They are possible predecessors of the masks on later bronzes (Lei Congyun 1996; see also Wengrow 2011 on the Late Bronze Age in Eurasia). These chimera are not ancestors but other, probably more feared and powerful spirits. The person with whom they were buried may have been reputed with the power to make them visible in other ways than their carved representations. In other words, it is possible that at the top of the hierarchy were shamans, as Chang Kwang-chih has argued (1983; 1989).

As soon as we encounter hierarchies of tombs, we also encounter fortified villages, then towns, and then cities. And within them, we encounter the theme of the relation between offerings to ancestors and offerings to the other spirits, and how each might establish claims not only to property in land and surplus (of gift or tribute) but also claims to gain from these powers to contact divinities. We could, along with Chang Kwang-chih, infer that the tombs of rulers were those of shamans and that their successors treated their forebears as mediators to more powerful spirits.

North Asian shamans might be a guide here. Take, for instance, Daur Mongolian *yadgan.* They embody spirits that are wild, counterintuitive, shape-changing, and animate as distinct from the marvelously plain mountains, rivers, and forests that elders address in rituals associated with ancestors. The spirits that Daur shamans embody are often spirits of former shamans. New shamans are trained and initiated by older shamans, but they are not usually their parents or ancestors (Humphrey and Urgunge Onon 1996, 29–64). Like spirit-mediums everywhere, shamans are cosmological innovators when negotiating conditions of uncertainty. They can become leaders. Perhaps the leaders of early Chinese states combined the two roles that in Mongolian Daur practice were separated into shaman and elder. Each divines in distinct ways. Indeed, Daur elders use cracks in the shoulderblades of sheep, similar to the oracle bones used by monarchs and nobles in China thousands of years ago. By contrast to these contemporary ethnographic descriptions of ritual divination among the Daur, the archaeological record in China reveals long processes of change. There is a similar separation in roles, but one associated with steepening hierarchy and therefore with different outcomes: shaman-ancestor becomes ancestor with shamanic advisors to his ruler-descendant, and that turns into a quest for immortality as a sage. I will trace this trajectory in more detail, to see how the hierarchy beneath this top level and the spread from its centers evolves. It is a process in which centricity and hegemony emerge, but the process has never been completed, so we cannot accept, as Mauss seems to do, a single starting point of spread from a center.

The elaboration of pottery in the late Neolithic and Chalcolithic period in China (3000–2000 BCE), often associated with a key site at Longshan, includes a spread south to the Yangzi River basin. More emphatically differentiated than Yangshao, the main sites of Longshan pottery are towns with rammed earth walls and moats. In addition to oracle bones, on which the interpretation of the cracks was written in a script that is already mature, a less mature and undeciphered writing has been found on pottery of this period. Rice is widespread, and the cultivation of silkworms is evident. A number of city and other sites of elaborate divination are indicated, rather than one dominant site. Oracle bones would have been one among a number of means of divination, but the others did not leave hard remains. The power or skill to divine is a kind of knowledge possessed by some, treated as experts, and so the bones indicate a ranking of knowledge of invisible beings and powers.

Apart from the remains of divination, there are plenty of offering vessels, now not just of pottery but also of bronze. The biggest tombs in the settlement found at Taosi, dating 2500–2000 BCE, contained ritual instruments that would be found in later settlements and finally recorded in the handbook on ritual, the *Zhou Li*, compiled under the former Han dynasty after 200 BCE. In one of these settlements, not far from Taosi at a place called Erlitou in north-central China (Henan Province), a palace and city were excavated. They have a north-south-oriented grid pattern, as all Chinese capitals had from then onward. In the early layers of this site and other sites of the same period (1900–1300 BCE), there are signs of steep hierarchy—palaces and three different sizes of house and of tomb. More elaborately prepared oracle bones have been found at other sites contemporary with Erlitou, equally hierarchical (Flad 2008). But for the later period of Erlitou (1300–1050 BCE), Sarah Allen (2007) argues that bronze ritual vessels made in the city were hegemonic because a number of the shapes and key design features of the Erlitou bronzes were found in sites covering a large area. They were used for ritual offerings of alcohol and food to ancestors and gods. But there were significant variations of form and feature in each region, so much that other centers of bronze and pottery production, ritual, and kingship could challenge the center. For instance, excavations near what is now the capital city of the western province of Sichuan show a wealth of bronze forms and features absent from other centers, such that the challenge in the present day to be the definitively "Chinese" bronze culture is impossible to decide. In this spread, there were many centers, and any of them could replace the hegemony of another.

Further elaboration of the preparation of oracle bones and the addition of inscriptions onto them is concentrated at the site in Zhengzhou known to be a capital of the dynasty of the Shang kings, north of Erlitou. They are not exclusive to that city, but this highest elaboration of oracle bone divination establishes its own hierarchy, at the top of which are diviners exclusively in the service of kings. The king's diviners were hierarchically above those employed by nobles, who in turn were higher than those who provided oracle bone divination for commoners; divination was increasingly elaborate with each rung of social hierarchy (Flad 2008, 413, citing Venture 2002a, 203–208). The Shang court distinguished itself by the almost exclusive use for divination of turtle plastrons (undershells) and some turtle carapaces, as well as by the elaboration of treatment before and after crack divination. It was also distinguished by yarrow stick divination that was eventually codified in the *Book of Changes* (*Yi Jing*). But other cities in the late Shang period (1250–1046 BCE), when the capital had moved to Yinxu (near Anyang), displayed almost equally prestigious oracle bones and prestige goods, such as jade and cinnabar (Fang 2008, 423). So, we have evidence of a politico-ritual hierarchy of a superior among peers in their similar centers.

The writing on the oracle bones and in the bronze sacrificial vessels now helps in the description of the rites themselves. The bronze vessels of the Shang are containers and heaters of millet-based alcohol, steamed millets, and cooked meats. One of the most prominent rites using such vessels was the guest ritual, in which the guest was either an ancestor or one of the spirits that could bring rain or drought. Through ancestors, human nobles and kings could approach the supreme deity Di (who according to some scholars may be a collective term for all supreme ancestors). The supreme deity was indirectly addressed as a decider of the fortunes and misfortunes of kings. Other rituals to which the oracle bone inscriptions refer include exorcisms of misfortune by addressing royal ancestors. Offerings to royal ancestors are also made to secure harvests. Divination was itself a ritual, including offerings, to know whether an action, such as creating a city or going into battle, would be approved by the highest deity, or whether a misfortune like flooding was the result of a curse by the supreme deity or an ancestor. After offering, the alcohol and millet would be shared by a group defined by descent from the ancestor addressed in the ritual. By the Shang, the ancestors of rulers were considered the main juridical authorities in the surrounding invisible world, forming their descendants as persons and groups at the top of steep hierarchies.

Michael Puett (2001) has worked through many oracle bone inscriptions to conclude that the earliest examples convey a conception of the highest deity as beyond human control, and as capricious as the Greek deities. Rites were, according to Puett's following volume (2002), a way to create ancestors out of the spirits of the royal dead, to make of them a genealogical pantheon. The recent dead who formed the lowest rung could be persuaded by ritual offerings to cease causing minor misfortunes, such as toothache, in specific persons. The highest ancestors could be persuaded to intercede by entertaining the supreme deity, to whom ritual offerings could not be made directly.

The relation of ancestors to the divinities of natural phenomena is similar to those of West African civilization. In West Africa, ancestors are invoked, and ritual pacts made with them, to bring into the center and the visible world what their descendants need from the invisible outside. But in China there was not the same dichotomy of two kinds of lineage, those of autochtonous earth cults and those of rulers, whose dynasties were from external ancestors. Instead, common people were denied the rites for creating ancestors but shared the common heritage of shamanically visible deities of fertility. Granet and others have used the *Book of Songs* and other compilations to detect popular fertility rites of song, dance, and legends; and to identify heroic figures who made agriculture possible and for whom there may have been popular cults that may well have included shamans who made contact with spirits of mountains, rivers, or stars. There must have been mortuary rites among commoners, but they were not allowed to build shrines to make ancestors out of their dead. In short, the ancestors of rulers and nobility in China are contrasted not so much with autochtony as with fertility rites and shamans.

The relationship between ancestors and gods is perhaps singularly fused in China. The ancestors of rulers and nobles are mediators to higher gods and both these gods and divine ancestors of the top ranks may have been shared with the common people as gods. The hymns and ritual dances compiled in the *Book of Songs* praise divine ancestors. Noblemen of this time knew the *Songs* by heart and would quote them in their diplomatic missions to tributary peer states (Hawkes 1985, 25–26). All of them are arranged in a hierarchy, at the top of which is a supreme and virtuous deity, of whom they are agents. The stories told of these deities in the *Songs* include dramas of miraculous birth (for instance from a stone or from the belly of their father) and of transgression and misrule. Divine ancestors were among the mythic heroes who had founded the possibilities of life and its production— such as Yu who completed the unfinished work of his father in dividing land from water, controlling flood; or the much later inventor of paper, or, for another later instance, the most skilled carpenter. For further instances, the founding ancestor of the kings of the state of Chu was the God of Fire and the founding ancestor of the kings of another Chinese state, the Zhou, which became the supreme state among its peers after defeating the Shang, was the God of Millet.

These deities could be reached either through royal ancestors or by shamans on spirit journeys. So, it is entirely possible that at one time kings were also shamans but over a long period, kings and nobles stressed their role as makers of ancestors, bringers of gifts, and avoiders of the misfortunes the ancestors could wreak. Shamans were still employed at court, but as prestigious experts brought from other parts of the kingdom. This continued into the Han dynasty while shamans among the common people were at the same time condemned as performers of lewd and excessive cults (Lewis 2007, 87, 97 and 179–81).

Later compilations, such as the *Songs of the South* (*Chu Ci*) attributed to the poet in exile Qu Yuan, but also what became the Daoist classics, the *Zhuang Zi, Huai Nan Zi,* and *Shan Hai Jing,* also contain shamanic songs or hymns that retell the myths of a great many divine heroes and kings. These songs were derived from earlier inscriptions and images of the invisible world (Hawkes 1985, 122–51). To their readers, they pose puzzles of contradiction and inconsistency. This is probably because the same myths spread across several kingdoms, each a rival to the others, who told these same myths to authenticate themselves and condemn the others. There are different myths about the same personae. Inconsistencies are also due to the fact that there were variants of a cosmology that over this same long period of time was being elaborated into systems of stars, and layers and fields of Heaven (*Tian*) and of Earth (*Di*), and of a cosmogony of the mating of two principles *Yin* and *Yang* that were at first more descriptive categories of the physical landscape, meaning respectively sun-facing and shadowed.

There seems to have been a transformation of the juxtaposition of shamans and ancestors. Rulers and nobles that may in previous times have been shamans came later to rely on mediation through their dead as ancestors, no longer themselves performing shamanic trances, whereas shamans dwelt among commoners. Their songs of spirit travel remain from the rituals they performed for both the nobility and commoners.

The theme of the outside conqueror, a version of the stranger king, is certainly traceable in China as it is in Africa and possibly worldwide (Sahlins 2014). Wars between small states resulted in conquests. The conqueror's ancestors carried a mandate of mediation with heaven, a power to make mountains sacred (as points of mediation with heaven), and a capacity to become immortal. The conquered dynasty's ancestors are relegated in favor of the conqueror's. The Zhou ancestors, for example, replaced the Shang in the Bronze Age with the help of horses and chariots from the steppes, bringing their powers from an outside that was considered higher, associated with mountains, and correspondingly with the powers of divinities and the supreme deity. The supreme deity was renamed *Tian* (Heaven) by the Zhou kings. In the renaming there was also a changed conception of the original ancestor into a descendent of Heaven. The king of Zhou was the first to call himself Son of Heaven (*Tianzi*) and thus to join Heaven into his offerings to his own ancestors, and so bring about the possibility of commanding the sun, clouds, mountains and rivers, grain, and soil through their gods and spirits.

By the Zhou dynasty (ninth century BCE), the inscriptions inside bronze vessels show that they were petitions to ancestors for protection and for aid in attaining promotion in the service of a ruling house (Marya Khayutina 2002). Alternately, the vessels celebrated legitimation by the supreme god of the rule of the Zhou kings themselves (Puett 2001, 33–34). In either case, the vessels distinguished those who offered them from the common run of humanity. The vessels themselves constitute sacred treasure for a noble line.

Bronzes also performed a civilizational function, as did all rites, according to the texts of the period. In particular, according to one text, the casting of bronzes with images made visible the forms of the spirits that governed the winds and other natural phenomena. One passage, for instance, referring to some mountain spirits, says, "They all have a human body and sheep horns. In sacrifices to them, use one sheep and, for grain offerings, use millet. These are the spirits. When they appear, the wind and rainwater make destruction"; the passage then prescribes rites to dissuade the spirits from such destruction (Puett 2002, 96–97). What might once have been the figure of a shaman or a shaman's spirit is here just the figure of a mountain spirit, and making it visible is an act of moral formation according to the same inscription.

Mark 2: Sage Rule and Self-Cultivation (Political Cosmocracy)

In the invisible world mediated by rulers, there is a supreme deity (*Tian*), imperial ancestors, the lesser ancestors of a landed nobility and of royal princes, and the ancestors and deities of tributary kings. There is also the dark side of ancestors who, if not propitiated, return to wreak harm. The afterlife includes bodily aspiration to immortality, by ritual discipline and self-cultivation, to be continued after death. In one tomb, in Fangmatan, a bamboo strip text relates the story of a man who died before his time and when the officials of the afterlife realized the mistake they released him back into life (von Falkenhausen 2006, 318). This allusion to an afterlife bureaucracy, in addition to the provision for luxurious life after death as prevention of return to life, is continued in mortuary ritual until the present.

The history of death rites in China from the ninth century BCE, particularly through the exemplary performance of rites and the learning of the classics that praise the early Zhou as an exemplary period of harmony and balance, rests on the praise of filial duty. This ancestral doctrine continues to exist alongside envisaging and making visible in ritual, painting, and writing the realms of the dead that could bring harm and the bureaucracy of command over the fate of the souls of the dead.

The period of the invention of iron smelting for tools and weapons and the intensification of agriculture is also the period of argumentative writing that produced the written classics of Chinese civilization and of what has been designated the axial age of human transcendence. Common to all these writings is that they are addressed to a class of literati, who advise rulers on governance and ritual matters. Each author always refers back to former sages and sage rulers, and, by implication, includes himself in the aspiration to sagehood. Yet, as Puett (2001) points out, each text is written to some extent against previously published texts, presenting a newly authoritative slant on a number of central issues. It is quite wrong to consider, as many do, that Chinese classical civilization was not adversarial. The issues over which writers disputed included the nature of common people and of humanity, and in particular the necessity for punishment and laws to control their potential evil. They debated whether priority should be given to regulations or to rituals, or whether harmony could be achieved through the self-cultivation practices of a sage ruler and his advisors who would become models of the way humans could achieve afterlife divinity. A related issue was whether invention of the arts of civilization, including those of farming, building, water control, and rule, was necessarily a conscious act on the part of heroes and sages, or whether the true sage is above such conscious creation. The supreme determinant of the movements of the universe, *Tian,* was described as the formation of patterns—*wen,* the same term used for cultivation. These patterns were for some authors revealed to sages, for others invented by sages. For all, these patterns were to be learned and transmitted through rites and prescribed norms of filial conduct bringing out the part of human nature that harmonizes, resonates, and responds spontaneously after learning not to give way to anger and other disruptive emotions. In sum, the debates were all about discipline and human self-constraint by means of either law or rite—a civilizing process long before that described for Europe by Norbert Elias. And they are also about the aspiration that the literate held for the sagehood and immortality attributed to heroes of the arts of civilization and revered rulers.

Tian was conceived as the source of normative conduct, but *Tian* could also go beyond, creating events that did not conform to ancient standards. This was recognition of transformative change, including changes by invention. The necessity to adjust to such transgressive events, chief of which was conquest, represented a dilemma between declaring a decline from the true pattern and accepting that the transgression was Heaven's will. Even Mencius, the most sagelike follower of Confucius, in his disappointment at the breech of norms and the nonacceptance of his advice, accepted that this was Heaven's fate or will (*ming*) (Puett 2002, 131–40).

Beside Axial Age contention and human transcendence, Morris (2011, 298ff) has detected another Eurasian parallel, a second axial age in which the salvation religions emerged out of the prophets and philosophers in what he calls high-end states: Paulian Christianity in the divided Roman Empire, and Daoist healing cults, Mahayana Buddhism, and Pure Land Salvation in the breakup of the Han dynasty. In China, these religions of salvation added the dimension that the soul, after death, needed to be redeemed from purgatory in an already established imagery of otherworld bureaucracy and its cosmos. One way or another, by military conquest or by civilizational absorption, the newly emerged center of the cosmos, which was also the political capital of imperial dynasties, was renewed from its outer regions and from other centers of civilization (see Wang Mingming 2014). The political act of conquering rival states and forming an empire, and the subsequent imperial sponsorship of the synchronization of several systems of divination and knowledge (Needham 1956; Henderson 1984) established the unification and singularity of political and civilizational centricity. Aspiration to this unification and singularity persisted through many divisions of empire and changes of the location of the capital city.

The mandate of heaven and the emperor's identification as the "son of heaven" meant that he was the supreme mediator between heaven and earth. We can add that a key guiding principle of the Chinese state, derived from Confucius's leading follower Mencius, was the warning that a ruler's success depended on "storing wealth among the people" (*cangfu yumin*), a regime of keeping tax low, storing grain for relief, and guaranteeing plots of land for subsistence cultivation (Deng 2003).

The sage ruler was the exclusive mediator with *Tian,* the source of the ordering principles of change and constancy. A poor ruler allowed his officials to be self-seeking, his court to be extravagant, and the common people to seek the aid of spirits and so to attempt to find their own mediations to *Tian*. In a phrase often cited, "cutting the [lay] communication between Heaven and Earth" was the ideal. The ruler, aided by ritual experts, through his sacrifices ordered the places of both the spirits in Heaven and the places of men on Earth, according to the fourth-century BCE text *Discourses of the State* (*Guoyu*), while the ruled simply revered the spirits and obeyed. Yet a later, Han dynasty classical compilation called the writings of *Master Guan* (*Guanzi*), including texts of the same period as the *Guoyu*, asserts that each person has an essence of vital energy that can be cultivated as a spirit, and that therefore each person can achieve sagehood through cultivation. This is the other principle beside sage rule of the civilization that emerged from Zhou rule onward, namely that knowledge and the attainment of sagacity or, in the Daoist tradition, of being a true person, was not just a question of birth, as in succession to an imperial dynasty. It was an attainment by means of learning, discipline, and technique in a system of discipleship and a line of masters.[3]

Mark 3: Absorbing Another Center of Civilization and Including the Commoner

Buddhism was introduced to China in the second century CE during one of many periods of disunity. It came from India via the central Asian steppes to the court of one of the northern dynasties. From the court, Buddhism's teachings seeped down the hierarchy and merged its highly moralistic versions of the underworld (as purgatory) and of rebirth with Daoist images of an underworld and its bureaucracy (Bokenkamp 2007). In this section I shall focus on the long-term process and effects of the absorption of Buddhism and its conception of a civilizational center into the imperial cosmocracy.

First, a political-economic note: from the Tang dynasty (618–905 CE), imperial codes protected private land ownership for all peasants and instituted equal inheritance among sons. This had the effect of breaking up landed estates that were not lineage, princely, or monastic trusts. This increase in central imperial power included the spread to commoners of access to the political class through education in literacy and passing civil service examinations. Those who did became a select, specialist, and almost exclusive elite.

The Tang were open to the influences of other civilizations but retained the centrality of their own universe. Indeed, the Tang expanded the extent of imperial rule to its greatest point westward, only surpassed by the last dynasty, the Qing. Like the Qing rulers, who were Manchu, the Tang rulers were not from the central areas of Chinese civilization, nor were they fully Chinese. Ethnically, the Tang rulers were of mixed Turkic and Chinese parentage. In this, they repeated a pattern: military and inspirational sources of renewal came from outside the centered polity. The Tang capital cities, Xi'an and Luoyang in northern China, were full of Turkic, Persian, Central Asian, Arabic, and other traditions (Hansen 2000, chs. 4 and 5). Most notable was the great number of Buddhist monasteries in which there were a number of Indian Buddhist monks, two of whom were also alchemists, providing the emperor with the means to prolong life and achieve immortality (Forte 1985).[4] The most famous Buddhists, however, were the Chinese monks Faxian and Xuanzang each of whom spent years traveling through central Asia to India, learning Sanskrit and Hindi, and making records of their journeys. Xuanzang brought back to the Chinese capital a large collection of Buddhist scriptures, which he proceeded to translate. Indian Buddhists at the same court had long before also been engaged in this work of translation alongside their Chinese brothers. For most Buddhists, China (where the Buddha had never lived) was marginalized with respect to India as a center of learning and teaching. India was the land of the Buddha, and its revered King Ashoka was a model of Buddhist monarchy (209–32 BCE). When Xuanzang told his fellow Indian monks in Nalanda, the center of learned

Buddhist life in India, that he wished to return to China, they were amazed. They considered China a land of barbarians, but Xuanzang responded by saying that the Chinese Empire was a land of exemplary rule and wisdom. This mutual marginalization between centers of the world and of civilization set up what Forte (1985, 27) calls a "borderland complex" for the Chinese Buddhists so highly favored by the Tang court. The response of rulers and monks was to compose new Buddhist sutras, in Sanskrit and in Chinese, hailing China as the land of Buddha (Forte 2010, 29). In other words, on one hand Xuanzang was a Chinese influence on the reputation of Buddhism in India, while on the other, Indian and Chinese monks in the Tang court helped to turn China into a land of the Buddha.

The next major transformation in this history came after a reaction against the landed power of monasteries, during the second half of the Tang.[5] In a revival of Han dynasty Confucianism, Buddhist monasteries were attacked, and monks and nuns were forced to work the land and pay taxes. The revenues from the monasteries acquired by the court helped pay Turkic generals and their armies assigned to fight off other, Altaic- or Turkic-speaking pastoralists and their federations threatening invasion. Buddhism was soon restored to imperial favor. But a result of the rebellion in 755 CE by the general An Lushan was the breaking down of imperial control from the center, transferring much military and tax-collecting power to local great landed families. Finally the northern federation of Khitans, one of the Altaic aristocratic tribal federations, took control of the northern region of Chinese provinces, exercising a dual rule, one federal and tribal, facing north, the other city-centered on the Tang model, facing south.

The reconquest of some Tang lands, but not the far north, left the succeeding dynasty, the Song, in a threatened relation to the successors of the Khitan and later the Jurchen Mongol federation. The Jurchen Mongols eventually took a much larger northern swath of China and formed its own Chinese dynasty, taking over the Song capital of Kaifeng and forcing the Song south to the new capital of Hangzhou. All these centuries of northern invasion had forced population movement and settlement south of the Great River (the Yangzi) where the new settlers drained and irrigated rice-growing lands and built new cities. In this newly prosperous south, the Song emperors were aware of the danger posed by their own generals, so they avoided armed attack and armed defense in the face of the northern threat, and resorted instead to diplomatic gift exchange with the aristocratic tribal federations to ward them off (Sneath 2007). Even before moving south, the Song had already increased the powers of civil officials, and expanded their recruitment beyond a privileged set of families who specialized in the passing of civil service examinations based on the texts attributed to the sage masters of the Zhou and Han. But factions among the Song's officials argued as fiercely as did the late Zhou hundred schools of thought over the way to rule and over the content of the examinations. The way to rule meant, eventually, to stimulate commerce as a tax base for the revenue to pay off the northerners. Long after the factions had weakened the Song and allowed them to be pushed south, the same pressures and means of ruling through civil administration and the use of revenues to keep the northerners at bay continued to favor commerce. The results of this Song ruling strategy, making commerce and the production of commodities respectable, brought about a rise in literacy for artisans and merchants; continued the rise in self-cultivation among commoners; and increased the pool of candidates for the examinations. All these results of symbiotic relations between militarily strong pastoral and trade-controlling outsiders and the agrarian inside replay the dynamic of transgression and adaptation by the self-proclaimed civilizational centers of sage rule.

The absorption of indigenous local cultures and the southern Song reliance on commerce as well as an enlarged and opened civil administration had the unintended consequence of a strong tendency to celebrate local officials and elite ancestors. This was interwoven with the building of local shrines to deities from elsewhere, often Daoist adepts who had achieved perfection and could now bring rain or heal illness (Hymes 2002). Another element of this localism of the high elite was a parallel building of local academies to study the works of commentators and reformers of the Confucian classics. Local academies that honored famous scholars of "the way of the learned" (*rujiao*), mountain temples and abbeys in which Daoists who had achieved perfection were worshipped, and other temples or monasteries where Buddhists sought personal and world salvation were the main, high level institutions of the literate. The temples and monasteries were also destinations of pilgrimage among commoners. At the same time, local temples to deities that embodied both virtue and the power to act in the visible world spread among commoners. Such temples and their gods were recommended by local elites for endorsement by the imperial court in increasing numbers during the Southern Song (1127–1229 CE) (Hansen 1990).

Privileges of birth for entry into the imperial bureaucracy were abolished completely in the Southern Song. In addition and partly as a result of the long absorption of Buddhism, commoners assumed for themselves the privilege of worshipping ancestors at their graves to save their souls from purgatory. A scholar named Zhu Xi from Wuyuan in what is now the southeast Chinese province of Jiangxi became a major figure in one of the new local academies. He advised the emperor to introduce this commoner piety as imperial orthodoxy, even though such forms of worship had been forbidden to those who were not from great land-owning families or of noble birth. He said it was a way of cultivating virtue in the population, including the landed magnates and nobility (Ebrey 1986). All officially endorsed rites had this aim, the cultivation of the hierarchic social relations that are summarized as filial—respect and affection between sons and fathers, loyalty and responsive care between subjects and rulers, propriety between rulers and ministers, differentiation between husband and wife, precedence between elder and younger brothers, trust between friends, and fidelity between business partners.

These upward aspirations of local elites and imperial attempts to control the proliferation of local deities were correctives to a process of differentiation of localities brought about by the absorption of northern steppe civilizations, of southern tributary kingdoms, lesser polities of non-Chinese indigenous people, and Indian Ocean traders in the increasing maritime commerce of the southeastern Chinese ports. For instance, the northern dynasties of the late Tang and Song periods started a fashion in Chinese writing that celebrated military prowess and pride (Lewis 2009, 226). Less elite, the cults of mountain and earth deities of the non-Chinese peoples south of the Yangzi were incorporated as minor deities, as were the local gods in western China border regions with Tibet in later centuries. The newly incorporated gods became the demonic and animalistic "saviors" of Buddhism, or were taken up by local cults administered by Daoist ritual masters, or became the lesser territorial guardians of the new cult of gods of walls and moats (*Chenghuang*) in Chinese towns and cities (Lewis 2009, 218).

Dynastic rule through its ancestral cult was challengeable by having an ancestor buried in a particularly auspicious grave. The quality of the grave itself was considered a matter of good locational selection and not associated with privileged birth. These and other arts and exercises of self-cultivation center body and location in relation to others in fields of vital forces, creating microcosms and relations to various externalities, insides to various outsides. Fields or circuits of vital forces are determined by the basic principles of Heaven-made authority or destiny (*ming*), but it is a destiny that itself shifts and fluctuates in the auspiciousness of time, direction, and place. Self-cultivation is always a cultivation of a relational self, in a flow of forces and the proper conduct of relations with others within an environment that is itself a circulation of vital energies and the principles upon which they combine or clash, are blocked, or are allowed to flow. Body and place are microcosms in which the forces and principles of the universe are tapped and can be concentrated. This is part of a cosmological system used for the location of graves, temples, capital cities, and imperial and ordinary residences, for traditional Chinese medicine and food, of how to eat well, for martial arts, as well as for the concentration and radiation of vital energies through breathing discipline and meditation.

All of these continue in practice until today. But of course they cultivate persons under a state that is not a mediation with *Tian,* but one that cultivates filial duty as heritage and Chineseness. The practices continue under a new version of "civilization," with a new temporality of future orientation, and in a world economic system through which many other kinds of moral person and aspiration have been absorbed. I have treated this elsewhere (Feuchtwang 2012).

Conclusion: Comparison of Civilizations with Themes

I have sketched three turning points—each of them lasting several centuries if not millennia—in the history of civilization in China. Note well that this is not a history of China. I assume no single subject identity of this history. But I think I have sufficiently indicated and shall here emphasize what I understand to be common themes in the histories of civilizations, as well as what might be the peculiar characteristics of those themes and their combination in China.

Hierarchy is central to all civilizations. But the nature, rake, and ranking of hierarchy, and the extent of exclusions for realizing the highest achievements in it or access to its highest reaches, are varied. The formation of visible insides and invisible and dangerous or potent outsides is also common to all civilizations, but again this takes distinctive forms, which can be described as variants of the stranger-king theme or less specifically by the concept of alterity. The placing—juxtaposition or ranking—of ancestors with gods and the privileging of ancestral lineage and canonization of gods are functions of steepening hierarchy. Writing adds to this steepening of hierarchy. Ritual practices for achieving immortality as an ancestor, or as a god, or as a person are probably common to many if not all civilizations. But the cosmology and cosmocracy described in these ritual practices can be distinctive, as for instance is the emphasis on ancestral, patrilineal lines in China.

Chinese civilization, in its own terms, is a concept of civilization as a process of centering and aspiration. This must be true of every civilization; it is what Chinese civilization teaches us about civilizations in general. What is distinctive in Chinese civilization is its conception of humanity as a centering activity, with the human being as mediator between a Heaven of change, deities, and human spirits and an Earth of material forms, including forms of human life. Both Heaven and Earth are substantiations of flows of materiality—*qi*—from the finest to the most solid that make up the universe. The relations of the interiority of the human, including human emotions, and outside forms are responsive or destructive, made visible and formed habitually in proper conduct or else in destructive abandon, possession by malign *qi,* chaos, and confusion.

These relations conceived through the universal substance of *qi* include the arts of adaptation and maneuver, through careful observation of the dispositions of topographic forms—the dynamic forces observable in the land—as well as of human forces, whether it be in military maneuvers, in diplomacy, or in other encounters, in which outcomes are unpredictable and to which there has to be constant readjustment. Francois Jullien (2004) has cited many early dynastic sources for this orientation of adjustment and maneuver, which he calls "efficacy." He contrasts the centrality of efficacy in Chinese thinking with the marginality of its equivalent in Greek and European philosophy and story, where it is just "cunning," the *metis* of Ulysses, or the tactics of Clausewitz.

Another comparison, hierarchy in Chinese civilization is not of caste but of statuses, or ranks, including divine statuses that, by the tenth century CE, were achievable by commoners through disciplines of self-cultivation, all of which were techniques of centering, accumulation, and response. The spread of this civilization is a spread of centers, each of them potentially a center of the same civilization or of that which will invigorate if not become its political center. Kingship is explained in the retrospective texts of the classical disputations as an effect of conquest, creation, and transgression, followed by sacrifice and alignment; this is a movement equivalent to the stranger-king syndrome of other civilizations, in which the transgressor is eventually authorized as a semi-divine being.

The temporality of this civilization is a centering of and an absorption or adjustment to transgressions of the norm of more ancient times. It is a temporality of return of the dead as ancestors and gods to the living, metaphorically manifesting what has been irreversibly changed. The archaism of the gods and ancestors reflects a dynamic of impossible return to an origin in a historicized chain of origins. This is Chinese civilization's version of what Schrempp (1992) has identified as basic paradoxical antinomies that pose questions such as, What was there before the Big Bang? All cosmologies probably have to deal with such antinomies. In China, the paradoxical antinomies are: If these are the ordained norms how then are transgressions from the norm ordained? If humans are intrinsically good and spiritual, why must they also be disciplined or cultivated in order to moderate their equally intrinsic and potentially destructive and chaotic passions and desires? If quietude is a return to the singleness of the universe, how is it also universal when there are multitudes of things and constant change?

Heaven can be as capricious as a Greek god. Humans have to be formed by good government, including law and punishment, and yet they can create their own cosmic effects; heroes of invention are honored as gods. But origin is not, as in monotheism, a creation by an external will and so the issue of sovereignty is not central (either as the sovereignty of a creator, or of those who know the ideal and theoretical forms of reality in a polis). Instead, authorization is the core concern of this civilization, achieved through the performance of hierarchy, ritual, hospitality, and social relations. It is a civilization of cosmic historicity. The gods are historical metaphors, not from a separate temporality of myth, as are Hindu and Greek gods, but from various pasts and places.

I have traced irreversible changes through a sequence: from shamanic ancestors to ultimate ancestors as hero-founders of the arts of civilization. At the same time, single hegemonic centers emerge from among a number of similar centers. Then appears a political cosmocracy of imperial ancestors as mediators to an ultimate deity accompanied by the art of self-cultivation as aspiration to immortality. This is eventually followed by the separation of territorial from ancestral centering strategies and rituals and the consolidation of a cosmology in which variant cosmologies and their experts and adepts can be accommodated. What then followed was the reversal of exclusion of commoners from ritual creation of ancestors and deities. These changes were all discernible only as long-term processes over hundreds of years.

I suggest that what persists through such irreversible changes is a distinctive way of learning and of transmission, which includes the historicity of a cosmology and its temporality. The content of transmission is the result of transgression and creation, changes of long or short duration through the absorption of influences, information, and whatever is confronted and exploited opportunistically as confusion, and then brought into several hierarchies of aspiration each with its own center, as well as the imperial center. The way of learning is through centering, by reference to the ideal of sage rule and the disciplines of aspiration and self-cultivation. From the Song dynasty, commoners too were performers of their own centricity of place and of a mediating body and emotion in ever-steeper hierarchies of rule. They aspired ultimately to reach immortality as ancestors, perhaps gods, through self-cultivation; and they sought to achieve personal perfection through material practices of ritual and the body. This is a sequence, a set of variations on themes common to other civilizations, which can be applied in more detailed comparisons.

Notes

1. There are nonhierarchical societies with encompassing hierarchical cosmologies. But I am not referring to those civilizations.

2. It also raises the issue that is omitted here of trading civilizations that inhabit such border regions of settled civilizations, within which trade goods, languages, and reciprocities of trust and exchange are elements from which an encompassing universe of their own is invoked and suggested.

3. For the contrast between these two classical points of reference, I rely on Puett (2002, 104–17), who also refutes previous scholars' taking these passages to mean that the emperor was a shaman. Rather, he was the unifying moral leader of humanity in its relation to Heaven. This was true of the time about which Puett writes but not necessarily of earlier periods when the ruler may well have been a shaman worshipping ancestors who are his spirit-masters.

4. Many thanks to Janine Nicol for sending me a copy of this article.

5. For much of the history in these two paragraphs I rely on Valerie Hansen (2000).

References

Allen, Sarah. 2007. "Erlitou and the Formation of Chinese Civilization: Toward a New Paradigm." *Journal of Asian Studies* 66, no. 2: 461–96.

Arnason, Johann P. 1988. "Social Theory and the Concept of Civilisation." *Thesis Eleven*: 87–105.

Bokenkamp, Stephen. 2007. *Ancestors and Anxiety; Daoism and the Birth of Rebirth in China.* Berkeley: University of California Press.

Chang Kwang-chih. 1983. *Art, Myth, and Ritual; the Path to Political Authority in Ancient China.* Cambridge and London: Harvard University Press.

———. 1989. "An Essay on Cong" *Orientations* (June): 37–43.

Ebrey, Patricia. 1986. "The Early Stages in the Development of Descent Group Organisation." In *Kinship Organisation in Late Imperial China 1000–1940*, edited by Patricia Buckley Ebrey and James L. Watson, 16–61. Berkeley: University of California Press.

von Falkenhausen, Lothar. 2005. "The Inscribed Bronzes from Yangjiacun: New Evidence on Social Structure and Historical Consciousness in Late Western Zhou China (c. 800 BC)." *Proceedings of the British Academy* 139: 239–95.

Fang Hui. 2008. Comment on Flad.

Feuchtwang, Stephan. 2012. "Chinese Civilisation in the Present." *The Asia Pacific Journal of Anthropology* 13, no. 2: 112–27.

———, and Michael Rowlands. 2010. "Re-evaluating the Long Term; Civilization and Temporalities." In *Archaeology and Anthropology*, edited by Duncan Garrow and Thomas Yarrow, 117–36. Oxford and Oakville: Oxbow Books.

Flad, Rowan. 2008. "Divination and Power: A Multiregional View of the Development of Oracle Bone Divination in Early China." *Current Anthropology* 49, no. 3: 403–37.

Forte, Antonino. 1985. "Hsi-chih (fl. 676–703 AD), a Brahmin Born in China." *Estratto da Annali dell'Instituto Universitario Orientale* 45: 106–34.

Hansen, Valerie. 1990. *Changing Gods in Medieval China 1127–1276.* Princeton: Princeton University Press.

———. 2000. *The Open Empire: A History of China to 1600.* New York and London: Norton.

Hawkes, David, trans., intro., annotate. 1985. *The Songs of the South: An Anthology of Ancient Chinese Poems by Qu Yuan and Other Poets.* London: Penguin Books.

Henderson, J. B. 1984. *The Development and Decline of Chinese Cosmology.* New York: Columbia University Press.

Humphrey, Caroline, and Urgunge Onon. 1996. *Shamans and Elders; Experience, Knowledge, and Power among the Daur Mongols.* Oxford: The Clarendon Press.

Hymes, Robert. 2002. *Way and Byway: Taoism, Local Religion, and Models of Divinity in Song and Modern China.* Berkeley: University of California Press.

Jullien, François. 2004 [1996]. *A Treatise on Efficacy; Between Western and Chinese Thinking.* Translated by Janet Lloyd. Honolulu: University of Hawai'i Press.

Lei Congyun. 1996. "Neolithic Sites of Religious Significance." In *Mysteries of Ancient China; New Discoveries from the Early Dynasties,* edited by Jessica Rawson, 220–24. London: The British Museum.

Lewis, Mark. 2007. *The Early Chinese Empires; Qin and Han.* Cambridge: Belknap, Harvard University Press.

———. 2009. *China between Empires: The Northern and Southern Dynasties.* Cambridge: Harvard University Press.

Mauss, Marcel. 2006. "Civilisations, Their Elements and Forms." In *Techniques, Technologies, and Civilisation* edited by N. Schlanger. Oxford and New York: Berghahn Books.

Morris, Ian. 2011. *Why the West Rules—For Now; The Patterns of History and What They Reveal About the Future.* London: Profile Books.

Needham, Joseph. 1956. "History of Scientific Thought." Volume 2 of *Science and Civilisation in China.* Cambridge: Cambridge University Press.

Puett, Michael J. 2001. *The Ambivalence of Creation: Debates Concerning Innovation and Artifice in Early China.* Stanford: Stanford University Press.

———. 2002. *To Become a God: Cosmology, Sacrifice, and Self-divinization in Early China.* Harvard Yenching Institute, Monograph 57. Cambridge: Harvard University Press.

Sahlins, Marshall. 2014. "Stranger Kings in General: The Cosmo-logics of Power." In *Framing Cosmologies; The Anthropology of Worlds,* edited by Allen Abramson and Martin Holbraad, 137–63. Manchester and New York: Manchester University Press.

Schrempp, Gregory. 1992. *Magical Arrows: The Maori, the Greeks, and the Folklore of the Universe*. Madison and London: University of Wisconsin Press.

Scott, James. 2009. *The Art of Not Being Governed: An Anarchist History of Upland Southeast Asia*. New Haven: Yale University Press.

Sneath, David, 2007. *The Headless State: Aristocratic Orders, Kinship Society, and Misrepresentations of Nomadic Inner Asia*. New York: Columbia University Press.

Venture, Olivier. 2002. "*Étude d'un emploi rituel de l'écrit.*" Dissertation Université de Paris 7.

Wang Mingming. 2014. *The West as the Other; A Genealogy of Chinese Occidentalism*. Hong Kong: Chinese University of Hong Kong Press.

Wengrow, David. 2011. "Cognition, Materiality and Monsters: The Cultural Transmission of Counter-intuitive Forms in Bronze Age Societies." *Journal of Material Culture* 16, no. 2: 131–49.

11

TECHNOLOGICAL CHOICES AND MODERN MATERIAL CIVILIZATION

Reflections on Everyday Toilet Practices in Rural South China

Gonçalo Santos

[E]ven the simplest techniques . . . take on the character of a system that can be analyzed, in terms of a more general system. The techniques can be seen as a group of significant choices, which each society—or each period within a society's development—has been forced to make, whether they are compatible or incompatible with other choices.

—Claude Lévi-Strauss, "The Scope of Anthropology"

Like other metropolitan anthropologists doing field research in relatively remote locations, one of the most immediate practical questions in the back of my mind when I first moved into the "single-lineage village" of Harmony Cave in the summer of 1999 was the question of pooing and peeing.[1] How do people "go to the toilet"? What kinds of technical procedures are in place for this purpose in Cantonese-speaking rural communities in the northern hilly regions of Guangdong province? At the time, I was already quite familiar with everyday life in major cities such as the provincial capital, Guangzhou, but I was not very familiar with the challenges of the local countryside, and I had never lived for long periods of time in a rural community in China or anywhere else.

259

My first host in Harmony Cave, a sixty-year-old man whose wife, sons, and daughters-in-law were working away from the village, provided a preliminary set of instructions. He mentioned three key places to sort out one's needs with discretion: the surrounding fields and hills, the village latrines, and the house. The surrounding fields and hills are particularly convenient when one is away from the village and its residential areas. As to the village latrines, he continued, they can be used whenever one is close to the village area. If not convenient, one can use a chamber pot or plastic basin at home and then pour the waste matter into a latrine. My host added that most villagers are users of communal latrines because their houses do not have private bathrooms with flush toilets, but he noted quite proudly that recently built modern houses like his own were equipped with such "advanced" (*sinjeun*) toilet arrangements.[2] He told me that these toilet arrangements are the most suitable for my "high-class identity" (*gou-kap san-fan*) as a "Western" foreign guest, but he insisted that at night time I should feel free to pee in the small plastic bucket near my bedroom to avoid the hassle of having to go to the manually flushed squat toilet on the ground floor.

I took this suggestion seriously and followed my host's advice. A few days later, however, I started to realize that what I took to be a last-minute toilet arrangement devised by my host—the bucket for nighttime peeing— was actually a fairly popular technical procedure to facilitate people's indoor peeing needs. My observations revealed that most families residing in the village kept one or two of these buckets in their houses for peeing purposes, not just at night time. Indeed, this practice was still so popular locally that even families like my host's who had already moved into a "modern" house with a private flush toilet continued to use these indoor urine buckets. I initially thought that this behavior was linked to the fact that village folks had still not adapted to the idea of having a private toilet at home, but it quickly became apparent that there was *something else* to it all.

My first confrontation with this *something else* occurred a few weeks later when I decided to empty the urine bucket placed next to my bedroom straight into the squat toilet downstairs. When my host realized what I was doing, he became very agitated and prompted me to stop. I soon realized that I was throwing away something that he considered highly valuable. Like most village households, my host was not accumulating urine in buckets simply to throw it away. Rather, he wanted to dilute the urine in water in order to produce high-quality fertilizer for his vegetable garden. This was not just about saving money; like many other villagers, my host was convinced that vegetables grown with this fertilizer are tastier than vegetables grown with more recent high tech fertilizing procedures involving farm chemicals. From his perspective, emptying the urine bucket into the toilet was a waste.

A similar dynamic was in place—so I subsequently learned—in the public latrines of each village hamlet. These latrines—locally called "shit pits" (*si-haang*)—are usually situated in a location somewhat removed from people's living quarters, quite often close to pigsties and cowsheds. Most latrines were built in the 1980s (the first decade of the Reform period) as part of a collective effort by each village hamlet. These latrines are small buildings (10–15m2) made of "traditional" yellow mud bricks and tiles. Inside, there is a pit, usually no more than two meters deep, where all waste matter accumulates. Users need to squat on two solid wooden boards hanging over the pit. The space inside the latrines is well ventilated because the entrance has no doors and the walls have small openings. Latrine users are expected to leave a hat or some other personal item by the entrance to signal their presence and thus avoid any embarrassing encounter.

I initially thought that the main function of these latrines was to enable villagers to sort out their bodily needs inside the village in a safe, secluded location that was sufficiently removed from people's residential quarters so as to prevent the spread of foul odors and other nuisances associated with excreta. But I quickly realized that—as with the urine buckets—there was another equally important function: to facilitate the accumulation of human waste for the purpose of producing agricultural fertilizer. Once the pit is full, the accumulated waste can be turned into liquid fertilizer simply by diluting it with water to initiate the fermentation process. This diluted "shit pit water" (*si-haang-sui*) can be applied directly to the rice plants in the paddies, or else to farm produce in the dryland, but this is a very laborious process. An alternative procedure is to treat the accumulated waste in the pit with lime, ashes, and other natural materials such as animal manure and chunks of muddy soil, and then sun-dry the resulting mixture in order to produce an entirely new substance called "mixed-soil fertilizer" (*tou-jaap-fei*). Applying this fertilizer to the fields during the dry season is thought to be a cheap, effective way of maintaining and enhancing the "soil's strength" (*tou-lik*), but it is also a very laborious and time-consuming method. In contrast to fertilizing procedures involving farm chemicals, very large amounts of shit-pit water and mixed-soil fertilizer need to be applied to the fields to achieve visible results, and these materials have to be transported to the fields in buckets strung on bamboo poles, and in handcarts. These practices were very popular during the Maoist period (1950s–1970s) because farm chemicals were still not widely available locally and human waste was politically regarded as a highly valued agrarian resource.

Historians of technology and civilization in China will not be surprised by these local practices of human waste management (Bray 1984; King 2004). These practices have a long history and are known to have reached particularly high levels of technical elaboration in the fertile subtropical region of South China (Bray 1984, 289–98; Zhou 2004, 178–214). By the late Ming (sixteenth and seventeenth centuries), an intensive trade in human excreta had emerged in many parts of China south of the Huai and Yangtze rivers (Xue 2005; Yu 2010; Zhou 2004, 180–85). At the time, peasant families were already relying on high levels of fertilizer input to sustain their soil-exhausting multicropping farming regime, and they had to supplement local fertilizing materials with human waste collected in cities and towns. Peasants were particularly keen on purchasing urban human waste because urbanites have a high-protein diet that was thought to improve the quality of human manure.

These rural-urban exchanges were at the heart of a sophisticated agro-urban sanitation system that was not reconfigured until after the collapse of the last imperial dynasty in 1911 under the influence of new "Western" concepts of public health (Zhu 1988; Zhou 2004; Rogaski 2004; Xue 2005; Yu 2010; Furth 2010; Huang 2016). After 1949, the Communists were ambivalent toward the "Western" flush-and-discharge model of human waste management, preferring instead to maintain traditional urban-rural synergies through a collectivist regime of public toilets and daily night soil collection (FAO 1977; Zhu 1988; Zhou 2004). Only after the reforms of the 1980s and 1990s was this collectivist people-centered infrastructure of urban sanitation discarded in favor of a more high tech, individualized approach based on private toilets and an expanding grid of sanitary sewers. This was a key turning point in the making of China's contemporary project of "hygienic modernity" (Rogaski 2004). By the 2000s, the burgeoning urban middle class was no longer satisfied with having home bathrooms with old-style squat toilets; they wanted to have sophisticated bathroom designs with "high quality" sitting toilets (Zhou 2004).

This chapter approaches China's ongoing "flush toilet revolution" not from the perspective of the wealthy urban middle class but from the perspective of impoverished rural areas in South China. My account highlights the centrality of the flush toilet and the wider waterborne system of waste disposal supporting its operation in the making of modern identities and modern civilizational processes (Laporte 2010; Bray 2012). This is not to say that there is only one kind of modern civilization. Just as there are many different kinds of flush toilet practices and infrastructures around the world, so there are many different conceptions and approaches to modern civilization (Seno Kappa 2011; Zhu 1988; Srinivas 2002; Molotch 2003; Szczygiel 2016). While the spread of what is usually called modernity has reached many different parts of the world, it did not give rise to just one civilizational configuration, one pattern of ideological, practical, and institutional response, but to at least several basic versions, which in turn are subject to further variations. The diversity of contemporary global flush toilet practices and infrastructures reflects these multiple civilizational configurations, while demonstrating the centrality of "technological choices" (Lemonnier 1993) in the making of "multiple modernities" (Eisenstadt 2003).

The term *technological choice* requires clarification. In most instances, it is only by analogy that one can say—as in the opening epigraph by Claude Lévi-Strauss—that it seems as though a community or a society has chosen a particular sociotechnical arrangement from a whole range of possible avenues. My approach to such collective "technological choices" privileges the point of view of ordinary users over that of powerful actors such as designers, experts, politicians, and/or entrepreneurs (Cowan 1983; Wajcman 2016, 111–35). I argue that the spread of private flush toilets in Chinese rural communities is not just a mere byproduct of macrolevel "civilizing" forces such as national development policies, industrial marketing campaigns, and global aid programs; these macrolevel forces are important but they are themselves entangled in complex user-mediated negotiations at the local level (Santos 2016a; 2016b, 2017). It is by looking at these negotiations at the local level—including the tensions embodied in emerging flush toilet practices and assemblages—that the anthropologist can illuminate how "multiple modernities" are actively constituted on the ground.

In addition to focusing on local-level reverberations of larger transformations, I show how the Northern Guangdong model of flush toilet modernity is not uncommon in other parts of rural China, and I argue that these cross-regional commonalities can be attributed to large-scale civilizational processes and long-term historical tensions between older "civilizational legacies" and newer "civilizing missions." I draw theoretically on the traditions initiated by Mauss (1950; 1969; 2006) and Elias (1994) to reconnect with what the historian Fernand Braudel (1992 [1979]) famously called "material civilization" (see also Bray 1997). Like Braudel, I use this concept as a corrective to approaches that privilege the ideational dimensions of civilizational processes.

A New Material Civilization of "Mansions" with Private Bathrooms

The move away from human manure production in the Harmony Cave region is linked to the rise of new forms of housing with private flush toilets, but this shift was initially triggered by the introduction of farm chemicals. Advertised as "advanced scientific products" (*sin-jeun fo-hok mat-ban*), farm chemicals started being sold in local markets in the 1980s, becoming increasingly popular from the 1990s onward. What was attractive about farm chemicals, when compared to human manure and other "traditional" techniques of soil fertilization, was the fact that farm chemicals enabled local smallholding families to achieve higher levels of food production with significantly less effort. This allowed village families to continue farming their land at home while sending migrant workers to Guangzhou and the neighbouring Pearl River Delta region to make additional income (Santos 2011).

By the late 1990s, the first modern-style houses with private flush toilets were being built with savings earned mostly through temporary labor migration. I noticed that their occupants remained regular users of communal latrines, even as they boasted about the "advanced" toilet arrangements of their new "mansions" (*lauh*). These mansion dwellers saw themselves as the first local representatives of a superior, "modern material civilization." However, these claims to superiority did not represent a consensus. Stories circulating in the village suggested that the new mansions did not represent a superior form of housing. It was said that they were too hot during the summer because their walls and windows were excessively insulated and because their location—the open fields in the middle of the valley—had too much sun exposure. These problems were often framed in terms of *feng shui*. Bad *feng shui* helped explain, for example, why so many mansions were infested with ants, or why their groundwater did not taste so good. Despite these counternarratives, the idea that the new mansions represented the most "advanced" form of housing became a hegemonic representation.

The new mansions are indeed very different materially from earlier forms of housing locally known as "mud brick houses" (*nai-jyun-nguk*) (Santos and Donzelli 2009). The latter look "old" because they use construction techniques dating from a much earlier period, but most were built as recently as the 1980s, if not later. These single-story houses are constructed with yellow-colored clay bricks made out of mud extracted from the local fields. The tiles covering the roofs of these houses are also made of local mud, but they are darker than the bricks because they are fired in a wood kiln to increase their resistance and impermeability to water. Local mud houses are rarely built as autonomous units; they are spatially aggregated in compact residential compounds comprising a whole village or hamlet. Because each mud house unit is small (15–25m2), the average local family uses several units including a kitchen, a bedroom, a rice granary, and more depending on family size and holdings. There is no separate unit called a "toilet" or "bathroom."

In contrast to these small low-tech bungalow units, the new mansions exude an impression of "higher-level scientific expertise" (*gou-kap fo-hok ji-sik*). This form of housing originated in the more affluent southern parts of the province where most local migrant workers sojourn. In Harmony Cave, the new mansions usually have two stories and a terrace on the roof that can be used to dry crops. Most have an automated system of piped water whereby groundwater is electrically pumped up into a stainless steel water tank on the terrace. The mansions look like solid white boxes. They are constructed by professional builders with "advanced" industrial materials such as bricks, cement, and glass. In the late 1990s, they cost about 70,000 RMB (about US$8,400), a sum that represented roughly a decade of savings by a village family with a couple of thrifty labor migrants working in the city.

One of the most important innovations associated with the new mansions was the "home toilet" (*ga-geui chi-so*) or "home bathroom" (*ga-geui sai-san-gaan*), alternative labels for a room devoted to personal hygiene. Usually located next to the kitchen in accordance with local *feng shui* principles, the home bathroom is a very small room (3–8m2) with four key components: a squat toilet fixture connected to a small underground septic tank, an outlet of piped water, a plastic bucket to store water, and a plastic ladle to flush the toilet and shower the body. In 1999–2001, I had the impression that villagers were still in the process of negotiating the best way to use these new home toilets. Through participating in informal discussions and gatherings, I came to realize that there were important disagreements between villagers.

These disagreements played an important role in shaping the reconfiguration not just of practices of pooing and peeing, but also of practices of bathing.

According to local customs, people need to "wash the body" (*sai-san*) every evening, usually immediately before or after dinner. Adults, unlike children, are expected to wash their bodies indoors, using specific techniques. They are expected to use a small plastic or wooden ladle to shower the body with water scooped from a plastic or wooden bucket, and to use a small cloth towel to clean the body and wipe it dry. Another important bathing requirement for adults is that they are expected to use hot water. This water is usually heated with the same fire that is used to cook dinner in the kitchen's firewood stove, to avoid additional fuel costs. In the mud brick houses, adults usually washed their bodies in a secluded corner of the kitchen, using fresh water that was supplied by means of a manual borehole water pump installed in the kitchen. While appreciating the privacy afforded by the introduction of a separate room for bathing in the new mansions, mansion dwellers did not completely discard earlier bathing practices. Rather than "advanced" showerheads and gas water heaters, they continued to use plastic ladles to shower and firewood stoves to heat their bath water. Most mansion dwellers interviewed between 1999 and 2005 said that that these procedures were at once more economic (i.e., wasted less water, and required no electricity), more practical (easier to implement), and more effective (they produced better results). The "advanced" devices, they admitted, served primarily as indicators of wealth and social status.

The number of mansions increased from six in 2001 to almost three-quarters of all houses in the village in 2016, but most residents continue to use "traditional" (*chyun-tung*) procedures not only for bathing but also for pooing and peeing. Villagers are aware that defecation in the surrounding fields and hills is no longer an adequate practice, but many have not entirely discarded open defecation. It is true that a growing number of villagers have access to a private flush toilet at home, but even mansion dwellers continue to use urine buckets inside their homes, and some continue to favor the option of using communal latrines outside the home, even though latrines are no longer being used to produce human manure. Mansion dwellers explain this preference for communal latrines by saying that flush toilets are very wasteful of household water and are very expensive in terms of maintenance. Some say that they prefer communal latrines because they find it inappropriate to poo inside the home.

This preference for pooing outside the home is not homogenously disseminated in village society, but is common enough to count as a shared *habitus* or embodied subjectivity.[3] Even young villagers with significant city exposure through labor migration (i.e., villagers born in the 1980s or later) are not reluctant to use communal latrines when they return to the village. An important factor here is that their toilet experiences in the city (most live in factory dorms or in zinc huts constructed in peri-urban vegetable gardens) continue to be framed around communal toilets. This emphasis on communal toilets outside the home is not very different from the experiences of older generations of villagers, but there are significant intergenerational differences in terms of ideals. During interviews in 2012 and 2015, I asked many young village migrants based in Guangzhou and Foshan why they are not using the communal pit toilets of their vegetable gardens to produce human manure. Their answers initially echoed the older generations when they said that farm chemicals are better than human manure because they are more productive and less labor intensive, but they added something to this earlier discursive pattern. They said that the practice of recycling human waste for agricultural purposes is no longer an option for them because it is too "backward" (*lok-hau*) and "non-hygienic" (*ng wai-saang ge*). The proper way to dispose of human waste in modern society is to use a private bathroom with a flush toilet.

Emerging Flush Toilet Infrastructures

Flush toilet technologies vary depending on context. The flush toilet in Harmony Cave is not a sitting toilet with a partially or fully automatic flushing mechanism, as found nowadays in most urban middle-class homes in China (Zhou 2004). It is a very basic squat toilet fixture that is flushed manually with the same plastic ladle that is used to shower the body, by scooping water from a bucket and pouring it directly into the toilet hole. Villagers say that getting rid of all excreta in this way is an act of "scientific hygiene" (*fo-hok wai-saang*) that is as important as cleaning the body with toilet paper instead of the wood chips used in the past. A toilet paper bin is kept next to the squat toilet fixture to avoid the toilet becoming clogged with paper and overflowing, but the paper accumulated in the bin is not always burned outside the house or in the kitchen's firewood stove. Instead, it is commonly discarded, or even flushed down the toilet, thus defying the very purpose of the bin.

One of the arguments frequently put forward by mansion dwellers for the superiority of the flush toilet arrangements of the new mansions is that they are more "hygienic" (*wai-saang*), but it is not really clear what is meant by "hygienic." It is certainly true that users of mansion toilets are not so directly confronted with excreta because they can flush the toilet to make excreta disappear; but this does not mean that all nuisances associated with excreta disappear with water dilution and flushing. This is never really the case, even when it comes to flush toilet infrastructures relying on centralized sewers. These large-scale infrastructures are very good at removing excreta from private homes and moving these waste materials to faraway sewage treatment facilities for further processing, but even these infrastructures have problems and moments of breakdown (Rockefeller 1996; George 2008; Black and Fawcett 2008; Jewitt 2011). Local flush toilet infrastructures, by contrast, are small-scale sewage systems based on septic tanks, and for this reason, they are not capable of evacuating waste materials to faraway places. This is not a problem in itself. Small-scale sewage systems can be very efficient at handling waste materials, but this is not the case in the Harmony Cave region. The most popular local model is a "three chamber septic tank" (*saam-gaak-sik fa-fan-chi*) that is constructed immediately outside the house, usually next to the bathroom. This tank is very functional if properly maintained, but many villagers are reluctant to spend money to service and empty the tank.

Under these conditions of poor maintenance, local septic tanks lead to frequent toilet overflowing. This overflowing is exacerbated by the frequent disposal of toilet paper into the squat toilet fixture, but this is not the only aggravating factor. There is also the fact that too much wastewater is discharged into the septic tanks because people are using the toilet to get rid of both bathwater and sewage. As a consequence, the home is regularly invaded by all kinds of nuisances associated with human excreta—something that did not happen when people were using communal latrines outside the home. Another consequence of the sociotechnical specificities of local flush toilet infrastructures is the increasing prevalence of negative externalities in the environment. Without a separate soak pit or drain field, untreated wastewater seeps more rapidly and deeper into the ground. As a result, the spread of contagion to local underground water sources is a genuine risk, even though local people usually boil the water before consumption (Santos 2011).

The Flush Toilet as a Technopolitical Project

Most human-centered accounts of the spread of flush toilets around the world focus on powerful macrolevel "civilizing" forces in the fields of public health and urban sanitation (Black and Fawcett 2008; George 2008; Jewitt 2011). These accounts draw at least implicitly on an approach to technological change that focuses on "technopolitics" (Hecht 1998, 15), or the "mutual constitution" of political culture and material forms (Jasanoff 2004; 2016). This chapter is also concerned with "co-production" but draws particular attention to the significance of microhistorical realities. Large-scale processes of technological change in the household inevitably require the support of broader social and political forces at both the national and the global levels, but these macrolevel forces are themselves entangled in complex social and political negotiations at the local level (Santos 2016a; 2016b, 2017).

The shift to private bathrooms and flush toilets in the hills of Guangdong did not result from a local consensus on the superiority of these "advanced" technologies, but from a work of "translation" (Callon 1986) of particular social strategies and interests. I refer to the strategies and interests of a local elite of high-earning migrant workers who played a key role in promoting a creative process of mimetic engagement with a schema of bodily hygiene and public sanitation that had emerged in the more affluent parts of the province. This elite sought to benefit from the high status associated with "advanced" flush toilet practices and related forms of housing, even though sustaining this image of superiority was costly and replete with ambiguities. In time, the shift to the new mansions with private flush toilets started to promote the development of new attitudes to human waste, new models of waste disposal, and new procedures of bodily hygiene, but it has also allowed the reproduction of earlier practices and structures, considered more appropriate and efficacious.

This account suggests that the shift to the flush toilet in the Harmony Cave region resulted less from inherent material benefits associated with the new technologies than from cultural values and social relations associated with these technologies. This analysis echoes a longstanding anthropological tradition that challenged the idea that human technological activity is "culture free" (Lemonnier 1993; Latour 1996; Bray 1997, 1998, 2012).[4] Bryan Pfaffenberger (1992) notes how the work of anthropologists such as Bronislaw Malinowski (1965a; 1965b) and Marcel Mauss (1950; 2006) opened the way for questioning the assumption that technology is primarily about the extension of human physical capacities to alter the natural world—a key assumption behind nineteenth-century evolutionist schemes of cultural evolution and technological progress. Malinowski and Mauss argued that it is misleading to evaluate technical artifacts *strictly* according to their functional efficiency as part of a system of material production, thus treating them independently of the human relations surrounding their use. In the following section, I suggest that the Maussian tradition is particularly helpful for grasping the linkages between microhistorical realities and large-scale historical transformations.

The Flush Toilet as Civilizational Process

My account so far has focused on technopolitical negotiations at the local level, but it is obvious that these microhistorical negotiations are connected to broader historical exchanges that one could call, following Mauss, "civilizational processes" (Mauss and Durkheim 1969; Mauss 1969, 2006; see also Febvre 1973; Schlanger 2006; Arnason 2010). The spread of the flush toilet in rural Guangdong is a civilizational process not in the sense that it leads to a higher stage of civilization (i.e., modernity), but because it connects many different "sociotechnical" entities—techniques, technologies, artifacts, institutions—in dynamic ways. These processes of creative assembling result in expanding networks of interdependency, which have multiple scales. When villagers in Northern Guangdong introduce flush toilet technologies into their homes, they are also responding to broader national and global processes converging on a new normative "material civilization."[5]

My usage of this term follows closely that of Fernand Braudel (1992 [1979], 27), whose approach to the emergence of modern capitalism in Western Europe differed from conventional views. Rather than diagnose a "gradual progress towards the rational world of the market, the firm and capitalist investment" (1992, 23), Braudel drew attention to basic aspects of life shared by all members of society. "This rich zone," he wrote, "like a layer covering the earth, I have called for want of a better expression *material life* or *material civilization*" (ibid.; emphasis in the original). Like Braudel, I am critical of approaches that give priority to the abstract over the material level of existence (see also Dant 2006, 300). It seems to me, however, that if the work of Braudel is useful to highlight the materiality of civilizational processes, it is not so useful when it comes to making sense of the strongly normative dimensions of modern transformations.

Here, we need to introduce a new narrative about "civilization," one that is usually associated with the work of Norbert Elias (1994 [1939]) on postmedieval European court society. Like Mauss and Braudel, Elias too is interested in the intricate connections between *habitus* as the socially organized basis of physical movement—how people walk, sit, pee, poo, etc.—and the use of instruments or technologies. But he approaches modern material civilization as inherently transformational, a "civilizing process" that brings about important changes in everyday behavioral standards as well as material practices, as human societies become larger. These changes are usually initiated by elite social groups who become trendsetters and succeed in establishing new terms for the incorporation of ordinary individuals and communities into larger chains of inclusion and civilization. The work of Elias has been criticized for contributing to the reproduction of a Eurocentric view of the making of modernity (Goody 2006). I follow Stephen Mennell (2007), who argues that the Elias's approach can be applied in a variety of historical settings, and Susanne Brandtstädter (2003), who has applied it fruitfully to China (see also Hahn, this volume), but my approach is closer to Elias's original concern with everyday behavioral standards and material practices.

Elias's approach to modern material civilization allows us to connect the "civilizing" aspirations of local-level trendsetters in rural Northern Guangdong to a broader national and international civilizing mission promoting the flush toilet as the global standard of bodily hygiene and public sanitation. There is a growing body of literature showing how private flush toilet schemas of bodily hygiene and public sanitation have become globally hegemonic under the influence of imperialist policies and modernist ideologies (Black and Fawcett 2008; George 2008; Jewitt 2011). Today, this view of the world is very powerful, and is actively promoted by various kinds of national and international social policies, public health institutions, NGOs, development programs. China has received various forms of aid to promote this civilizing mission. In 1996, just to give one example, UNICEF supported the implementation of a development program in eight provinces to improve the sanitary conditions of rural villages, and a key part of this program was about introducing flush toilets and small-scale sewage systems to the Chinese countryside (Zhou 2004, 83).

It would be a mistake to ignore the impact of organizations such as UNICEF on China's national policies of public sanitation, but the effects of such international organizations are themselves mediated by technopolitical negotiations at the national level. From very early on, possibly since the first known Chinese descriptions of Western flush toilets were written in the 1860s, Chinese elites developed their own vision of a new hygienic modernity built around Western-style flush toilet technologies (Zhou 2004, 76). These visions of modernity were based on Western Enlightenment ideas of evolutionary progress as well as an older Confucian vision that Prasenjit Duara (2001, 122) describes as an active engagement with "bringing true and proper civilizational virtues to all." This civilizing mission would be significantly expanded and strengthened throughout the twentieth century. As Stevan Harrell (1995) and Sara Friedman (2004) note, early–twentieth-century intellectuals and officials advocated "civilization" ([P] *wen-ming*) as a national strategy for radical social transformation, and flush toilets were an important aspiration of this "civilizing mission." As early as 1933, in a special issue of *Dongfang Magazine*, the historian Zhou Yucheng describes the flush toilet as one of the key goals of China's project of modernization, expressing the hope that "everyone will one day be able to have their own flush toilet bowl to poo" (cited in Zhu 1988, 18).

This flush toilet civilizing mission was not abandoned after 1949, but the high cost of building centralized sewage infrastructures favored the temporary adaptation of earlier agrarian infrastructures of human waste management (Zhou 2004). Under Mao, the urban population was expected to poo for the most part in public toilets under a collectivist regime of daily collection; and night-soil workers such as Shi Chuanxiang (1915–1975) were celebrated in official propaganda as national heroes and model workers. But even in the Mao era, as Zhu Jiaming (1988, 2) vividly recalls, it was difficult for urbanites to understand why night-soil workers were still necessary, and why China was not using the power of science and technology to develop flush toilet waste disposal systems. By the 1980s, the idea that national toilet standards were "backward" was widespread in urban contexts, and the government started to increase investment on public sanitation (Zhu 1988, 3). This investment was intensified in the 1990s and the aughts, just as a housing construction boom started to take shape. It was during this period that a large number of urban homes were connected to sewers and the concept of the private bathroom with a flush toilet—as envisioned by early–twentieth-century Chinese elites—started to become an essential component of everyday life, not just in urban areas. The 1990s and the aughts were also the period when the government started promoting mass campaigns to improve national toilet standards. These campaigns included a five-grade system of classification of public toilets that would have an important impact in the popular imagination in terms of establishing the normativity of the flush toilet model.

It was around this time that an emerging elite of high-earning migrant workers in the Harmony Cave region started to construct new mansions in their villages, arguing that their brand new flush toilets were superior to earlier local toilet practices. This elite took advantage of state-managed programs to improve village housing and public sanitation infrastructures. One of these programs—the "civilized village" program—encourages villages to apply for governmental subsidies to help improve housing conditions and build mansions with home toilets (Perry 2011). One of the most economically successful lineage branches in Harmony Cave applied successfully in 2010 and went on to build a new village hamlet with more than thirty new mansions. We thus return to the significance of microhistorical realities. Situating microhistorical realities in the context of broader civilizing processes can be illuminating, but it is by showing how macrolevel forces are entangled in local level negotiations that we get to see how flush toilet modernities are actively constituted on the ground.

Conclusion

I have outlined the dissemination of flush toilet technologies—and the civilizing mission supporting them—to the rural areas of a country with a very different tradition of human waste management (see Santos 2011; Dombroski 2015; Kawa 2016 for a reappraisal of such alternative traditions). Similar transformations are taking place in other parts of rural China, especially in the richer eastern-southern coastal areas (Liu et al. 2014). Yet there remain tensions between older "civilizational legacies" and newer "civilizing missions."

The spread of flush toilet technologies in rural China is not just about the making of a new material civilization built around a fecal-phobic hygienic model of waste disposal. It is also about the transformation of an older material civilization built around a fecal-philic agricultural model of human waste management that emphasizes the value of "turning waste into treasure" (*bin-fai wai-bou*). The agricultural recycling of human waste has declined since the 1990s (when an estimated 95–100 percent of rural households were engaging in this practice), but overall levels of human manure usage in 2007 were still high, amounting to 85 percent of all rural households interviewed in different provinces (Liu et al. 2014, 437). Since then, the shift toward an urban-like "flush-and-discharge" model of waste disposal has accelerated, but it seems likely that this increasing engagement with flush toilet technologies will *not* lead to a complete dismissal of earlier traditions of "turning waste into treasure".

The popularity of household biogas plants in rural areas is a case in point. China plays a leading role in the development of innovative household biogas technologies since the 1950s and 1960s, but it was only in the last two decades that these technologies started to become very popular due to technical improvements and heavy government investment. Today, China is the world's largest producer and consumer of household biogas plants with more than thirty million rural households using biogas digesters to produce clean cooking fuel and organic fertilizer through the fermentation of human, animal, and plant wastes (Chen and Hu 2017; Xia 2013; George 2008, 123–44). This biogas revolution is fully compatible with contemporary flush toilet aspirations in rural areas, but it also highlights the continuing significance of earlier fecal-philic civilizational legacies. These ambiguities—I suggest—lie at the heart of the making of multiple modernities, including emerging flush toilet modernities.

Acknowledgments

I would like to acknowledge the support provided by several research funding institutions over the years: Fundação Para a Ciência a Tecnologia (SFRH/BPD/40396/2007, 2007–08), Max Planck Institute for Social Anthropology (2011–13), University of Hong Kong (Seed Funding Project Grant: 201411159201, 2014–17), and the Hong Kong Research Grants Council (GRF Project Grant: 17402014, 2014–17). Earlier versions of this chapter were presented at the Max Planck Institute for Social Anthropology, at University College London, and at the Chinese University of Hong Kong. I would like to thank also Francesca Bray, Suzanne Gottschang, Patrice Ladwig, Jerome Lewis, Zhang Jun, and my students at HKU for their critical suggestions.

Notes

1. All names of places and persons referring to my research area in Northern Guangdong are pseudonyms. The chosen pseudonyms attempt to capture the spirit of local naming practices. I lived in the Harmony Cave

region in the years 1999–2001 and have returned to the area intermittently in the years 2005–2016.

2. All Chinese expressions quoted in this text refer to the Cantonese language as spoken in the region of Northern Guangdong (Yingde region). Cantonese is transcribed with a simplified version of the Yale System of Romanization. All expressions quoted in Putonghua are marked with [P] and follow the Standard Pinyin System of Romanization.

3. Villagers who have moved to the local market town have developed flush toilet practices that are closer to urban lower social strata expectations. A Bourdieusian analysis of the intersections between local toilet practices and social stratification would reveal the exact extent of these internal variations (see Sterne 2003).

4. I have tried to integrate this theoretical tradition with the study of human-environment relations in another publication (Santos 2011). In this chapter, I am not concerned with the linkages between sociotechnical systems and ecological systems.

5. This concept is not to be confused with Chinese official narratives of progress in the Reform period calling for the need to promote a harmonious relationship between "material civilization" (meaning material and economic development) and its opposite "spiritual civilization" (meaning good socialist values) (Dynon 2008).

References

Arnason, Johann P. 2010. "Domains and Perspectives of Civilizational Analysis." *European Journal of Social Theory* 13, no. 1 (February 1, 2010): 5–13.

Black, Maggie, and Ben Fawcett. 2008. *The Last Taboo: Opening the Door on the Global Sanitation Crisis*. London: Earthscan.

Brandtstädter, Susanne. 2003. "With Elias in China: 'Civilizing Process', Local Restorations and Power in Contemporary Rural China." *Anthropological Theory* 3, no. 1: 87–105.

Braudel, Fernand. 1992 [1979]. *The Structures of Everyday Life: The Limits of the Possible*. Berkeley and Los Angeles: University of California Press.

Bray, Francesca. 2012. *American Modern. The Foundation of Western Civilization*. Website: http://www.anth.ucsb.edu/faculty/bray/toilet/; accessed June 26.

———. 1998. "Technics and Civilization in Late Imperial China: An Essay in the Cultural History of Technology." *Osiris* 13, 2nd Series: 11–33.

———. 1997. *Technology and Gender. Fabrics of Power in Late Imperial China*. Berkeley: University of California Press.

———. 1984. *Science and Civilization in China. Vol. 6, Biology and Biological Technology. Part 2. Agriculture*. Edited by Joseph Needham. Cambridge: Cambridge University Press.

Callon, Michel. 1986. "Some Elements of a Sociology of Translation: Domestication of the Scallops and the Fishermen of St Brieuc Bay." In *Power, Action, and Belief: A New Sociology of Knowledge?*, edited by John Law, 196–223. London: Routledge.

Chen, Hu, et al. 2017. "Household Biogas CDM Project Development in Rural China." *Renewable and Sustainable Energy Reviews* 67: 184–91.

Cowan, Ruth S. 1983. *More Work for Mother: The Ironies of Household Technology from the Open Hearth to the Microwave*. New York: Basic Books.

Dant, Tim. 2006. "Materiality and Civilization: Things and Society." *The British Journal of Sociology* 57, no. 2: 289–308.

Dombroski, Kelly. 2015. "Multiplying Possibilities: A Postdevelopment Approach to Hygiene and Sanitation in Northwest China." *Asia Pacific Viewpoint* 56, no. 3: 321–44.

Duara, Prasenjit. 2001. "The Discourse of Civilization and Pan-Asianism." *Journal of World History* 12, no. 1: 99–130.

Dynon, Nicholas. 2008. " 'Four Civilizations' and the Evolution of Post-Mao Chinese Socialist Ideology." *The China Journal* 60: 83–109.

Eisenstadt, Shmuel N. 2003. *Comparative Civilizations and Multiple Modernities*. Leiden: Brill.

Elias, Norbert. 1994 [1939]. *The Civilizing Process*. Oxford: Blackwell.

FAO, 1977. *China. Recycling of Organic Wastes in Agriculture*. Rome: Food and Agriculture Organization of the United Nations.

Febvre, Lucien. 1973 [1930]. "Civilisation: Evolution of a Word and a Group of Ideas." In *A New Kind of History and Other Essays*, edited by Peter Burke, translated by K. Folca. New York: Harper and Row.

Friedman, Sara. 2004. "Embodying Civility: Civilizing Processes and Symbolic Citizenship in Southeastern China." *Journal of Asian Studies* 63, no. 3: 687–718.

Furth, Charlotte. 2010. "Hygienic Modernity in Chinese East Asia." In *Health and Hygiene in Chinese East Asia. Policies and Publics in the Long Twentieth Century*, edited by Angela K. C. Leung, and Charlotte Furth, 1–21. Durham and London: Duke University Press.

George, Rose. 2008. *The Big Necessity. The Unmentionable World of Human Waste and Why it Matters*. New York: Holt.

Goody, Jack. 2006. *The Theft of History*. Cambridge: Cambridge University Press.

Harrell, Stevan. 1995. "Introduction." In *Cultural Encounters on China's Ethnic Frontiers* edited by Stevan Harrell, 3–36. Seattle: University of Washington Press.

Hecht, Gabrielle. 1998. *The Radiance of France: Nuclear Power and National Identity after World War II*. Cambridge: MIT Press.

Huang, Xuelei. 2016. "Deodorizing China. Odour, Ordure, and Colonial (Dis)order in Shanghai, 1840s–1940s." *Modern Asian Studies* 50, no. 3): 1092–1122.

Jasanoff, Sheila. 2016. *The Ethics of Invention. Technology and the Human Future*. New York: W. W. Norton.

———, ed. 2004. *States of Knowledge. The Co-production of Science and the Social Order*. London: Routledge.

Jewitt, Sarah. 2011. "Geographies of Shit. Spatial and Temporal Variations in Attitudes towards Human Waste." *Progress in Human Geography* 35, no. 5: 608–26.

Kappa, Seno. 2011. *Kuishi cesuo [Taking a Peep at Toilets]*. Beijing: Sanlian shudian.

Kawa, Nicholas. 2016. "What Happens When We Flush?" *Anthropology Now* 8, no. 2: 34–43.

King, Franklin H. 2004 [1911]. *Farmers of Forty Centuries. Organic Farming in China, Korea, and Japan*. Mineola, NY: Dover.

Laporte, Dominique. 2010. *History of Shit*. Cambridge: MIT Press.

Latour, Bruno. 1996. *Aramis or the Love of Technology*. Cambridge: Harvard University Press.

Lemonnier, Pierre, ed. 1993. *Technological Choices: Transformation in Material Cultures Since the Neolithic*. London: Routledge.

Lévi-Strauss, Claude. 1983 [1976]. "The Scope of Anthropology [1960]." In *Structural Anthropology, Volume 2*, 3–32. Chicago: University of Chicago Press.

Liu, Ying, Ji-kun Huang, and Precious Zikhali. 2014. "Use of Human Excreta as Manure in Rural China." *Journal of Integrative Agriculture* 13, no. 2: 434–42.

Malinowski, Bronislaw. 1965a. *Coral Gardens and their Magic, vol. 1, Soil-tilling and Agricultural Rites in the Trobriand Islands.* Bloomington: Indiana University Press.

———. 1965b. *Coral Gardens and their Magic, vol. 2, The Language of Magic and Gardening.* Bloomington: Indiana University Press.

Mauss, Marcel. 1950 [1936]. "Les Techniques du Corps." In *Sociologie et Anthropologie*, 363–86. Paris: Presses Universitaires de France.

———. 1969 [1929]. "Les civilisations. Éléments et formes." In *Oeuvres. 2. Représentations collectives et diversité des civilisations*, 456–479. Paris: Les Éditions de Minuit.

———. 2006. *Techniques, Technology, and Civilisation.* Edited and introduced by Nathan Schlanger. Oxford: Berghahn.

———, and Emile Durkheim. 1969 [1913]. "Note sur la notion de civilisation." In *Oeuvres. 2. Représentations collectives et diversité des civilisations*, by Marcel Mauss, 451–55. Paris: Les Éditions de Minuit.

Mennell, Stephen. 2007. *The American Civilizing Process.* London: Polity.

Molotch, Harvey. 2003. *Where Stuff Comes From: How Toasters, Toilets, Cars, Computers, and Many Other Things Come to Be as They Are.* London: Routledge.

Perry, Elizabeth J. 2011. "From Mass Campaigns to Managed Campaigns: 'Constructing a New Socialist Countryside.'" In *Mao's Invisible Hand: The Political Foundations of Adaptive Governance in China*, edited by Sebastian Heilmann and Elizabeth J. Perry, 30–61. Cambridge: Harvard University Press.

Pfaffenberger, Bryan. 1992. "Social Anthropology of Technology." *Annual Review of Anthropology* 21: 491–516.

Rockefeller, Abby. 1996. "Civilization and Sludge. Notes on the History of the Management of Human Excreta." *Current World Leaders* 39, no. 6: 99–113.

Rogaski, Ruth. 2004. *Hygienic Modernity. Meanings of Health and Disease in Treaty-Port China.* Berkeley: University of California Press.

Santos, Gonçalo. 2011. "Rethinking the Green Revolution in South China: Technological Materialities and Human-Environment Relations." *East Asian Science, Technology, and Society: An International Journal* 5, no. 4: 479–504.

————. 2016a. "On Intimate Choices and Troubles in South China." *Modern Asian Studies* 50, no. 4: 1298–1326.

————. 2016b. "Birthing Dramas and Generational Narratives. Coping with Medicalization in Rural South China, 1960s–2010s." Paper presented at the Annual Meeting of the *Society for the History of Technology*, Singapore, June 25.

————. 2017. "Love, Family, and Gender in 21st Century China." In *Socialism with Neoliberal Characteristics*, edited by Kirsten W. Endres and Chris Hann, 31–35. Halle, Saale: Max Planck Institute for Social Anthropology.

————, and Aurora Donzelli. 2009. "Rice Intimacies: Reflections on the 'House' in Upland Sulawesi and South China." *Archiv für Völkerkunde* 57–58: 37–64.

Schlanger, Nathan. 2006. "Introduction. Technological Commitments. Marcel Mauss and the Study of Techniques in the French Social Sciences." In *Techniques, Technology, and Civilisation*, 1–30. Berghahn Books.

Srinivas, Tulasi. 2002. "Flush with Success. Bathing, Defecation, Worship, and Social Change in South India." *Space and Culture* 5, no. 4: 368–86.

Sterne, Jonathan. 2003. "Bourdieu, Technique, and Technology" *Cultural Studies* 17, no. 3/4: 367–89.

Szczygiel, Marta E. 2016. "From Night Soil to Washlet. The Material Culture of Japanese Toilets." *Electronic Journal of Contemporary Japanese Studies* 16, no. 3. http://www.japanesestudies.org.uk/ejcjs/vol16/iss3/szczygiel.html.

Wajcman, Judy. 2016. *Pressed for Time. The Acceleration of Time in the Digital Age*. Chicago: Chicago University Press.

Wang Yuhua, Fang Ying, and Jiao Juan. 2008. "Jiangsu nongcun / sangeshi huafenchi wushui chuli xiaoguo pingjia) [Evaluation of Night Soil Treatment Efficiency of 'Three-grille-mode' Septic Tanks in the Rural Area of Jiangsu]." *Shengtai yu nongcun huanjing xuebao* [*Journal of Ecology and Rural Environment*] 24: 80–83.

Xia, Zuzhang. 2013. *Domestic Biogas in a Changing China: Can Biogas Still Meet the Energy Needs of China's Rural Households?* London: International Institute for Environment and Development.

Xue, Yong. 2005. " 'Treasure Nightsoil as if It Were Gold'. Economic and Ecological Links between Urban and Rural Areas in Late Imperial Jiangnan." *Late Imperial China* 26, no. 1: 41–71.

Yu, Xinzhong. 2010. "The Treatment of Night-soil and Waste in Modern China." In *Health and Hygiene in Chinese East Asia. Policies and Publics in the Long Twentieth Century*, edited by Angela K. C. Leung, and Charlotte Furth, 51–72. Durham and London: Duke University Press.

Zhou, Lianchun. 2004. *Xueyin xunzong-cesuo de lishi jingji fengsu* [*Looking for Traces of the Toilet. History, Economy, and Social Customs*]. Hefei: Anhui renmin chubanshe.

Zhu Jiaming, ed. 1988. *Zhongguo: xuyao cesuo geming* [*China: Needs a Toilet Revolution*]. Shanghai: Sanlian shudian Shanghai fendian.

12

THEORETICAL PARADIGM OR METHODOLOGICAL HEURISTIC?

Reflections on *Kulturkreislehre*
with Reference to China

YANG Shengmin and WU Xiujie

Kulturkreislehre was one of the most influential theories in the German-speaking humanities (*Geisteswissenschaften*) during the first half of the twentieth century, and the dominant theoretical paradigm from 1910 to the 1940s (Rössler 2007, 10; see also Gingrich 2005). "Cultural circle teaching," as it might be literally translated (Brandewie 1982), is usually associated with the Vienna School of Ethnology, in particular the Catholic priest Wilhelm Schmidt (1868–1954), diffusionism, and the historical-geographical method. Though German ethnologists born before the 1930s were well educated in these approaches, *Kulturkreislehre* was increasingly neglected in the postwar era. Wilhelm Schmidt became known for his anti-Semitic statements, and emotional resistance toward his teachings on these grounds hindered recognition of the contribution of *Kulturkreislehre* to the history of anthropology. When, in the late 1970s, an alumna of Vienna University (Andriolo 1979) set out to consider Schmidt's theory in the context of the social and intellectual milieu of Vienna and the late Habsburg Empire (i.e., the so-called Austrian Mind), the reaction of one German anthropologist was strong (Braukamper 1979). This provoked a long defensive article by an American anthropologist (Brandewie 1982). Eventually, the debate calmed down without being satisfactorily resolved, but many facets of the "Vienna teachings" are still worth scrutinizing.

Some recent publications indicate that *Kulturkreislehre* has been influential not only in anthropology (*Völkerkunde*), but also in related disciplines such as *Volkskunde* (folklore) and *Humangeographie* or *Kulturgeographie* (cultural geography). In Central European archaeology, *Kulturkreislehre* has been an influential but hidden paradigm (Rebay-Salisbury 2011; Schmoll 2009). It is well known that *Kulturkreislehre* influenced leading American anthropologists such as Alfred Kroeber and Clyde Kluckhohn. Even Robert Lowie's emphasis on the relevance of mutual influences between cultures reflects the indirect influence of the ideas of *Kulturkreislehre*.

Our aim in this chapter is threefold. First, we review *Kulturkreislehre* as a relevant chapter in the history of German-speaking anthropology, without shirking the controversies. Second, we examine its intellectual impacts in China. Third, we apply its methodological and theoretical tenets to a case study in China.

Rediscovering the *Kulturkreislehre*

Kulturkreis is an ambivalent keyword. According to Paul Leser (1963), it was originally introduced as a technical, methodological term with which to investigate the diffusion of cultural elements. Fritz Graebner and Wilhelm Schmidt shared this understanding of *Kulturkreislehre* as a culture-historical method, indeed the only way of doing culture-history according to Schmidt. His emphasis was on the collection and documentation of cultural elements—mainly concerning kinship, religion and material culture—for ethnographic description. On the empirical level, this implied that, contrary to the method of all-around participant observation, researchers could focus exclusively on certain subjects or objects while neglecting the "total social facts." It was thus (for example) central to the culture-historical method to draw maps of the spatial distributions of the cultural elements. The success of this method depended in large measure on two basic factors: the simplicity of the chosen elements and the quantity of collected data. It is not surprising that archaeologists were also attracted by this method of mapping their findings (Rebay-Salisbury 2011, 43). The focus on material culture can offer insight into broader processes, including those of modernization. We will come back to this point later in our case study.

One popular misunderstanding is that the term *Kulturkreis* refers to a concrete cultural area, and, accordingly, that *Kulturkreislehre* aims at describing a circumscribed cultural area and its boundaries. Archaeologists frequently interpret the concept in this way (Rebay-Salisbury 2011, 46). This interpretation is also prevalent in contemporary China, where "cultural circles" have been located in certain ethnic or regional cultures, as in the formulation "cultural circle of Alashan (Alxa) Mountains." But the term *Kulturkreis* is better understood as an abstract methodological concept. The key theoretical assumption is that culture-historical connections are made through time and space. Accordingly, the same cultural elements can be found in different cultures due to migration and cultural contacts; similar elements can be traced back to a common origin (Braukämper 2005). This basic idea can be traced to Friedrich Ratzel (1844–1904), who proposed that human beings invented primary cultural elements in very early times, and that the spread of these elements through migration was the major impetus for development in humanity's cultural history. The ambitious aim of *Kulturkreislehre* was to investigate diffusion of cultural elements in order to generate an alternative interpretation of human history to that of unilineal evolution.[1]

Andriolo's criticism concentrated on its "atomistic image of culture" and alleged a sterile and formalistic approach to culture, disengaged from substantive problems (1979, 138, 140). In practice, adherents of *Kulturkreislehre* in the second half of the twentieth century did highlight the social context of the objects they studied. Another line of attack suggested that they lacked a theory of history, but Ernest Brandewie defended Schmidt subtly by distinguishing between a philosophy of history and a theory of history:

> His epistemology . . . was one of moderate realism. . . . He would also, as a result, have held a philosophy of history such that history was knowable, and therefore, within broad limits, capable of being reconstructed. In fact, if anybody were working with culture and were not doing history, that person, as far as Schmidt was concerned, was not really doing anything worthwhile. (Brandewie 1982, 152)

For Schmidt, the key term in defining culture was *Geist* (mind) because the fundamental human capacity to symbolize and make abstractions relies on the mind. "Anthropology," he wrote, "is a science of the mind. All that it deals with has proceeded from the mind, has gone through the mind and bears its impress, and it is precisely through this process that it becomes a culture object. A mere object of nature as such does not belong to the field of investigation of ethnology" (Schmidt 1937, 7, cited in Brandewie 1982, 160). Thus, the collections of material culture would never be merely a "butterfly collection" and anthropology (*Ethnologie*) had its place in the ranks of the *Geisteswissenschaften*.

In *Volkskunde*, the *Atlas der deutschen Volkskunde* project applied the culture-historical method to German culture. Wilhelm Peßler, a pupil of Ratzel, outlined the project's goal: not the nostalgic collection of static objects, but a contribution to the knowledge of the essence (*Wesen*), becoming (*Werden*), and changing nature (*Wandern*) of cultural forms, kinship organization, and human migrations (Peßler 1943, 32). The project was initiated in 1928 with financial support from the Deutsche Forschungsgemeinschaft (DFG) which expected this pioneering application of the theoretical paradigm of *Volkskunde* to explain the deep cultural strata of the nation (Schmoll 2009, 21). Contributors to the project attempted to give culture-historical answers to acute problems such as modernization and nation building. But their claims to apply culture-historical investigations to substantive problems were perhaps overdone and this kind of applied science became a Damocles sword for the discipline of *Volkskunde*'.[2]

Tracing *Kulturkreislehre* in the Anthropology of China

In China, evolutionism was the dominant paradigm in the very beginning of the twentieth century. The Vienna School of Ethnology and *Kulturkreislehre* were never in the mainstream or very influential because diffusionism was perceived as a counterpole to evolutionism and not—as Marvin Harris has argued—one of its variants.[3] *Kulturkreislehre* was perceived as incompatible with Marxism because Wilhelm Schmidt denied the existence of natural laws of historical development and held that cultural contact could enable cultures to skip stages of development. Moreover, the spread of *Kulturkreislehre* in China was inhibited by its image as being dominated by Catholic priests. Even influential Chinese ethnologists such as Tao Yunkui (1904–1944), trained in Germany during *Kulturkreislehre*'s peak, were rarely influenced by it because they had more interest in physical anthropology. Cai Yuanpei (1868–1940), who was a senior researcher at the Ethnographic Museum of Hamburg between 1924 and 1926, and who introduced the term *minzu xue* (lit. the study of peoples' ethnicity) instead of *minzhong xue* (lit. the study of people races) as the Chinese for *Ethnologie*/anthropology, showed no special interest in the theoretical assumptions of *Kulturkreislehre*.[4]

Nevertheless, the Vienna School did have some subtle influences on anthropology in China during the first half of the twentieth century. The main representatives of the Vienna School, both Wilhelm Schmidt and Wilhelm Koppers, belonged to the Catholic Congregation *Societas Verbi Divini* (SVD), also known as the Divine Word Missionaries or Steyler Missionaries. In 1922, the society's missionaries reached the province of Gansu in China's northwest. About ninety missionaries were sent to China's vast northwestern regions, today's Qinghai and Gansu Provinces and the Xinjiang Autonomous Region, in the following decades. Among these missionaries, Mathias Hermanns, Dominik Schröder, and Johann Frick were especially interested in anthropology. The ethnic groups they described ethnographically included Han-Chinese, Tu, Uyghur, Tibetans, and Hui (see Horlemann 2009, 75–78, for a comprehensive list of their ethnographies). Primarily missionaries, these men lacked the conditions and the necessary objectivity to conduct academic research and writing (Quack 1994, 5). Mathias Hermanns's (1935) attempt to explain the history of China through ideas of the *Kulturkreislehre* was ambitious but not convincing. This monograph of more than three hundred pages titled *Chinas Ursprung. Vom Urmenschen zur Hochkultur* (*The Origin of China: From the Primeval Humans to the High Culture*) was not published by an academic publishing house, but printed in Yenchowfu by the central mission station. Wilhelm Koppers criticized this work as erroneous (*Fehlleistung*) because based on insufficient Sinological knowledge and a too mechanical and dogmatic application of the classical works of the Vienna School (Koppers 1935, 609). The other ethnographies produced by missionaries did not have such an ambitious and abstract scope. They aimed merely to describe concrete "cultural elements" such as the processing of fur; the use of blood in magic and medicine; wedding rituals; wages for female agricultural laborers; and peasant oral traditions. Since most of these works were published in German after the authors left China (mostly in the 1950s), they are generally neglected by Chinese anthropologists. A collected volume of five articles concerning rituals and customs in Qinghai by Johann Frick of the SVD only saw the light of day in Germany in 1995, when he was already ninety-two years old (Frick 1995).

Two professional scholars who have done anthropological research in China should be singled out, Mathias Eder SVD (1900–1980) and

Willem A. Grootaers (1911–1999). Both were employed as academics at the Catholic Fujen University in Peking in the 1930s and 1940s. Mathias Eder joined the SVD when he was still a young man and was sent to Japan as a missionary schoolteacher.[5] He felt himself more passionate about academic work than missionizing, and applied for academic training in Europe. Schmidt and Koppers were his mentors both academically and within the SVD. In 1938, he finished his doctoral dissertation and examinations in Berlin, where his major subjects were Japanese Studies and anthropology, and his minor subject was Sinology. On Schmidt's suggestion, Eder was sent to Peking (then under Japanese occupation) and nominated "Editorial Secretary of *Monumenta Serica*" at Fujen Catholic University. While other universities retreated to the hinterland to locations such as Kunming, Fujen was still allowed to continue normal teaching schedules.[6] Mathias Eder was assigned multiple responsibilities: teaching in Japanese Studies and anthropology; the establishment of a Museum of Oriental Ethnology; and the editing of the museum's yearbook, which later became the journal *Folklore Studies*.[7]

The SVD seems to have envisioned a long-term anthropological research program in China, to be developed by Eder. He invited the well-known Russian anthropologist S. M. Shirokogoroff to contribute a statement to the journal about the prospects for developing the discipline in China, based on his expertise and experience. Due to financial problems, the publication of the first volume was delayed until 1942, and the leading article by Shirokogoroff appeared three years after his death. In this article, the distinguished Russian scholar argued that an ethnographic investigation of China should cover the entirety of the cultural adaptations of its population. He stressed that any ethnographer had to master specific historico-ethnographical methods in order to understand the observed cultural complex. For him, the preliminary steps were to draw an ethnographical map and build up an adequate history of ethnography. He called for the establishment of a special Ethnographic Institute with the prime task being "the collection of the material for an ethnographical map of China by means of comparison of the published data and special investigation at the spot" (Shirokogoroff 1942, 7). Shirokogoroff's interest in mapping paralleled that of *Kulturkreislehre,* but it remains uncertain how extensively or deeply he engaged with the Vienna School's overall agenda.[8] Shirokogoroff appreciated the historico-geographical concerns of *Kulturkreislehre,* but he did not hide his preference for documenting cultural differentiations and complexes over dispersed "cultural elements." He considered that the description of cultural elements "cannot become clear until the relative value and relative weight of elements are defined after the elements have been grouped into complexes" (ibid., 1). Moreover, for a country with many written documents such as China, Shirokogoroff concluded that it was too simplistic to reconstruct its cultural history on the basis of ethnographic data alone.

Mathias Eder seems to have been influenced by the new ideas. In October 1940, he began to do field research on the streets of Peking, documenting the forms of the fronts and the decorations of the houses (a typical cultural element for the *Kulturkreislehre*). An article based on this study was published in his journal in 1943, using parallel data from the Shandong, Henan, and Shanxi Provinces in the Yellow River Region. At that time it was almost impossible to conduct any field research outside Peking. Eder hoped to be able to conduct fieldwork in other regions and then to arrange the collected data cartographically (Eder 1943, 54). In November 1940, he wrote to Adolf Spamer in Berlin, who held Germany's first university chair in *Volkskunde,* requesting information about literature on folklore methodology with the argument that "the methodology of German folkloristics is the only one appropriate for work (in China)" (ibid.). Unfortunately, we do not know how Spamer, at the time an enthusiastic supporter of the *Atlas der deutschen Volkskunde* project, responded to this inquiry. His sympathy with Nazi politics later made his work suspect. Certainly, Eder was familiar with what was going on in Europe, but his position within Japanese-occupied China would have made it difficult for him to publicly advocate strong political opinions. Personally and academically Eder had much sympathy for Japanese language and culture, but he was in a marginal position as a foreigner living in a city occupied by Japan, and was obliged to maintain a neutral position. In spite of all the practical obstacles, he endeavored to consider geographic variations in his research. For example, in one substantial text he analyzed 230 pieces of poetry that he and his assistants had collected from different regions to discuss the reflection of seasonal rhythms in folk poetry (Eder 1946). For another large-scale study about children's games and toys, he circulated a twenty-question form in five provinces (Eder 1947).

Eder's Belgian colleague Willem Grootaers was more concerned with tracing the historical development of customs. Grootaers was a trained linguist, well acquainted with the geographic distribution of dialects throughout China. In order to document popular religions in Chahar, a multiethnic region in northern China through which the historic frontier between the Han and Mongols passed, he and his Chinese assistants traveled to selected places to conduct short-term fieldwork, document the number of temples and the names of gods worshipped, and copy temple inscriptions (Grootaers 1948). Grootaers conducted similar research in Datong, in the north of Shangxi Province (Grootaers 1945). In both cases, he used the materials he gathered to attempt a reconstruction of the historical development for the cults of specific gods (Grootaers 1951). Like Eder, Willem Grootaers was satisfied with case studies, and did not aspire to make general conclusions, as Mathias Hermanns had done.

In 1950 the Fujen Catholic University was taken over by the Chinese Communist Party. Mathias Eder left China to continue work in Japan. In a farewell article he expressed a few considerations about the methodological problems of folklore studies. He used the term *Volkstum* (Folk culture) and described it as being characterized by acquisitions (*Übernahmen*), interferences (*Überschneidungen*), alterations (*Abänderungen*), and reinterpretations (*Umdeutungen*) (Eder 1950, 208). In order to understand the dynamics of the *Volkstum* he considered it necessary to draw maps of the spread of the custom under consideration over different eras. Such mapping would allow conclusions as to whether a custom was a functional part of a structural complex, a survival, or a new invention (ibid.). In his view, conducting such historically and geographically oriented research would require teams containing thousands of members (ibid., 211).[9] Eder's farewell article indicates that his thinking about studying folklore in China had been influenced equally by S. M. Shirokogoroff and by his mentors in Vienna. Eder had developed an openmindedness in his efforts to adapt *Kulturkreislehre* to China. He understood that the use of historical documents provided special opportunities and even suggested the integration of information found in Chinese encyclopedic compilations (*lei shu*), but he underestimated the methodological difficulties of assessing these historic materials. Indeed, despite his focus on the dynamic aspect of the *Volkstum*, Eder's own works rarely considered the dynamics of change.

The research undertaken at Fujen Catholic University before 1950 certainly contributed to the history of anthropology in China, but the extent of its influence is unclear. Eder's preference for drawing maps on the basis of spatially comprehensive but superficial investigations was also manifest in later historico-geographical studies in China.[10] However, no direct references to Eder, or to anyone else, are to be found in these later studies, making it difficult to trace early intellectual influences. Recently, however,

Chinese scholars have been sympathetic to Willem Grootaers, whose work has been rediscovered and feted by historians.[11]

In the following we dedicate attention to approach a small ethnic group—Salar—from those aspects that have been implemented by those pioneering researchers of China oriented to the *Kulturkreislehre* such as Eder and Grootaers—namely, to pick up those oral traditions, material culture. However, we set the aim of a better understanding of the modernization processes instead of identifying those origins of certain cultural elements.

A Case Study: Intercivilizational Encounters of the Salar in Qinghai Province

The Salar are one of fifty-five officially acknowledged ethnic minorities in China. They are Turkic-speaking Muslims, but language alone does not distinguish the Salar as an ethnic group. As Nicholas Poppe notes, "Although Salar differs from the remaining dialects of East Turkic, it is only one of its dialects and is not an independent language" (1953, 477). The Salar number about 120,000 people. The majority of these, more than one hundred thousand, live in Xunhua (35,8N, 102,5E), an autonomous county in Qinghai Province. A smaller part of the population lives scattered among a few villages in Yining, Xinjiang, along the border with Kazakhstan. Historical documents from imperial China verify that the Salar migrated to Qinghai at the end of the Yuan Dynasty during the thirteenth century. Their location prior to the migration is less clear. According to oral narratives of the locals, recorded in 2004–05, the Salar originally stem from Samarkand in Central Asia. Following Kubily Khan, they settled down in Qinghai and served the Khan as guardians of the frontier against invaders. In the eighteenth century, it is known that some Salar traveled back to Central Asia due to lack of arable land, and their search for subsistence led them to settle on the banks of the Yili River. Some current discourses trace the origin of the Salar even farther west in Central Asia to Turkmenistan—perhaps because a shared genealogy six hundred years in the past helps to naturalize close economic cooperation between Xunhua County and Turkmenistan in the present.

In Qinghai, the Salar have lived in close proximity to other ethnic groups including Tibetans, Han, Hui, and Mongols. It is not certain whether the Salar people were pastoral nomads or sedentary farmers before they came to Qinghai. But in Qinghai, they have been long occupied with agriculture, the cultivation of fruit trees, handicrafts, and trading. In the local context, the Salar people are distinguished from neighboring ethnic groups in terms of language, religion, and—in some cases—modes of subsistence. It can be said that over time they experienced intercivilizational encounters on multiple layers.

It is difficult to reconstruct contemporary civilization as the "historical outcome of exchanges and borrowings" (Wengrow, cited in Hann 2012, 113) between the Salar people and their neighbors. The Salar have no written history in their own language; nor do they have a script with which to begin recording it. Their history, and contacts with others, can therefore only be reconstructed with documents produced by other groups or with the techniques of a historically oriented folklore. One such technique would be oral narratives; these often present immediate incongruities if taken only as statements about Salar lifeways. According to oral narratives, for example, a white camel guided their ancestors to a beautiful place with a spring. They decided to stay there and built a mosque, naming the spring *luotuo quan* (camel's spring).[12] For folklorists, two things in this narrative contradict reality: camels play no role in the Salars' daily life; and white camels do not exist. Could this narrative be taken not as a statement of historical fact, but as a record of the encounter between the Salar and the Mongols? After all, camels and the color white are sacred elements for the western Mongols.

Alternatively, one might look to social organization and kinship for reconstructing the Salar past and their encounters with others. The social organization of the Salar is based on a patrilineal kinship system. The core unit is *aghing* or *agni,* consisting of *aga* (elder brother) and *ini* (younger brother). Below the *aghing* is the household (*oychi*), the basic unit for production and reproduction. The size of one *aghing* varies from two to ten households. The *aghing* is a closed group that excludes any member who is not related by blood through the patriline. Above *aghing* is the *kumsan,* an alliance of dozens of *aghing*. A *kumsan* can accept a household from another descent group, but this is rare in practice. One or more *kumsan* form a natural village (*agil*). Historically, villages were administered by the state in a regional-social unit called the *gon,* equivalent to today's township. In the Ming and Qing Dynasties, the imperial court nominated two *tusi* to be responsible for administering the twelve *gon* in Qinghai.[13] This created a pyramidal structure with the *oychi* (household) subordinate to the successive layers of authority of the *aghing* (patrilineal descent group), *kumsan* (lineage), *agil* (village), *gon* (township), and *tusi* (local chief).[14]

The Salar did and do not fully exclude intermarriage with other ethnic groups. The most accepted interethnic marriage relation is with the Hui because they share the Islamic religion and similar customs. According to oral narratives, the ancestors of the Salar asked the Tibetans for marriage alliance. Due to differences in religion and customs, the Tibetans stipulated a number of requirements, but an agreement was finally reached that allowed Salar men to marry Tibetan women (Ma 2011, 63). Over several generations, cultural mixing was thus possible through marriage. Recently, such marriages have become rare: marriage alliances with Tibetans exist only among the older generations; marital exchanges with other Salar patrilines within a ten kilometer range are preferred; and marriages with Han are avoided (Wang 2011, 9).

Some Han influence is reflected in Salar family names. Among the more than thirty family names used by the Salar, "Han" is the most popular. But the family name marks the boundaries of an *aghing* and does not reflect deeper Han influence. The Salar do not share a concept of patriliny with the Han, for whom cultural elements such as an ancestor's cult, genealogy, or lineage rules support the patriline's multifunctional role in religion, society, and culture. By contrast, the Salar lineage has a more limited scope: "[T]he role of the Salar patrilineal lineage serves to arrange marital exchanges, [provide] support and care within the lineage, [and] coordinate economic and ritual activities. Its functions are limited within the local society; [they] serve [the] integration and adaptation of small-scale communities. Seldom [do] they spread to the areas of politics, religions [or] related ideologies" (Wang 2011, 7).

Oral narratives, kinship and social organization, interethnic marriages, and some family names all point to the existence of cultural exchange between the Salar and their neighbors, but they do not suffice to enable a reconstruction of the historical processes of exchange. To solve this puzzle we turn our focus to the house, the favorite starting point of *Kulturkreislehre,* to trace historical changes and investigate the fine distinctions between the Salar and their neighbors. We profit greatly from a detailed report of four nineteenth-century farm buildings in Xunhua and one building of the 1980s in Xinjiang. The investigations were conducted between 2005 and 2006 by an interdisciplinary team of archaeologists, ethnologists, and architects coordinated by Mayke Wagner of the German Archaeological Institute's Eurasia Department (Wagner, Flitsch et al. 2007).

In the countryside of Qinghai Province, as well as in north China generally, a dwelling unit is a building complex enclosed by walls. The complex consists of the main house located on the south end, often accompanied by houses located to the east and/or to the west, as well as some space for livestock, a toilet, and a garden plot for vegetables and fruit trees. Seen from the outside, the traditional Salar house differs from the dwellings of neighboring ethnic groups in three aspects: the main house is two stories; the back wall of the house which has a height of four to five meters serves as the courtyard wall; and the whole homestead resembles a fort. The distinctiveness of the Salar house is also marked by the Chinese term used to describe it: *liba lou* (lit. fences storied-building). The term also describes the Salar's distinctive building technique. The Salar's Han and Hui neighbors traditionally made their walls by piling earth, but the Salar used wood to make a stable frame which they filled with fences made of thin brittle stems and branches (*liba*), and then secured everything by covering it with mud on both sides. *Liba* fences marked courtyard boundaries and livestock enclosures. This unique building technology has been acknowledged as cultural heritage at the provincial level, but architectural historians have not yet been able to identify its origin. References to such "fence walls" are not found in the documents about vernacular buildings in Central Asia, nor in the architecture of other ethnic groups nearby. Similar ways of building walls, however, are found among nomadic Tibetans in Qinghai who build their winter shelters in Aba, Sichuan Province. This finding supports the proposition that the Salar were nomads in close contact with Tibetans before they settled in Xunhua (Zhou, Li et al. 2011, 65). If further evidence is found to support such a hypothesis, it will help to reconstruct the history of cultural contacts on the Qinghai-Tibet Plain.

The research team led by Mayke Wagner focused on the documentation of housing construction, building materials, and the history of building use within the complexes. By comparing Salar and Han dwellings they hoped to ascertain which elements of Salar culture had been maintained from the nomadic period (Wagner, Flitsch et al. 2007, 127). It is possible to identify exactly the building dates of the four homesteads under investigation by examining the wood in the main frameworks. The oldest parts of the houses, still inhabited, were built between 1816 and 1859. Repairs and changes have been made continually, and new buildings were regularly added according to the needs of the family cycle and kinship relations, the availability of space and of financial resources. The foundations of the original buildings are comprised of big stones placed on the ground on which pillars were erected. Timber was used to build the house structure including windows, doors, and stairs; walls were filled in as *liba*; clay and straw were used for walls and roofs. Newer building materials include bricks, cement, and glass windows.

We have no space in this chapter to go into the many ornate decorative items that have symbolic meanings for Salar culture and Islam more generally. We focus instead on the arrangement of the kitchen in comparison with that of neighboring Han dwellings. In the dwelling culture of north China, the heated brick-platform (*kang*) plays a central role for all family members. It has multiple functions, and provides space for living, hosting guests, sleeping, and working (Flitsch 2004). The *kang* is found among both the Salar and the Han, but the two groups heat it differently. When entering a traditional Han house through the southern door, the first room is the kitchen with its cooking ovens. The living room or rooms to the east or west of the kitchen, double in size, hold the *kang*. The kitchen's cooking oven is connected with the *kang* in the living room; smoke and heat pass through channels in the base of the *kang* to heat it, before being released through the chimney. In contrast, the entry to a Salar house opens into a living room for hosting guests with an unheated *kang*. The family's living rooms are located beyond the guest room, and each is heated separately from outside the house or with a special oven within the living room. Although the Salar kitchen is much larger than the Han kitchen, and usually the largest of all the Salar rooms, it is separated from the living rooms and the heat produced from cooking is lost immediately.

In terms of technological effectiveness, the Salar arrangement of the kitchen and living rooms is disadvantageous. However, it reflects core values in kinship relations. The Salar kinship system prioritizes the regulation and control of exchanges with other patrilines, partially through consideration of physical distances. The cognition of kinship tends to be horizontal rather than vertical, and cultivating kinship relations can be described as an "art of arranging distances" structurally and spatially (Wang 2011, 11). The kitchen materializes the cultural logic of kinship because this is where family members prepare food to share within their social support network. In the case of arranging lifecycle rituals like births, weddings, and funerals, the kitchen is used to offer warm food for up to 150 visitors (Wagner, Flitsch et al. 2007, 223).

The houses built by the Salar since the 1980s and 1990s, both in Xunhua and in Xinjiang, are outwardly more similar to those of the Han. They are no longer two-storied constructions. Instead a cement platform about 40cm in height supports a single-floor house. Increasingly, timber has been replaced by industrially produced brick, cement, and stainless steel window casings. Symbolic aspects, however, continue to distinguish Salar houses. For example, the kitchen is still built in the northwestern corner of the compound, and it is still separated from the living rooms. The *kang* is also still used to mark fine social distinctions among the Salar in a way that it cannot be used by the Han. In Han houses, the *kang* in various rooms must all be of uniform height because they are connected to a single heating system. In Salar houses, the *kang* differ in form and height between rooms, denoting subtle status differences between those who inhabit the various rooms in the compound.[15]

From the preceding discussion of the Salar, it might seem that cultural elements might change through contact with immediate neighbors. A new phenomenon has been observed among Han in Hebei Province, two thousand kilometers away from the Salar, but reminiscent of traditional Salar building styles. Here, economically well-off villagers have begun to build new residences with two "Salar" characteristics: two-storied houses and kitchens that are separate from the living rooms. However, these changes have nothing to do with contact with Salar culture. They are attempts to emulate the modern style of urban apartment buildings. Cooking is fueled by gas or electricity by those who can afford them, and the *kang* is used as an unheated platform for sleeping. People over the age of forty are neither accustomed to the use of mattresses like urban residents, nor to sleeping on a cold *kang*, so they place electric mattresses on the *kang* in winter. By the same logic, if the Salar resume the construction of two-storied houses, it should not be assumed that they are "returning" to their traditional practices.

Conclusions

In this chapter, we discussed some basic ideas of *Kulturkreislehre* and then traced the tracks of its Chinese variant in the work of missionary scholars during the 1930s and 1940s. By rethinking this historico-geographic methodology in the context of China, we hoped to (re)discover analytical tools for examining modernization and interethnic relations, especially in multiethnic regions such as Qinghai. We used the phrase intercivilizational encounter to describe the selected case of the Salar, not least because "civilization" carries a double meaning. Civilization refers to a large-scale cultural entity, and at the same time implies that the culture is advanced and developing along a clearly defined trajectory. The findings of our intellectual tour might be summarized as following:

1. The historico-geographic method of *Kulturkreislehre* was a promising conception that cast an unfortunate curse on the ambitions of historical anthropology to reconstruct human activities over time. China, a country with a long-standing written tradition, gives ethnologists some hope for reconstructing relatively recent episodes of cultural contact and change by applying this methodology. The availability of historical documents implies the two tasks outlined by Shirokogoroff: the reconstruction of a history of ethnography and ethnographic mapping. In fact, however, China's written documents often provide insufficient material to answer historically phrased ethnographic questions, such as those relating to the origins of the Salar. Juxtaposed pieces of data, scattered temporally and spatially, provide no satisfactory basis for theoretical insight. The diligently undertaken but rather fruitless folkloristic work done in China has given no cause for euphoria. We therefore need to consider what constitutes a good historico-geographic method very critically and cautiously.

2. The methodological strength of *Kulturkreislehre* lies in its focus on material culture as much as on religion and kinship as relevant cultural elements. To use the documentation of certain objects during short-term field trip(s) as an ethnological method is likely to provoke criticism from those who value long-term participant observation. The advantage of short-term visits to the field, however, is the fresh curiosity that guides the researcher before he or she gets accustomed to the many practices of daily life.[16] As the case of the Salar shows, the remarkable technological inefficiency of heating the living rooms led the attention of the newly arrived ethnologist Mareile Flitsch first to the kitchen, then to the customs of cooking food, hosting guests, and finally to practices and cognition of kinship.[17]

3. Qinghai is a multiethnic region, and the Salar are a small ethnic group who came to this region about seven hundred years ago. Multilateral ethnic contacts are unavoidable, but there are no obvious conflicts between the Salar and other groups. Why,

under these circumstances, did the Salar remain an independent cultural entity? We assume that in the "societal self-understanding" (Wagner 2011, 94) of the Salar two core values are regarded as unalterable: adherence to Islam and a horizontal patrilineal kinship system that regulates social capital. Wang Jianxin's observations (cited above) about increased endogamy in recent decades are consistent with both core values. As the Salar are a small group that has never had any institutional power, its societal self-understanding has remained an "oasis" unaffected by sociopolitical transformations. Conflicts within the Salar community—such as those between "new" and "old" religious practices during the Qianlong Era (eighteenth century) that were brought before the mandarin of the Qing court for arbitration (Yang 2011), or river-use disputes that lasted until the Republican Era (Ma 2009)—neither violated the basic rules and values of the Salar nor caused a splintering within the group. Indeed, the existence of such conflicts in the past is barely known today.

4. Salar vernacular buildings have undergone many changes during the last hundred years. Like the Han, the Salar have begun to use industrially produced building materials. The popularity of such new products goes beyond regional boundaries. What interests us are the dynamics of this process of change. The *Kulturkreislehre* proposes that cultural elements are diffused in space primarily by migration. But the diffusion of cultural elements can also occur through virtual passageways such as the media, especially when a "civilizing mission" is present. The progressive aspect of the term *civilization* is well established and accepted in China, where rural populations view urban lifestyles as the epitome of "modern civilization." Translated into material culture, such visions of modernity are reflected in the choice of building materials, ownership of seldom-used electric appliances, and a car parked in the courtyard. The Chinese government has encouraged all of these new forms of consumption to support market development under slogans like "cars into the countryside."

In his study of Japan, Johann P. Arnason asserted that "modernity always coalesces around civilizational legacies which contextualize it and to which it is responsive" (cited in Smith 2011, 42). This statement stimulates us to contextualize the modernity that is imagined nowadays in rural communities in China (cf. Santos, this volume). As concerns the vernacular buildings, for example, there are more changes than continuities. In the village in Hebei Province where Wu Xiujie did her fieldwork, an environmentalist architect constructed two "model" houses. The concept was to build environmentally friendly houses from recyclable materials without timber, cement, or bricks. The house walls were made from earth with a width of one meter to provide efficient insulation that kept the house warm in winter and cool in summer. But this pioneering design was not accepted by the villagers. In their view even though the two-storied houses were "modern," they were made of earth (*tufang*) and still carried connotations of rural poverty.

The case of the Salar leads us to conclude that civilizational legacies can be categorized into at least two types. One type of legacy includes the cultural elements that are retained during the process of transformation toward modernity because they help an ethnic group retain its distinction as a cultural entity. A second type of legacy includes the elements that are rejected because they contradict images of modern life. If we stress cultural elements and their diffusion in the manner of the scholars of the *Kulturkreislehre*, we have a better chance of distinguishing these two legacies. In this sense, the keywords *civilization* and *civilizational analysis* have much potential for understanding the modernization processes of multiethnic China.

Notes

1. 1. *Kulturkreislehre* has also been criticized as relying on the concept of *Urmonotheismus* (primitive monotheism). Wilhelm Schmidt propagated the belief in a unique god being at the foundation of all religions in his twelve-volume work *Der Ursprung der Gottesidee* (1926–1955). It has been assumed that the author's religious conviction and a certain missionary agenda influenced his academic thinking (Gingrich 2005, 96). Schmidt's vocation as a "Catholic cleric" has negatively influenced the reception of the *Kulturkreislehre* as a whole. Yet he did not invent the concept of *Urmonotheismus*, which can be traced back to Andrew Lang (1844–1912) and was much used by other scholars (Rössler 2007, 13, note 18).

2. After World War II, it was alleged that this project had involved the military in collecting data and in occupied Eastern European territory (Schmoll 2009). Moreover, its results (such as the detailed documentation of local forms of gabled roofs) came to be considered outdated and were

often ridiculed, even within folklore as well as in the later intellectual communities of "European ethnology" (Bausinger, Kaschuba et al. 2006).

3. This is so even though the first Chinese introduction to Western anthropology was *Völkerkunde* by Michael Haberland, first published in 1898. The Chinese version, based on its English translation, came out in 1903 with the title *Minzhong xue* (Wang 1997, 74).

4. Cai Yuanpei defined anthropology as a discipline that documents all the cultural creations of humankind; he regarded ethnography as its basic method, and distinguished descriptive ethnography from systematic comparative ethnography.

5. Information concerning Eder's academic background was compiled by Dr. Peter Knecht at Wu Xiujie's request. The accounts are based on Eder's diaries. Eder was not a person who sustained many contacts, but he wrote diary entries every day. After his death, these documents were kept in the Divine Word Seminary in Nagoya, Japan. Peter Knecht is also a member of SVD and an ethnologist focusing on Shamanism in northeastern Asia. In 2007, he became Eder's successor as the editor-in-chief of the journal *Asian Ethnology*. We are very grateful for his generous help in preparing this article.

6. It is said that the university was tolerated by the Japanese occupying authorities because its rector was German.

7. When Eder was relocated to Japan, the journal was renamed *Asian Folklore Studies*. In 2007, it became *Asian Ethnology*.

8. In 1935, when S. M. Shirokogoroff had just published his Shamanism studies, Wilhelm Schmidt visited China. They met each other in Qingdao, but the personal relation between them was very tense.

9. The original text is: "Eine vollwertige Volkskundeforschung muß geographisch und historisch vorgehen, eine Aufgabe, die eine große Organisation und nicht nur hunderte, sondern tausende von Mitarbeitern auf höheren und niederen Arbeitsstufen erfordert."

10. Ethnological investigations of China have also been conducted on the scale similar to that which Eder imagined as necessary. Giant projects were organized for social-historical surveys of ethnic minorities in the 1950s; to collect oral traditions in the 1980s; and to register intangible cultural heritage in the 2000s. These projects produce huge quantities of raw data which are difficult for successors to use, and might better be seen as the curse of ethnological investigations in China than as their salvation.

11. Willem A. Grootaers's research articles on popular religions were edited and printed in 1995 (Grootaers, Li et al. 1995). In his review, David

Johnson recommends the book for the richness of the material it contains, but points out its major defect by noting that the work "is concerned with things—buildings, inscriptions, murals—not people" (Johnson 1998, 187). The Chinese version of the article "The Hagiography of the Chinese God Chen-Wu: The Transmission of Rural Traditions in Chahar" (Grootaers 1952) was published in 2006 in *Journal of Historical Anthropology* with a long, effusive afterword by the translator Deng Qingping, a historian (He and Deng 2006). Grootaers's study of Han dialects was translated into Chinese in 2003 and has been well received by linguists.

12. See http://www.56china.com/2009/1014/69027.html, a website devoted to the "Ethnic Cultures of China."

13. Two *tusi* authorities were created to control the area surrounding the Yellow River. In the Qing Dynasty, one general and five hundred soldiers were assigned to a garrison in Xunhua, in the center of the twelve *gon,* to prevent rioting among the Salar people who were believed to be strong, tough (*qiang han*), and difficult to subordinate (Zhu 2005, 43).

14. This description of Salar social organization is based on two articles by Chinese anthropologists (Wang 2011, 6; Ma 2011, 63), but uses the transcription of terms provided by Ma.

15. In Xinjiang, for example, the *kang* in the guest room may be 20 cm lower than those in the other living rooms (Wagner, Flitsch et al. 2007, 214–15).

16. As Willem Grootaers and his assistants investigated the temples in Chahar, they found that the sculptures of different gods had the same styles because they were made by the same craftspeople.

17. Although the housing culture of the Salar is a hot topic in the anthropology of China, details of the kitchen have never been discussed (Wagner, Flitsch et al. 2007).

References

Andriolo, Karin R. 1979. "Kulturkreislehre and the Austrian Mind."
    Man. New Series 14, no. 1: 133–44.
Bausinger, Hermann, Wolfgang Kaschuba, Gudrun M. König, Dieter
    Langewiesche, and Bernhard Tschofen. 2006. *Ein Aufklärer des
    Alltags. Der Kulturwissenschaftler Hermann Bausinger im Gespräch.*
    Wien: Böhlau Verlag.

Brandewie, Ernest. 1982. "Wilhelm Schmidt: A Closer Look." *Anthropos* 77, no. 1/2: 151–62.

Braukämper, Ulrich. 1979. "The Enigma of the Austrian Mind." *Man. New Series* 14, no. 3: 560–61.

———. 2005. "Kulturkreis." In *Wörterbuch der Völkerkunde*, edited by Walter Hirschberg. Berlin: Reimer.

Eder, Matthias. 1946. "Das Jahr im chinesischen Volkslied." *Aisan Folklore Studies* 4: 1–160.

———. 1950. "Gedanken zur Methode der chinesischen Volkskundeforschung." *Asian Folklore Studies* 9: 207–12.

———. 1943. "Hausfrontdekorationen in Peking. Mit Parallelen aus Shantung und Nord-Honan." *Folklore Studies* 2: 51–78.

———. 1947. "Spielgeräte Und Spiele Im Chinesischen Neujahrsbrauchtum." *Folklore Studies* 6, no. 1: 1–202.

Flitsch, Mareile. 2004. *Der Kang. Eine Studie zur materiellen Alltagskultur bäuerlicher Gehöfte in der Manjurei*. Wiesbaden: Harrassowitz.

Frick, Johann. 1995. *Zwischen Himmel und Erde. Riten und Brauchtum in Nordwestchina*. Sankt Augustin: Academia Verlag.

Frings, Theoder, and Edda Tille. 1925/1926. "Kulturmorphologie." *Teuthonista* 2, no. 1: 1–18.

Gingrich, Andre. 2005. "Ruptures, Schools, and Nontraditions: Reassessing the History of Sociocultural Anthropology in Germany." In *One Discipline, Four Ways: British, German, French, and American Anthropology*, 59–153. Chicago: University of Chicago Press.

Grootaers, Willem A. 1945. "Les Temples Villageois De La Région Au Sud De Tat'ong (Chansi Nord), Leurs Inscriptions Et Leur Histoire." *Folklore Studies* 4: 161–212.

———. 1948. "Catholic University Expedition to Hsüanhua (South Chahar). Preliminary Report." *Folklore Studies* 7: 135–38.

———. 1952. "The Hagiography of the Chinese God Chen-Wu (the Transmission of Rural Traditions in Chahar)." *Asian Folklore Studies* 11, no. 2: 139–81.

———. 1951. "Rural Temples around Hsüan-Hua (South Chahar), Their Iconography and Their History." *Asian Folklore Studies* 10, no. 1: 1–116.

———, Shih-Yü Li, and Fu-Shih Wang. 1995. *The Sanctuaries in a North-China City. A Complete Survey of the Cultic Buildings in the*

City of Hsüan-Hua (Chahar). Bruxelles: Institut Belge des Hautes Etudes Chinoises.

Hann, Chris. 2012. "Civilizational Analysis for Beginners." *Focaal* 62: 113–21.

He, Dengsong (Willem A. Grootaers), and Qingping Deng. 2006. "Zhenwu Shen Zhi—Chahaer Xiangtu Chuantong de Liubian." *Lishi renleixue xuekan/Journal of Historical Anthropology* 4, no. 2: 127–70.

Hermanns, Mathias. 1935. *Chinas Ursprung. Vom Urmenschen zur Hochkultur*. Yenchowfu: SVD.

Horlemann, Bianca. 2009. "The Divine Word Missionaries in Gansu, Qinghai, and Xinjiang, 1922–1953: A Bibliographic Note." *Journal of Royal Asiatic Society, Series 3* 19, no. 1: 59–82.

Johnson, David. 1998. "Book Review to the Sanctuaries in a North-China City. A Complete Survey of the Cultic Buildings in the City of Hsüan-Hua (Chahar)." *The Journal of Asian Studies* 57, no. 1: 186–88.

Kaschuba, Wolfgang. 1999. *Einführung in die Europäische Ethnologie*. Hamburg: C. H. Beck.

Koppers, Wilhelm. 1935. "Review Chinas Ursprung by Mathias Hermanns." *Anthropos* 30, no. 3/4: 609–11.

Leser, Paul. 1963. "Zur Geschichte des Wortes Kulturkreis." *Anthropos* 58: 1–36.

Ma, Chengjun. 2009. "Bainian Susong: Cunluo Shuili Ziyuan De Jingzheng Yu Quanli-Dui Jiacang Cunluo Wenshu De Lishi Renleixue Yanjiu." *Xibei minzu yanjiu/Northwestern Ethno-National Studies* 2: 80–88.

Ma, Yan. 2011. "Lishi Shang Hehuang Diqu Huizu Yu Sala Zu De Shehui Jiaowang." *Huizu yanjiu/Journal of Hui Muslim Minority Studies* 1: 61–65.

Peßler, Wilhelm. 1943. "Der Heutige Stand Der Sachgeographie." *Volkswerk. Jahrbuch des Staatlichen Museums für Deutsche Volkskunde* 3: 15–35.

Poppe, Nicholas. 1953. "Remarks on the Salar Language." *Harvard Journal of Asiatic Studies* 16: 438–77.

Quack, Anton. 1994. "Missionar und Ethnologe. Zum 90. Geburtstag von P. Johann Frick SVD." *Anthropos* 89: 3–13.

Rebay-Salisbury, Katharina C. 2011. "Thoughts in Circles: Kulturkreislehre as a Hidden Paradigm in Past and Present

Archaeological Interpretations." In *Investigating Archaeological Cultures: Material Culture, Variability, and Transmission*, edited by Benjamin W. Roberts and Marc Vander Linden, 41–60. New York: Springer.

Rössler, Martin. 2007. "Die Deutschsprachige Ethnologie Bis Ca. 1960: Ein Historischer Abriss." *Kölner Arbeitspapiere zur Ethnologie* 1: 1–29.

Schmidt, Wilhelm. 1937. *Handbuch der Methode der Kulturhistorischen Ethnologie*. Münster: Aschendorffsche Verlagsbuchhandlung.

Schmoll, Friedemann. 2009. *Die Vermessung der Kultur. Der "Atlas der Deutschen Volkskunde" und die Deutsche Forschungsgemeinschaft 1928–1980*. Stuttgart: Franz Steiner Verlag.

Shirokogoroff, S. M. 1942. "Ethnographic Investigation of China." *Folklore Studies* 1, no. 1: 1–8.

Smith, Jeremy C. A. 2011. "Modernity and Civilization in Johann Arnason's Social Theory of Japan." *European Journal of Social Theory* 14, no. 1: 41–54.

Wagner, Mayke, Mareile Flitsch et al. 2007. "Traditionelles Bauen und Wohnen der Salar in Nordwest-China." *Deutsches Archäologisches Institut, Eurasien-Abteilung, Aussenstelle Teheran* 39: 127–234.

Wagner, Peter. 2011. "From Interpretation to Civilization—and Back: Analyzing the Trajectories of Non-European Modernities." *European Journal of Social Theory* 14, no. 1: 89–106.

Wang, Jianmin. 1997. *Zhongguo Minzuxue Shi Shangjuan* [*The History of Ethnology in China, Part I*]. Kunming: Yunnan jiaoyu chubanshe.

———. 2011. "Sala Zu De Jiazu Zuzhi Yu Hunyin Guizhi - Jiyu Xueyuan Renzhi De Wenhua Luoji Fenxi." *Beifang minzu daxue xuebao (zhexue shehui kexue ban)/Journal of Beifang University of Nationality* 4: 5–12.

Yang, Yanxi. 2011. "1781 Nian Xinjiu Liangjiao Zhizheng Shuping." *Heilongjiang shizhi*: 22–23.

Zhou, Jing, Xuxiang Li, and Xiangjie Meng. 2011. "Sala Zu 'Zhuangke-Libalou' Minju De Huanjing Shiyingxing Yanjiu." *Qinghai minzu daxue xuebao (shehui kexue ban)/Journal of Qinghai Nationalities University (social sciences)* 37, no. 4: 62–65.

Zhu, Puxuan. 2005. "Qinghai Tusi Zhidu Yanjiu." *Xizang minzu xueyuan xuebao (zhexue shehui kexue ban)/Journal of Tibet Nationalities Institute (Philosophy and Social Sciences)* 26, no. 3: 40–44.

13

NOMADS AND THE THEORY OF CIVILIZATIONS

Nikolay N. Kradin

Introduction

The world of nomads has always been terra incognita for residents of the settled agricultural civilizations, both scaring and intriguing them. The centaur, itself a mysterious creature, was a symbol of the steppe world. It is no coincidence that the former crusader William of Rubruck, who had seen much in his lifetime, included in the first chapter of his writings a description of a trip to the ruler of the Mongolian Empire (Rockhill 1900, 52): "When I found myself among them it seemed to me of a truth that I had been transported into another century." The economy, culture, mode of life, and social-political organization of the inhabitants of steppe regions have all differed significantly from those of agricultural and urban populations.

The nomads of the Old World lived in arid steppes and semi-desert environments where agriculture was practically impossible. They were able to breed grass-grazing animals, which proved to be an effective mode of existence in these zones. The nomadic lifestyle originated in Inner Asia approximately at the transition from the second to the first millennium BCE. It could not compete with the industrial economy of modernity. The development of repeating firearms and modern artillery gradually ended the military power of nomadic peoples. Later attempts to sedentarize nomads, the creation of cattle-breeding markets, and the conversion of pastures to arable lands combined to upset ecological balances, although traces of nomadization still remain in the postsocialist period. This chapter probes the extent to which we can speak of a distinct civilization of nomads throughout these millennia, as distinct from mere lifestyle traits that reflect adaptations to an ecology or cultural area.

The World of the Nomads

The climate of the arid Eurasian steppes horrified the residents of the agricultural states. Pastoral nomadism was shaped strongly by the cataclysms of nature and climate. Snowstorms (Mong. *dzut*), droughts, and epidemics were perpetual hazards. Researchers have long suspected that major losses of cattle were characterized by particular climatic cycles (e.g., Kradin 1992, 54–55; Masanov 1995, 100). One can attribute the decimation of the stock to the incidence of extreme cold, storms, and/or droughts every ten to twelve years. Typically, about half of the whole herd would perish in each cycle. Restoring the herd required roughly between ten and thirteen years. Livestock reproduced at a faster rate than the human population and thus the number of domestic animals and the number of cattle breeders varied in accordance with a complex cyclical model.

Cattle breeding is strongly associated with dispersed settlement. The concentration of large herds in one place resulted in overgrazing, excessive grass trampling, and a higher risk of contagion for infectious diseases among the animals. It was impossible to accumulate cattle ad infinitum due to the limited capacity of the steppe. Irrespective of rank, the stock keeper could always lose his entire herd. This made it rational either to apportion the livestock among his poor kinsmen for pasture, or to distribute them as gifts and thereby raise his social status. In any case, pastoral nomadism could not provide the stable food surplus necessary to support large groups of people (aristocrats, officials, soldiers, priests) who did not participate in food production.

The mode of life and culture of nomads did not change during preindustrial times. The famous treatise of the Chinese historian Ssu-ma Ch'ien *Shih chi* (*Historical Records*) describes the composition of cattle herds characteristic of Xiongnu,: "Most of their domestic animals are horses, cows, sheep, and they also have rare animals such as camels, donkeys, mules, hinnies and other equines known as *t'ao-t'u* and *tien-hsi*. They move about according to the availability of water and pasture, have no walled towns or fixed residences, nor any agricultural activities, but each of them has a portion of land" (Watson 1961, 129). A thousand years later, Mongols had the same herd composition. "The Tartars are quite rich in animals: camels, cattle, sheep, goats, and they have so many horses and mares that we did not believe there were that many in all the world, but they have few pigs or other animals" (Plano Carpini 1996, 41). And several hundred years later, the situation on the steppes of Inner Asia had not changed (Radloff 1989, 130, 153–62, 168, 260, 335, passim).

All nomads invested in livestock, which were not just their source of material life but also the prime indicator of success and social standing. In the headquarters of chiefs and khans, beef, mutton, and horsemeat dishes were essential dietary components. Most people, however, only consumed the meat of slaughtered animals when entertaining guests. Cattle breeders generally relied on a diet consisting mainly of the different milk products of mares, sheep, and camels, *slum,* the occasional cereals, and "Mongolian" tea (Plano Carpini 1996, 53; Juvaini 1997, 21).

Because the animals constantly required fresh pasture, their herders were forced to move several times a year. Similar descriptions to those of Xiongnu nomads cited above were recorded for Turks, Uigurs, Mongols, and other nomads. Household necessities were few, and dishes were commonly made of unbreakable materials such as wood and leather. Clothes and footwear were sewn, as a rule, of leather, wool, and fur. The mobile way of life required nomads to live unpretentiously in light collapsible dwellings such as yurts and tents. The yurt was a major architectural invention of the nomads. Its circular form allows the greatest amount of interior living space. The yurt protects against cold in winter and against heat in summer. It has optimal aerodynamic qualities, rendering it tolerant of strong winds and hurricanes.

> Tartar homes are round and prepared like tents made cleverly of laths and sticks. In the middle of the roof there is a round window through which light comes in and smoke can leave, because they always have a fire in the center. The walls and the roof are covered by felt and even the doors are made of felt. Some huts are large and some are small, depending upon the wealth or poverty of the owners. Some are taken apart quickly and put back together again and carried everywhere; some cannot be taken apart but are moved on carts. The smallest are put on a cart drawn by one ox, the larger by two or three or more depending upon how large it is and how many are needed to move it. Whenever they travel, whether to war or other places, they always take their homes with them. (Plano Carpini 1996, 41).

Without its timber floor, a yurt weighs about 200kg, 75 percent of which is made up by the felt. Yurts could be assembled within one hour. Felt carpets could be utilized for up to five years, while a timber frame lasted more than twenty years.

When migrating, Mongols placed yurts on special carts, as noted by Marco Polo: "On the carts, the rooms [are arranged] in which one can sit and lie. They are called 'carts-marquees' (Mong. *Ger-tergen*). Into the four corners of the cart, sticks or planks are driven and they connect crosswise above" (2001, 77). The migratory clusters of yurts and carts could stretch out for many kilometers over the steppe:

> When migrating, the carts move in one row of five each. [When preparing for migrating, they], as the strings of ants, as the fibers for plaiting of cord, reach [to one place] from the right and left at a [distance] of fifteen *li* (about six kilometers). When (a column of moving carts) becomes straight and half [of them] reach the water source a [column] makes a stop. (Lin and Munkuev 1960, 138)

Such movement of such large masses of people sparked deep awe in the farmers of the settled agricultural states.

Nomadism: From Dawn Till Dusk

Possibly the most intriguing question in the history of Inner Eurasia is: What compelled nomads to undertake mass migrations and destructive campaigns against agricultural civilizations? A great many diverse answers have been proposed. These opinions can be classified as follows: (1) diverse global climatic changes (aridization, according to Arnold Toynbee [1934–61] and Grigory Grumm-Grzhimailo [1926]; humidification, according to Lev Gumilev [1993, 237–340]); (2) the warlike and intrinsically greedy nature of nomads; (3) overpopulation of the steppe; (4) the growth of productive forces and class struggle, that is, the weakening of agricultural societies as a consequence of feudal division (Marxist conceptions); (5) the recurrent need to replenish an extensive cattle-breeding economy by means of raids on more stable agricultural societies; (6) unwillingness on the part of settled peoples to trade with nomads (the cattle breeders then had nowhere to sell their surplus products); (7) personal acts of aggression on the part of the rulers of the steppe societies; (8) ethnic mobilization (*passionarity*) (see Gumilev [1989]).

While most of these factors have a certain plausibility, the importance of some of them has been overestimated. Present paleogeographic data refute any tight correlation between humidification or aridification and periods of decline or prosperity (Ivanov and Vasilyev 1995, table 24, 25). The Marxist class struggle thesis concerning nomads has proved to be erroneous (Markov 1976; Khazanov 1984; Kradin 1992). The role of demography is unclear because the livestock increased faster than the human population. An increase in livestock catalyzed grass depletion and a crisis of the ecosystem. While nomadic life can, of course, contribute to the development of certain military characteristics, farmers outnumbered the nomads many times over, and they also had an ecologically complex economy, reliable fortresses, and a more powerful handicraft-metallurgical base.

It seems to me that the following factors are crucial:

1. As many ethnohistorical studies in Asia and Africa have shown, pastoral nomads do not require any sort of legitimated hierarchy, let alone a fully fledged state (e.g., Markov 1976; Irons 1979; Khazanov 1984; Fletcher 1986; Barfield 1992; Masanov 1995).

2. The degree of centralization among nomads is directly proportional to the extent of the neighboring agricultural civilization. In terms of world-systems analysis, nomads have always occupied the status of a "semi-periphery" (Chase-Dunn and Hall 1997). Different regional economies were consolidated into a common space (whether local civilizations or world-empires). In each local regional zone, the political structuring of the nomadic semi-periphery was in direct proportion to the size of the core. Hence, in order to trade with oases or attack them, the nomads of North Africa and the Near East united into "tribal confederations" of chiefdoms, the Eastern European steppe nomads living on the margins of the Ancient Rus' established quasi-imperial statelike, while in Inner Asia the "nomadic empire" became the most important mode of adaptation (Lattimore 1940; Khazanov 1984; Barfield 1992; Golden 1992; Kradin 1992; Honeychurch, Amartuwshin 2006; Kradin, Skrynnikova 2006; Rogers 2007, 2012).

3. The imperial and quasi-imperial organization of Eurasian nomads took shape during the axial age (Jaspers 1949), that is, from the middle of the first millennium BCE onward. It began where

large spaces favorable to nomadic pastoralism were most readily available (e.g., regions of the Black Sea, Volga steppes, and Khalkha-Mongolia), Some nomads were forced into active contact with more highly organized agricultural urban societies (e.g., Scythians interacted with old oriental and ancient states; the nomads of Inner Asia interacted with China).

Nomadic empires were organized in the form of "imperial confederations" (Barfield 1992). From the outside, these confederations appeared autocratic and statelike (they were created to withdraw the surplus products outside the steppe), but on the inside they were consultative and tribal. The stability of steppe empires depended directly on the skill of the supreme power in organizing the production of silk, agricultural products, handicraft articles, and fine jewelry in settled territories. As these products could not be produced under conditions of a cattle-breeding economy, obtaining them by force and extortion was the nomadic ruler's priority. Being the sole intermediary between China and the steppe, the ruler strengthened his own power by redistributing booty from China. The nomadic empire could not have survived on the basis of an extensive pastoral economy alone.

The fortunes of the nomadic empire depended on the skill of the ruler in solving this problem and in redirecting the energies of his numerous relatives and brothers-in-arms outside the polity. In addition to his superior personal qualities, an aspirant needed talent in the fields of policymaking and warfare. He needed charisma in order to renew his authority over the pastoralist tribes and chiefdoms that had submitted to his predecessor. He had to show generosity and magnanimity when dividing spoils and distributing gifts. If he failed to do so, the nomadic empire was doomed to collapse into historical oblivion.

Nomadic empires shared the following characteristics: (1) the hierarchical character of social organization, which was affected at all levels by tribal and supra-tribal genealogical ties; (2) dualistic (into wings) or triadic (into the wings and center) principles of administrative division; (3) the military-hierarchical character of the social organization of the empire's center, usually according to the decimal principle; (4) the horse relay messenger service (Mong. *yam*) as a precise way of organizing the administrative infrastructure; (5) a particular system of power inheritance (empire is a property of the whole khan clan, institution of co-government, Mong. *kuriltai*); (6) the specific nature of relations with the agricultural world (Kradin 1992, 2000).

With the onset of industrial modernity and the transformation of military technology, the steppe societies turned into the colonial periphery of the new world-system. If, in the nineteenth century, the practice of indirect rule of nomads was normal, then with the establishment of socialism, direct rule prevailed. More recently, environmental crises and new sociopolitical institutions have posed new challenges to the resilience of the nomad, although numerous scholarly analysts have advocated giving them a chance to carry on traditional forms of nature management (e.g., Salzman, Galaty 1990; Humphrey, Sneath 1999; Ikeya, Fratkin 2005; Janzen, Enkhtuvshin 2008; Scholz 2008).

Between Barbarism and Civilization

In the years of perestroika and after the collapse of the USSR, many researchers from the countries of the former socialist camp have turned their back on Marxism and turned instead to civilizational theory (Erasov 1990; Barg 1991; Shemyakin 1991). In some new states, a civilizational paradigm became the official methodology for representatives of human sciences. However, post-Soviet scholars do not share a common definition of civilization, and several different civilizational approaches can be identified: (1) civilization as a local or regional variant of a mode of production (e.g., "Chinese feudalism"); (2) civilization as a postprimitive stage (or stages) of historical development (see above); (3) civilization as a shift away from Marxist terminology rooted in materialism (i.e., investigating socioeconomic relations and class structure) to the superstructure of mentality, ideology, and religion); (4) civilization as the key unit in large-scale local historical patterns; estimates of the number of such civilizations vary greatly (Kradin 2008).

Two opposing conceptions have dominated (Ito 1997). The first dates from the Scottish philosopher of the eighteenth century Adam Ferguson, who was the first to divide the history of humankind into the stages of ferity, barbarity, and civilization. This idea was developed in the works of Lewis Henry Morgan and Friedrich Engels, and, later, by Vere Gordon Childe, who attempted to specify the criteria of civilization in archaeological sources. This stadial approach defines civilization as a "postprimitive" society, (or postprimitive social formation, in Marxist terminology). Some scholars have simply renamed social formations (stages) as civilizations (e.g., Yakovets 1994). In this case, history was still perceived to be unilinear, a feature shared by Marxism and modernization theory, both of which had a tendency to divide the peoples of the world into the categories of "civilized" and "uncivilized."

A stadial approach to nomadism has long focused on the question as to whether nomads were capable of arriving at civilization by bypassing the stage of barbarity. The distinguished Kemerovo archaeologist Anatoly Martynov answered in the affirmative on the basis of his investigations of the ancient nomads of South Siberia. The elaborate, monumental burials of the nomadic elite required considerable expense and suggest a significant social stratification and cultural differentiation (Martynov 1989, 2003). This idea was highly controversial among Russian archaeologists (Brief Reports 1993). Martynov adopted his criteria of civilization from Childe's concept of the urban revolution, which specified ten features:

1. central urban places;
2. full-time specialists (craftsman, merchants, officials, priests, etc.), who worked for organizations that could command surplus from peasants;
3. monumental public buildings;
4. sizeable surplus product appropriated by elites through taxes or tribute;
5. demarcation of ruling groups, including priests, civil, and military leaders and officials;
6. written language and numerical notation, enabling the emergence of arithmetic, geometry, and astronomy;
7. sophisticated artistic style;
8. long-distance trade;
9. social solidarity, represented and misrepresented ideologically in temples and sepulchral shrines;
10. state formation. (Childe 1950)

Much later, writing about the Ancient Greeks, Colin Renfrew proposed a shorter list of features: (1) social stratification; (2) highly developed handicraft specialization; (3) towns; (4) written language; (5) monumental spiritual construction. For Renfrew, development in any two of the last three features was sufficient to warrant the classification *civilization* (Renfrew 1972, 3–7). Russian archaeology has a similar tradition. For example, according to Vadim Masson the archaeological "triad" of town, monumental architecture, and written language was decisive (1989, 8–11).

Charles Maisels, drawing on more recent analyses of the four most ancient civilizations of the Old World (Egypt, Mesopotamia, India, and China), concluded that well-marked social stratification, writing systems, long-distance trading, and monumental cultic structures were found only in three of the four cases (Maisels 1999, 343).

Martynov argued that the early nomads of South Siberia had already created a specific steppe civilization by the middle of the first millennium BCE. (1993; 2003). However, the Tagars and Pazyryk cultures did not have a sufficient number of civilizational features to qualify as such. They had no towns and no written language. The same conclusion can be drawn with respect to the Xiongnu Power. However, the Turkic and Uighur Kaganates, though lacking towns, can be considered nomadic civilizations. The Mongolian Empire, at its zenith in the thirteenth century, fulfilled the criteria comprehensively. A huge capital city was raised on the territory of the Mongolian steppes. The foreign architects and craftsmen erected beautiful palaces in Karakorum and the East Baikal region (Kiselev 1965). The Mongols invented a script and around 1240 produced a unique literary work, *Secret History of the Mongols*. Although no distinctive graves of the royal house have been found, from the written reports of European travelers it is known that that their funerals were accomplished with magnificence and mystery.

Nomadism as Local Civilization

The above delineation of some nomadic groups into "civilization," with the majority excluded from this category, is based on a stadial interpretation of the historical process. The other approach is to define a civilization in terms of shared local or regional cultural specificities. According to this perspective, each civilization is a gigantic organism that, like a living being, evolves through successive stages of development—from the cradle to the grave. In contrast to stadial theories, this approach considers the historical process in its spatial or "horizontal" dimension rather than diachronically or "vertically." Compared with the stadial approach, more sophisticated methodological tools are required; but the effort is worthwhile because it enables analysis to overcome the bias of Western scholarship.

One pioneer of this approach was Nikolai Danilevsky in his book *Russia and Europe* (1920). Another was Oswald Spengler, best known for his *Decline of the West* (1932; the German original was written at the end of World War I). However, the outstanding formulation of this type of civilizational theory was that of Arnold Toynbee in the twelve volumes of his *A Study of History* (1934–1961) Toynbee distinguished about thirty civilizations, each of which originated as a response to the "challenges" of its external environment. Each experienced processes of growth, rupture, and collapse. The internal structure of civilizations was based on functional divisions between a creative minority, the general population, and a proletariat (see also Kumar 2014).

Neither Danilevsky nor Spengler included the nomads in their lists of civilizations. Danilevsky assigned nomads a purely negative role in the historical process, as destroyers of other civilizations. Spengler placed nomads on a lower level than the *Hochkulturen* (i.e., civilizations), in the category of "clans, tribes and peoples." By contrast, Toynbee identified among his many civilizations the nomadic one, albeit viewing it as frozen and stagnant (Toynbee 1934, Vol. III: 7–22, 391–454). Toynbee's nomads were the eternal captives of climatic and vegetative cycles. Their expansion was triggered by nature and it was bound to be ephemeral, since there was nothing in their culture to nurture any long-term development. The nomads thus have no progressive history; these hordes can make no contribution to a dynamic world economy. Nevertheless, Toynbee deserves credit as the first scholar to begin to theorize nomadic civilization (see Wescott 1970; Melko 1995; Huntington 1996; Blaha 2007; Targovsky 2007, 2009).

Before perestroika in the 1980s, the civilizational approach was associated with so-called bourgeois science. In the USSR, Lev Gumilev was its only significant advocate. In recent Western scholarship it has become fashionable to abuse Gumilev as a Russian nationalist and anti-Semite. This criticism is undeserved. Gumilev was a tolerant man and a fine scholar who developed original perspectives on the lives of steppe people. While earlier xenophobic Russian historiography had portrayed nomads as barbarians who did nothing but plunder and slaughter the ancient Slavs. Gumilev opened up more positive interpretations for Russian readers. It is no accident that the national university in the Kazakhstan capital is named after him and that a monument has been erected to him in Kazan, the capital of the Republic of Tatarstan.

Gumilev's philosophy of history transcends the discriminatory stadial barrier between barbarism and civilization by postulating instead a process of interaction between separate macrosystems, which he terms *super-ethnoses*.

This concept has much in common with Toynbee's concept of civilization. Each super-ethnos went through the stages of birth, growth, and decline over a span of some 1,200–1,500 years. The dynamics were shaped by energetic impulses on the part of individual agents (Gumilev 1989). Thanks to Gumilev's contributions, nomads have gained recognition as a distinctive civilization in post-Soviet science (Suleimenov 1999; Abayev, Feldman 2003; Enkhtuvshin 2003; Kumekov 2003; Orazbaeva 2005).

No matter how self-evidently different the world of the nomads from that of sedentary agriculturalists, the question remains as to how valid it is to view them as a civilization. Is the term also to be applied to hunter-gatherers of Australia, to Arctic fishermen and hunters, and indeed to any human group? If this is to be acceptable, a new scientific definition must be agreed.

A second, quite different question asks whether some features are unique to nomadic civilization. Similarities in notions of time and space, hospitality customs, kinship, the limitation of ostentatious consumption, powers of endurance, epics, and the militarization of society tend to display an evolutionist character and are not restricted to nomads. Perhaps only the special cult relation to livestock serves to distinguish them.

Thirdly, if we accept that each civilization is based on a particular psychocultural unity that experiences stages of growth, prosperity, and collapse, we have to concede that nomadism is something different. Nomads flourished in the Old World over a very long period from the first millennium BCE to the middle of the second millennium CE. Many sedentary civilizations emerged and collapsed during this period, but there was no unity on the nomadic side, either. The ethnic and cultural differences between the Hyksoses peoples and Xiongnu nomads, between medieval Arabs and Mongolian Kereyid, or between Nuer from Sudan and Arctic reindeer breeders, are enormous. One way to proceed in the face of this diversity is to classify some groups of nomadic societies as constituting a civilizational core (e.g., Arabians), and others as the "barbarian" periphery of another civilization (e.g., Hyksoses before the conquest of Egypt). Yet others might be classified as beyond the civilization processes, which impacted on them only with the beginning of modern colonialism (e.g., Nuer, Chukchi).

This complexity suggests that we approach nomadism as a quasi-civilizational network rather than a specific civilization (Pavlenko 2002, 312–21). The quasi-civilizational network, as opposed to civilization, has no common spiritual core. Nomads have played a key role in translating ideas and technologies in world history (Allsen 2001) and they have contributed to the artistic achievements of many other civilizations (Khazanov 1993; 1994). Yet it is not mere chance that nomads have not invented a world religion.

Civilizational Pluralism in the Service of Postcolonial Nationalism

Lev Gumilev (1989) associated the processes of the origin and development of civilization with particular geographical zones, such as the Arabian Peninsula in the seventh century CE. Inner Asia was another such zone, enabling the emergence of a more or less unified steppe civilization since the Xionhnu or earlier (Perlee 1978; Urbanaeva 1994). This civilization was characterized by administrative division into wings, decimal numeration, enduring ideas about power, enthroning ceremonies, love of horse and camel races, and a particular world outlook. As a nomadic empire, the Mongolian civilization deserves special attention in this context (Zelezniakov 2000; cf. Wescott 1970; Melko 1995; Ito 1997). It is clear that the Mongolian civilization had a genetic code distinct from other Eurasian nomads, but neither the circumstances of its emergence in the eleventh century, when Mongols settled in the eastern part of Central Asia, nor the spread of Buddhism in later centuries have been adequately explored to date. In short, the basic stages of Mongolian civilization and the effect of Mongols on civilizational processes elsewhere during the Middle Ages require further scholarly investigation.

Another civilization identified by post-Soviet scholars is that of the Golden Horde. This idea was advanced by a number of Tatarstan specialists from Moscow and Saint Petersburg (Kramarovsky 2003; Kulpin 2004; 2008). The important almanac *Zolotoordynskaya tsivilizatsiia* (*The Golden Horde Civilization*) was published in Russian but it fails to substantiate the concept satisfactorily (Kradin 2005). The relatively short duration (no more than three centuries) and limited cultural commonalities do not warrant classification of the Golden Horde as a united civilization. Archeological excavations have revealed that two absolutely different worlds existed alongside each other: the Turkic-Mongolian world of pastoral nomads and the hybrid world of several great towns. In these urban cultures, we can find elements of a plethora of civilizations and cultures, among them the Chinese, Central Asian, Western European, and Russian.

Numerous other candidates for recognition as nomadic civilizations have been advanced in recent years, for instance, in Kazakhstani historiography. The theory of nomadic civilization is introduced to correct for the inadequacy of the old Marxist theories (Sembinov 2003, 183 184). Similarly, local scholars in Kyrgyzstan have identified a Kyrgyz civilization. If, in the Soviet times, it was necessary to demonstrate "nomadic feudalism," after the collapse of the USSR it was necessary to construct of one's own nation and state. Already under President Askar Akaev in 2003, ambitious actions to commemorate the 2,200th anniversary of local statehood were carried out in Kyrgyzstan. Local historians found this date in Chinese annals where it was recorded that the ruler of the Xiongnu Empire reached the territory of the ancient Kyrgyz in 200 BCE (Kakeev, Ploskikh 2003; Ploskikh 2003). There is no need to expand here on the scholarly accuracy of such calculations, which function to legitimate new power holders. It is a similar story in many national republics of the Russian Federation, where scholars have busily documented the existence of specific civilizations on the territories in question. Civilizational analysis for peoples such as the Bashkir, Buryat, Kalmyk, Tatar, and Yakut is thus primarily an instrument of nationalism, which helps each nation to construct its past and prove its antiquity. This is consistent with earlier instances of postcolonial nation building (Wallerstein 1984). For example, it is nowadays common practice in Yakutia to relate the past to the medieval Kyrgyz and even the Xiongnu Empire. While some practitioners may defend this form of civilizational analysis as a legitimate move to emerge from the shadow of the previous colonial masters, in practice it has become a form of nationalism.

Conclusions

In this chapter, I have not considered recent variations of civilizational analysis by leading Western scholars (Mazlish 2001; Arnason 2001; 2010; Knöbl 2010; Hann 2012). These have had little impact on the discourses of historians in the post-Soviet countries. While many scholars have become increasingly skeptical of theoretical generalizations, preferring to focus on local communities, everyday life, and microhistory, the comparative study of civilizations has by no means disappeared. Notable examples include Hord (1987), Ito (1997), Alaev and Korotayev (2000), Targovsky (2007), Melko (2008), and Hamilton (2010). Yet several fundamental challenges remain unresolved to date. Firstly, there is still no agreement concerning the objective criteria on which to base classification. There is thus no agreement concerning the number of civilizations, up to and including the point at which every ethnic group can be given recognition as a civilization. Secondly, to identify civilizations with living organisms is unhelpful. The evolution of civilizations is different, and unidirectional rise and fall is not the only trajectory. We need to recognize that different civilizations have different dynamics, and more profoundly, that civilizational uniqueness does not contradict universal or at least general-historical regularities (e.g., Axial Age or globalization).

In the USSR, where civilizational theory was associated with so-called bourgeois science, Lev Gumilev was the only major practitioner of the civilizational approach. In the years of perestroika and after the collapse of the USSR, many researchers turned to the civilizational approach, believing that it should replace historical materialism. Several different variants of the civilization theory interpretation were proposed, of which the most popular has been to view civilization as a distinctive historical pattern with a local or regional basis. This view of civilization has become the statutory historical methodology in many postsocialist countries as well as in the national republics of the Russian Federation. The appearance of so many new civilizations results from the need to rewrite the past, justify new technologies of power and explain economic backwardness. Not infrequently, invoking the specific characteristics of (a) nomadic civilization can be used to buttress the new national ideology.

References

Abaev, Nikolay V., and Vladimir R. Feldman. 2003. "K voprosu o roli sotsialnoy samoorganizatsii v geneticheskoy strukture kochevogo obshchestva [Towards the Role of Social Self-organization in Genetic Structure of the Nomadic Society]." *Nomadic Studies Bulletin* 6: 73–78.

Alaev, Leonid B., and Andrey V. Korotayev. 2000. "Perspektiva primeneniia kross-kulturnykh baz dannykh dlia sravnitelnogo izucheniia tsivilizatsiy [Perspective of the Cross-cultural Data Bases for the Comparative Study of Civilizations]." In *Sravnitelnoe izuchenie tsivilizatsiy mira*, edited by K. V. Khvostova, 159–80. Moscow: Institute of World History of the Russian Academy of Sciences.

Allsen, Thomas 2001. *Culture and Conquest in Mongol Eurasia.* Cambridge: Cambridge University Press.

Arnason, Johann P. 2001. "Civilizational Patterns and Its Sources." *International Sociology* 16: 387–405.

———. 2010. "Domanis and Perspectives of Civilizational Analysis." *European Journal of Social Theory* 13: 5–13.

Barfield, Thomas 1992 [1989]. *The Perilous Frontier: Nomadic Empires and China, 221 BC to AD 1757.* Cambridge: Blackwell.

Barg, Mikhail A. 1991. "Kategoriia 'tsivilizatsiia' kak metod sravnitel-no-istoricheskogo issledovaniia [The Category 'Civilization' as a Method of Contemporary Historical Study]." *Istoriia SSSR* 5: 70–86.

Blaha, Stephen. 2007. "The Origin and Sequences of Civilizations." *Comparative Civilizations Review* 57: 70–92.

Chase-Dunn, Christopher, and Thomas D. Hall. 1997. *Rise and Demise: Comparing World-Systems.* Boulder: Westview.

Childe, V. Gordon 1950. "The Urban Revolution." *Town Planning Review* 21: 3–17.

Golden, Peter 1992. *An Introduction to the History of the Turkic Peoples: Ethnogenesis and State Formation in Mediaeval and Early Modern Eurasia and the Middle East.* Wiesbaden: Otto Harrassowitz.

Grumm-Grzimailo, Grigory G. 1926. *Zapadnaia Mongoliiia i Uiriankhai Krai* [*Western Mongolia and the Uiriankhai Country*]. Vol. II. Leningrad: Russian Geography Society.

Gumilev, Lev N. 1989. *Etnogenes i biosfera zemi* [*Ethnogenesis and the Biosphere of the Earth*]. 2nd ed. Leningrad: Leningrad University Press.

———. 1993. *Ritmy Evrasii* [*The Cycles of Eurasia*]. Moscow: Ekopros.

Danilevsky, Nikolay Y. 1920. *Russland und Europa.* Stuttgart Berlin: Deutsche Verlags-Anstalt.

Enkhtuvshin, Batbold. 2003. "Nomadic Society and Some Aspects of Civilizations Studies." In *Chinggis Khaan and Contemporary Era,* edited by B. Enkhtuvshin and J. Tsolmon, 65–90. Ulaanbaatar: International Institute of the Study of Nomadic Civilizations.

Erasov, Boris S. 1990. *Kultura, religiia i tsivilizatsiia na Vostoke* [*Culture, Religion, and Civilization in the Orient*]. Moscow: Nauka.

Fletcher, John. 1986. "The Mongols: Ecological and Social Perspectives." *Harvard Journal of Asiatic Studies* 46, no. 1: 11–50.

Hamilton, Gary G. 2010. "World Images, Authority, and Institutions: A Comparison of China and the West." *European Journal of Social Theory* 13: 31–48.

Hann, Chris. 2012. "Civilizational Analysis for Beginners." *Focaal: Journal of Global and Historical anthropology* 62: 113–21.

Honeychurch, William, and Chunag Amartuwshin. 2006. "States on Horseback: The Rise of Inner Asian Confederations and Empires." In *Archaeology of Asia*, edited by Miriam T. Stark, 255–78. London: Blackwell.

Hord, John. 1987. "The Civilizational Tree." In *The Boundaries of Civilizations in Space and Time*, edited by Matthew Melko, 32–46. Lanham, MD: University Press of America.

Humphrey Caroline, and David Sneath. 1999. *The End of Nomadism?* Durham: Duke University Press.

Huntington, Samuel. 1996. *The Clash of Civilizations and the Remaking of World Order*. New York: Simon and Schuster.

Ikeya, Kazunobo, and Elliot Fratkin, eds. 2005. *Pastoralists and Their Neighbors in Asia and Africa*. Osaka: National Museum of Ethnology (Senri Ethnological Studies 69).

Irons, William. 1979. "Political Stratification among Pastoral Nomads." In *Pastoral Production and Society*, 361–74. Cambridge: Cambridge University Press.

Ito, Shuntaro. 1997. "A Framework for Comparative Study of Civilizations." *Comparative Civilizations Review* 36: 4–15.

Ivanov, Igor, and Igor Vasiljev. 1995. *Chelovek, priroda i pochvy Ryn-peskov Volgo-Uralskogo meshdurechya v golocene* [*Ryn-Sands Country during the Holocene: A Man and Nature*]. Moscow: Intellect.

Janzen, Jörg, and Batbold Enkhtuvshin, eds. 2008. *Proceedings of the International Conference "Dialog between Cultures and Civilizations: Present State and Perspectives of Nomadism in a Globalizing World*. Ulaanbaatar: Admon Printing Press.

Jaspers, Karl. 1949. *The Origin and Goal of History*. New Haven: Yale University Press.

Juvaini. 1997. *Genghis Khan. The History of the World Conqueror by 'Ala ad-Din 'Ata-Malik Juvaini*. Translated by J. A. Boyle. Manchester: Manchester University Press.

Kakeev, Askar Ch., and Vladimir M. Ploskikh. 2003. "Renesans idei gosudarstvennosti v Kyrgyzstane [Renaissance of Statehood Idea in Kyrgyzstan]." *Dialog tsivilizatsiy* 2 (Bishkek): 11–14.

Khazanov, Anatoly M. 1984. *Nomads and the Outside World.* Cambridge: Cambridge University Press; 2nd ed. Madison: University of Wisconsin Press.

———. 1993. "Muhammed and Jenghiz Khan Compared: The Religious Factor in World Empire Building." *Comparative Studies in Society and History* 35: 461–79.

———. 1994. "The Spread of World Religions in Mediaeval Nomadic Societies of the Eurasian Steppes." In *Nomadic Diplomacy, Destruction and Religion from the Pacific to the Arctic,* edited by M. Gervers and W. Schlepp, 11–33. Toronto: Joint Centre for the Asia Pacific Studies, Toronto Studies in Central and Inner Asia, No 1.

Kiselev, Sergey V., ed. 1965. *Drevnemongolskie goroda* [*Ancient Mongolian Towns*]. Moscow: Nauka.

Knöbl, Wolfgang. 2010. "Path Dependency and Civilizational Analysis: Methodological Challenges and Theoretical Tasks." *European Journal of Social Theory* 13: 83–97.

Kradin, Nikolay N. 1992. *Kochevye obshchestva* [*The Nomadic Societies*]. Vladivostok: Dal'nauka.

———. 2000. "Nomadic Empires in Evolutionary Perspective." In *Alternatives of Social Evolution,* edited by N. N. Kradin, A. V. Korotayev, D. M. Bondarenko, V. de Munck, and P. Wason, 274–88. Vladivostok: Far-Eastern Branch of the Russian Academy of Sciences.

———. 2005. "Kochevnichestvo i teoriia tsivilizatsiy [Nomadism and Civilization Theory]." In *Mongolskaya imperiia i kochevoy mir,* edited by B. V. Bazarov, N. N. Kradin, T. D. Skrynnikova, Vol. 1, 14–23. Ulan-Ude: Buryat Scientific Center of Siberian Division of RAS Press.

———. 2008. "Problemy periodisatsii istoricgeskikh makroprotsessov [Problems of Periodization Historical Macroprocesses]." In *Istoriia i metematika: Modeli i teorii,* edited by L. E. Grinin, A. V. Korotayev, and S. Y. Malkov, 166–200. Moscow: URSS.

———, and Tatiana D. Skrynnikova. 2006. *Imperiia Chngis-khana* [*Chinggis Khan Empire*]. Moscow: Vostochnaya literatura.

Kramarovsky, Mark. 2003. "Velikaia Orda Zlataia: Ulus Dzuchi kak tsivilizatsiia [The Great Golden Horde: Jochi Polity as a Civilization]." *Rodina* 11: 66–74.

Kulpin, Edward S. 2004. "Tsivilizatsiia Zolotoy Ordy [Golden Horde Civilization]." In *Mongolskaya imperiia i kochevoy mir,* edited B.

V. Bazarov, N. N. Kradin, and T. D. Skrynnikova, Vol. 1, 167–86. Ulan-Ude: Buryat Scientific Center of Siberian Division of RAS Press.

———. 2008. "Spor o tsivilizatsii [Dispute about civilization]." *Zolotoordynskaya tsivilizatsiia* 1: 7–13.

Kumekov, Bulat. 2003. "O stepnoy tsivilizatsii [About the Steppe Civilization]." In *Kazakhskaya tsivilizatsiia v kontekste mirovogo istoricheskogo protsessa*. Proceedings of international conference, 72–77. Almaty.

Lattimore, Owen. 1940. *Inner Asian Frontiers of China*. New York and London: American Geographical Society.

Lin, Chiun-yi, and Nikolay Munkuev, trans. 1960. "Hei-Ta shih-lue (Kratkie svedeniia o chernykh tatarakh) [Hei-Ta shih-lue (Brief Notes on the Black Tatars), by P'eng Ta-ya and Hsu T'ing]." *Problemy vostokovedeniia* 5: 132–58.

Maisels, Charles. 1999. *Early Civilizations of the Old World*. London and New York: Routledge.

Marco Polo. 2001. *The Travels of Marco Polo*. Translated by M. Komroff. New York: Modern Library.

Markov, Gennady E. 1976. *Kochevniki Asii [The Nomads of Asia]*. Moscow, Moscow University Press.

Martynov, Anatoly I. 1989. "O stepnoy skotovodcheskoy tsivilizatsii I tys. do n.e. [On the Steppe Nomadic Civilization in the I Millennium BC]." In *Vzaimodeistvie kochevykh kultur i drevnikh tsivilizatsiy*. Edited by V. M. Masson, 284–92. Alma-Ata: Nauka.

———. 2003. "Model tsivilizatsionnogo razvitiia v stepnoy Evrasii [The Model of Civilizational Development in the Eurasian Steppe]." In *Sotsialno-demograficheskie protsessy na territorii Sibiri (drevnost I srednevekovie)*, edited by V. V. Bobrov, 7–15. Kemerovo: Kemerovo State University.

Masanov, Nurbulat E. 1995. *Kochevaia civilizatsiia kazakhov [The Nomadic Civilization of the Kazaks]*. Moscow and Almaty: Gorizont and Sotsinvest.

Masson, Vadim M. 1989. *Pervye tsivilisatsii [The First Civilizations]*. Leningrad: Nauka.

Mazlish, Bruce. 2001. "Civilization in a Historical and Global Perspective." *International Sociology* 16: 293–300.

Melko, Matthew. 1995. "The Nature of Civilizations." In *Civilizations and World Systems: Studying World-Historical Change*, edited by

Stephen K. Sanderson, 25–45. Walnut Creek, CA: AltaMira Press.

———. 2008. "The Origin of Civilizations: Essay with Notes." *Comparative Civilizations Review* 59: 9–36.

Orazbaeva, Altainy I. 2005. *Tsivilizatsiia kochevnikov evraziiskikh stepey* [*The Civilization of the Eurasian Steppe Nomads*]. Almaty: Daik-Press.

Pavlenko, Yury V. 2002. *Istoriia mirovoy tsivilizatsii* [*History of the World Civilization*]. Kiev: Phoenix.

Perlee Khodoo 1978. *Nokotorye voprosy istorii kochevoy civilizatsii drevnikh mongolov* [*Some Questions of the History of the Nomadic Civilization of Ancient Mongols*]. Unpublished DrSc Dissertation. Ulanbaatar.

Plano Carpini, Giovanni. 1996. *The Story of the Mongols Whom We Call the Tartars*. Translated by E. Hildinger. Boston: Branden.

Ploskikh, Vladimir M. 2003. "Istoriia Kyrgyzskoy gosudarstvenno-sti: itogi i perspektiva issledovaniia [History of Statehood in Kyrgyzstan: Results of Studies and Perspectives]." *Dialog tsivilizatsiy* 2 (Bishkek): 51–53.

Radloff, Friedrich Wilhelm. 1989. *Iz Sibiri* [*From Siberia*]. Moscow: Nauka.

Renfrew, Colin. 1972. *The Emergence of Civilization: The Cyclades and Aegean in the Third Millenium B.C.* London: Methuen.

Rockhill, William W., trans. 1990. *The Journey of William of Rubruck to the Eastern Parts of the World, 1253–55, as narrated by himself, with two accounts of the earlier journey of John of Pian de Carpine.* London: Hakluyt Society.

Rogers, Daniel J. 2007. "The Contingencies of State Formation in Eastern Inner Asia." *Asian Perspectives* 46: 249–74.

———. 2012. "Inner Asian States and Empires: Theories and Synthesis." *Journal of Archaeological Research* 20: 205–56.

Salzman, Peter C., and John Galaty, eds. 1990. *Nomads in a Changing World*. Naples: Instituto Universitario Orientale.

Scholz, Frederik. 2008. *Nomadism: A Socioecological Mode of Culture*. Ulaanbaatar: International Institute of the Study of Nomadic Civilizations.

Schorkowitz, Dittmar. 2012. "Historical Anthropology in Eurasia … and the Way Thither." *History and Anthropology* 23, no. 1: 37–62.

Sembinov, Murat. 2003. "Stanovlenie natsionalnoy istoriografii v Kazakhstane [The Creation of National Historiography in

Kazakhstan].” In *Nacionalnye istorii v sovetskom i postsovetskikh gosudarstvakh*, edited by K. Imermacher and G. Bordiugov, 176–91. 2nd ed. Moscow: Friedrich Haumann foundation; AIRO-XX.

Shemyakin, Yakov G. 1991. “Problema tsivilizatsii v sovetskoy nauchnoy literature 60–80-kh godov [The Problem of Civilization in Soviet Literature in 1960–80 Years].” *Istoriia SSSR* 5: 86–103.

Suleymenov, Timur. 1999. “Kategoriia ‘tsivilizatsiia’ v trudakh issledovateley nomadisma [The ‘Civilization’ Category in the Studies of Researchers of Nomadism].” *Evrasiiskoe soobshchestvo* 2: 24–29.

Spengler, Oswald. 1932. *Decline of the West*. New York: Knopf.

Targovsky, Andrew. 2007. “The Civilization Index.” *Comparative Civilizations Review* 57: 93–113.

———. 2009. “Towards a Composite Definition and Classification of Civilization.” *Comparative Civilizations Review* 60: 79–98.

Toynbee, Arnold. [1934] 1961. *A Study of History*. Vol. I–XII. London: Oxford University Press.

Urbanaeva, Irina S. 1994. *Chelovek u Baikala i mir Centralnoy Asii [Man at the Baikal and the World of the Central Asia]*. Ulan-Ude: Publishing House of Buryatian Scientific Centre of the Siberian Branch of the Russian Academy of Sciences.

Wallerstein, Immanuel. 1984. *The Politics of the World-Economy*. Paris: Maison de Science de l’Homme.

Watson, Burton, trans. 1961. *Records of the Grand Historian of China from the Shih Chi of Ssu-ma Ch’en*. Vols. 1. New York: Columbia University Press.

Wescott, Roger. 1970. “The Enumeration of Civilizations.” *History and Theory* 9, no. 1: 59–75.

Yakovets, Yury V. 1994. *Ritm smeny tsivilizatsiy i istoricheskie sudby Rossii [The Rhythm of Civilizations Changes and Historical Fates of Russia]*. Moscow: Institute of Economy of the Russian Academy of Sciences.

Zelezniakov, Alexandr. 2000. “Is Mongolia a Civilization?” *Nomadic Studies Bulletin* 1 (Ulaanbaatar): 20–23.

14

THE "ORTHODOX," "EURASIAN," OR "RUSSIAN ORTHODOX" CIVILIZATION?

Milena Benovska-Sabkova

Discussions about "Orthodox civilization" have appeared and disappeared periodically in different periods of Russian history. Since the end of the Soviet era and along with the liberalization of religious life, the term *Orthodox civilization* again has a significant presence in various public discourses in Russia: secular and religious, academic, quasi-scientific, journalistic, and political. These most recent theories about "Orthodox civilization" form part of wide-ranging ideological discourses about Russia's identity that developed in the early 1990s. Although the theories vary widely, they partially overlap with each other and use as synonyms terms such as *Russian civilization, Slavic civilization, Eastern-Slavic civilization, Eastern European civilization,* or *Eurasian civilization.* This last term is deployed under the influence of the philosophical-political project of Eurasianism (*евразийство*) discussed below. Orthodox traditions outside of Russia are rarely mentioned in these discourses; Russia and its civilizational peculiarities are the sole focus of attention.

This chapter analyzes the significance of "Orthodox civilization" in public and political discourses in post-Soviet Russia. I concentrate on messianic ideas in academic literature, including history, literary studies, and political science. Due to the essentialist bias of Russian conceptions of "Orthodox civilization," not even academic writers engage with recent international debates concerning the concept of civilization.[1] Although I analyze how discourses are engendered "from above" among Russian intellectual, religious, and political elites and draw my examples from published texts, the impetus for this study comes from the oral versions I encountered during my fieldwork in Russia.[2]

International and Russian scholars alike emphasize the proliferation of radical nationalist movements in Russia toward the end of the first decade of the twenty-first century. As Andreas Umland puts it, "Radical anti-Westernism has become a significant intellectual and political movement, and the pronouncement of anti-Western views has become politically correct" (2009, 5). Views and discourses on "Orthodox civilization" should be interpreted in this political context. Russian Orthodox Christianity has undoubtedly influenced political doctrines at the highest levels, and the idea of an "Orthodox civilization" is considered a key component of Russia's historical faith and its political future. A number of influential political Russian ideologies, Eurasianism prominent among them, can be considered to have "Orthodox Christian roots" (Sidorov 2006, 318).

Early and Neo-Eurasianism

Eurasianism is a political movement created by Russian émigrés in Western Europe in the beginning of the 1920s. Most authors characterize it as an (ethno)nationalistic movement (Bicilli 2004 [1927], 109; Laruelle 2009a, 85; Shnirelman 1996, 4; Shnirelman 2006; Umland 2008; Wiederkehr 2012, 10; Bassin, Glebov, Laruelle 2015, 2). But some define it as a "different kind of unitary religious ideology—'political Orthodox Christianity'" (Mitrofanova 2009, 148). The publication of the collection *Ishod k Vostoku* (*Turn to the East*) by Georgii Florovskii, Petr Savickii, Petr Suvchinskii, and Nikolai Trubetzkoy in 1921 is considered to mark the beginning of the movement. In this collection, "Eurasia" was a synonym for Russia—a multinational empire with unique geographic characteristics that unified Eastern Europe and a large part of Asia. The "Eurasia" of the Eurasianists refers solely to Russia; it should not be confused with the efforts of social scientists to elaborate on a neutral *etic* concept of "Eurasia" (see Hann 2016; Arnason 2015, 483–512)

The small intellectual circle of Eurasianists increased rapidly in the 1920s, gathering followers until Eurasianism became a political platform. The development of different wings, including a left wing that was positively disposed toward Bolshevism (due to the infiltration of Soviet secret services—see Bassin, Glebov, Laruelle 20015, 3), led to disagreements and the dissolution of the movement in the 1930s. A special role in the history of the movement was played by the historian and ethnographer Lev Gumilev (1912–1992) who, as a public intellectual, was associated with both the early Eurasianists and the neo-Eurasianism that established itself in the beginning of the 1990s. Gumilev's theories about Eurasianism are quite specific, however, and although he refers to the early Eurasianists as authorities, he deviates considerably from their ideas (Shnirelman 2006; Laruelle 2008, 50–82; Wiederkehr 2012, 9; Bassin 2015, 165–186).[3]

The neo-Eurasianism of the 1990s has clear political connections, thanks above all to the contributions of Alexander Dugin. In the 2000s, it continued to attract supporters across the Russian political spectrum. Eurasianism now occupies a central place in Russian political life (Mitrofanova 2009), especially since the establishment of the Eurasian Economic Union in 2011. There is no doubt that, from its first appearance, the "main pathos of the Eurasian movement came down to the preservation at any cost of the wholeness of the Russian state, whether it is called the Russian Empire, USSR or Eurasia" (Shnirelman 2006). The actual concept of "Eurasia" was advanced by Petr Savickii on the basis of certain traditions in Russian geography (Shnirelman 2006; see also Laruelle 2007, 13–14). Savickii's formulation recognized the positive impact of the Asian peoples of the Russian Empire on Russian statehood, history, and culture. This positive view of Asia was innovative because Russian political and cultural theory had previously venerated only Western European traditions (Wiederkehr 2012, 10). Like the founding fathers of Eurasianism, contemporary neo-Eurasians consider the ethnic Russian population to be culturally closer to Russia's non-Slavic Asian populations than to Southern and Western Slavs. This position is correlated with anti-Western views. Eurasianists have always seen the "expansion of Roman-German culture" as a threat and deplored Roman-German "cosmopolitan chauvinism" (Shnirelman 2006). In this respect, the early Eurasianists were continuing the anti-Western traditions of nineteenth-century Slavophiles. One of their leaders proclaimed that an "Asian orientation" was the only one possible for a true Russian nationalist (Trubetzkoy 1922, 306).

Eurasianism has been distinguished by its internal heterogeneity and dogged by controversy from the beginning. The multiplicity of ideas encompassed by the doctrine makes Eurasianism a flexible ideology that can be incorporated by multiple political, cultural, and scientific projects (Laruelle 2007, 13). Early Eurasianism contributed to the construction of numerous scientific theories in Russia and the Soviet Union. For example, Trubetzkoy developed a theory of cultural difference close to what is known in English as cultural relativism in which he rejected the term *underdeveloped* (*слабо развитые*) peoples. His concept of a "language union" has been widely accepted in linguistics, even outside Russia (Shnirelman 1996, 10). Yet even the works of individual Eurasianists were internally contradictory: Trubetzkoy pleaded for the preservation of Russia's ethnic cultures, but he nonetheless thought that the Russian language and Orthodox Christianity should lead and unify the peoples of the Eurasian conglomerate. Such ideas were criticized as soon as they appeared (e.g., Bicilli 2004 [1927], 106–107), but it still "remains unclear how [early Eurasianists] imagined the change of religion without any damage to the genuine picture" (Shnirelman 1996, 6). Geographic determinism was also a part of the initial Eurasian theories. Petr Savickii, for example, considered the openness of continental Eurasia to be opposed to the "oceanic" characteristic of Western Europe as a cultural region (Florovskii et al. 1921). All these ideas were grafted onto those of Slavophilism and Russian messianism (Mitrofanova 2009, 149).

Eurasianism was easily resurrected by the political project of the illiberal Right after 1991. Unlike their predecessors, however, contemporary neo-Eurasianists are not opposed to maintaining contact with extreme Right and ultranationalistic parties in Western Europe (Laruelle 2009a; Umland 2008; Laruelle 2015, 1–32). Supported by different segments of the Russian political spectrum, neo-Eurasianism has a radical understanding of Eurasia's geographical boundaries and a provocative assessment of the cultural and political influences of Islam. Unlike the early Eurasianists, for whom "Eurasia" corresponded with the boundaries of the Russian Empire, contemporary Eurasianists boldly expand the concept to include much of continental Eurasia: the entire Asian continent and a large part of Europe (Umland 2008). Supporters of neo-Eurasianism do not seem to be bothered by the geographic and cultural imprecision.[4] Today, the Turkic peoples of the former Soviet Union are no longer just a "subject of the Orientalist discourse of Eurasianism" (Laruelle 2009a, 79–80). Political elites among Russia's Turkic and Muslim peoples but also in the independent republics of Central Asia actively endorse Eurasian projects.[5] According to these "Asian" versions of Eurasianism, "the Turkic-Muslim peoples are the only ones who completely personify Eurasia . . . .[T]he Russian nation is considered extremely European, foreign to Eurasia, and Russia [is considered]—not as a great country, but the most underdeveloped part of Europe" (ibid., 80–81). As Laruelle points out, this formulation of Eurasianism enables "a genuine blackmail" of Russia by its non-Russian peoples, and helps regional institutions to seize power from the federal government (ibid.).

This brief overview of the development of the Eurasianist movement and ideology shows its variability, incoherence, and power. The popularity of Eurasianist ideas expresses the unwillingness of Russian intellectuals to accept the realities of the Soviet Union's decay, post-Soviet transformations, or Western social models (Wiederkehr 2012, 7–9). Neo-Eurasianism plays the role of an integrative ideology in post-Soviet society (ibid., 13–14). It is, practically speaking, "the only viable ideology which . . . legitimises . . . Russia as a multiethnic state" (Laruelle 2007, 13).

Secular and Religious "Orthodox Civilization"

Contemporary discourses about "Orthodox civilization" appear in both secular and religious varieties. Both tend to originate in traditions of Russian messianism, in which the "redeemer" or "Messiah" may be a "nation, class or party, or an individual person" (Duncan 2000, 6). Russian messianism proclaims Moscow as the "Third Rome," which Dimitrii Sidorov has described as "the main Russian Orthodox geopolitical metaphor" (Sidorov 2006, 320). The idea most probably has its origins in Russian monasteries following the fall of Constantinople in 1453, or the ultimate victory of Muscovy over Mongolian Islamic invaders in 1480 (Stremouhov 2002, 425–32). It is first documented in a letter from the monk Filofei (Philotheus) to Tsar Vasilii III in 1511. In his letter, Filofei used the figure of the "Third Rome" to affirm a unique religious and political role for the Muscovite kingdom as a successor to imperial Rome and Byzantium (Duncan 2000, 10–12). The letter explains the fall of the "First Rome" as a retribution for Apollinarian heresy and ends with the eschatological warning: "For two Romes have fallen, and the Third stands, and a fourth shall never be" (Duncan 2000, 11). For three hundred years, the message from Filofei, though known in religious circles and widely accepted among common people and Old Believers, had no influence on Russia's political development (Duncan 2000, 13–14). This changed following the publication of his texts in 1861–63, after which the metaphor of Moscow as the "Third Rome" circulated widely within

Russian academic circles and in the popular press. The eminent Russian philosophers Vladimir Solovyev and Nikolai Berdyaev both reflected on "Moscow—the Third Rome," though under quite distinct historical conditions. Solovyev's writings on the theme were concentrated during the period 1877–1881, while Berdyaev's works appeared from 1924–1947. The latter argued that Bolshevism had religious features and had transformed some of the main messages of Orthodoxy: "[I]nstead of monk Filofei's Third Rome, we get Lenin's Third International" (Berdyaev 1971 [1931], 41; see also Duncan 2000, 55).

A half-century earlier, in 1877, Vladimir Solovyev had formulated a vision of Moscow as the Third Rome corresponding to the ideas of early Slavophiles, who held that Orthodox Russians were called upon to mediate between the Muslim East and the Christian West, as well as between the world of God and the human world. Russians were considered to be in a position of spiritual leadership among the Orthodox nations (Duncan 2000, 44–45; Sidorov 2006, 323). For Solovyev, the ambition to conquer Constantinople also served to project the metaphor of the Third Rome into the context of the Russian-Turkish War ongoing at the time of his writing (1877–78) (Duncan 2000, 44–45; Sidorov 2006, 323). Unlike Solovyev, the early Slavophiles were not particularly familiar with the writings of Filofei (Poe 2000, 68). Nor did this group of writers, thinkers, and intellectuals use the term *Orthodox civilization*. However, they did consider Orthodox Christianity to provide the basis for Russian specificity (*самобытность*). Ironically, the name *Slavophiles* was given to them by their opponents. In fact, the Slavophiles took little interest in Slavic peoples outside of Russia, since not all Slavic peoples were Orthodox, and it was Orthodox Christianity that mattered most to them. Slavophiles wanted this tradition to be accepted not only by all the Slavic peoples but by the whole of humanity (Duncan 2000, 22–25).

Nikolay I. Danilevskii (1822–1885), the ideologist of the pan-Slavism that came to replace the early Slavophilism, can also be considered as the founder of the civilizational approach to the history of Russia. In *Russia and Europe* (1895 [1869]), he opposed the idea of a unitary human civilization and put forward instead eleven "cultural-historical types." For Danilevskii, Slavic "civilization" was synonymous with Slavic "culture" and "race," but Orthodox Christianity also figured prominently in his messianic ideas (Duncan 2000, 32–33). According to Danilevskii, the Slavic nations, along with the Greeks, have the determination to be "the chief guardians of the living tradition of religious truth, Orthodoxy, and in this way—the continuers of the great cause, which was the lot of Israel and Byzantium: to be the God-chosen peoples" (Danilevskii 1895 [1869], 525). With his theory of cultural-historical types, Danilevskii can also be viewed as a predecessor of Oswald Spengler, Arnold J. Toynbee, and Samuel Huntington. Certainly his ideas influenced Russia's political and military projects during the last quarter of the nineteenth century (Duncan 2000, 32–33).

At the end of the Soviet era, ideas about "Orthodox civilization" proliferated at a remarkable rate, partly thanks to new media possibilities for reproducing them. The organization of several conferences marked the significance and social resonance of such ideas. In 2006, "Orthodox civilization: past, present and future" was the title of a conference in the city of Samara (Larkina 2006; Sergii 2006). In Moscow in 2008, "Moscow—the Third Rome" was organized as part of the Orthodox Christmas Readings, the most prestigious public forum of the Russian Orthodox Church.[6] This latter conference featured the participation of the church elite, influential representatives of Russian academia, politicians, and high-ranking government officials.

My analysis of more than one hundred academic, political, and church publications since the 2000s demonstrates that the topics "Orthodox civilization" and "Moscow—the Third Rome" are intersecting semantic fields. The "Third Rome" metaphor is an ingredient of the concept of "Orthodox civilization," and the latter is invariably related to ideas and perceptions of Russian statehood. Discussions and publications on both topics can be found in secular and in religious environments with no significant conceptual differences. Lay authors actively publish in religious editions, such as the Orthodox magazine *Blagovest*, and vice versa. Orthodox priests release publications in secular editions, such as the extreme Right's monarchist website Pravaia.ru. The most relevant distinction between the versions is whether "Orthodox civilization" is presented as an exclusively Russian phenomenon (the secular viewpoint) or as a unified Orthodox area dominated by Russia (the religious view, which tends to be less widely expressed).

How is "Orthodox civilization" characterized in these publications? Its features are very close to (often identical with) those of Russian civilization, while indivisibly connected to the history of Russian statehood. The definitions "civilization" and "culture" are used in the spirit of the classic German distinction: civilization denotes material, technological achievement, while culture, embracing art, literature, and creativity, is more highly valued. The perception of "Orthodox civilization" is often characterized as a normative discourse, with statehood filtering moral messages. In practice, proponents of Orthodox civilization hold that what is good for the Russian state is morally good and just.

According to a rather typical church view, expressed by Archbishop Sergii, Orthodox civilization is characterized by specific power models combined with a number of values, among them patriotism and the "symphony of both powers." In his view, church and civil powers both aim to stabilize the state through an emphasis on faith, morality, and the sacred. The archbishop calls special attention to *"messianism and the sacrifice of the Russian Orthodox population in the creation of the spiritual-moral revival of contemporary society"* (Sergii 2006; original italics). He calls for a gradual restoration of the image of God in the soul of the contemporary human being, which is represented in the formula "Moscow—the Third Rome." Finally, he concludes that the spiritual transformation of Russia will be of significance for all humanity: *"[B]y witnessing its accomplishments, the rest of world will reform spiritually"* (ibid.).

Like many other texts of this kind, this one is built through a polemic perspective. Faith is opposed to faithlessness, which is equated with a rejection of the national idea; cosmopolitism is synonymous with spiritual regress; spiritual values are opposed to the material prosperity that is ascribed to (Western) European countries. *"Satiety and comfort are insufficient for the human being"* (Sergii 2006; original italics). Pacifism, tolerance, and the concept of human rights are presented as contradictory to Christian values. Socialism was a period in which Russia rejected its own traditions; but the loss of its superpower role is nevertheless incompatible with "Orthodox civilization": *"Russia—as a historical civilization and powerful cultural tradition, cannot be satisfied by the pupil's secondary role on the world scene"* (ibid). The archbishop's ideas may be encountered daily in different configurations in Russian Orthodox parishes and religious periodicals.

Panarin's Orthodox Civilization

In secular circles, the philosopher Alexander Panarin (1940–2003) is deemed to "have succeeded to represent in the most complete way the political postulates which are spread amongst the nationalistic circles, as well as wider circles of the Russian society" (Laruelle 2009b, 157). I will introduce Panarin's views about "Orthodox civilization" by comparing him with other contemporary authors, although comparison between his book (2002) and other contributions is hampered by differences of length and genre. Panarin's views are significant because of his "incredible popularity" in Russia (Peunova 2009, 167); his reputation is that of a man who has undoubtedly made "academic contributions," and whose views demonstrate nonconformism and civil bravery (Verhovskii and Pain 2010, 86). He has been variously described as a representative of a moderate Eurasianism (Laruelle 2009a, 84–85) and of neo-Eurasianism (Mitrofanova 2009, 152–53); as an expressionist of "civilizational nationalism" (Verhovskii and Pain 2010, 69–99); and as a guide for how the ideas of the French "New Right" can be transferred to Russia (Peunova 2009, 159–75). The presence of Panarin at the inaugural congress for the political movement "Eurasia" in 2001 (along with the popular television journalist Michail Leont'ev) was considered the most significant event of the congress because of his exceptional reputation (Umland 2008).

Alexander Panarin's conceptions have undergone transformation over time. In the last days of his life, his preoccupation with Eurasianism as an expression of the "great tradition, synthesizing Christianity and Islam," gave way to a singular accent on Orthodox Christianity (Laruelle 2009b, 156). For the elderly Panarin, "the term civilization is burdened by ethnographical, geographical, culturally-anthropological senses related to everything which emphasizes the local, regional, and the distinctive" (Panarin 2002, 182). A short analysis of his voluminous works bears a risk of simplification, but I shall emphasize those features of his theory which bring him close to other exponents of "civilizational nationalism." An anti-Westernism related to the idea of Russia's uniqueness permeates his major book (e.g., Panarin 2002, 6, 19). In harmony with the unanimous voice of Russian clergy, Panarin expresses intolerance toward the contemporary concept of human rights (especially in the post-Soviet context), and assesses the large-scale modernization projects of Peter the Great negatively (ibid., 15, 157). Both are described as misguided "Western" influences on Russia. Panarin condemns Marxism and Bolshevism as Western modernization projects which were alien influences on authentic Russian traditions with catastrophic consequences (ibid., 112). His association of all negative influences in Russian society with "the West" follows a pattern shared by numerous other authors of both religious and secular backgrounds.

Panarin's thought also incorporates the metaphor "Moscow—the Third Rome." In the style of historical Russian Orthodoxy, Panarin specified that "in the Third Rome must be seen not the new imperial center of the world, but a New Jerusalem." In other words, he emphasized a spiritual connotation for the metaphor rather than an imperial one: "The church-city is not quite like the city-castle, into which Peter I tried to turn the capital" (Panarin 2002, 177–79). Relying on the early Slavophiles and more generally on Russian messianic traditions, Panarin (like church authors) sees Orthodox Christianity as a universal project: the future "worldwide Orthodox Christianity" is designated to rediscover the unity of humankind (ibid., 485). Also common to other commentators is the way in which Panarin differentiates between Western Europe and the United States. For him, Europe embodies the refined spirituality of the ancient Greek civilization, while the United States is the reincarnation of rational and militaristic Rome (2002, 53–57). He also distinguishes Bolshevism from the Soviet Union. In his assessment, Bolshevism was a "foreign object" of Western origin that harmed "Orthodox civilization," but the disintegration of the Soviet Union was a tragic mistake (ibid., 14–15, 113–14, 379).

Panarin also offers a slightly more unusual perspective that strips the power of Orthodox Christianity as a religious impulse outside of Russian lands: "Orthodox Christianity itself, inherited from Byzantium and without attachment to the Russian cosmic space, cannot give such powerful impulse to be sufficient for the whole continental Eurasia. Orthodox Christianity outside Russia, pressured in the narrow urban spaces of Greece and Eastern Europe, inevitably takes the form of some stylization" (ibid., 133). Panarin's dismissive gloss of Greek and Eastern European societies as "urban" is patently untrue in empirical terms, but that is to miss the point of his hermeneutic argumentation. The symbolic dimensions of history and the contemporary world serve as a "pool" of meanings from which he carefully selects the most appropriate fragments to build the complex puzzle of the "Orthodox civilization." Finally, perhaps the most significant original contribution of Alexander Panarin is his assertion that "Orthodox civilization" is not based on masculine self-affirmation, but on feminine self-denying love (2002, 179). In this respect, his ideas hark back to those of Berdyaev, even though Panarin does not refer to him directly.

Orthodox Civilization and Eurasianism as Metatexts

The numerous texts and discourses devoted to "Orthodox civilization" and Eurasianism, and other expressions of Russian messianism, might be best viewed as ideological metatexts. As such, these concepts create moods in

Russian society that can be politically mobilized. Although these metatexts are ideological, they depend on certain ideas about what characterizes "civilization" at a conceptual and theoretical level. Orthodox civilization is seen in unitary terms (see Arnason 2003, 1), and its messianic features reach out to utopian horizons. But the term *civilization* is mostly used as a narrow correlate of "empire," and an anticipated synthesis between state and religion.

According to such a definition, is there such a thing as a united "Orthodox civilization"? There are few arguments in support (Sidorov 2006, 333). Paradoxically, even proponents of "Orthodox civilization" reveal its impossibility when they confine it to Russia rather than the whole geographic space in which Orthodox Christians form the largest communities. Empirically, Orthodox space is not culturally or politically homogenous. Significant distinctions in institutional and cultural models, for example, marriage patterns and kinship systems, exist between the Orthodox countries. Even if the concept were to be reduced to "Russian Orthodox civilization," it would seem necessary to acknowledge some plurality in view of the radical transformations of the Russian state and culture in specific historical periods, not least during the Soviet era.

The concepts of "Orthodox civilization" and related ideologies such as Eurasianism are thus best interpreted as relics of past theoretical and political arguments that have been revived in the contemporary context of the Soviet Union's disintegration and Russia's search for a new future that maintains as much as possible from former Soviet spheres of influence. In this sense, the production of theories in support of "Orthodox civilization" may be viewed as a specific form of the politics of memory and as a means of political mobilization.

Notes

1. For an overview see Arnason 2003; Arnason, Eisenstadt, and Wittrock 2005; Eisenstadt 2003; Hann 2012.

2. Fieldwork was conducted for three months during 2006 and 2007, and was supported by the Max Planck Institute for Social Anthropology in Halle/Saale.

3. Gumilev's work defies easy categorization because he mixed empirical observation with elaborate fantasy. In recent years, he has been criticized from several directions. Between 2003 and 2012, the magazine *Scepsis* published a series of thirteen articles on "The Pseudo-cholar Gumilev" (see

http://scepsis.net/tags/id_24.html. Accessed April 30th, 2013). Specific criticisms of Gumilev's ethnographic and historical views are presented by Shnirelman 2006, while Wiederkehr (2012, 12) defines him as a proponent of "biologically-determined racism." For a more positive view of Gumilev, see Kradin, this volume.

4. During the late Soviet period, Lev Gumilev promulgated occult-influenced ideas about cosmic influences on the formation of the *ethnos*; his work "Ethno-genesis and the Bio-sphere of the Earth" (1989) was widely popular.

5. For example, see the manifesto of Kazakhstan's President Nazarbaev (1997). On the "widespread appropriation" of the Eurasian idea by the peoples of Asia, see Humphrey 2002.

6. www.Pravaia.ru 2008; accessed May 30, 2012.

References

Arnason, Johann. 2003. *Civilizations in Dispute: Historical Questions and Theoretical Traditions*. Leiden: Brill.

———. 2015. "State Formation and Empire Building, 500–1500". In *Expanding Webs of Exchange and Conflict, 500 CE–1500 CE, vol. 5 of The Cambridge World History*, edited by Benjamin Z. Kedar and Merry E. Wiesner–Hanks, 483–512. Cambridge: Cambridge University Press.

———, Shmuel N. Eisenstadt, and Björn Wittrock. 2005. *Axial Civilization and World History*. Leiden: Brill.

Bassin, Mark, Sergey Glebov, and Marlene Laruelle. 2015. "What Was Eurasianism and Who Made It?" In *Between Europe and Asia. The Origins, Theories, and Legacies of Russian Eurasiansim*, edited by Mark Bassin, Sergey Glebov, and Marlene Laruelle, 1–12. Pittsburgh: University of Pittsburgh Press.

Bassin, Mark. 2015. "Lev Gumilev, Russian Nationalists, and the Troubled Emergence of Neo-Eurasianism." In *Between Europe and Asia. The Origins, Theories, and Legacies of Russian Eurasiansim*, edited by Mark Bassin, Sergey Glebov, and Marlene Laruelle, 165–86. Pittsburgh: University of Pittsburgh Press.

Berdyaev, Nikolaj. 1971 [1931]. *The Russian Revolution*. Ann Arbor: University of Michigan Press.

Bicilli, Petâr. 2004 [1927]. "Dva lika na evrazijstvoto [Two Images of the Eurasianism]" In *Natsija i kultura*, edited by Petâr Biċilli, 102–25. Sofia: Iztok-Zapad.

Danilevskii, Nikolaj. 1895 [1869]. *Rossia i Evropa. Vzgliad na kul'turnye i politicheskie otnoshenia Slavianskogo mira k Germano-Romanskomu. Izdanie piatoe [Russia and Europe. An Outlook to the Cultural and Political Relations of the Slavic World towards German-Roman World]*. Fifth ed. Sankt-Peterburg: Tipografia brat. Panteleevyh.

Duncan, Peter J. S. 2000. *Russian Messianism: Third Rome, Holy Revolution and After*. London: Routledge.

Eisenstadt, S. N. 2003. *Comparative Civilizations and Multiple Modernities*. Brill, Leiden.

Florovskii, Georgii, Petr Savickii, Petr Suvchinskii, and Nikolai Trubetzkoy. 1921. *Ishod k Vostoku: predchuvstvija i sovershenija. Utverzhdenija evrazijcev [Turn to the East: Premonitions and Deeds. The Statements of Eurasianists]*. Kniga 1. Sofia: Rossijsko-bolgarskoe knigoizdatel'stvo.

Gumilev, Lev N. 1989. *Etnogenez i biosfera zemli [The Ethno-genesis and the Bio-sphere of the Earth]*. Leningrad: Izdatel'stvo Leningradskogo Gosudarstvennogo universiteta.

Hann, Chris. 2012. "Civilizational Analysis for Beginners." *Focaal* 62: 113–21.

———. 2016. "A Concept of Eurasia." *Current Anthropology* 57, no. 1, 1–27.

Humphrey, Caroline. 2002. " 'Eurasia', Ideology and the Poliitical Imgination in Provincial Russia." In *Postsocialism. Ideas, Ideologies and Practices in Eurasia*, edited by C. M. Hann, 258–76. London and New York: Routledge.

Larkina, Olga. 2006. "Pravoslavnaja civilizacia: proshloe, nastojashchee i budushchee [Orthodox Civilization: Past, Present and Future]." *Blagovest*, 22 September 2006.

Laruelle, Marlène. 2007. "The Orient in Russian Thought at the Turn of the Century." In *Russia between East and West. Scholarly Debates on Eurasianism*, edited by Dmitry Shlapentokh, 9–38. Leiden: Brill.

———. 2008. *Russian Eurasianism: An Ideology of Empire*. Washington, DC: Woodrow Wilson Center Press.

———. 2009a. "Pereosmislenie imperii v postsovetskom prostranstve: novaja evrazijskaja ideologija [Rethinking Empire in the Post-Soviet Space: The New Eurasian Ideology]." *Форум новейшей восточноевропейской истории и культуры* (русское издание) 1: 78–92.

———. 2009b. "Aleksandr Panarin i 'civilizacionnyj nacionalizm' v Rossii [Alexadre Panarin and Civilizational Nationalism in Russia]." *Форум новейшей восточноевропейской истории и культуры* (русское издание) 2: 143–58.

———. 2015 "Dangerous Liaisons: Eurasianism, The European Far Right, and Putin's Russia." In *Eurasianism and the European Far Right. Reshaping the Europe-Russia Relationship*, edited by Marlene Laruelle, 1–32. Lanham, MD, Boulder, New York, London: Lexington Books.

Mitrofanova, Anastasia. 2009. "Blesk i nishcheta neoevrazijskogo religiozno-politicheskogo proekta [Brilliance and Misery of the New-Eurasian Religio-political Project]." *Форум новейшей восточноевропейской истории и культуры* (русское издание) 1: 148–65.

Nazarbaev, Nursultan A. 1997. *Evrazijskij sojuz: idei, praktiki, perspektivy 1994–1997 [The Eurasian Union: Ideas, Practices, Perspectives 1994–1997]*. Moskva: Fond sodejstivija razvitiju social'nyh i politicehskih nauk.

Panarin, Alexandre. 2002. *Pravoslavnaja civilizacija v global'nom mire [The Orthodox Civilization in the Global World]*. Moskva: Algoritm.

Peunova, Marina. 2009. "Vostochnaja inkarnacija evropejskih 'novyh pravyh': Aleksandr Panarin i neoevrazijskij diskurs v sovremennoj Rossii [The Eastern Incarnation of the European 'New Rights': Alexandre Panarin and New-Eurasionist Discourse in Contemporary Russia]." *Форум новейшей восточноевропейской истории и культуры* (русское издание) 2: 159–74.

Sergii, Archbishop. 2006. "Russia: Rossija—preemnica i hranitel'nica pravoslavnoj civilizacii [Russia—Successor and Guardian of the Orthodox Civilization]." Plenary paper at the conference "Orthodox Civilization: Past, Present and Future," Samara, 15–17 September 2006. www.samara.orthodoxy.ru/archierey/dokald/10; accessed: 30 May 2012).

Shynkarenko, Oleg. 2014. "Alexander Dugin: The Crazy Ideologue of the New Russian Empire." www.thedailybeast.com/

articles/2014/04/02/alexander-dugin-the-crazy-ideologue-of-the-new-russian-empire.html.

Shnirelman, Viktor. 1996. "Evrazijskaja ideja i teorija kul'tury." *Etnograficheskoe obozrenie* 4: 3–16.

———. 2006. "Evrazijcy i evrei [Eurasionists and Jews]." *Skepsis*: http://scepsis.net/library/id_952.html; accessed: 30 May 2013.

Sidorov, Dmitrii. 2006. "Post-Imperial Third Romes: Resurrections of a Russian Geopolitical Metaphor." *Geopolitics* 11: 317–43.

Stremouhov, Dmitrii. 2002. "Moskva—Tretii Rim i istochnik doktriny [Moscow—The Third Rome and the Source of the Doctrine]." In *Iz istorii russkoj kul'tury*, T. II. Kn. 1.Kievskaja i Moskovskaja Rus', 425–32. Moskva.

Trubetzkoy, Nikolai. 1922. "Russkaja problema [The Russian Problem]." In *Na putiah. Utverzhdenie evrazijcev [On the Road. Statements of the Eurasianists]*. Kniga 2, Berlin.

Umland, Andreas. 2008. "Postsovetskie pravoekstremistkie kontrelity i ih vlijanie v sovremennoj Rossii [The Post-Soviet Right-extremist Counter Elites and Their Influence in Contemporary Russia]." *Neprikosnovennyj zapas* 1. http://www.intelros.ru/readroom/nz/nz_57/2286-postsovetskie-pravojekstremistskie.html; accessed 1 June 2013.

———. 2009. "Rasscvet russkogo ul'tranacionalizma i stanovlenie soob-shshestva ego issledovatelej [The Bloom of Russian Ultra-nationalism and the Establishment of Its Researchers]." *Форум новейшей восточноевропейской истории и культуры* (русское издание) 1: 5–39.

Verhovskii, Alexandre, and Emil Pain. 2010. "Civilizacionnyj nacio-nalizm: rossijskaja versija osobogo puti [The Civilizational Nationalism: Russian Version of the 'Special Road']." *Форум новейшей восточноевропейской истории и культуры* (русское издание) 2: 69–100.

Wiederkehr, Stefan. 2012. "Vosprijatie trudov L. N. Gumileva v pozd-nesovetskij i postsovetskij periody: intelligentsija v Rossii v poiskah orientirov [The Perception of Works by L. N. Gumilev in the Late Soviet and Post-Soviet Periods: Intelligentsia in Russia in Search for Orientation]." *Форум новейшей восточноевропейской истории и культуры* (русское издание) 1: 7–20.

Afterword

ANTHROPOLOGY, EURASIA, AND GLOBAL HISTORY

Chris Hann

Readers of, this volume will make up their own minds as to whether social and cultural anthropology has a contribution to make to civilizational analysis; and if so, then which particular strands of anthropology, and how exactly they should be applied. Similarly, readers are free to decide for themselves whether the concept of civilization would help to expand the horizons of anthropologists. If so, which particular version of civilizational analysis should they take up? Should it be Maussian strand, elaborated in chapter 1 by Johann Arnason? Or does the Weberian approach, perhaps as modified by S. N. Eisenstadt and others, have more to offer the anthropologist? The Workshop in 2012 in Halle was exploratory. Johann Arnason and I deliberately invited colleagues representing very different viewpoints. The diversity was enhanced by others who we recruited through a Call for Papers, and by still other voices at the meeting, too heterogeneous to summarize here.

We are acutely conscious of many limitations. Civilizational analysis knows no spatiotemporal restrictions. Yet the empirical studies in, this volume deal mainly with recent centuries and are almost all concerned with Asia (chapter 14 by Milena Benovska-Sabkova is the sole exception). Our focus on Eurasia was deliberate, but we would have liked to include more case studies from other parts of Europe, including the Mediterranean, and also from Inner Eurasia. However, just as we did not aspire to reach intellectual consensus, we did not aim at comprehensive geographical coverage. Our intention was to open up a debate. We hope to have succeeded in this minimal goal, and that the debates will continue in years to come.

Miracles and Modernity

It is a commonplace that, ever since its origins in the European Enlightenment, the discipline known nowadays as (social or cultural) anthropology has wavered between the study of what is common to all human beings and the study of that which makes particular groups of human beings (usually called cultures or societies) unique. This ever-present tension is still with us in the twenty-first century, but it takes certain new forms, and boundaries are drawn in new ways. Some contemporary anthropologists describe themselves as posthumanist and claim to be interested in the minds and cultures of other species, and even in the agency of inanimate things, as they investigate the deep history of the planet Earth. Some are pursuing new ways to combine evolutionary approaches, deriving from biology and ecology, with approaches that focus on the emergence of particular cultures (human and other). Comparable tensions have long existed in history between those scholars concerned to chronicle the particular and those more interested in identifying general patterns and even universal laws. Concepts such as civilization and *Kulturwelt* are attractive to the latter type of historian, including scholars such as Spengler and Toynbee, whose works have reached wider publics. But the risks are obvious: with academic life becoming ever more professionalized and the public sphere ever more susceptible to sensationalized distortion, terms like civilization, which for many cannot be stripped of their value connotation, become objects of polemic and suspicion. The discipline of anthropology has therefore retreated from the word, even when numerous practitioners continue to address the issues for which it was theorized in earlier generations.

Within the field of universal history it is becoming common to draw a distinction between world history and global history. The former refers to the history of the entire planet as an entity, for instance, as it now enters into a new era that some call the Anthropocene (Hann 2017). World historians are expected to pay attention to all parts of the world, or at least all those parts touched by humans, no matter how unequally distributed the sources for recovering the past. Global historians place more emphasis on connectivity and usually end up paying much more attention to recent centuries, and to some parts of the world rather than others, namely, those parts for which written sources are available. These are characterized by more complex systems of government, economy, and knowledge, as well as demographic expansion. (Use of the term *complex* here has no normative connotations, as Arnason stresses in the introduction.)

Irrespective of this rather fuzzy divide between world history and global history, Western scholars working at supranational levels (including the pioneers of so-called universal history over the centuries) have frequently been accused of Eurocentric bias (Goody 1996; 2006). History is still commonly told as a story in which the most dramatic leap was made some five hundred years ago, following European voyages of discovery. According to these narratives, in the wake of the Renaissance and the Reformation, scientific and industrial revolutions combined with the result that Europe became the first continent to enter "modernity." Social and cultural anthropology can be viewed as products of this Western modernity. Scholars in numerous disciplines have written of a "European miracle." The model has even been endorsed by a few anthropologists (e.g., Gellner 1988).

It is important to place such theories in context. By the second half of the twentieth century, the United States was the hegemonic power and modernization and decolonization were keywords in the social sciences. Alfred Kroeber, student of Franz Boas (the most important source for the transmission of impulses from German humanities traditions into North American anthropology), used the concept of civilization alongside that of culture. He distinguished them primarily in terms of scale (as did Samuel Huntington later). Both culture and civilization were open systems, which, however, could congeal to form "patterns" that varied in intensity at different locations and had little to do with utilitarian adaptations. They were based ultimately on a common style or "value culture" (see Arnason's introduction to, this volume). Kroeber negotiated a division of labor with sociologist Talcott Parsons, confirming fieldwork as the dominant method of the anthropologists and granting them the leading role in the study of culture in this idealist sense, particularly the "value culture" of people very different from ourselves (Kuper 1999). This reached its apotheosis in the Geertzian paradigm of "the interpretation of cultures." Arnason is therefore quite right to classify Geertz as a "reluctant civilizationist" (Introduction, p. xxvi).

It may be instructive to dig a little deeper into American contributions of the postwar era. Clifford Geertz was also an influential contributor to modernization theory, in the years when studies of exotic "tribesmen" were gradually being displaced by closeup investigations of "peasants." Whether studied in East or South Asia, the Mediterranean or Latin America, peasant communities were evidently embedded in wider systems that could be extensively documented historically. Robert Redfield, building on Kroeber's ideas, argued that peasant communities were "part societies" whose "little tradition" had to be analyzed in dynamic interaction with the "great tradition" to which they belonged. He was the main inspiration behind a project on "comparative civilizations" at the University of Chicago (Arjomand 2010). Redfield and his colleagues were fully aware of the domination of the West, but for them it was important to draw attention to the continued partial autonomy of intracivilizational dynamics within what became known eventually as the third world.

India provided particularly rich materials for scholars of this generation. Sanskritization proceeded in accordance with the logic of a distinctive South Asian, primarily Hindu civilization, even as new intercivilizational encounters had resulted in the rise of the English language in an independent developmental state (influenced also by Soviet models). These complexities were ignored in Louis Dumont's modeling of this civilization as an exemplar of hierarchy, rooted in religion, in opposition to the secularized egalitarianism of the modern West. Although a student of Mauss, Dumont's binary approach had little in common with the Maussian approach to civilization. It is heavily criticized in, this volume by Martin Fuchs.

Eric Wolf (1967) sympathized with Redfield's conceptualization of the "social organization of tradition," which he viewed as a corrective to the culturalist idealism of Kroeber. Every "coagulation" or "crystallization" (Kroeber's terms) that we might wish to call a civilization had to be accounted for sociologically, distinguishing internal and external factors. At the same time, Wolf insisted on the need to integrate what he termed cognitive and ideological dimensions. By the time he wrote *Europe and the People without History* (1982), however, he seems to have lost interest in the concept of civilization. His master concept, at least in this phase of his life, was a neo-Marxist concept of "mode of production," of which civilizations were "cultural counterparts . . . . [C]ultural interaction zones pivoted upon a hegemonic tributary society central to each zone" (1982: 82). In his later work Wolf continued to rely heavily on the concepts of culture and ideology, but he never returned to any serious engagement with civilization. If the word becomes prominent once again at the end of the century in anthropological writings, it is usually with the sole purpose of critiquing the "closed," essentialist usage of Samuel P. Huntington (1996).

Of course, as Arnason stresses in chapter 1 of, this volume, the absence of the word in any positive register does not mean that substantive civilizational themes are no longer addressed. The nearest to an American equivalent of Philippe Descola is Marshall D. Sahlins. Sahlins began his career as a materialist evolutionist colleague of Eric Wolf, but he has spent most of the last half-century following a unique trajectory in historical anthropology. An association with Claude Lévi-Strauss in the late 1960s inspired him to synthesize a notion of structure with a strong version of the German American culture concept, which emphasized the dominance of the symbolic in every aspect of behavior, including the economic. Sahlins's modeling of the "structure of the conjuncture" was applied most famously to Hawai'i, where it allowed him to explain the death of Captain James Cook in terms of a cultural performance. Yet neither in this work nor in later meticulous ethnohistorical explorations (Sahlins 1992) does he use the vocabulary of civilizational encounters. For Sahlins, the notion of civilization remains the non-pluralizable concept that it was for the *philosophes* who coined the term in the middle of the eighteenth century; only the German countercurrent to the French Enlightenment, spearheaded by Herder, offers an opening to anthropology in the form of a relativist concept of culture. This is a pity because an application of the Maussian concept of *civilisation,* as elaborated in, this volume by Arnason, would seem potentially very helpful in analyzing the religio-political nexus (Arnason 2014) and complex hierarchies of preindustrial Polynesia. Instead we are left (as with Descola) with culture reigning supreme, but no guidance as to how particular cultural units are formed, scaled, and differentiated from each other.

It is a similar story of opportunities missed in Britain, where civilization has not figured prominently in anthropologists' vocabulary since the nineteenth century.[1] The only figure of comparable stature to Wolf and Sahlins in British social anthropology was the late Jack Goody.[2] Contrary to those who privilege Europe, Jack Goody (2010) prefers to speak of a "Eurasian miracle." Spatially, he concentrates on the belt between the Mediterranean and the East China Sea (this is very far from including the entire land surface of Eurasia; but proponents of the "European miracle" did not claim that it referred to the entire landmass of what they considered to be a separate continent). Temporally, Goody follows archaeologist Gordon Childe in reaching back over three thousand years to the "urban revolution of the Bronze Age." His argument is that changes in the technologies of production and communication facilitated the emergence of "connoisseurship," by which he means cultural discrimination and status competition within increasingly unequal populations, for instance, concerning cuisine, clothing, and the use of flowers. In earlier work, Goody pinpointed plough agriculture and increasingly individualized forms of property holding as the ultimate causes of these developments (Goody 1976). Religion and ideology were emphatically *not* significant causes. Belief systems are viewed by Goody as epiphenomena. He argues that the so-called world religions oscillated between promoting the growth of knowledge and repressing scientific enquiry in favor of theological dogma. More significant than this religious oscillation (or "internal alternation") in Goody's account was a process of long-term alternation in the relative contributions and power of East and West. Goody does not deny the remarkable ascent of Europe in recent centuries, but insists on placing this in a longer time frame. The validity of this approach is confirmed, in his view, by the reemergence of China as a major economic, political, and scientific-technological player in the twenty-first century. Europe and China are thus comparable, "roughly equal" units. Goody sees Eurasia (including North Africa) as a unity, to be compared and contrasted with other world regions such as sub-Saharan Africa (where he had begun his career as an anthropologist).[3]

This is not the place to present a fuller exposition and critique of Goody's work. Elsewhere, while applauding his criticism of Eurocentric traditions, I have suggested that he places excessive emphasis on "merchant cultures" in the transmission of ideas and goods, and that he pays too little attention to expanding scales of political and religious organization (Hann 2015). Whether or not one subscribes to the notion of an "Axial Age," new forms of cosmology and morality developed across Eurasia in the first millennium BC, in association with complex changes in governance, economy, and communication. Goody is no doubt right to insist that the *details* of the new forms of religion (their dogmas and their rituals) cannot function as causal variables; but many attach great significance to monotheism and the *general* shift in the direction of transcendence seems indisputable. Can these transformations be theorized using the term *civilization*? Goody does not use the term consistently. Like many others, he frequently slips between a singular, evolutionist usage and a plural usage. Civilizational approaches do not feature significantly in his books.[4] I argue that this shortcoming can be remedied, first by distinguishing between the different senses of civilization, and second by combining evolutionary and pluralist usages to demonstrate why, when the goal is to grasp global history, it is legitimate to privilege Eurasia, where this term refers to a belt of agrarian civilizations evolving in unprecedented encounters with each other and with other forms of civilization since the Bronze Age.

Three Senses of Civilization

If civilization is defined in the Maussian sense as a macrosocial formation or "family of societies," it is obvious that Eurasia in the larger sense contains a great many *civilisations,* including many that come nowhere near to fulfilling Childe's archaeological criteria (see Kradin, chapter 13). In addition to the nomadic empires reviewed by Kradin, whose key role in the larger story of Eurasian history no one questions, populations of more or less isolated nonliterate hunters and gatherers and swidden cultivators were until recently common in many parts of the landmass, usually interacting with the carriers of quite different forms of literate "high culture." There is no reason to privilege Eurasia in the comparative anthropological study of these civilizations. Research should proceed in a framework that is truly global; this has been the aspiration of various ethnological schools since the nineteenth century.[5] As Arnason argues in chapter 1, Mauss and Durkheim took this aspiration to a new level with their efforts to theorize the concept of civilization. The timing of their first intervention, shortly before the publication of Durkheim's *Elementary Forms of Religious Life* in 1912, suggests that religion was central to their concept. While their concept of civilization was nonevolutionist and its potential was universal, they clearly considered its prime field of application to be all those populations excluded from history as told by modern Europeans.

Gordon Childe's criteria specify a very different, evolutionist notion of civilization. They are nowadays considered outmoded, even among archaeologists—who have not, however, given up on the term altogether (Wengrow 2010). At least in Anglophone archaeological anthropology, the evolutionist usage remains dominant. For Bruce Trigger, adhering to the materialist tradition initiated by Lewis Henry Morgan in the nineteenth century and continued by Childe, the emergence of economic classes is decisive: an early civilization is "the earliest and simplest form of *class-based society*" (2003, 46; emphasis in original). On the basis of this definition, Trigger conducts a rigorous comparative analysis of seven early civilizations, only three of which fall within Goody's "Old World" definition of Eurasia (Egypt, Mesopotamia, and China). Again, therefore, there is no justification for prioritizing Eurasia in this form of civilizational analysis.

But Trigger's comparative study is limited to *early* civilizations. It excludes the later story as taken up by Goody.[6] The Aztec, Inca, Maya, and Yoruba cases did not achieve the scalar consolidation and intercivilizational connectivity that have been characteristic of Eurasia over the last three millennia. Only Eurasia has witnessed a more or less continuous expansion from the original belt of agrarian civilizations to a landmass characterized not only by far-reaching dependence on markets but also by the values and institutions of socially inclusive industrial civilizations.[7] In this third sense of the term *civilization,* some of the central questions asked by ethnologists, such as those concerning the "independent invention" or "diffusion" of technologies and concepts, become redundant. Contacts are intensive, the flows of people, goods, and knowledge continuous. Thanks to literacy, however restricted it may be, new cosmological ideas are widely diffused through texts and are crucial to the legitimation of the polity. Religious specialists and their differentiated institutions play a key role in the order of society. In short, in these later, more complex forms of civilization, the religio-political nexus functions as the main determinant of commonality and distinction from other populations. This is not adequately recognized by Jack Goody, who fails to see how, alongside the expansion of inequality and class differences, religion contributes to principles of redistribution and inclusive citizenship that correct the divisive and destructive potential of the market principle. This dynamic has long played out on a global scale but Eurasia remained its most important forum, at least until late in the twentieth century. From this point of view, socialism is a continuation of earlier forms of religious ideology. The rise and fall of various forms of socialist redistribution, democratic as well as Marxist-Leninist-Maoist, across a much expanded Eurasian landmass, is a continuation of the *longue durée* dialectic between market and redistribution, between economic efficiency and the "self-protection" of society (see Hann 2016, building on Polanyi 1944).

We can thus distinguish at least three ways in which anthropologists might practice civilizational analysis. In the most general sense of the older ethnological schools, all inhabited places of the landmass are eligible for consideration in all historical eras. Given the origins of their discipline, the anthropologists have a penchant to pay special attention to nonliterate societies with economies based on hunting and gathering. The ethnographer of Siberian hunters, or of the Achuar Indians of Amazonia (Philippe Descola), is even today more readily classified as an archetypal anthropologist than the ethnographer of, say, European bankers or Chinese factory workers. It is not possible to do fieldwork in the Paleolithic, but some anthropologists continue to do the next best thing—even if, as Arnason points out for the case of Descola, they seldom work with the concept of civilization.

In the second sense, civilization is an evolutionary form that is *not* found everywhere on the surface of Eurasia, and one which also turns up in various other parts of the world. There is scope to broaden the definition offered by Trigger (2003). One might wish to include many other forms of early state, from Hawai'i to Zimbabwe. As at the first level, at this second level of comparative analysis (not just of the early civilizations themselves but also of their relations with other social formations, such as nomadic pastoralists or upland cultivators) has to be worldwide; there is no justification for privileging Eurasia.

The third sense is different. This refers to a social formation that is more advanced in terms of its productive technology and its means of communication (as argued by Goody). It also features new forms of religion and morality (neglected by Goody). This form of civilization did not develop in isolation. It emerged through dynamic connectivity across Eurasia, during which the torch "alternated" periodically between East and West (Goody 2010). It is this Eurasian history, rather than the dominance in recent centuries of one part of this supercontinent (Europe), that gave birth to the modern world we inhabit today, and to the Anthropocene whose threshold humanity has recently crossed. Of course, this globalized world is still incredibly diverse. Civilization can still be a helpful concept in grasping this diversity, even if today's plural societies are very different from the civilizational pluralism of the preindustrial era. In this way, civilizational analysis flows into a large body of literature on "multiple modernities" (Eisenstadt 2002).

Given this pluralism, is there any sense in which a singular application of the term *civilization* to Eurasia might still be justified? Just as Mauss in the closing pages of his analysis of "The Gift" felt able to generalize about "the great Neolithic civilization" (1990, 92), which evidently comprised a very large number of *civilisations* as he defines this term elsewhere, so one might invoke a singular "Eurasian civilization" to denote that discontinuity in human history which, long after the Neolithic transition, decisively accelerated the speed of planetary transformation. It did so by creating new bases for social relations at multiple levels: from divisions of labor in the domestic domain to emulation and cultural connoisseurship within local societies, the payment of tribute to the centers of civilizational power, and expanding encounters with other civilizational centers. Like the Neolithic transition which preceded it, this was a gradual process rather than a sudden rupture. If Goody is right, it began several centuries before even the earliest dating of the Axial Age, which would imply that material transformations are prior to the spiritual and philosophical; but more research is needed to clarify these causalities.

The human beings who created the multiple variants of Eurasian civilization, with their innovative political economies and cosmologies, are cognitively the same animal as their neighbors within Eurasia and human beings elsewhere. Some of the problems they addressed through "inventions" such as political democracy and redistributive welfare states can be viewed as replicating arrangements pioneered at the other levels: in earlier forms of civilization in Trigger's sense, and also in the smaller-scale societies that formed *civilisations* in the original Maussian sense.[8] The Eurasian "miracle" should not be exaggerated. Even today, as several chapters in, this volume document, the civilizations that evolved here during the last three millennia in senses two and three have by no means eliminated other forms of civilizational diversity in their midst.

Nearly twenty years ago, Dipesh Chakrabarty published an influential study titled *Provincializing Europe* (2000). While critiquing Eurocentrism, the postcolonial historian nonetheless argued that it was hardly possible to theorize modernity outside of the categories of the European Enlightenment. He celebrated culturally diverse translations, but Europe (and specifically the conceptual resources of modern English) retained their preeminence. But if Goody's analysis is to be preferred, a more thoroughgoing provincialization of Western Eurasia is called for. European concepts and institutions should be investigated comparatively on an equal footing with those of other Eurasian civilizations. Some anthropologists (those more interested in exploring civilizations in senses one and two) might view this as an unsatisfactory substituting of Eurocentrism with a new Eurasia-centrism. But Chakrabarty's accusatory notion of provincializing has no traction at the level of Eurasia. For anthropologists interested in how the world has changed in the last three thousand years, Eurasia can hardly be provincialized; it is the fulcrum of global history.

Conclusion: Anthropology and Civilizations

The Halle meeting of 2012 and the subsequent work in preparing, this volume have helped me to a better understanding of diverse forms of civilizational analysis—and also of why many anthropologists are still reluctant to use this term, either for the past or the present. Setting aside the above argument concerning Eurasia, which I have elaborated in more detail elsewhere (Hann 2016), I see many compelling reasons why social and cultural anthropologists should engage with long-term processes of resilience and transformation at levels above those of community or region, nation or state:

1. The study of such macroformations is a corrective to the bias of paradigms such as cultural relativism; as a result of the dominance of ethnographic methods throughout the last century, the concept of culture has too often been invoked with insufficient attention to dynamic processes, and on too small a scale.

2. Work at the civilizational level helps to overcome the pitfalls of methodological nationalism, that is, the tendency to generalize categories determined by the prime political and sociological units of recent times; (this is analytically distinct from the bias associated with the concept of culture, though the two often coincide in practice).

3. Paying attention to the macroformations is conducive to rejuvenating links between anthropology and other disciplines, notably sociology and history, in the interests of reestablishing a holistic science of social relations.

4. Work at this level can also help mainstream social and cultural anthropologists reconnect with colleagues who work with one or another version of evolutionary theory. The concept of civilization lies beyond those of culture and society, and is better suited to brokering a renewal of anthropology's most basic dialectic—that between the universal (that which applies to all human beings) and that which is determined in particular historical contexts.

5. Finally and more parochially, engaging with the concept of civilization may have the salutary effect of helping contemporary social and cultural anthropologists (some of whom have been brought up to believe that almost every text written before the 1980s was flawed and can be safely ignored) to rediscover their own disciplinary history.

Far from being of antiquarian interest, civilizational analysis shows us ways in which to renew anthropology in the globalized world of the present. While other disciplines also have their built-in propensities to search for new paradigms and even to question ultimate foundations, a synchronically oriented anthropology is under strong pressure to reinvent itself with each new generation. Is there a canon at all? A few classics from the past are ritually invoked, but I am not sure how widely they are read. Every student knows that Marcel Mauss wrote about the gift and the category of the person.

However, the texts of Mauss and Durkheim that deal with civilization are not well known and seldom taught, even in France. Nathan Schlanger (2006) deserves credit for his efforts to disseminate this work in English, but even he does not probe far into the German ethnological materials on which Mauss and Durkheim relied. Those German sources have largely vanished from view although, as Yang and Wu show in chapter 12 of, this volume, they might still have much to offer. In short, to take up terms such as *civilisation* and *Kulturkreis* can facilitate productive connections between different strands of the discipline's past (overcoming political prejudice as necessary) in order to retrieve what is still relevant for the present.

My own enthusiasms are eclectic, but I do of course have my own preferences when it comes to linking the analysis of past macroformations to contemporary challenges. I find it important to balance the study of the imaginative and ideological dimensions, which have tended to attract more attention from civilizational analysts in sociology, with investigation of the material, infrastructural dimensions of civilizations, as explored by the anthropologists Goody and Wolf. More specifically, historical anthropologists should explore how different civilizations have contributed to the overall advance of a Eurasian ratchet based on the dialectic between the principle of market exchange and Polanyian redistribution. Karl Polanyi's substantivist economic anthropology (in which the third main "form of integration" is reciprocity or mutuality, which continuously adapts to the evolving exchange-redistribution dialectic in ways consistent with the traditions of the civilization) offers a better approach to the dynamics of *longue durée* history than the more deterministic models of world systems theory. Although Polanyi (like Goody) did not contribute to civilizational analysis in any explicit way, it has long seemed to me that his approach offers a healthy balance between, on the one hand, the idealist bias that characterizes much of the sociological literature (not to mention the new "anthropology of ethics"), and on the other the "vulgar materialist" bias of most Marxist and neo-Marxist paradigms.

Notes

1. Publication of the original contributions of Mauss and Durkheim (Schlanger 2006) has not changed this substantially. There has, however,

been a revival of interest in some quarters, notably in collaborations with material culture specialists and archaeologists. Michael Rowlands is the driving force behind the *Centre for Research on the Dynamics of Civilisation* (CREDOC) at University College London.

2. This is not to imply that Goody engaged significantly with his North American contemporaries. Rather, he aligned himself with the tradition of A. R. Radcliffe-Brown and defined social anthropology as "comparative sociology," in opposition to the American emphasis on culture(s). Goody nonetheless wrote extensively about cultural themes. Goody (2010, 43) applauded Eric Wolf for rejecting the term *feudalism* in favor of a more general "tributary mode of production," and for recognizing the equivalence of Europe and East Asia in the preindustrial era. Yet major differences remain. The title and periodization of Wolf's magnum opus are consistent with the Eurocentric bias of the postwar modernization paradigm. For Goody, the emergence in the last three hundred years of industrial capitalism (the critical rupture for Wolf) is but a further episode in the rise of mercantile capitalism over three thousand years.

3. For a synthesis published in the month of his death see Goody 2015.

4. Goody's failure to engage systematically with civilizational analysis may derive in large part from his aversion to the work of Norbert Elias, an antipathy that seems to have been influenced by their personal encounters in postcolonial Ghana. See Goody 2006.

5. Notably the German traditions of *Kulturgeschichte* (including the proponents of *Kulturkreislehre*), but also in North American "culture area" theories.

6. Only Trigger's northern Chinese case (1200–950 BCE) falls within Goody's time frame; however, the dating of the "Bronze Age" in East Asia remains controversial.

7. I term this process "realizing Eurasia." This is the title of a research project supported by the European Research Council devoted to investigation of the links between civilizational background and moral economy at the level of households and small businesses across contemporary Eurasia, from Protestant Scandinavia to Confucian China (Grant agreement no. 340854: REALEURASIA).

8. For example, Jack Goody (2003) offers a suggestive analogy between socialist redistribution and sorcery accusations in the nonliterate societies of sub-Saharan Africa.

References

Arjomand, Saïd Amir. 2010. "Three Generations of Comparative Sociologies." *European Journal of Sociology* 52, no. 3: 363–99.

Arnason, Johann P. 2014. "The Religio-political Nexus. Historical and Comparative Reflections." In *Religion and Politics: European and Global Perspectives*, edited by Johann P. Arnason and Ireneusz Pawel Karolewski, 8–36. Edinburgh: Edinburgh University Press. Chakrabarty, Dipesh 2000. *Provincializing Europe. Postcolonial Thought and Historical Difference*. Princeton: Princeton University Press.

Eisenstadt, Shmuel N., ed. 2002. *Multiple Modernities*. New Brunswick, NJ.: Transaction.

Gellner, Ernest. 1988. *Plough, Sword, and Book. The Structure of Human History*. London: Collins.

Goody, Jack. 1976. *Production and Reproduction. A Comparative Study of the Domestic Domain*. Cambridge: Cambridge University Press.

———. 1996. *The East in the West*. Cambridge: Cambridge University Press.

———. 2003. "Sorcery and Socialism." In *Distinct Inheritances. Property, Family, and Community in a Changing Europe*, edited by Hannes Grandits and Patrick Heady, 391–406. Münster: LIT.

———. 2006. *The Theft of History*. Cambridge: Cambridge University Press.

———. 2010. *The Eurasian Miracle*. Cambridge. Polity.

———. 2015. "Asia and Europe." *History and Anthropology* 26, no. 3: 263–307.

Hann, Chris. 2015. "Goody, Polanyi, and Eurasia: An Unfinished Project in Comparative Historical Economic Anthropology." *History and Anthropology* 26, no. 3: 308–20.

———. 2016. "A Concept of Eurasia." *Current Anthropology* 57, no. 1: 1–27 (including critical symposium).

———. 2017. "The Anthropocene and Anthropology. Micro and Macro Perspectives." *European Journal of Social Theory* 20, no. 1: 183–96.

Huntington, Samuel P. 1996. *The Clash of Civilizations and the New World Order*. New York: Simon and Schuster.

Kuper, Adam. 1999. *Culture. The Anthropologist's Account.* Cambridge: Harvard University Press.

Mauss, Marcel. 1990 [1925]. *The Gift. The Form and Reason for Exchange in Archaic Societies.* London: Routledge.

Polanyi, Karl 1944. *The Great Transformation. The Political and Economic Origins of Our Time.* New York: Rinehart.

Sahlins, Marshall. 1992. *Anahulu: The Anthropology of History in the Kingdom of Hawaii. Volume I: Historical Ethnography.* Chicago: Chicago University Press.

Schlanger, Nathan, ed. 2006. *Marcel Mauss. Techniques, Technology, and Civilization.* New York: Berghahn.

Trigger, Bruce G. 2003. *Understanding Early Civilizations. A Comparative Study.* Cambridge: Cambridge University Press.

Wengrow, David. 2010. *What Makes Civilization? The Ancient Near East and the Future of the West.* Oxford: Oxford University Press.

Wolf, Eric R. 1967. "Understanding Civilizations: A Review Article." *Comparative Studies in Society and History* 9, no. 4: 446–65.

———. 1982. *Europe and the People without History.* Berkeley: The University of California Press.

Contributors

Johann P. Arnason. Emeritus Professor of Sociology, La Trobe University, Melbourne, Australia; associated with the Department of Historical Sociology, Faculty of Human Studies, Charles University, Prague.

Milena Benovska-Sabkova. Professor of Anthropology, New Bulgarian University, Sofia, Bulgaria.

Stephan Feuchtwang. Emeritus Professor of Anthropology, Department of Anthropology, London School of Economics, Great Britain.

Martin Fuchs. Professor of Indian Religious History, Max Weber Center for Advanced Cultural and Social Studies, Erfurt, Germany.

David N. Gellner. Professor of Social Anthropology, Institute of Social and Cultural Anthropology, Oxford University, Great Britain.

Andre Gingrich. Director, Institute of Social Anthropology, Austrian Academy of Sciences, Vienna, Austria.

Hans Peter Hahn. Professor of Anthropology, Institute for Anthropology, Goethe University, Frankfurt (Main), Germany.

Chris Hann. Director of the Department "Resilience and Transformation in Eurasia," Max Planck Institute for Social Anthropology, Halle, Germany.

Joel S. Kahn [1946–2017]. Sometime Professor of Anthropology, University of Melbourne, Australia.

Nikolay N. Kradin. Professor of Anthropology, Institute of History, Archaeology and Ethnography of the Peoples of the Far-East, Russian Academy of Sciences, Vladivostok, Russian Federation.

Patrice Ladwig. Senior Research Fellow, Max Planck Institute for the Study of Religious and Ethnic Diversity, Göttingen, Germany.

Yulia Prozorova. Research Fellow, Sociological Institute of the Russian Academy of Sciences, Moscow, Russian Federation.

Gonçalo Santos. Assistant Professor of Anthropology, Institute for the Humanities and Social Sciences, University of Hong Kong, China.

Oliver Tappe. Senior Researcher, Global South Studies Center, University of Cologne, Germany.

WU Xiujie. Senior Research Fellow, Max Planck Institute for Social Anthropology, Halle, Germany.

YANG Shengmin. Professor of Ethnology, *Minzu* University, Beijing, China.

Index

Adams, Suzi, 174

Adorno, Theodor, 39

agriculture: and fertilizer production, 260–62, 264, 267, 273; in Goody's notion of civilization, 343; in Lao-Vietnamese upland frontier, 200; and Malays, 221–22, 225; and nomads, 303, 304–5, 306

Akaev, *Askar*, 315

Allen, Michael, 102

Allen, Sarah, 239

analogism, 26, 27–28, 29, 31n3

anarchy, 198

ancestors: and afterlife bureaucracy, 244; juxtaposition of shamans and, 242–43; relationship between Chinese gods and, 240–42, 251–52

ancient Greek civilization, 8, 60–61, 64, 65–67

Andriolo, Karin R., 283

animism, 26, 31n3

Annales School, 44–45

anthropology: approaches to civilization in, 99–100; changes in understanding of goals of, 219–20; civilization as problematic concept for, 99; cultural, xix, xx–xxii; defined by Cai Yuanpei, 298n4; Descola on, 25; Durkheim and Mauss on, 17; economic, 350; interrelations between civilizational studies and, xvii–xix; and levels of civilizational analysis, 155–56; Lévi-Strauss on predicament of anthropologist, 19; linguistics-based convergence between civilizational analysis and, xxii–xxviii; and objections to civilizational analysis, xx–xxii; problem of Malay, 222–23; Schmidt on, 283–84; social, xix, xx–xxii, 343–44, 351n2; as source of knowledge of civilizations, 5–6; tension within, 340. *See also* historical anthropology

anti-Westernism, 324, 325, 331

Arabic, 80, 93n4

Arab-Islamic civilization, 79–87

archaeology, 53–54; analysis of early civilizations, 58–59; chronological and typological approaches to civilizations, 54–58; cognitive, 62–63; intercultural and intercivilizational encounters, 65–67; social, 63; temporal limits, theories, and concepts of civilizational analysis, 59–64

area of civilization, 10, 13–14

Arnason, Johann P.: on Axial Age, 67n2; on Axial Age formations, 55; on axial transformations, 57; on Buddhist monks, 160;

Arnason, Johann P. (*continued*)
on civilizations as patterns, 155; on conceptualizing civilizational dimensions, 143; defines civilizations, 195; on diversity of civilizational formations, 58; on Indianization, 157; on modernity, 296; on open notion of imaginary, 174–75; on state formation, 56; on strength of premodern Southeast Asian kingdoms, 163; on structural constraints of cultural ordering, 63; on Theravada Buddhism, 162
artha, 181n22
arthaśāstra, 169, 170–71, 174, 181n22
Art of Not Being Governed: An Anarchist History of Upland Southeast Asia, The (Scott), 110–11
Askew, Marc, 166
Aśoka, 162, 163
Aśokāvadāna (*The Legend of* Aśoka), 162
Assavavirulhakarn, Prapod, 163
Atlas der deutschen Volkskunde project, 284, 297–98n2
Australian religions, 9
autonomy, 29
Axial Age, xviii, xxx, 3, 67n2; second, 245
Axial Age (theory), 44, 62
Axial Age civilizations, 54–55
Ayyubids, 85

Babylonian province, 57
Bali, Geertz's analysis of theatre state in, xxvii–xxviii
Balinese peasants, 111
Banks, Marcus, 91
barbarians, 65–67

barbarism, 38
bathing, in South China, 265–66
Bellah, Robert, 61
Benedict, Ruth, xvii
Benjamin, Walter, 42–43
Berdyaev, Nikolai, 328
Beret, Moshe, 68n6
Berr, Henri, 11
Bhaktapur, 101
bhaktas, 133–36
bhakti: Champakalakshmi on, in Tamil region, 149n36; congregational dimension of, 134; consequences of new civilizational approach to, 136–38; as derivative of *samnayasi*-hood, 149–50n40; dissemination of, 137; Dumont on, 126–27, 128–30, 132, 146–47nn14–17; *Gitagovinda* and relational and interactional character of, 148n29; Hardy and Prentiss on, 146n12; neglect of, 125–31; orality and textuality in, 150n44; recognition in, 133, 148nn29,30; understanding and analyzing, 131–36; Weber on, 126–30, 132, 145n9, 149n33; world-indifference in, 146n10
Bogner, Artur, 39
Bolshevism, 324–25, 328, 331, 332
Book of Songs, 241–42
Borkenau, Franz, 44
Bosporan Kingdom, 66–67
Bourlet, Antoine, 206, 207
Bowden, Brett, 44
Brahmanism, 157, 168, 169
Brahmin, 180n20
Brandewie, Ernest, 283
Brandtstädter, Susanne, 41, 271

Braudel, Fernand, xv–xvi, 263–64, 270

Bronkhorst, Johannes, 169

Bronze Age, xxx–xxxi

bronze ritual vessels, 239–40, 243–44

Buddhism: absorbed into Chinese civilization, 246–51; connection between Pali and, 179n12; development of, in Laos, 182nn27,30; Eisenstadt on, 130; in Indian culture, 122, 145n3; Lévi-Strauss on, 21–22; spread of, 157–58, 178n8; trends in study of, 177–78n4. *See also* Theravada Buddhist statecraft

Buddhist monks, 160–61, 178n7, 180n18, 247–48

Burghart, Richard, 101

Burke, Peter, 40

Busche, Hubertus, 45

Byzantine civilization, 7–8

Cai Yuanpei, 284–85, 298n4

camels, 290

camouflage borrowing, 172

capitalism, global, 220–24

Casanova, José, 124

caste system, 104–5, 113nn4,11, 114n15

Castoriadis, Cornelius, 150n42, 156, 174, 175

cattle breeding, 304–5, 307

Chakrabarty, Dipesh, 348

chamber pots, 260, 266

Champakalakshmi, R., 149n36

chamra, 173

Chang Kwang-chi, 238

chemicals, farm, 261–62, 264, 267

Chevalier, Sophie, 37, 46

Childe, V. Gordon, 53, 309, 310, 345

China: and analogism, 27; and change in relations between Inner and Outer Eurasia, xxxiv; and common themes in histories of civilizations, 251–54; in comparative perspective, 233–34, 236–37; emerging flush toilet infrastructures in, 267–68; ethnological investigations of, 298n10; everyday toilet practices in rural South, 259–64, 273–74; flush toilet as civilizational process in, 270–73; flush toilet as technopolitical project in, 269–70; Granet's work on, 16–17; history and development of, xxxi–xxxii; inclusion of commoner and absorption of Buddhism in, 246–51; interactions with, xxxiii; *Kulturkreislehre* and case study regarding intercivilizational encounters of Salar in, 289–97; *Kulturkreislehre* in anthropology of, 284–89, 294–97; mansions with private bathrooms in, 264–67; political cosmocracy in, 244–46; from Stone to Iron Age, 237–44

Chinese classics, 242, 244–45

Christians and Christianity, 22, 55, 93n3

Chu, 242

Chutintaranond, Sunait, 163

cinema, 15

city-state, 56, 58

civilisation matérielle, xv–xvi, 263–67, 270–71, 275n5

civilizational analysis: anthropologists' reactions to, 177n1; approaches to, xiv–xvii, 54–58; classical legacy of, 1–3; Elias on, 44–46; in Eurasia, 344–48; goals of, 122–23;

civilizational analysis (*continued*)
interrelations between anthropology and, xvii–xix; linguistics-based convergence between anthropology and, xxii–xxviii; methods of, 344–48; obstacles to dialogue concerning, xx–xxii; process categories in, 123–26; revival of, 1, 2–3, 4; scale and levels of, 155–56; secularization in, 123, 124; temporal limits, theories, and concepts of, 59–64

civilizational crossroads, xxix–xxx

civilizational decline and collapse, 57–58

civilizational legacies, 297

civilizational process(es), 196, 197, 199, 263–64, 270–73

civilizational ruptures, 141–42

civilizational sequence, 8–9

civilizational spread, 233–34

civilizational theory, 309, 312, 316

civilization(s): analysis of, as study of everyday life, 44–46; anthropological approaches to, xxvii, 35–37, 99–100; Arab-Islamic, 79–87; archaeological investigations of early, 58–59; area of, 10, 13–14; Arnason's definition of, 195; Childe's criteria for, 345; chronological and typological approaches to, 54–58; common themes in histories of, 251–54; conceptualizing civilizational dimensions, 143–44; conceptual usage of term in historical anthropology, 76–79, 87–92; critique of traditional concept of, 121–22; Descola's use of term, 29–30; development of, 210; differentiation in, 8; Durkheim and Mauss on, xiv, 3–10, 54, 345; Durkheim's concept of, xix, xxi; elements of, 10–12, 14; as elements of sociocultural formations, 121; Elias and, as anthropological tool, 37–40, 46–47; Elias on concept of, 37–40; evolution of, 316; figuration and anthropological approach to, 40–42; form of, 10, 12–13, 14; heterogeneity of, 229; as hierarchies of aspiration and exclusion, 233; influences on Elias's anthropological approach to, 42–44; Kroeber on, 341; layers of, 13–14; Lévi-Strauss on, 18–23; Mauss and definition of, 2, 233–34; Mauss on, 10–18, 230n3, 234; modernity as new, 29; moral person at heart of, 236–37; nomadism as local, 311–14; objects versus elements of, 11; phenomena of, 10–12, 14; post-Soviet scholars on, 309–11; as problematic concept for anthropologists, 99; relationship between frontier and, 194–95; Sahlins on, 342–43; in South Asia, 107–10, 112; spread of, 7–8; and territorial and cultural boundaries, 122; traditions of thought regarding South Asian, 100–101; universal, 14–16; use of term, 123, 234–36

Claessen, Henry J. M., 68n4

Clash of Civilizations, The (Huntington), xvii

Clastres, Pierre, xxv

climatic cycles, impact of, on nomads, 304

Coedès, Georges, 157, 164, 195–96

cognition, development of human, 61

cognitive archaeology, 62–63

cold and hot societies, xxv

"collapse of civilization," 38

Collins, Steven, 158, 159–60, 179n12, 179n14

colonialism: and abuses of concepts of civilization, 91–92; and intercivilizational dynamics and cultural borrowings in Southeast Asian uplands, 206; and interethnic relations in Southeast Asian uplands, 203, 205; in Malay World, 225–26; and martial tribes, 113n3; millenarian movements under, 212n5; and sociocultural dynamics of Southeast Asian uplands, 193–94, 201–3

commoner, access to political class of Chinese, 246–51, 254

Comte, Auguste, 6

Condominas, Georges, 166, 167, 182n29

conqueror, outside, 243, 251, 252–53

consciousness, structures of, 62

cosmopolitanisms, 142

cultural anthropology, xix, xx–xxii

cultural difference, Trubetzkoy's theory of, 326

cultural integration, Spengler's conception of, xvii

cultural ontologies, 23, 30n2, 54

culture: in civilizational analysis, 54; development of, 210; Kroeber on, 341

Dalit *bhaktas*, 135

Danilevsky, Nikolai, 311, 312, 328–29

Daur Mongolian shamans, 238–39

death rites, in China, 244

Deo Van Tri, 193, 202, 203, 208

Descola, Philippe, 23–30, 31n3, 346

deterritorialization, 223

development: in civilizational analysis, 67n1; Elias on, 37, 38; in Malay World, 225–26

devotionalist Hinduism, 129

Di, 240

Dien Bien Phu, battle of, 202

diffusionism, 284

divination, 239, 240–41

Donald, Merlin, 61

Dostal, Walter, 88

dreaming, in totemism, 27

Duara, Prasenjit, 272

Dugin, Alexander, 325

Dumont, Louis, 88, 100–101, 113n4, 126–30, 132, 146nn14–16, 342

Durkheim, Émile: on anthropology, 17; conception of human conceptual and reflective competences, 26; conceptual guidelines for civilizational analysis, xviii; on criteria for civilizations, 54; foundational work on religious life, xxi; on internationalization of social phenomena, 210; on *nai*, 208; notion of civilization, xiv, xix, xxi, 345; person and center of sociology and anthropology of, 236; on power, 17–18; and revival of civilizational analysis, 2, 3; on society and civilization, 3–10; on transformation of civilization, 168; writings on civilization, 350

economic anthropology, 350

ecumenic zones, 7

Eder, Mathias, 285–86, 287, 288, 298n5

efficacy, in Chinese thinking, 252

Eisenstadt, Shmuel: and analysis of axial civilizations, 55; Axial Age theory of, 44; on bhakti, Buddhism, and Jainism, 130; on Buddhist monks, 160; on civilizational dimension of human societies, xiv; contributions of, to civilizational analysis, xv; on mundane and transmundane, 179–80n16; on pre-axial civilizations, 68n5; on rationalization, 145n5; and revival of civilizational analysis, 2, 4; on state collapse, 57–58; on Theravada Buddhism, 162

elementary form, xxi, xxiv

Elias, Norbert, 35–37, 46–47; on analysis of civilization, 44–46; on concept of civilization, 37–40; distanced from dominant sociological and anthropological theories, 36–37; on figuration, 40–42; Goody's aversion to, 351n4; and historical comparison of societies, 42–44; on material civilization, 271; originality of, 36; and processual analysis, xvi; self-alienation of, 45; self-evaluation of, 36

elitism, 122

emotions, 38–39

emperor(s): Chinese, as shaman, 254n3; Chinese, as "son of heaven," 246; diplomacy of Song, 248; Mauryan, 163

empire, use of term in anthropology, 77–78

Engels, Friedrich, 309

Erlitou, 239

ethnography, 5–6, 219–20, 298n4

Eurasia, xxviii–xxxiv, 20–21, 344–48; "realizing," 345, 351n7

Eurasianism, 323, 324–27, 331, 332–33

Eurasian nomads, 65, 307–8n3, 314

Eurocentrism, 341–42, 348

"European miracle," 341, 343

evolutionism, 67n1

Evrard, Olivier, 197

external symbolic storage, 61, 63

"family of societies," 9, 13–14

farm chemicals, 261–62, 264, 267

Faxian, 247

Febvre, Lucien, 39

fences, of Salar, 292

feng shui, 264

Ferguson, Adam, 309

Ferguson, John P., 161

fertility rites, 241

fertilizer, 260–62, 264, 267, 273

festivals, in Newar culture, 105–6

fieldwork, xxi–xxii, xxvi–xxvii, 19

figuration, 39, 40–42, 43, 47

filial duty, 244, 250, 251

Filofei (Philotheus), 327–28

Finot, Louis, 169

First Indochina War (1946–1954), 202

Fiskesjö, Magnus, 212n2

Florovskii, Georgii, 324

flush toilet: as civilizational process, 270–73; emerging infrastructures for, 267–68; and mansions with private bathrooms, 264–67; as marker of modernity, 262–63; as technopolitical project, 269–70

Forte, Antonino, 248

Frankfurt School, 42–43

Frick, Johann, 285

Friedman, Sara, 272

Frobenius, Leo, 43

frontier: creation and shaping of, 197; defined, 209; dynamics, 193–94; relationship between civilization and, 194–95

Fujen Catholic University, 286, 288, 298n6

Fuller, Chris J., 113n12, 126, 127, 129, 130, 147nn19,21

galactic polity, xxviii, 108, 163. See also *mandala*

Gandhi, Mahatma, 99

Gauchet, Marcel, xxv–xxvi

Geertz, Clifford, xiii, xxvi–xxviii, 110–11, 114n20, 341

Gestalt Theory, 43

Giddens, Anthony, 4

Gift, The (Mauss), 16

global capitalism, 220–24

global history, versus world history, 340

globalization, xxix–xxx

Godelier, Maurice, xxvi

gods, relationship between Chinese ancestors and, 240–42, 251–52

Golden Horde, 314

Gombrich, Richard, 108

Goody, Jack, xxx, xxxii, 90, 343–44, 346, 351nn2,4

Grabowsky, Volker, 167, 180n18

Graebner, Fritz, 282

Granet, Marcel, 16–17

"Great Traditions," 227

Greek civilization, 8, 21, 60–61, 64, 65–67

Grootaers, Willem A., 285–86, 287–89, 298–99nn11,16

Guanzi, 246

guest ritual, 240

Gumilev, Lev, 312–13, 314, 316, 325, 333–34nn3,4

Haberland, Michael, 298n3

Habermas, Jürgen, 174

Hallisey, Charles, 133

Han, 291, 294

Hann, Chris, 155, 172

Hardy, Friedhelm, 135, 146n12, 148n32

Harijans, 113n12

Harrell, Stevan, 272

Harris, Marvin, 284

Hawley, John, 131

Hermanns, Mathias, 285

hierarchy: as central to all civilizations, 251–52; and Chinese civilization, 237–44, 252–53, 254; in Dumont's conception of South Asian civilization, 100–101; in South Asia, 104–5, 113nn4,11, 114n15

Hinduism: devotionalist movements in, 129; Fuller on, 127; in Kathmandu, 103–5; patterns of, 137–38; and Theravada Buddhist political imaginaries, 161–62. *See also* bhakti

Hindutva, 110

historical anthropology, 75; Arab-Islamic civilization in, 79–87; conceptual usage of civilization in, 76–79, 87–92; conceptual usage of term in historical anthropology, 76–79

historical change, long-term, 42–44, 47

historical sociology, xv–xvi, xxiv, 1, 36, 155–56

Ho Chinese, 201, 203, 204

Hochkulturen, 2

Hodgson, Marshall, xiv, xxii

Hogarth, D. G., 166

Honneth, Axel, 148n30

hot and cold societies, xxv

Houaphan, 199–203, 206, 207, 209, 211

Houaphan Tang Hok, 201

household biogas, 274

houses: of Salar, 291–94, 296–97; in South China, 264–67

Hridaya, Chittadhar, 106–7

Huizinga, Johan, 45

human cognition, development of, 61

Huntington, Samuel, xvii, 92

al-Husayn, Yahya b., 84

Huxley, Andrew, 171

hygiene: in South Asia, 271–72; in South China, 265–66. *See also* toilet practices in rural South China

India: Islam and Buddhism in culture of, 122, 145n3; Lévi-Strauss on, 20–21; and Mauss's relationship with Lévi, 30n1; and neglect of bhakti, 126–30; reconceptualization of culture and society, 139–43; relationship of Brahmin and king in, 180n20; religious diversity in, 131, 136, 139–41; and Sanskritization, 342. *See also* bhakti

Indianization. *See* Theravada Buddhist statecraft

individualization: bhakti and studying processes of, 125–26; in civilizational analysis, 123, 124

Indus Valley civilization, 58–59

Inner Eurasia, xxxii–xxxiv

intercivilizational encounters, 65–67

intercultural encounters, 65–67

interdependencies, 39, 40, 160, 270

intermarriage, Salar and, 291

Ishi, Yoneo, 182n33

Islam: arrival of, in Yemen, 83–84; civilizational approaches to, xiv–xv; Eisenstadt on, 55; Geertz's study of, xxvii; Hodgson's analysis of, xxii; in Indian culture, 122, 145n3; Lévi-Strauss on, 21–22; mobilization of political, 91; rise of, 80; spread to Southeast Asia, 224

Islamic expansion, xxxii

Izikowitz, Karl G., 206

jades, 237–38

Jainism, 130

Jaspers, Karl, 55, 67n2

Jews, in Southwest Arabia, 93n3

Jinakālamālīpakaraṇa, 158, 178n7

Johnson, David, 298–99n11

Joly, Mark, 42

Jonsson, Hjorleifur, 197

Juju, Baldev, 102

Jullien, François, 252

Jurchen Mongols, 248

Kabir, 135–36

Kachin, 197

Kahn, Joel S., 209

kampong, 222, 223

kang, 293, 294, 299n15

karma, 146n11

Kathmandu Valley, 101–7, 110

Kautilya, 181nn22,23

Kha, 203–6

Kha Cheuang rebellions, 204, 205

Khmu, 204–5

kings and kingship: in Chinese civilization, 240, 242, 243, 252–53; in Indus Valley civilization, 58–59; of Sanskrit cosmopolis, 109; in South Asia, 105, 106. *See also* Theravada Buddhist statecraft

Knecht, Peter, 298n5

Koppers, Wilhelm, 285

Kroeber, Alfred L., xix, 13, 90, 341

Kulke, Hermann, 180n19, 181n25

Kulturkreislehre, 281–82; in anthropology of China, 284–89, 294–97; case study regarding intercivilizational encounters of Salar, 289–97; criticism of, 18, 297n1; review of, 282–84

Kyrgyzstan, 315

Lalitpur, 101

Lamet, 204, 206–7

Lamprecht, Karl, 43

land tenure, 206–9, 247

Language of the Gods in the World of Men, The (Pollock), 108

language(s): in Arab-Islamic civilization, 82–83; ideological link between Southeast Asian politics and, 159; of Nepal, 107; in South Asia, 108–10; and Theravada Buddhist political imaginaries, 158

Lan Xang, 182n27

Lao people, 199–200, 203, 204, 205–6, 209

Laos. *See* Southeast Asian uplands; Theravada Buddhist statecraft

Laruelle, Marlene, 327

latrines, 260, 261, 264, 266–67

Lattimore, Owen, 197, 212n3

Leach, Edmund, 181, 197

Lefort, Claude, xxvii

legitimation theory, 114n16

Leser, Paul, 282

Lévi, Sylvain, 30n1, 101–2

Lévi-Strauss, Claude, xxii–xxv, 18–24, 235, 259

Levy, Robert I., 104, 105, 107

liba fences, 292

Liebermann, Victor, 161

Lingat, Robert, 169, 171

linguism, 110

literacy and writing: in Arab-Islamic civilization, 82–83; as intrinsic feature of civilizational formations, 59, 68n7; in Sanskrit cosmopolis, 109

literature: bhakti and, 135–36; of Newars, 106–7; in Sanskrit cosmopolis, 109

"Little Traditions," 227

livestock, and nomads, 304–5, 307

local civilization, nomadism as, 311–14

localization: of imaginary, 170–75; as process of scaling down civilizational patterns, 156, 176–77; of Theravada statecraft in Laos and northern Thailand, 164–70

Longshan pottery, 239

longue durée, 44, 142–43, 177n1

Lorrillard, Michel, 181–82n26

Lowie, Robert, 210, 282

Luoyang, 247

macroformations, 219–20, 227, 349

Maisels, Charles, 311

Malay World: anthropology and civilizational analysis of, 219–20; and civilizational analysis, 227–29; colonialism, state, modernization, and development in, 225–26;

Malay World (*continued*)

    and global capitalism, 220–24; heterogeneity of, 227, 228–29, 230n1; leading sites of economic and capitalist development in, 230n7; power of rulers in, 224; social, cultural, and economic life in, 224–25

Malinowski, Bronislaw, 269–70

Malla, K. P., 102, 106–7

Malla kings, 106

mana, 12

mandala, 162–63, 165–67, 174, 181n23, 200. *See also* galactic polity

Mann, Michael, 4

Mannheim, Karl, 41–42, 43

marriage, among Salar, 291

martial tribes, 113n3

Martynov, Anatoly, 310, 311

Masson, Vadim, 310

material civilization, xv–xvi, 263–67, 270–71, 275n5

material culture, 61

material life, xv–xvi

material symbolism, 61–63

Mauss, Marcel: conception of civilization, xiv, xix, 230n3, 234, 345; conceptual guidelines for civilizational analysis, xviii; on conceptual orientations of civilization, 10–18; on criteria for civilizations, 54; and definition of civilization, 2, 233–34; on evaluation of technical artifacts, 270; on internationalization of social phenomena, 210; Lévi and, 30n1; on *nai*, 208; person and center of sociology and anthropology of, 236; on power, 17–18; and revival of civilizational analysis, 2, 3; on society and civilization, 3–10; on transformation of civilization, 168; writings on civilization, 350

McDaniel, Justin, 173, 174

McNeill, William H., 7

memory preservation, 62

Mencius, 245, 246

Mennell, Stephen, 37, 271

Merleau-Ponty, Maurice, 143

Mesopotamia, 56, 57, 58, 60

microhistorical realities, 273

millenarian movements, 212n5

Minangkabau "peoples," 219, 227

modernity and modernization: Axial Age civilizations as paving way for, 54; civilizational and geopolitical shifts marking onset of early, xxxiv; Descola on, 29; Eisenstadt on, 29, 145n5; and Eurocentrism, 341–42, 348; Goody on capitalism and, 351n2; Hridaya and, 107; hygienic, 262–63, 271–72; and *Kulturkreislehre* in China, 296–97; in Malay World, 222–23, 225–26, 227; multiple modernities, 54, 145n5, 263, 274, 347; as new civilization, 29; and nomadism, 303, 309–10; Panarin on Maxism and Bolshevism as, projects, 331; and progressive process categories, 123–24

modernization theory, xxii, 222, 309–10, 341

monastic communities, 161, 180n19, 248

Mongols and Mongolian civilization, 311, 314

Mon-Khmer, 199

monks, 160–61, 171–72, 173, 178n7, 180n18, 247–48

Mon monks, 171–72

morality, and use of term *civilization*, 234–35, 236–37

moral milieux, 6–7, 234

Morgan, Lewis Henry, 309, 345

Morris, Ian, 245

Moscow, as Third Rome, 327–28, 329, 331–32

mud brick houses, in South China, 265, 266

Mughals, xxxii

multiple modernities, 54, 145n5, 263, 274, 347

mundane, 179–80n16

Nadel, Siegfried, 90

nation, Durkheim and Mauss's use of term, 5

nationalism, 314–15. *See also* Eurasianism

naturalism, 25–26, 29, 31n3

Negeri Sembilan, 219, 230n1

Nelson, Benjamin, xv, 2, 4, 23, 57, 62

neo-Eurasianism, 324–27

Neolithic period, 60

neolithic revolution, xxiv–xxv

neolithic societies, 20

Nepal, 101–7

Newar society and culture, 102–7, 110, 113nn9,11

Niestroj, Brigitte, 43

nomadic empire, 307–8

nomads and nomadism, 303–4, 315–16; challenges to resilience of, 309; factors influencing migration of, 306–8; lifestyle and culture of, 304–6; as local civilization, 311–14; and postcolonial nationalism, 314–15; and post-Soviet conceptions of civilization, 309–11

Nordholt, Henk Schulte, xxviii

Novetzke, Christian, 134

O'Connor, Richard, 166, 167

Oman, 80, 81, 93n2

oracle bones, 239, 240

oral narratives and transmission of knowledge, 150n44, 290

Orthodox civilization, 323–24; and early and neo-Eurasianism, 324–27; and Eurasianism as metatexts, 332–33; Panarin on, 330–32; secular and religious, 327–30

Ottomans, xxxii

Outer Eurasia, xxxiii–xxxiv

outside conqueror, 243, 251, 252–53

Pali: adoption of, as language, 158; connection between Buddhism and, 179n12; as transregional language of religious and political elite, 159

Pali Buddhist canon, 158–59

Pali imaginaire, 159–60, 162, 167, 168, 169–70, 175, 179n14

Panarin, Alexander, 330–32

paradoxical antinomies, 253

Parsons, Talcott, 341

Patterns of Culture (Benedict), xvii

Paul, Axel, 40, 46

Pavie, Auguste, 193, 202

peer polity interaction, 63–64

pensée sauvage, xxiii–xxv, 22

Perdue, Peter, 209

Persian, 80

Peßler, Wilhelm, 284

Pfaffenberger, Bryan, 269–70

Philotheus (Filofei), 327–28

phono-semantic matching, 172

Polanyi, Karl, 350

political cosmocracy, in China, 244–46

Pollock, Sheldon, 108–10, 112, 114n16, 142, 156, 163–67, 175–77

Polo, Marco, 306

Poppe, Nicholas, 289

power: Durkheim and Mauss on, 17–18; Elias on, 39, 40–41

Präzisionsdruck, 45

pre-axial civilizations, 55, 59–60, 68n5

Prentiss, Karen Pechilis, 133–34, 146n12

"primal symbol," 13

primitive societies: Clastres and Gauchet on, xxv; Elias on, 38; Lévi-Strauss on, xxiii–xxv

Privat, Jean-Marie, 37

process categories, 123–26

processual analysis, clarification and integration of, xvi–xvii

progressive rationalization, 145n5

progressive secularization, 124

property relations: in China, 247; in Southeast Asian uplands, 206–9

psychology, 37

Puett, Michael, 241, 244, 254n3

Qing empire, xxxii

Qing rebels, 201–2

quan ban, 208

quasi-civilizational network, 313–14

Radcliffe-Brown, A. R., 220

Raendchen, Jana, 167–68

Ramayana, 172

Rasulids, 85–86

rationalization, 123, 124, 145n5

Ratzel, Friedrich, 283

recognition, in bhakti, 133, 148nn29,30

Redfield, Robert, 90, 99, 220, 227, 341–42

reflexivity, problem of, 227–28

Reid, Anthony, 161

"relative universalism," 25

religion(s): in Arab-Islamic civilization, 83–85; Durkheim on, 9; and empire, xxix; Goody on, 343–44; interplay of politics and, xxv–xxvi; Lévi-Strauss on, 21–22; Mauss on, 11–12; patterns of Indian, 137–38; and reconceptualization of Indian culture and society, 139–43; of salvation, 245. *See also* bhakti; Buddhism; Christians and Christianity; Hinduism; Islam

religious diversity, in India, 131, 136, 139–41

Renfrew, Colin, 53, 60, 61, 310

Rispaud, Jean, 207

rituals: Chinese, 240–41; in Newar culture, 106

Roman empire, xxxi–xxxii

Rowlands, Michael, 235, 351n1

Rubruck, William of, 303

Russia: and change in relations between Inner and Outer Eurasia, xxxiv; and early and neo-Eurasianism, 324–27; and Orthodox civilization and Eurasianism as metatexts, 332–33; and Panarin's

Orthodox civilization, 330–32; and
postcolonial nationalism, 315, 316;
and secular and religious Orthodox
civilization, 327–30; significance of
Orthodox civilization in post-Soviet, 323–24
Russian archaeology, 310–11
Russian messianism, 327

sage-rule, 244–46
Sahlins, Marshall D., 342–43
Saka dynasty, 108–9
Saladin, 85
Salar, 289–94, 295–96, 297
Salemink, Oscar, 212n5
salvation, religions of, 245
sanitation. *See* toilet practices in rural
South China
Sanskrit, 108–10, 158, 179n12
Sanskrit cosmopolis, 108–9, 112, 172,
178n9
Sanskritization, 342
"savage thought," xxiii–xxv
Savickii, Petr, 324, 325, 326
Schlanger, Nathan, 350
Schmidt, Wilhelm, 281, 282, 283–84,
285, 297n1, 298n8
Schober, Juliana, 158
Schöttker, Detlev, 42–43
Schröder, Dominik, 285
Scott, James C., 110–11, 178n6, 195,
196, 197, 198, 204
Scythians, 65–67
second axial age, 245
secularization, in civilizational analysis,
123, 124
self-cultivation, in China, 244–46,
251
Sergii, Archbishop, 330

shamans, 238–39, 242–43, 254n3
Shi Chuanxiang, 272
Shirokogoroff, S. M., 286–87, 295,
298n8
Sidorov, Dimitrii, 327
Singer, Milton, 99
Sipsong Chau Tai, 199–203, 209,
211
Sipsong Panna, 200–201
Skalnik, Peter, 68n4
Skilling, Peter, 157
Slavophiles, 325, 328
Smith, Dennis, 46
social anthropology, xix, xx–xxii,
343–44, 351n2
social archaeology, 63
social change, Mannheim and Elias
on, 41, 43
social imaginary: application of,
to "nonmodern" constellations,
150n42; Descola's refusal to engage
with, 28; examples of improvisation
and localization of, 170–75; influence on Arnason's conceptualization
of civilization, 156; localization
and vernacularization of, 156–57;
production of, 176; and Theravada
Buddhist political imaginaries,
157–64, 175–77
socialism, 206–7, 309, 330, 346
Societas Verbi Divini (SVD), 285, 286
society/societies: *Annales* School and
understanding, 44–45; in context of larger civilization, 14–15;
Durkheim and Mauss on civilization and, 3–10; Elias and historical
comparison of, 42–44; formation
of, xxvi; primitive, xxiii–xxv, xxv, 38
sociocultural deterritorialization, 223

sociology: comparative civilizational approaches brought back to, 1; Durkheim and Mauss on, xxiii, 3–6, 234, 236; Elias on, 36, 45; Lévi-Strauss on, xxiii–xxiv; Mannheim and Elias on, 41–42

Solovyev, Vladimir, 328

Song dynasty, 248–49, 254

Songs of the South, 242

South Asia: Kathmandu Valley as microcosm of classical pre-Islamic civilization in, 101–7; notion of civilization in, 107–10, 112; state-evading behavior in, 110–12; traditions of thought regarding civilization in, 100–101; unity of south Indian villages, 113n12

Southeast Asia. See Malay world; Southeast Asian uplands; Theravada Buddhist statecraft

Southeast Asian uplands: historical contextualization of, 197–99; inter-civilizational dynamics and cultural borrowings in, 206–9; interethnic relations in, 203–6; political and cultural trajectories of, 199–203; sociocultural dynamics in, 193–97, 209–12

Southern Song dynasty, 249–50

Southwest Arabia: early Arabic speakers in, 93n4; historical studies of civilization in, 79–87; Jewish and Christian enclaves in, 93n3

Soviet Union, xxxiv

Spamer, Adolf, 287

Spengler, Oswald, xv, xvii, xix, 13, 43, 311–12

spiritual civilization, 275n5

Sri Lanka, 158, 178n7

Ssu-ma Ch'ien, 304

state: long-term relationship between periphery and, 57; in Malay World, 225–26; new ideology of, 56–57, 68n4; use of term in anthropology, 77

state collapse, 57–58

state-evasion, 110–12, 197, 198

state formation, 55–57, 68n4, 181n25, 226

stateless societies, xxv, xxvi

Strabo, 66–67

stranger king, 243, 251, 252–53

Strong, John, 162

structural anthropology, 22–24

structures of consciousness, 62

Stuart-Fox, Martin, 167

substantialization, 113n4

Sugata Saurabh (Life of the Buddha, Hridaya), 107

Suksamran, Somboon, 160

super-ethnoses, 312–13

Suriyavongsa, 173

Suvchinskii, Petr, 324

Sweepers, 104–5

symbolic material culture, 61–63

symmetrization, strategies of, 25

synchoronic civilizational ruptures, 141–42

Szakolczai, Árpád, 44

Taiization, 197

Taillard, Christian, 166

Tai Neua, 205–6, 209

Tai societies, 167–68, 178n5, 182n29, 193–94, 199–206

Tambiah, Stanley, xxviii, 90, 108, 161, 163, 169, 182n34

Tang dynasty, 247

Taosi, 239

Tao Yunkui, 284

Tarot, Camille, 11–12, 30n1

Taxila, 20–21

Taylor, Charles, 150n42

technological choice, 263

temporality, 24, 31n3, 253, 254

territorial expansion and contraction, 82

territorial state, 56

Thailand, 161. *See also* Southeast Asian uplands

theatre state, xxvii–xxviii, 107–8

theoretical culture, 62

theoretic stage, 61

Theravada Buddhist statecraft, 155–57, 175–77; continuing relevance of, 177n3; and distinction between mundane and transmundane, 179–80n16; and improvisation and localization of imaginary, 170–75; localizations of, 164–70; and Theravada Buddhist political imaginaries, 157–64

Third Rome, Moscow as, 327–28, 329, 331–32

Tian, 245, 246

Tibetans, 291, 292

Tilly, Charles, 144n1

Toffin, Gérard, 102, 106

toilet paper, 267–68

toilet practices in rural South China, 259–64, 273–74; emerging flush toilet infrastructures in, 267–68; and flush toilet as civilizational process, 270–73; and flush toilet as technopolitical project, 269–70; and mansions with private bathrooms, 264–67

tombs, hierarchies of Chinese, 237–38, 239

totemism, 26–27, 31n3

Touraine, Alain, 4

Toynbee, Arnold, xv, 43, 312

trade, xxix, 64, 66, 85, 86

trans-locality, 158–59

transmundane, 179–80n16

Treibel, Annette, 40

Trigger, Bruce, 56, 58, 59, 68n5, 345

Tristes Tropiques (Lévi-Strauss), 19–23

Trubetzkoy, Nikolai, 324, 325–26

Turkic-Muslim peoples, 326–27

Turner, Frederick Jackson, 195

Tylor, E. B., xix

Umland, Andreas, 324

UNICEF, 271

universal civilization, 14–16

"universalism, relative," 25

urbanism and urbanization, 59, 101, 103

urban revolution, 310

Urmonotheismus, 297n1

van Schendel, Willem, 196

Van Velzen, Thoden, 40

Vasilii III, Tsar, 327–28

vernacularization, 109–10, 156, 170–75, 176–77

Vienna School of Ethnology, 281, 284, 285

Vietnam. *See* Southeast Asian uplands

Voegelin, Eric, 43

Völkerkunde (Haberland), 298n3

Volkskunde, 284

Volkstum, 288

Wagner, Mayke, 291, 292

Wallerstein, Immanuel, 221

walls, of Salar, 292

Wang Jianxin, 296

waste management. *See* toilet practices in rural South China

Weber, Max: and ambiguity of classical civilizational analysis, 1–2; as anthropological landmark, xviii–xix; on *arthaśāstra*, 181n22; bhakti in model of Indian civilization of, 126–30, 132, 145n9, 149n33; Descola and, 23; and Elias's concept of power, 39; on Occidental trajectory, 13–14; on rationalization, 124, 145n5; and revival of civilizational analysis, 2–3; on world-rejection, 130, 145–46n10

wen, 245

Wengrow, David, 172

West Africa, 241

Whitehead, Alfred North, xvi

Wilson, Constance, 172

Wolf, Eric R., 76, 87, 342, 351n2

Wolters, Oliver, 167, 181n23

women, bhakti and, 134–35

world history, versus global history, 340

world-rejection, 130, 145–46n10

writing. *See* literacy and writing

Wundt, Wilhelm, 43

Xi'an, 247

Xiongnu, 314, 315

Xuanzang, 247–48

Yangshao period, 237

Yemen, 80, 81, 83–87, 93n2

Yoffee, Norman, 56

Yu, 242

yurts, 305–6

Zaydis and Zaydism, 84–85, 93n5, 94n6

Zhengzhou, 240

Zhou dynasty, xxxi, xxxiii, 243, 249

Zhou Yucheng, 272

Zhuang Zi, 242

Zhu Jiaming, 272

Zhu Xi, 250

Zomia, 110–11, 196, 198, 211